EMPLOYEE BENEFIT PLANS

IN A NUTSHELL

THIRD EDITION

By

JAY CONISON
Dean and Professor
Valparaiso University School of Law

Mat # 40195975

To Nancy, Alex and David

*

PREFACE TO THE THIRD EDITION

The Law of employee benefit plans, once a small part of labor and tax law, is now an independent field with a distinctive character. Its growth was catalyzed by ERISA, a statute premised on the importance of plans and designed to remedy plan problems systematically. While plan law builds on established rules of tax law, labor law, trust law, and other fields, its special principles and policies set it apart and demand independent study.

Plan law is remarkably pervasive, largely because plans are ubiquitous features of modern life. An employer who has an informal practice of paying severance benefits to employees; a creditor of a plan participant in bankruptcy; an individual who seeks division of a spouse's pension rights in a divorce proceeding; and an individual who disputes a denial of a health insurance claim; all may be affected by the law of plans.

Lawyers need to become familiar with this distinctive and pervasive body of law. Yet gaining familiarity can be difficult because the law is heterogeneous and in many parts highly complex. The law contains highly detailed rules for actuaries to follow in establishing plan funding levels, for administrators to follow in supplying information to participants and government agencies, and for employers and benefit recipients to follow in their tax planning and tax payment. It also contains a great deal of common law governing benefit payment and fiduciary conduct, much of which is not obviously compelled by the statutory language. Rather than finding unifying themes, the newcomer may see only disconnected detail.

The aim of this book is to help the student or nonexpert achieve a basic, yet thorough, understanding of the law. The book is not a diluted or popular account. Where a body of law is detailed or difficult, the student gains nothing from a superficial text. Rather, this book provides tools that the reader can use to better understand the law and apply it intelligently. The book does this in two ways. First, it provides essential background on, among other things, actuarial principles, legislative history, uses for plans, and comparisons of ERISA with other bodies of law. Second, it presents the various topics in plan law as coherent units implementing general principles. It also presents the more difficult topics by moving from general principles and rules to ones that are increasingly detailed. As the reader will see, in even the most complex parts of plan law the basic principles and rules are quite easy to understand. The detailed rules may numb the mind initially, but once their purpose and place are grasped, they become much less formidable.

The reader should be aware of several pedagogic matters. First, the law of plans can be presented in many different ways. The order of presentation in this book is substantially the order in which the author teaches the subject. But because other approaches are possible, the book's chapters are designed to be relatively independent and can be read in whatever order the reader finds most appropriate. A caveat, however, is that everyone should initially read the first five chapters to obtain an overview and the background needed for a thorough understanding of the law.

Second, this book is not a substitute for original texts; space limitations prevent extensive quoting of statutes and regulations. To fully understand a statute or a case, it is essential to read it.

Third, the law of benefit plans changes rapidly. Important changes were made by statute, regulation, and caselaw between the second edition of the book and this writing, and many more are impending. Nonetheless, because this book aims to help the reader understand the purpose and context of the rules, one who reads the book carefully should have little difficulty mastering new developments.

JAY CONISON

October 2003

*

ACKNOWLEDGMENT

I wish to thank my research assistant, Lori Marschke, a member of the Valparaiso University School of Law Class of 2005, for her excellent help in the preparation of this third edition.

*

OUTLINE

Page

PREFACE --- v
TABLE OF CASES -------------------------------------- xxvii
TABLE OF STATUTES AND REGULATIONS --------------- xlv

**Chapter 1. Overview and Basic Con-
cepts** --- 1
A. Plans and the Scope of ERISA ------------------- 1
   1. What Is a Plan? ----------------------------------- 1
   2. Varieties of Plans ------------------------------- 3
      a. Pension Plans ----------------------------------- 3
      b. Welfare Plans ---------------------------------- 7
      c. Multiemployer Plans -------------------------- 8
   3. Pension and Welfare Plans Covered by
      ERISA -- 9
      a. Title I -- 9
      b. Title II -- 11
B. Persons Associated With Plans ----------------- 12
C. Overview of ERISA Regulation ----------------- 15
   1. The Structure of Title I ----------------------- 16
   2. The Structure of Title II ---------------------- 19
   3. The Structure of Title IV --------------------- 20
   4. The Allocation of Regulatory Authority ---- 21

Page

Chapter 2. Basic Plan Finance and Taxation 23
A. Present Value 23
B. Valuing Pensions 25
C. Individual Tax Advantages 27
D. Firm Tax Advantages 30

Chapter 3. Economic Aspects of Plans 33
A. Plans as Business Activities 33
B. Plans as Retirement Security Programs 38
    1. National Policy 39
    2. Plan Design 44
C. Plans and Compensation 45
D. Plans and Corporate Finance 48
E. Plans and Financial Markets 53

Chapter 4. Traditional Frameworks for Plan Regulation 56
A. The Problem of Expectations 56
B. The Common Law Answers 57
C. Statutory Regulation Before ERISA 64

Chapter 5. The Legislative Background to ERISA 70
A. The Motivations for ERISA 70
B. The Policy Underpinnings of ERISA 72
C. The Incompleteness of ERISA 74

Chapter 6. Benefit Protection: Vesting .. 78
A. The Vesting Problem 78
B. Vesting Standards 79
    1. Vesting of the Normal Retirement Benefit 80
    2. Vesting of Accrued Benefits 81
    3. Forfeitures 86
    4. Vesting Upon Plan Termination 88

	Page
5. Vesting Rules for Top–Heavy Plans	90
C. What Benefits Are Nonforfeitable?	91

Chapter 7. Benefit Protection: Participation, Accrual and Non–Interference | 96

A. Participation	96
B. Accrual of Benefits	98
1. Accrued Benefits in General	98
2. Defined Benefit Plans: Anti–Backloading Rules	100
a. The 3 Percent Rule	100
b. The 133–1/3% Rule	102
c. The Fractional Rule	104
d. Insurance Plans	105
3. Defined Benefit Plans: Age Discrimination Rules	106
4. Defined Contribution Plans	106
5. Top–Heavy Plans	106
6. Plan Amendments and Accrued Benefits	107
7. Cash Balance Plans	111
C. Protection of Benefit Rights in the Workplace	114

Chapter 8. Benefit Distribution: Substantive Standards | 118

A. Annuities	118
1. Annuities and Actuarial Principles	119
2. Annuities and Spousal Protection	121
a. The Need for Spousal Protection	121
b. Required Forms for Annuities	123
c. Who is a Spouse?	125

Page

     d. Waiver and Election................... 125
B. Non–Annuity Payments 127
  1. Lump Sum Payments of Benefits 127
  2. Cash Outs................................ 129
  3. Spousal Consent 130
  4. Plan Loans............................. 130
C. Non–Retirement Benefits 134
  1. Allowable Benefits 135
  2. Death Benefits.......................... 136
  3. Payments of Accrued Benefits to Bene-
    ficiaries 138
D. Timing of Distributions 139
  1. Consent................................. 139
  2. Required Beginning...................... 139
  3. Limits on Participant Delay............. 139
  4. Death Distributions..................... 140
E. Anti–Alienation Rules 141
  1. The Basic Provision..................... 141
  2. Welfare Benefit Plans 142
  3. Personal Bankruptcy 143
  4. Qualified Domestic Relations Orders 145
  5. Other Statutory Exceptions 148
  6. Benefit Offsets......................... 148

Chapter 9. Taxation of Distributions...... 150
A. Annuities 150
  1. Amounts Received as an Annuity—Ba-
    sic Rules 151
  2. Simplified Exclusion Method 152
  3. Amounts Not Received as an Annuity ... 153
  4. Separate Contracts...................... 154
B. Lump Sum Distributions 155

Page

C. Rollovers and Trustee–to–Trustee Transfers... 157
   1. Rollover Distributions 158
     a. Eligible Rollover Distributions 158
     b. Transfer to the New Plan 159
     c. Distributions to Spouses.................... 160
     d. Withholding Tax 161
     e. Notice.. 161
   2. Direct Transfer of Rollover Distributions 162
D. Additional Tax on Early Distributions 162

Chapter 10. Benefit Payment: Procedure... 165
A. Plan Claims Procedures............................... 165
   1. The Meaning and Purpose of the Requirement....................................... 165
   2. Standards for a Reasonable Claims Procedure 169
     a. Basic Standards 170
     b. Claim Determination—All Plans...... 171
     c. Claim Determination—Group Health Plans—Initial Determination 173
     d. Claim Determinations—Group Health Plans—Review.................... 175
     e. State Law.. 177
B. Suits for Benefits....................................... 178
   1. Policy Considerations 178
   2. The Character of the Suit for Benefits .. 179
     a. The Labor–Law Model 179
     b. The Trust–Law Model........................ 181
     c. Caselaw Development 182

Page

3. The Proper Defendant 188
4. The Availability of Jury Trial 189
C. Liabilities Incidental to Benefit Payments .. 190

Chapter 11. Plan Information 194
A. Reporting and Disclosure 194
1. The Rationale for the Requirements 195
2. The Required Reports and Documents .. 196
   a. Summary Plan Description 197
   b. Summary of Material Modifications
      and Changes 199
   c. Annual Report 199
   d. Summary Annual Report 202
3. Reporting to Government Agencies 203
4. Disclosure to Participants 204
5. Determination of Qualified Status 207
6. Additional Requirements 208
7. Remedies and Sanctions 209
B. The Writing Requirement 211
1. The Rationale for the Writing Require-
   ment 212
2. Conflicts Between the Plan Document
   and the SPD 213
3. The Status of Oral Plans 217
   a. The Existence of Oral Plans 217
   b. The Amendability of Oral Plans 217
4. Oral Representations at Variance With
   Plan Terms 218
   a. Purported Oral Amendments 218
   b. Individualized Oral Representations 219

Chapter 12. Fiduciary Regulation 224
A. Plan Fiduciaries 224

Page

1. Basic Characteristics of Plan Fiducia-
   ries --- 224
2. Denominated Fiduciary Roles -------------- 226
   a. Named Fiduciary--------------------------- 226
   b. Trustee-- 227
   c. Allocation of Fiduciary Responsibili-
      ty--- 228
   d. Administrator ------------------------------- 229
   e. Investment Manager---------------------- 230
   f. Investment Advisor ---------------------- 231
3. Other Fiduciaries------------------------------- 232
   a. The Function and Discretion Stan-
      dard --- 232
   b. Attorneys and Other Professionals--- 234
4. The Employer as Fiduciary------------------ 235
5. Term of Fiduciary Office --------------------- 236
B. Trust and Related Requirements -------------- 237
   1. Plan Assets -------------------------------------- 237
      a. Plan Assets vs. Funds or Other
         Property ------------------------------------- 237
      b. Time of Asset Acquisition -------------- 238
      c. Mutual Fund Interests ------------------- 239
      d. Other Investments ------------------------ 239
      e. Guaranteed Benefit Policies ----------- 240
   2. The Trust Requirement --------------------- 243
   3. Non–Inurement---------------------------------- 244
   4. Bonding Requirements ------------------------ 245
   5. Prohibited Persons----------------------------- 247
C. Fiduciary Standards---------------------------------- 248
   1. The Structural Character of ERISA Fi-
      duciary Duties ----------------------------------- 249
   2. The Duty of Loyalty ---------------------------- 250

Page

    a. To Whom Is The Duty Owed? 251

    b. What Employer Conduct Is Subject to the Duty? 253

    c. *Pegram* and the Functional Approach 255

    d. Employer Conflicts of Interest......... 257

  3. Other Fiduciary Duties 263

    a. Prudence...................................... 263

    b. Diversification 265

    c. Non–Deviation............................. 267

    d. Truthfulness and Information 267

  4. Cofiduciary Responsibility 269

D. Limitations on Fiduciary Responsibility..... 270

  1. Limitations Resulting From Allocation Rules.. 270

  2. Directed Trustees 272

  3. Exculpatory Provisions, Insurance and Indemnification 273

  4. Participant–Directed Accounts 274

E. Remedies for Breach of Duty 275

  1. Suits Against Fiduciaries 275

    a. ERISA § 409 275

    b. ERISA § 502(a)(3)......................... 278

  2. Civil Penalties 279

  3. Suits Against Non–Fiduciaries 280

Chapter 13. Prohibited Transactions 282

A. Parties in Interest 282

B. Prohibited Fiduciary Conduct..................... 283

  1. The Party in Interest Rules 284

    a. Property Transactions..................... 285

    b. Loans 286

    c. Goods and Services 286

Page

    d. Asset Transfer ------------------------------ 287
    e. Employer Stock and Employer Real
       Property ------------------------------- 287
    f. Corresponding Code Provisions ------ 288
  2. The Self–Dealing Rules --------------------- 288
    a. Self–Dealing and Adverse Interest --- 288
    b. Kickbacks---------------------------------- 291
C. Exemptions --- 292
  1. Statutory Exemptions------------------------ 292
    a. Participant Loans------------------------ 293
    b. Operating Contracts -------------------- 293
    c. Banks and Insurers -------------------- 294
  2. Statutory Clarifications--------------------- 294
  3. Administrative Exemptions ---------------- 295
D. Remedies-- 297
  1. Fiduciaries----------------------------------- 297
  2. Parties in Interest--------------------------- 297

**Chapter 14. Employer Securities and
    Employee Stock Ownership Plans** 300
A. Employer Securities----------------------------- 301
  1. Definitions------------------------------------ 301
  2. Prohibited Transactions and Exemp-
    tions -- 303
  3. Exceptions to Fiduciary Requirements -- 305
B. ESOPS--- 306
  1. ESOPS in General ------------------------- 306
  2. Leveraged ESOPS--------------------------- 307
  3. ESOP Loans---------------------------------- 309
    a. Primary Benefit ------------------------- 309
    b. Release of Collateral ------------------- 310
  4. Further ESOP Requirements-------------- 310
    a. Designation ------------------------------- 311

Page

    b. Integration 311
    c. Allocation to Accounts 311
    d. Voting Rights 311
    e. Distribution Options 312
    f. Timing of Distributions 313
    g. Diversification 314
    h. Appraisal 314
  5. Additional Tax Advantages 314
    a. Dividend Deduction 315
    b. Deferral of Capital Gains 315
C. ESOPS and Corporate Control Contests 317
  1. Fiduciary Considerations in Voting and
    Tendering 317
  2. State Corporation Law 322
    a. The Business Judgment Rule 322
    b. Preemption Issues 324

Chapter 15. Preemption 326
A. "Relate To" 327
  1. The Interpretive Problems 327
  2. Limits to Preemption 329
    a. "Relate to": The Broad Reading 329
    b. "Relate to": The Narrower Reading 331
B. A Plan 333
  1. The *Dillingham* Test 333
  2. The Functional Test 335
  3. Group Insurance 336
C. State Insurance Regulation 337
  1. "Regulates Insurance" 337
  2. The Deemer Clause 341
D. Preemption and Remedies 342

	Page
Chapter 16. Procedure	348
A. Jurisdiction, Process and Venue	348
1. Subject Matter Jurisdiction	348
2. Process and Venue	350
B. Limitations Periods	351
C. Attorney's Fees	352
D. Privilege	354
Chapter 17. Nondiscrimination: Coverage	357
A. Highly Compensated Employees	358
1. 5–Percent Owners	358
2. Compensation	359
3. Top–Paid Group	359
4. Former Employees	360
B. Plans Tested for Nondiscrimination	360
1. Single Plans	360
2. Disaggregation	361
3. Aggregation	361
C. The Coverage Tests	362
1. Ratio Percentage Test	363
2. Nondiscriminatory Classification and Average Benefit Percentage Tests	363
a. Nondiscriminatory Classification Test	364
b. Average Benefit Percentage Test	365
c. Compensation	367
d. Special Rules	368
e. Former Employees	368
D. Employee Inclusion Rules	369
1. Business Aggregation Rules	369
2. Leased Employees	370
E. Excludable Employees	370
1. Collective Bargaining Units	371

Page

2. Minimum Age and Service Requirements.. 371
3. Former Employees 372
F. Separate Line of Business Rules 372
   1. LOBs 374
   2. SLOBs.. 374
   3. QSLOBs 376
G. Minimum Participation Test 377
   1. Plans Tested 378
   2. Employees Considered 379
   3. Other Rules 380
   4. Exemptions.................................... 381

Chapter 18. Nondiscrimination: Contributions or Benefits............... 382
A. The Basic Standard 383
B. Nondiscrimination in Amount of Contributions or Benefits............................. 384
   1. Defined Contribution Plans 385
      a. Safe Harbors 385
      b. General Test.............................. 387
   2. Defined Benefit Plans........................ 388
      a. Safe Harbors 388
      b. General Tests 391
   3. Cross–Testing................................ 392
   4. Complicating Factors........................ 394
      a. Former Employees......................... 394
      b. Employee Contributions 394
      c. Combined Plan 395
      d. Plan Restructuring 395
C. Integration and Disparities 396
   1. Section 401(*l*) Permitted Disparity 397
      a. Defined Contribution Excess Plans .. 398

Page

  b. Defined Benefit Excess Plans 399
  c. Defined Benefit Offset Plans 400
  d. Additional Requirements for Defined Benefit Plans 402
  e. Overall Permitted Disparity 402
  2. Imputed Disparity 404
  a. Adjusted Allocation Rate 404
  b. Adjusted Accrual Rate 405
  3. Social Security Offset Plans 406
D. Nondiscrimination in Benefits, Rights and Features 406
E. Nondiscrimination in Amendments 408
F. Retroactive Corrections 409

Chapter 19. Additional Limitations on Contributions and Benefits 411
A. Defined Contribution Plans 412
B. Defined Benefit Plans 413
C. Aggregate Limitations 414

Chapter 20. Cash or Deferred Arrangements 416
A. Qualified Cash or Deferred Arrangements.. 417
  1. Basic Qualification Requirements 417
  2. Contributions to CODAs 418
  3. Other Benefits 419
B. Nondiscrimination Standards 419
  1. Coverage 419
  2. Contributions 420
  a. The Actual Deferral Percentage Test 420
  b. Calculating the ADP 421
  c. Safe Harbor 423
  3. Excess Contributions 424

	Page
4. Catch–Up Contributions	426
C. SIMPLE 401(k) Plans	426
1. Eligible Employers	427
2. SIMPLE Plan Requirements	427
Chapter 21. Funding and Contributions	429
A. Basic Actuarial Principles	430
1. Actuarial Present Value	430
2. The Calculation of Benefit Costs	431
a. Unit Credit Method	432
b. Entry Age Normal Method	434
B. Funding Standards	437
1. The Basic Funding Rules	437
a. Required Contribution	437
b. Funding Standard Account	438
c. Alternative Minimum Funding Standard	439
d. Actuarial Cost Methods	440
e. Timing	441
2. Modifications of the Basic Rules	442
a. Additional Funding Requirements	442
b. Full Funding Limitation	443
c. Money Purchase Plans	444
3. Employer Inability to Meet Funding Standard	445
a. Variances	445
b. Change in Funding Method	446
c. Retroactive Amendments	446
4. Notices	447
5. Penalties	447
C. Deductions for Contributions	449
1. Stock Bonus and Profit Sharing Plans	449

Page

   2. Defined Benefit and Money Purchase
      Plans -- 450
   3. Combinations of Plans ---------------------- 451
   4. Penalties ------------------------------------ 452

Chapter 22. Plan Termination -------------- 453
A. Overview of Regulation ---------------------- 453
   1. Internal Revenue Code --------------------- 453
   2. Title I -- 454
   3. Title IV ------------------------------------- 454
B. The PBGC and the Benefit Guaranty Pro-
    gram -- 455
   1. The PBGC ----------------------------------- 455
   2. Plans Covered ------------------------------- 456
   3. Plan Termination Insurance --------------- 456
   4. Single-Employer Plan Benefits Guaran-
      teed -- 458
   5. Multiemployer Plan Benefits Guaran-
      teed -- 460
   6. The PBGC Financial Position ------------- 461
C. Reporting to the PBGC ---------------------- 462
D. Single–Employer Plan Terminations -------- 464
   1. Standard Terminations --------------------- 464
   2. Distribution of Plan Assets ---------------- 466
   3. Distress Terminations --------------------- 468
   4. Liability for Underfunding ----------------- 471
   5. Involuntary Terminations ------------------ 472
      a. Triggering Events --------------------- 472
      b. Appointment of Trustee --------------- 473
      c. Termination Proceedings --------------- 473
      d. Sponsor Liability --------------------- 474
   6. Plan Restoration ---------------------------- 475
E. Reversions -------------------------------------- 476

OUTLINE

		Page
F.	The Purchase of Annuities	480
G.	Withdrawal Liability	482
INDEX		485

TABLE OF CASES

References are to Pages

Adams v. Avondale Industries, Inc., 905 F.2d 943 (6th Cir.1990), cert. denied 498 U.S. 984, 111 S.Ct. 517, 112 L.Ed.2d 529 (1990), *217, 218*

Adams v. Cyprus Amax Minerals Co., 149 F.3d 1156 (10th Cir.1998), *190*

Administrative Committee of the Sea Ray Employees' Stock Ownership and Profit Sharing Plan v. Robinson, 164 F.3d 981 (6th Cir.1999), cert. denied Robinson v. Administrative Committee of Sea Ray Employees' Stock Ownership and Profit Sharing Plan, 528 U.S. 1114, 120 S.Ct. 931, 145 L.Ed.2d 810 (2000), *89*

Agency Holding Corp. v. Malley–Duff & Associates, Inc., 483 U.S. 143, 107 S.Ct. 2759, 97 L.Ed.2d 121 (1987), *352*

Airparts Co., Inc. v. Custom Ben. Services of Austin, Inc., 28 F.3d 1062 (10th Cir.1994), *280*

Alday v. Container Corp. of America, 906 F.2d 660 (11th Cir. 1990), cert. denied 498 U.S. 1026, 111 S.Ct. 675, 112 L.Ed.2d 668 (1991), *93, 95*

Alessi v. Raybestos–Manhattan, Inc., 451 U.S. 504, 101 S.Ct. 1895, 68 L.Ed.2d 402 (1981), *329*

Amalgamated Clothing & Textile Workers Union, AFL–CIO v. Murdock, 861 F.2d 1406 (9th Cir.1988), *276*

Amato v. Bernard, 618 F.2d 559 (9th Cir.1980), *166, 167, 168*

Anderson v. Alpha Portland Industries, Inc., 836 F.2d 1512 (8th Cir.1988), cert. denied Anderson v. Slattery Group, Inc., 489 U.S. 1051, 109 S.Ct. 1310, 103 L.Ed.2d 579 (1989), *94*

Anderson v. Alpha Portland Industries, Inc., 752 F.2d 1293 (8th Cir.1985), cert. denied Alpha Portland Industries, Inc. v. Anderson, 471 U.S. 1102, 105 S.Ct. 2329, 85 L.Ed.2d 846 (1985), *167*

TABLE OF CASES

Arakelian v. National Western Life Ins. Co., 680 F.Supp. 400 (D.D.C.1987), *227*

Arizona Governing Committee for Tax Deferred Annuity and Deferred Compensation Plans v. Norris, 463 U.S. 1073, 103 S.Ct. 3492, 77 L.Ed.2d 1236 (1983), *119*

Armistead v. Vernitron Corp., 944 F.2d 1287 (6th Cir.1991), *221, 353*

Baker, Matter of, 114 F.3d 636 (7th Cir.1998), *144*

Ballone v. Eastman Kodak Co., 109 F.3d 117 (2nd Cir.1997), *268*

Bartkus, United States v., 816 F.2d 255 (6th Cir.1987), cert. denied Bartkus v. United States, 484 U.S. 842, 108 S.Ct. 132, 98 L.Ed.2d 90 (1987), *211*

Batchelor v. International Broth. of Elec. Workers Local 861 Pension and Retirement Fund, 877 F.2d 441 (5th Cir.1989), *188*

Baxter v. C.A. Muer Corp., 941 F.2d 451 (6th Cir.1991), *168*

Baxter v. Lynn, 886 F.2d 182 (8th Cir.1989), *183*

Beddall v. State Street Bank and Trust Co., 137 F.3d 12 (1st Cir.1998), *228*

Bennett v. Gill & Duffus Chemicals, Inc., 699 F.Supp. 454 (S.D.N.Y.1988), *92*

Berger v. Edgewater Steel Co., 911 F.2d 911 (3rd Cir.1990), cert. denied 499 U.S. 920, 111 S.Ct. 1310, 113 L.Ed.2d 244 (1991), *169*

Bergt v. Retirement Plan for Pilots Employed by Markair, Inc., 293 F.3d 1139 (9th Cir.2002), *214*

Berlin v. Michigan Bell Telephone Co., 858 F.2d 1154 (6th Cir.1988), *253*

Bidlack v. Wheelabrator Corp., 993 F.2d 603 (7th Cir.1993), cert. denied Wheelabrator Corp. v. Bidlack, 510 U.S. 909, 114 S.Ct. 291, 126 L.Ed.2d 240 (1993), *95*

Bill Gray Enterprises, Inc. Employee Health and Welfare Plan v. Gourley, 248 F.3d 206 (3rd Cir.2001), *342*

Bittner v. Sadoff & Rudoy Industries, 728 F.2d 820 (7th Cir. 1984), *354*

Black v. TIC Investment Corp., 900 F.2d 112 (7th Cir.1990), *220, 221, 222*

Blessitt v. Retirement Plan For Employees of Dixie Engine Co., 848 F.2d 1164 (11th Cir.1988), *478*

Boggs v. Boggs, 520 U.S. 833, 117 S.Ct. 1754, 138 L.Ed.2d 45 (1997), *122, 330*

Bogue v. Ampex Corp., 750 F.Supp. 424 (N.D.Cal.1990), aff'd 976 F.2d 1319 (9th Cir.1992), cert. denied 507 U.S. 1031, 113 S.Ct. 1847, 123 L.Ed.2d 471 (1993), *222*

Boyle v. United Technologies Corp., 487 U.S. 500, 108 S.Ct. 2510, 101 L.Ed.2d 442 (1988), *344*

Brandt v. Grounds, 687 F.2d 895 (7th Cir.1982), *250*

Brant v. Principal Life and Disability Ins. Co., 195 F.Supp.2d 1100 (N.D.Iowa 2002), aff'd 50 Fed.Appx. 330 (8th Cir.2002), *221*

Brewer v. Lincoln Nat. Life Ins. Co., 921 F.2d 150 (8th Cir.1990), cert. denied 501 U.S. 1238, 111 S.Ct. 2872, 115 L.Ed.2d 1038 (1991), *185*

Brink v. DaLesio, 496 F.Supp. 1350 (D.Md.1980), aff'd in part, rev'd in part 667 F.2d 420 (4th Cir.1981), *291*

Brock v. Citizens Bank of Clovis, 841 F.2d 344 (10th Cir.1988), cert. denied sub nom. Citizens Bank of Clovis v. McLaughlin, 488 U.S. 829, 109 S.Ct. 82, 102 L.Ed.2d 59 (1988), *286, 290*

Brock v. Hendershott, 840 F.2d 339 (6th Cir.1988), *280*

Brock v. Robbins, 830 F.2d 640 (7th Cir.1987), *278*

Brock v. Self, 632 F.Supp. 1509 (W.D.La.1986), *263*

Brown v. Blue Cross and Blue Shield of Alabama, Inc., 898 F.2d 1556 (11th Cir.1990), cert. denied Blue Cross and Blue Shield of Alabama v. Brown, 498 U.S. 1040, 111 S.Ct. 712, 112 L.Ed.2d 701 (1991), *186, 187*

Brown v. Retirement Committee of Briggs & Stratton Retirement Plan, 797 F.2d 521 (7th Cir.1986), cert. denied 479 U.S. 1094, 107 S.Ct. 1311, 94 L.Ed.2d 165 (1987), *191*

Brown v. Roth, 729 F.Supp. 391 (D.N.J.1990), *231, 234*

Bruch v. Firestone Tire and Rubber Co., 828 F.2d 134 (3rd Cir.1987), *180*

Brundage–Peterson v. Compcare Health Services Ins. Corp., 877 F.2d 509 (7th Cir.1989), *336*

Buckhorn, Inc. v. Ropak Corp., 656 F.Supp. 209 (S.D.Ohio 1987), aff'd mem. 815 F.2d 76 (6th Cir.1987), *323*

Budd Co. Pension Plan Litigation, In re, 1991 WL 236473 (E.D.Pa.1991), *482*

California Div. of Labor Standards Enforcement v. Dillingham Const., N.A., Inc., 519 U.S. 316, 117 S.Ct. 832, 136 L.Ed.2d 791 (1997), *332*

Call v. Sumitomo Bank of California, 881 F.2d 626 (9th Cir. 1989), *277*

Campbell v. BankBoston, N.A., 327 F.3d 1 (1st Cir.2003), *112, 114*

Carducci v. Aetna United States Healthcare, 247 F.Supp.2d 596 (D.N.J.2003), *188*

Cefalu v. B.F. Goodrich Co., 871 F.2d 1290 (5th Cir.1989), *213, 219*

Central Trust Co., N.A. v. American Avents Corp., 771 F.Supp. 871 (S.D.Ohio 1989), *319*

Chalmers v. Quaker Oats Co., 61 F.3d 1340 (7th Cir.1995), *187*

Chambers v. Kaleidoscope, Inc. Profit Sharing Plan and Trust, 650 F.Supp. 359 (N.D.Ga.1986), *230*

Charter Canyon Treatment Center v. Pool Co., 153 F.3d 1132 (10th Cir.1998), *216*

Chauffeurs, Teamsters and Helpers, Local No. 391 v. Terry, 494 U.S. 558, 110 S.Ct. 1339, 108 L.Ed.2d 519 (1990), *189*

Chemung Canal Trust Co. v. Sovran Bank/Maryland, 939 F.2d 12 (2nd Cir.1991), cert. denied 505 U.S. 1212, 112 S.Ct. 3014, 120 L.Ed.2d 887 (1992), *346*

Chiles v. Ceridian Corp., 95 F.3d 1505 (10th Cir.1996), *216*

Citrus Valley Estates, Inc. v. Commissioner, 49 F.3d 1410 (9th Cir.1995), *441*

Cleary v. Graphic Communications Intern. Union Supplemental Retirement and Disability Fund, 841 F.2d 444 (1st Cir.1988), *223*

Coleman Clinic, Ltd. v. Massachusetts Mut. Life Ins. Co., 698 F.Supp. 740 (C.D.Ill.1988), *275*

Commissioner v. _____ (see opposing party)

Confer v. Custom Engineering Co., 952 F.2d 41 (3rd Cir.1991), *219*

Cooper v. IBM Personal Pension Plan, 2003 WL 21767853 (S.D.Ill.2003), *112*

Cullen v. Riley (Masters Mates & Pilots Pension Plan and IRAP Litigation, In re), 957 F.2d 1020 (2nd Cir.1992), *346*

Curcio v. John Hancock Mut. Life Ins. Co., 33 F.3d 226 (3rd Cir.1994), *221*

Curtis v. Loether, 415 U.S. 189, 94 S.Ct. 1005, 39 L.Ed.2d 260 (1974), *189*

Curtiss–Wright Corp. v. Schoonejongen, 514 U.S. 73, 115 S.Ct. 1223, 131 L.Ed.2d 94 (1995), *253*

Custer v. Sweeney, 89 F.3d 1156 (4th Cir.1996), *280*

TABLE OF CASES

Dallas County Hosp. Dist. v. Associates' Health and Welfare Plan, 293 F.3d 282 (5th Cir.2002), *143*

Danaher Corp. v. Chicago Pneumatic Tool Co. (II), 635 F.Supp. 246 (S.D.N.Y.1986), *320*

Danaher Corp. v. Chicago Pneumatic Tool Co. (I), 633 F.Supp. 1066 (S.D.N.Y.1986), *322*

Daniels v. Thomas & Betts Corp., 263 F.3d 66 (3rd Cir.2001), *269*

Danti v. Lewis, 312 F.2d 345, 114 U.S.App.D.C. 105 (D.C.Cir. 1962), *63*

Davidowitz v. Delta Dental Plan of California, Inc., 946 F.2d 1476 (9th Cir.1991), *143*

Davidson v. Cook, 567 F.Supp. 225 (E.D.Va.1983), aff'd mem. 734 F.2d 10 (4th Cir.1984), cert. denied sub nom. Accardi v. Davidson, 469 U.S. 899, 105 S.Ct. 275, 83 L.Ed.2d 211 (1984), *266*

De Buono v. NYSA–ILA Medical and Clinical Services Fund, 520 U.S. 806, 117 S.Ct. 1747, 138 L.Ed.2d 21 (1997), *333*

Deeming v. American Standard, Inc., 905 F.2d 1124 (7th Cir. 1990), *117*

Defoe Shipbuilding Co., Matter of, 639 F.2d 311 (6th Cir.1981), *456*

Delgrosso v. Spang and Co., 769 F.2d 928 (3rd Cir.1985), cert. denied Spang & Co. v. DelGrosso, 476 U.S. 1140, 106 S.Ct. 2246, 90 L.Ed.2d 692 (1986), *479*

Dewitt v. Penn–Del Directory Corp., 106 F.3d 514 (3rd Cir.1997), *187*

Dobson v. Hartford Financial Servs., 196 F.Supp.2d 152 (D.Conn. 2002), *193*

Doe v. Blue Cross & Blue Shield United of Wisconsin, 112 F.3d 869 (7th Cir.1997), *352*

Donovan v. Bierwirth, 754 F.2d 1049 (2nd Cir.1985), *277*

Donovan v. Bierwirth, 680 F.2d 263 (2nd Cir.1982), cert. denied Bierwirth v. Donovan, 459 U.S. 1069, 103 S.Ct. 488, 74 L.Ed.2d 631 (1982), *258, 260, 261, 290, 291*

Donovan v. Dillingham, 688 F.2d 1367 (11th Cir.1982), *217, 333, 334, 337*

Donovan v. Fitzsimmons, 90 F.R.D. 583 (N.D.Ill.1981), *355, 356*

Donovan v. Mercer, 747 F.2d 304 (5th Cir.1984), *227*

Donovan v. Walton, 609 F.Supp. 1221 (S.D.Fla.1985), aff'd sub nom. Brock v. Walton, 794 F.2d 586 (11th Cir.1986), *263*

Eaton v. Onan Corp., 117 F.Supp.2d 812 (S.D.Ind.2000), *112*

Edwards v. State Farm Mut. Auto. Ins. Co., 851 F.2d 134 (6th Cir.1988), *215*

Egelhoff v. Egelhoff, 532 U.S. 141, 121 S.Ct. 1322, 149 L.Ed.2d 264 (2001), *330*

Ehm v. Phillips Petroleum Co., 583 F.Supp. 1113 (D.Kan.1984), *89*

Eley v. Boeing Co., 945 F.2d 276 (9th Cir.1991), *184*

Ellenburg v. Brockway, Inc., 763 F.2d 1091 (9th Cir.1985), *223*

Ellis v. Metropolitan Life Ins. Co., 126 F.3d 228 (4th Cir.1997), *187*

Emporium Capwell Co. v. Western Addition Community Organization, 420 U.S. 50, 95 S.Ct. 977, 43 L.Ed.2d 12 (1975), *166*

Evans v. Midland Enterprises, Inc., 704 F.Supp. 106 (M.D.La. 1989), *168*

Evans, United States v., 796 F.2d 264 (9th Cir.1986), *355*

Everett v. USAir Group, Inc., 165 F.R.D. 1 (D.D.C.1995), *356*

Fallick v. Nationwide Mut. Ins. Co., 162 F.3d 410 (6th Cir.1998), *169*

Farm King Supply, Inc. Integrated Profit Sharing Plan and Trust v. Edward D. Jones & Co., 884 F.2d 288 (7th Cir.1989), *231*

Farr v. United States West Communications, Inc., 151 F.3d 908 (9th Cir.1998), *269*

Feroleto Steel Co., Inc. v. Commissioner, 69 T.C. 97 (U.S.Tax Ct.1977), *65*

Firestone Tire and Rubber Co. v. Bruch, 489 U.S. 101, 109 S.Ct. 948, 103 L.Ed.2d 80 (1989), *13, 179, 180, 181, 182, 185, 186, 190, 343*

Fischer v. Philadelphia Elec. Co., 96 F.3d 1533 (3rd Cir.1996), *268*

FMC Corp. v. Holliday, 498 U.S. 52, 111 S.Ct. 403, 112 L.Ed.2d 356 (1990), *341*

Folz v. Marriott Corp., 594 F.Supp. 1007 (W.D.Mo.1984), *116*

Forsyth v. Humana, Inc., 114 F.3d 1467 (9th Cir.1997), cert. denied 522 U.S. 996, 118 S.Ct. 559, 139 L.Ed.2d 401 (1997), *279*

Fort Halifax Packing Co., Inc. v. Coyne, 482 U.S. 1, 107 S.Ct. 2211, 96 L.Ed.2d 1 (1987), *333, 335*

Frahm v. Equitable Life Assur. Soc. of United States, 137 F.3d 955 (7th Cir.1998), cert. denied 525 U.S. 817, 119 S.Ct. 55, 142 L.Ed.2d 43 (1998), *219, 221*

Freund v. Marshall & Ilsley Bank, 485 F.Supp. 629 (W.D.Wis. 1979), *270*

Friedrich v. Intel Corp., 181 F.3d 1105 (9th Cir.1999), *186*

Gavalik v. Continental Can Co., 812 F.2d 834 (3rd Cir.1987), cert. denied Continental Can Co. v. Gavalik, 484 U.S. 979, 108 S.Ct. 495, 98 L.Ed.2d 492 (1987), *115*

Gelardi v. Pertec Computer Corp., 761 F.2d 1323 (9th Cir.1985), *189*

Gilbertson v. Allied Signal, Inc., 328 F.3d 625 (10th Cir.2003), *191, 192*

GIW Industries, Inc. v. Trevor, Stewart, Burton & Jacobsen, Inc., 895 F.2d 729 (11th Cir.1990), *266*

Graham v. Federal Exp. Corp., 725 F.Supp. 429 (W.D.Ark.1989), *168*

Great–West Life & Annuity Ins. Co. v. Knudson, 534 U.S. 204, 122 S.Ct. 708, 151 L.Ed.2d 635 (2002), *252, 278, 346*

Gruber v. Hubbard Bert Karle Weber, Inc., 675 F.Supp. 281 (W.D.Pa.1987), *276*

Guidry v. Sheet Metal Workers International Ass'n, Local No. 9, 39 F.3d 1078 (10th Cir.1994), cert. denied Guidry v. Sheet Metal Workers' Nat. Pension Fund, 514 U.S. 1063, 115 S.Ct. 1691, 131 L.Ed.2d 556 (1995), *141*

Guidry v. Sheet Metal Workers Nat. Pension Fund, 493 U.S. 365, 110 S.Ct. 680, 107 L.Ed.2d 782 (1990), *148*

Guiles v. Metropolitan Life Ins. Co., 2002 WL 229696 (E.D.Pa. 2002), *188*

Hackett v. Pension Ben. Guaranty Corp., 486 F.Supp. 1357 (D.Md.1980), *459*

Hackett v. Xerox Corp. Long–Term Disability Income Plan, 315 F.3d 771 (7th Cir.2003), *191, 192*

Hall v. Unum Life Ins. Co. of America, 300 F.3d 1197 (10th Cir.2002), *184*

Halliburton Co. v. Commissioner, 100 T.C. No. 15, 100 T.C. 216 (U.S.Tax Ct.1993), aff'd mem. Halliburton Co. v. I.R.S., 25 F.3d 1043 (5th Cir.1994), cert. denied sub nom. Nash v. Halliburton Co., 513 U.S. 989, 115 S.Ct. 486, 130 L.Ed.2d 398 (1994), *89*

Hamilton v. Air Jamaica, Ltd., 945 F.2d 74 (3rd Cir.1991), cert. denied 503 U.S. 938, 112 S.Ct. 1479, 117 L.Ed.2d 622 (1992), *216*

Hamilton v. Allen–Bradley Co., Inc., 244 F.3d 819 (11th Cir. 2001), *188*

Hansen v. Continental Ins. Co., 940 F.2d 971 (5th Cir.1991), *214, 215, 216, 336, 339*

Hansen v. Western Greyhound Retirement Plan, 859 F.2d 779 (9th Cir.1988), *219*

Hansen v. White Farm Equipment Co. (White Farm Equipment Co., In re), 788 F.2d 1186 (6th Cir.1986), *93*

Harold Ives Trucking Co. v. Spradley & Coker, Inc., 178 F.3d 523 (8th Cir.1999), *230*

Harris v. Arkansas Book Co., 794 F.2d 358 (8th Cir.1986), *334*

Harris Trust and Sav. Bank v. Salomon Smith Barney, Inc., 530 U.S. 238, 120 S.Ct. 2180, 147 L.Ed.2d 187 (2000), *280, 281, 298, 345*

Harrow v. Prudential Ins. Co. of America, 279 F.3d 244 (3rd Cir.2002), *169*

Held v. Manufacturers Hanover Leasing Corp., 912 F.2d 1197 (10th Cir.1990), *351*

Helfrich v. Carle Clinic Ass'n., P.C., 328 F.3d 915 (7th Cir.2003), *215*

Helt v. Metropolitan Dist. Com'n, 113 F.R.D. 7 (D.Conn.1986), *355*

Herman v. NationsBank Trust Co. (Georgia), 126 F.3d 1354 (11th Cir.1997), *320*

Herzberger v. Standard Ins. Co., 205 F.3d 327 (7th Cir.2000), *183, 184*

Hickey v. Chicago Truck Drivers, Helpers and Warehouse Workers Union, 980 F.2d 465 (7th Cir.1992), *108*

Hickman v. Tosco Corp., 840 F.2d 564 (8th Cir.1988), *253*

Hicks v. Fleming Companies, Inc., 961 F.2d 537 (5th Cir.1992), *214*

Horvath v. Keystone Health Plan East, Inc., 333 F.3d 450 (3rd Cir.2003), *269*

Howe v. Varity Corp., 896 F.2d 1107 (8th Cir.1990), *93*

Hozier v. Midwest Fasteners, Inc., 908 F.2d 1155 (3rd Cir.1990), *255*

Hummell v. S. E. Rykoff & Co., 634 F.2d 446 (9th Cir.1980), *87*

Ingersoll–Rand Co. v. McClendon, 498 U.S. 133, 111 S.Ct. 478, 112 L.Ed.2d 474 (1990), *115, 330*

TABLE OF CASES

Inland Steel Co. v. N.L.R.B., 170 F.2d 247 (7th Cir.1948), cert. denied 336 U.S. 960, 69 S.Ct. 887, 93 L.Ed. 1112 (1949), *45*

In re (see name of party)

Inter–Modal Rail Employees Ass'n v. Atchison, Topeka and Santa Fe Ry. Co., 520 U.S. 510, 117 S.Ct. 1513, 137 L.Ed.2d 763 (1997), *116*

International Ass'n of Heat and Frost Insulators Local 17 Pension Fund v. American Nat. Bank and Trust Co. of Chicago, 13 F.Supp.2d 753 (N.D.Ill.1998), *276*

International Broth. of Teamsters, Chauffeurs, Warehousemen and Helpers of America v. Daniel, 439 U.S. 551, 99 S.Ct. 790, 58 L.Ed.2d 808 (1979), *68*

International Union, United Auto., Aerospace & Agr. Implement Workers of America, U.A.W. v. Skinner Engine Co., 188 F.3d 130 (3rd Cir.1999), *95*

International Union, United Auto. Workers v. Yard–Man, Inc., 716 F.2d 1476 (6th Cir.1983), cert. denied Yard–Man, Inc. v. International Union, United Auto., Aerospace & Agr. Implement Workers of America, 465 U.S. 1007, 104 S.Ct. 1002, 79 L.Ed.2d 234 (1984), *94*

Jacobs v. Pickands Mather & Co., 933 F.2d 652 (8th Cir.1991), *353*

Jass v. Prudential Health Care Plan, Inc., 88 F.3d 1482 (7th Cir.1996), *188*

Jebian v. Hewlett Packard Co., 310 F.3d 1173 (9th Cir.2002), *192*

Jerome Mirza & Associates, Ltd. v. United States, 882 F.2d 229 (7th Cir.1989), cert. denied 495 U.S. 929, 110 S.Ct. 2166, 109 L.Ed.2d 496 (1990), *441*

John Hancock Mut. Life Ins. Co. v. Harris Trust & Sav. Bank, 510 U.S. 86, 114 S.Ct. 517, 126 L.Ed.2d 524 (1993), *242, 243*

Jones v. Kodak Medical Assistance Plan, 169 F.3d 1287 (10th Cir.1999), *186*

Jones & Laughlin Hourly Pension Plan v. LTV Corp., 824 F.2d 197 (2nd Cir.1987), *474*

Kane v. Aetna Life Ins., 893 F.2d 1283 (11th Cir.1990), cert. denied Aetna Life Ins. Co. v. Kane, 498 U.S. 890, 111 S.Ct. 232, 112 L.Ed.2d 192 (1990), *221*

Katsaros v. Cody, 744 F.2d 270 (2nd Cir.1984), cert. denied sub nom. Cody v. Donovan, 469 U.S. 1072, 105 S.Ct. 565, 83 L.Ed.2d 506 (1984), *263*

Kearney v. Standard Ins. Co., 175 F.3d 1084 (9th Cir.1999), cert. denied Standard Ins. Co. v. Kearney, 528 U.S. 964, 120 S.Ct. 398, 145 L.Ed.2d 310 (1999), *183*

Kennedy v. Electricians Pension Plan, 954 F.2d 1116 (5th Cir. 1992), *188*

Kentucky Ass'n of Health Plans, Inc. v. Miller, ___ U.S. ___, 123 S.Ct. 1471, 155 L.Ed.2d 468 (2003), *340, 341*

Keystone Consol. Industries, Inc., Commissioner v., 508 U.S. 152, 113 S.Ct. 2006, 124 L.Ed.2d 71 (1993), *285*

Kidder v. H & B Marine Inc., 932 F.2d 347 (5th Cir.1991), *336*

Kochendorfer v. Rockdale Sash and Trim Co., Inc. Profit Sharing Plan, 653 F.Supp. 612 (N.D.Ill.1987), *215*

Kolentus v. Avco Corp., 798 F.2d 949 (7th Cir.1986), *215*

Kreis v. Charles O. Townley, M.D. & Associates, P.C., 833 F.2d 74 (6th Cir.1987), *90*

Kunin v. Benefit Trust Life Ins. Co., 910 F.2d 534 (9th Cir.1990), cert. denied Benefit Trust Life Ins. Co. v. Kunin, 498 U.S. 1013, 111 S.Ct. 581, 112 L.Ed.2d 587 (1990), *184*

Kwatcher v. Massachusetts Service Employees Pension Fund, 879 F.2d 957 (1st Cir.1989), *344*

Lambos v. Commissioner, 88 T.C. No. 80, 88 T.C. 1440 (U.S.Tax Ct.1987), *299*

Lancaster v. United States Shoe Corp., 934 F.Supp. 1137 (N.D.Cal.1996), *215*

LeBlanc v. Cahill, 3 Fed.Appx. 98 (4th Cir.2001), *281*

Leigh v. Engle, 858 F.2d 361 (7th Cir.1988), cert. denied Engle v. Estate of Johnson, 489 U.S. 1078, 109 S.Ct. 1528, 103 L.Ed.2d 833 (1989), *277*

Leigh v. Engle, 727 F.2d 113 (7th Cir.1984), *258, 260, 261, 278, 287, 290, 291*

Levy v. Local Union Number 810, 20 F.3d 516 (2nd Cir.1994), *237*

L.I. Head Start Child Development Services, Inc. v. Frank, 165 F.Supp.2d 367 (E.D.N.Y.2001), *281*

Lincoln Mut. Cas. Co. v. Lectron Products, Inc., Employee Health Ben. Plan, 970 F.2d 206 (6th Cir.1992), *342*

Lister v. Stark, 890 F.2d 941 (7th Cir.1989), cert. denied 498 U.S. 1011, 111 S.Ct. 579, 112 L.Ed.2d 584 (1990), *331, 349*

Livestock Feeds v. Local Union No. 1634, 221 Miss. 492, 73 So.2d 128 (Miss.1954), *62*

Local Union 598, Plumbers & Pipefitters Industry Journeymen & Apprentices Training Fund v. J.A. Jones Const. Co., 846 F.2d 1213 (9th Cir.1988), aff'd 488 U.S. 881, 109 S.Ct. 210, 102 L.Ed.2d 202 (1988), *329*

Lockheed Corp. v. Spink, 517 U.S. 882, 116 S.Ct. 1783, 135 L.Ed.2d 153 (1996), *253, 287*

Lockrey v. Leavitt Tube Employees' Profit Sharing Plan, 766 F.Supp. 1510 (N.D.Ill.1991), *222*

Lockrey v. Leavitt Tube Employees' Profit Sharing Plan, 748 F.Supp. 662 (N.D.Ill.1990), *220*

Lodge v. Shell Oil Co., 747 F.2d 16 (1st Cir.1984), *272*

Long Island Lighting Co., In re, 129 F.3d 268 (2nd Cir.1997), *356*

Lowen v. Tower Asset Management, Inc., 829 F.2d 1209 (2nd Cir.1987), *291, 292*

Luby v. Teamsters Health, Welfare, and Pension Trust Funds, 944 F.2d 1176 (3rd Cir.1991), *185*

Lucas v. Seagrave Corp., 277 F.Supp. 338 (D.Minn.1967), *62*

Mackey v. Lanier Collection Agency & Service, Inc., 486 U.S. 825, 108 S.Ct. 2182, 100 L.Ed.2d 836 (1988), *330, 331*

Makar v. Health Care Corp. of Mid–Atlantic (Carefirst), 872 F.2d 80 (4th Cir.1989), *169*

Marshall v. Kelly, 465 F.Supp. 341 (W.D.Okla.1978), *284*

Martin v. Arkansas Blue Cross and Blue Shield, 299 F.3d 966 (8th Cir.2002), cert. denied ___ U.S. ___, 123 S.Ct. 967, 154 L.Ed.2d 893 (2003), *353*

Martin v. Raymark Industries, Inc., No. 592–00614 EBB (D.Conn. filed Oct. 22, 1992), *482*

Martin v. Valley Nat. Bank of Arizona, 140 F.R.D. 291 (S.D.N.Y. 1991), *356*

Martinez v. Schlumberger, Ltd., 338 F.3d 407 (5th Cir.2003), *268*

Martorano, United States v., 767 F.2d 63 (3rd Cir.1985), cert. denied Martorano v. United States, 474 U.S. 949, 106 S.Ct. 348, 88 L.Ed.2d 296 (1985), *211*

Massachusetts v. Morash, 490 U.S. 107, 109 S.Ct. 1668, 104 L.Ed.2d 98 (1989), *47, 335*

Massachusetts Mut. Life Ins. Co. v. Russell, 473 U.S. 134, 105 S.Ct. 3085, 87 L.Ed.2d 96 (1985), *193, 251, 343, 346*

Matter of (see name of party)

Matz v. Household Intern. Tax Reduction Inv. Plan, 265 F.3d 572 (7th Cir.2001), *89*

TABLE OF CASES

McDougall v. Donovan, 552 F.Supp. 1206 (N.D.Ill.1982), *285*

McGann v. H & H Music Co., 946 F.2d 401 (5th Cir.1991), cert. denied sub nom. Greenberg v. H & H Music Co., 506 U.S. 981, 113 S.Ct. 482, 121 L.Ed.2d 387 (1992), *116*

McGarrah v. Hartford Life Ins. Co., 234 F.3d 1026 (8th Cir. 2000), *192*

McGee v. Equicor–Equitable HCA Corp., 953 F.2d 1192 (10th Cir.1992), *215*

McNevin v. Solvay Process Co., 32 A.D. 610, 53 N.Y.S. 98 (N.Y.A.D. 4 Dept.1898), aff'd mem. 167 N.Y. 530, 60 N.E. 1115 (N.Y.1901), *58*

Mead Corp. v. Tilley, 490 U.S. 714, 109 S.Ct. 2156, 104 L.Ed.2d 796 (1989), *467*

Meredith v. Navistar Intern. Transp. Corp., 935 F.2d 124 (7th Cir.1991), *354*

Mers v. Marriott Intern. Group Accidental Death and Dismemberment Plan, 144 F.3d 1014 (7th Cir.1998), cert. denied 525 U.S. 947, 119 S.Ct. 372, 142 L.Ed.2d 307 (1998), *186*

Mertens v. Hewitt Associates, 508 U.S. 248, 113 S.Ct. 2063, 124 L.Ed.2d 161 (1993), *251, 278, 280*

Metropolitan Life Ins. Co. v. Massachusetts, 471 U.S. 724, 105 S.Ct. 2380, 85 L.Ed.2d 728 (1985), *338, 339, 340*

Metropolitan Life Ins. Co. v. Taylor, 481 U.S. 58, 107 S.Ct. 1542, 95 L.Ed.2d 55 (1987), *348*

Mett, United States v., 178 F.3d 1058 (9th Cir.1999), *356*

Michael Reese Hosp. and Medical Center v. Solo Cup Employee Health Ben. Plan, 899 F.2d 639 (7th Cir.1990), *183*

Miller v. United Welfare Fund, 72 F.3d 1066 (2nd Cir.1995), *187*

Misic v. Building Service Employees Health and Welfare Trust, 789 F.2d 1374 (9th Cir.1986), *142*

Mobile, Alabama–Pensacola, Florida Bldg. and Const. Trades Council v. Daugherty, 684 F.Supp. 270 (S.D.Ala.1988), *236*

Moench v. Robertson, 62 F.3d 553 (3rd Cir.1995), cert. denied Robertson v. Moench, 516 U.S. 1115, 116 S.Ct. 917, 133 L.Ed.2d 847 (1996), *305*

Moon v. American Home Assur. Co., 888 F.2d 86 (11th Cir.1989), *184*

Moore v. Metropolitan Life Ins. Co., 856 F.2d 488 (2nd Cir.1988), *95*

Morgan v. Contractors, Laborers, Teamsters and Engineers Pension Plan, 287 F.3d 716 (8th Cir.2002), *192*

TABLE OF CASES

Morse v. Stanley, 732 F.2d 1139 (2nd Cir.1984), *252*

Nachwalter v. Christie, 805 F.2d 956 (11th Cir.1986), *213, 219*

Nance v. Sun Life Assur. Co. of Canada, 294 F.3d 1263 (10th Cir.2002), *183*

National Companies Health Ben. Plan v. St. Joseph's Hosp. of Atlanta, Inc., 929 F.2d 1558 (11th Cir.1991), *223*

Nationwide Mut. Ins. Co. v. Darden, 503 U.S. 318, 112 S.Ct. 1344, 117 L.Ed.2d 581 (1992), *13*

NCR Corp. v. American Tel. and Tel. Co., 761 F.Supp. 475 (S.D.Ohio 1991), *323*

Nemeth v. Clark Equipment Co., 677 F.Supp. 899 (W.D.Mich. 1987), *116*

New York State Conference of Blue Cross & Blue Shield Plans v. Travelers Ins. Co., 514 U.S. 645, 115 S.Ct. 1671, 131 L.Ed.2d 695 (1995), *332*

Nieto v. Ecker, 845 F.2d 868 (9th Cir.1988), *234*

N.L.R.B. v. Amax Coal Co., a Div. of Amax, Inc., 453 U.S. 322, 101 S.Ct. 2789, 69 L.Ed.2d 672 (1981), *66*

Noorily v. Thomas & Betts Corp., 188 F.3d 153 (3rd Cir.1999), cert. denied 529 U.S. 1053, 120 S.Ct. 1555, 146 L.Ed.2d 460 (2000), *254*

Norlin Corp. v. Rooney, Pace Inc., 744 F.2d 255 (2nd Cir.1984), *323*

Northeast Dept. ILGWU Health and Welfare Fund v. Teamsters Local Union No. 229 Welfare Fund, 764 F.2d 147 (3rd Cir. 1985), *349*

Oddino v. Oddino, 65 Cal.Rptr.2d 566, 939 P.2d 1266 (Cal.1997), *146*

Pagan v. NYNEX Pension Plan, 52 F.3d 438 (2nd Cir.1995), *187*

Painters of Philadelphia Dist. Council No. 21 Welfare Fund v. Price Waterhouse, 879 F.2d 1146 (3rd Cir.1989), *234*

Pappas v. Buck Consultants, Inc., 923 F.2d 531 (7th Cir.1991), *234*

Paramount Communications, Inc. v. Time Inc., 571 A.2d 1140 (Del.Supr.1989), *324*

Patterson v. Shumate, 504 U.S. 753, 112 S.Ct. 2242, 119 L.Ed.2d 519 (1992), *141, 144*

Pegram v. Herdrich, 530 U.S. 211, 120 S.Ct. 2143, 147 L.Ed.2d 164 (2000), *255, 256, 340*

Pension Ben. Guar. Corp. v. LTV Corp., 496 U.S. 633, 110 S.Ct. 2668, 110 L.Ed.2d 579 (1990), *476*

Pension Ben. Guar. Corp. v. Solmsen, 671 F.Supp. 938 (E.D.N.Y. 1987), *233*

Perry v. P*I*E Nationwide Inc., 872 F.2d 157 (6th Cir.1989), cert. denied P*I*E Nationwide, Inc. v. Perry, 493 U.S. 1093, 110 S.Ct. 1166, 107 L.Ed.2d 1068 (1990), *342*

Perry v. Simplicity Engineering, 900 F.2d 963 (6th Cir.1990), *184*

Peterson v. Continental Cas. Co., 282 F.3d 112 (2nd Cir.2002), *353*

Phillips v. Bebber, 914 F.2d 31 (4th Cir.1990), *464*

Pierre v. Connecticut General Life Ins. Co., 932 F.2d 1552 (5th Cir.1991), cert. denied 502 U.S. 973, 112 S.Ct. 453, 116 L.Ed.2d 470 (1991), *185*

Pilot Life Ins. Co. v. Dedeaux, 481 U.S. 41, 107 S.Ct. 1549, 95 L.Ed.2d 39 (1987), *178, 330, 331, 339, 340*

Pinto v. Reliance Standard Life Ins. Co., 214 F.3d 377 (3rd Cir.2000), *186*

Plumbing Industry Bd., Plumbing Local Union No. 1 v. Howell Co., Inc., 126 F.3d 61 (2nd Cir.1997), *349*

Pokratz v. Jones Dairy Farm, 771 F.2d 206 (7th Cir.1985), *180*

Pompano v. Michael Schiavone & Sons, Inc., 680 F.2d 911 (2nd Cir.1982), cert. denied 459 U.S. 1039, 103 S.Ct. 454, 74 L.Ed.2d 607 (1982), *128*

Pressroom Unions–Printers League Income Sec. Fund v. Continental Assur. Co., 700 F.2d 889 (2nd Cir.1983), cert. denied 464 U.S. 845, 104 S.Ct. 148, 78 L.Ed.2d 138 (1983), *275*

Provident Life & Acc. Ins. Co. v. Waller, 906 F.2d 985 (4th Cir.1990), cert. denied Waller v. Provident Life & Acc. Ins. Co., 498 U.S. 982, 111 S.Ct. 512, 112 L.Ed.2d 524 (1990), *345, 349*

Quesinberry v. Life Ins. Co. of North America, 987 F.2d 1017 (4th Cir.1993), *184*

Quinn v. Blue Cross and Blue Shield Ass'n, 161 F.3d 472 (7th Cir.1998), *192*

RCM Securities Fund, Inc. v. Stanton, 928 F.2d 1318 (2nd Cir.1991), *322*

Rhoades, McKee & Boer v. United States, 43 F.3d 1071 (6th Cir.1995), *441*

Richardson v. United States News & World Report, Inc., 623 F.Supp. 350 (D.D.C.1985), *233*

Rinard v. Eastern Co., 978 F.2d 265 (6th Cir.1992), cert. denied Eastern Co. v. Rinard, 507 U.S. 1029, 113 S.Ct. 1843, 123 L.Ed.2d 468 (1993), *479*

Roberts v. Taussig, 39 F.Supp.2d 1010 (N.D.Ohio 1999), *347*

Rodrigue v. Western and Southern Life Ins. Co., 948 F.2d 969 (5th Cir.1991), *219*

Rowan v. Unum Life Ins. Co. of America, 119 F.3d 433 (6th Cir.1997), *185*

Rubio v. Chock Full O'Nuts Corp., 254 F.Supp.2d 413 (S.D.N.Y. 2003), *214*

Rush Prudential HMO, Inc. v. Moran, 536 U.S. 355, 122 S.Ct. 2151, 153 L.Ed.2d 375 (2002), *340*

Russo v. Health, Welfare & Pension Fund, Local 705, Intern. Broth. of Teamsters, 777 F.Supp. 1429 (N.D.Ill.1991), aff'd 984 F.2d 762 (7th Cir.1993), *222*

Sage v. Automation, Inc. Pension Plan and Trust, 845 F.2d 885 (10th Cir.1988), *90*

Sandoval v. Simmons, 622 F.Supp. 1174 (C.D.Ill.1985), *290*

Sanford v. Harvard Industries, Inc., 262 F.3d 590 (6th Cir.2001), *191*

Sanson v. General Motors Corp., 966 F.2d 618 (11th Cir.1992), cert. denied 507 U.S. 984, 113 S.Ct. 1578, 123 L.Ed.2d 146 (1993), *343*

Sarault, United States v., 840 F.2d 1479 (9th Cir.1988), *211*

Saret v. Triform Corp., 662 F.Supp. 312 (N.D.Ill.1986), *219*

Scardelletti v. Bobo, 897 F.Supp. 913 (D.Md.1995), *276*

Scheider v. United States Steel Corp., 486 F.Supp. 211 (W.D.Pa. 1980), *168*

Schneider Moving & Storage Co. v. Robbins, 466 U.S. 364, 104 S.Ct. 1844, 80 L.Ed.2d 366 (1984), *167*

Schwartz v. Interfaith Medical Center, 715 F.Supp. 1190 (E.D.N.Y.1989), *191, 262*

S. E. C. v. Evans, [1989–90] Transfer Binder Fed.Sec.L.Rep. ¶ 94,802 (S.E.C. Release No.1989), *317*

S.E.C. v. W.J. Howey Co., 328 U.S. 293, 66 S.Ct. 1100, 90 L.Ed. 1244 (1946), *68*

Sedlack v. Braswell Services Group, Inc., 134 F.3d 219 (4th Cir.1998), *193*

Senkier v. Hartford Life & Acc. Ins. Co., 948 F.2d 1050 (7th Cir.1991), *216*

Senn v. United Dominion Industries, Inc., 951 F.2d 806 (7th Cir.1992), cert. denied 509 U.S. 903, 113 S.Ct. 2992, 125 L.Ed.2d 687 (1993), *94*

Shamrock Holdings, Inc. v. Polaroid Corp., 559 A.2d 257 (Del.Ch. 1989), *323, 324, 325*

Shaw v. Delta Air Lines, Inc., 463 U.S. 85, 103 S.Ct. 2890, 77 L.Ed.2d 490 (1983), *10, 329, 331*

Shea v. Esensten, 107 F.3d 625 (8th Cir.1997), cert. denied 522 U.S. 914, 118 S.Ct. 297, 139 L.Ed.2d 229 (1997), *269*

Sheffield v. Allstate Life Ins. Co., 756 F.Supp. 309 (S.D.Tex. 1991), *9*

Sigman v. Rudolph Wurlitzer Co., 57 Ohio App. 4, 11 N.E.2d 878 (Ohio App. 1 Dist.1937), *35, 60*

Smith v. Hartford Ins. Group, 6 F.3d 131 (3rd Cir.1993), *222*

Sokol v. Bernstein, 812 F.2d 559 (9th Cir.1987), *352*

Sprague v. General Motors Corp., 133 F.3d 388 (6th Cir.1998), cert. denied 524 U.S. 923, 118 S.Ct. 2312, 141 L.Ed.2d 170 (1998), *94, 221*

Springer v. Wal–Mart Associates' Group Health Plan, 908 F.2d 897 (11th Cir.1990), *169*

Straub v. Western Union Telegraph Co., 851 F.2d 1262 (10th Cir.1988), *219*

Successor Trust Committee of Permian Distributing, Inc. Employees' Profit Sharing Plan and Trust v. First State Bank, Odessa, N.A., 735 F.Supp. 708 (W.D.Tex.1990), *270*

Sutton v. Weirton Steel Div. of Nat. Steel Corp., 724 F.2d 406 (4th Cir.1983), cert. denied 467 U.S. 1205, 104 S.Ct. 2387, 81 L.Ed.2d 345 (1984), *92*

S & Vee Cartage Co., Inc., United States v., 704 F.2d 914 (6th Cir.1983), cert. denied S & Vee Cartage Company, Inc. v. United States, 464 U.S. 935, 104 S.Ct. 343, 78 L.Ed.2d 310 (1983), *211*

Taft v. Equitable Life Assur. Soc., 9 F.3d 1469 (9th Cir.1993), *189*

Tango Transport v. Healthcare Financial Services LLC, 322 F.3d 888 (5th Cir.2003), *142*

TABLE OF CASES

Tenneco Inc. v. First Virginia Bank of Tidewater, 698 F.2d 688 (4th Cir.1983), *141*

Texas Industries, Inc. v. Radcliff Materials, Inc., 451 U.S. 630, 101 S.Ct. 2061, 68 L.Ed.2d 500 (1981), *344*

Thomas v. Oregon Fruit Products Co., 228 F.3d 991 (9th Cir. 2000), *190*

Time Oil Co. v. Commissioner, 258 F.2d 237 (9th Cir.1958), *65*

Tolton v. American Biodyne, Inc., 48 F.3d 937 (6th Cir.1995), *343*

Union Labor Life Ins. Co. v. Pireno, 458 U.S. 119, 102 S.Ct. 3002, 73 L.Ed.2d 647 (1982), *338*

United Food & Commercial Workers & Employers Arizona Health & Welfare Trust v. Pacyga, 801 F.2d 1157 (9th Cir. 1986), *342*

United Independent Flight Officers, Inc. v. United Air Lines, Inc., 756 F.2d 1274 (7th Cir.1985), *254*

United States v. _____ (see opposing party)

United Steelworkers of America v. Warrior & Gulf Nav. Co., 363 U.S. 574, 80 S.Ct. 1347, 4 L.Ed.2d 1409 (1960), *167*

University of Tennessee William F. Bowld Hosp. v. Wal–Mart Stores, Inc., 951 F.Supp. 724 (W.D.Tenn.1996), *143*

Unocal Corp. v. Mesa Petroleum Co., 493 A.2d 946 (Del. Supr.1985), *323*

Useden v. Acker, 947 F.2d 1563 (11th Cir.1991), cert. denied sub nom. Useden v. Greenberg, Traurig, Hoffman, Lipoff, Rosen & Quentel, 508 U.S. 959, 113 S.Ct. 2927, 124 L.Ed.2d 678 (1993), *234*

Van Boxel v. Journal Co. Employees' Pension Trust, 836 F.2d 1048 (7th Cir.1987), *180, 236*

Varity Corp. v. Howe, 516 U.S. 489, 116 S.Ct. 1065, 134 L.Ed.2d 130 (1996), *193, 251, 252, 254, 255, 268, 278, 279*

Wardle v. Central States, Southeast and Southwest Areas Pension Fund, 627 F.2d 820 (7th Cir.1980), cert. denied 449 U.S. 1112, 101 S.Ct. 922, 66 L.Ed.2d 841 (1981), *189*

Warner v. Ford Motor Co., 46 F.3d 531 (6th Cir.1995), *349*

Washington–Baltimore Newspaper Guild, Local 35 v. Washington Star Co., 543 F.Supp. 906 (D.D.C.1982), *355*

Watts v. BellSouth Telecommunications, Inc., 316 F.3d 1203 (11th Cir.2003), *168*

TABLE OF CASES

Weaver v. Phoenix Home Life Mut. Ins. Co., 990 F.2d 154 (4th Cir.1993), *192*

Weldon v. Kraft, Inc., 896 F.2d 793 (3rd Cir.1990), *168*

Wheeler v. Dynamic Engineering, Inc., 62 F.3d 634 (4th Cir. 1995), *185*

White v. Jacobs Engineering Group Long Term Disability Benefit Plan, 896 F.2d 344 (9th Cir.1989), *216*

Whitfield v. Cohen, 682 F.Supp. 188 (S.D.N.Y.1988), *231*

Whitfield v. Lindemann, 853 F.2d 1298 (5th Cir.1988), cert. denied sub nom. Klepak v. Dole, 490 U.S. 1089, 109 S.Ct. 2428, 104 L.Ed.2d 986 (1989), *280*

Whitfield v. Torch Operating Co., 935 F.Supp. 822 (E.D.La.1996), *217*

Wickman v. Northwestern Nat. Ins. Co., 908 F.2d 1077 (1st Cir.1990), cert. denied 498 U.S. 1013, 111 S.Ct. 581, 112 L.Ed.2d 586 (1990), *337*

Williams v. Midwest Operating Engineers Welfare Fund, 125 F.3d 1138 (7th Cir.1997), cert. dismissed Midwest Operating Engineers Welfare Fund v. Williams, 522 U.S. 1101, 118 S.Ct. 907, 139 L.Ed.2d 922 (1998), *216*

Winchester v. Pension Committee of Michael Reese Health Plan, Inc. Pension Plan, 942 F.2d 1190 (7th Cir.1991), *210*

Wineinger v. United Healthcare Insurance Co., 25 Employee Benefits Cas. 2692 (D.Neb.2001), *352*

Winpisinger v. Aurora Corp. of Illinois, Precision Castings Division, 456 F.Supp. 559 (N.D.Ohio 1978), *252*

Winstead v. J.C. Penney Co., Inc., 933 F.2d 576 (7th Cir.1991), *345*

Winters v. Costco Wholesale Corp., 49 F.3d 550 (9th Cir.1995), cert. denied sub nom. 516 U.S. 908, 116 S.Ct. 276, 133 L.Ed.2d 197 (1995), *185*

Woo v. Deluxe Corp., 144 F.3d 1157 (8th Cir.1998), *186*

Ziegler v. Connecticut General Life Ins. Co., 916 F.2d 548 (9th Cir.1990), *351*

Zwolanek v. Baker Mfg. Co., 150 Wis. 517, 137 N.W. 769 (Wis. 1912), *59*

TABLE OF STATUTES AND REGULATIONS

UNITED STATES CONSTITUTION

Amend.	This Work Page
7	189

UNITED STATES CODE ANNOTATED
11 U.S.C.A.—Bankruptcy

Sec.	This Work Page
Ch. 11	95
541(a)	143
541(c)(2)	144
704	474
1114	95
1114(e)(1)	95
1114(g)	95

15 U.S.C.A.—Commerce and Trade

Sec.	This Work Page
77b(1)	67
77c(a)(2)	69
1011	327
1012	337

18 U.S.C.A.—Crimes and Criminal Procedure

Sec.	This Work Page
1027	211

UNITED STATES CODE ANNOTATED
26 U.S.C.A.—Internal Revenue Code

Sec.	This Work Page
72	150
72	154
72	156
72(a)	150
72(b)(1)	151
72(b)(2)	152
72(b)(3)	152
72(b)(4)	152
72(c)(1)	152
72(c)(3)	152
72(d)	152
72(d)	153
72(d)(1)(D)	154
72(d)(2)	155
72(e)	153
72(e)	155
72(e)(2)(A)	154
72(e)(2)(B)	154
72(e)(8)(A)	154
72(e)(8)(B)—(e)(8)(C)	154
72(e)(8)(D)	154
72(f)	152
72(o)(5)(B)	133
72(p)	133
72(p)	134
72(p)(2)(A)	133
72(p)(2)(B)	134
72(p)(2)(C)	134
72(p)(2)(D)	133
72(t)	163
72(t)	425
72(t)(2)(A)	163
72(t)(2)(B)—(t)(2)(F)	164
125	368
132(f)(4)	368
162	449
212	449
213	163
401	19

TABLE OF STATUTES AND REGULATIONS

UNITED STATES CODE ANNOTATED
26 U.S.C.A.—Internal Revenue Code

Sec.	This Work Page
401	207
401(a)	243
401(a)	454
401(a)(2)	478
401(a)(4)	362
401(a)(4)	373
401(a)(4)	381
401(a)(4)	382
401(a)(4)	383
401(a)(4)	384
401(a)(4)	394
401(a)(4)	396
401(a)(4)	397
401(a)(4)	403
401(a)(4)	404
401(a)(4)	406
401(a)(4)	408
401(a)(4)	409
401(a)(4)	410
401(a)(4)	421
401(a)(4)	422
401(a)(4)	423
401(a)(4)	426
401(a)(4)—(a)(5)	19
401(a)(5)(B)	382
401(a)(5)(C)	44
401(a)(5)(C)	382
401(a)(5)(D)	44
401(a)(5)(D)	382
401(a)(5)(D)	397
401(a)(5)(D)	406
401(a)(9)	159
401(a)(9)(A)	140
401(a)(9)(B)(i)	140
401(a)(9)(B)(ii)	140
401(a)(9)(C)	140
401(a)(9)(G)	138
401(a)(11)	122
401(a)(13)	141
401(a)(16)	411

TABLE OF STATUTES AND REGULATIONS

UNITED STATES CODE ANNOTATED
26 U.S.C.A.—Internal Revenue Code

Sec.	This Work Page
401(a)(17)	368
401(a)(17)	422
401(a)(22)	312
401(a)(26)	373
401(a)(26)	378
401(a)(26)	381
401(a)(26)(B)(i)	379
401(a)(26)(G)	380
401(a)(27)	5
401(a)(28)(B)	314
401(a)(28)(C)	314
401(a)(30)	418
401(a)(31)(A)	162
401(a)(31)(B)	162
401(a)(31)(C)	162
401(a)(31)(E)	162
401(b)(1)	420
401(c)(1)	156
401(d)	11
401(f)	244
401(h)	135
401(k)	6
401(k)	12
401(k)	97
401(k)	361
401(k)	387
401(k)	396
401(k)	410
401(k)	416
401(k)	426
401(k)	427
401(k)	428
401(k)	449
401(k)(1)	417
401(k)(2)(B)(i)	417
401(k)(2)(B)(ii)	417
401(k)(2)(C)	417
401(k)(2)(D)	97
401(k)(2)(D)	417
401(k)(3)(A)	420

UNITED STATES CODE ANNOTATED
26 U.S.C.A.—Internal Revenue Code

	This Work
Sec.	Page
401(k)(3)(A)	423
401(k)(3)(A)(ii)	420
401(k)(3)(A)(ii)	423
401(k)(3)(A)(ii)	426
401(k)(3)(B)	421
401(k)(3)(C)	421
401(k)(3)(D)(i)	422
401(k)(3)(D)(ii)	422
401(k)(3)(E)	421
401(k)(4)(A)	419
401(k)(8)(A)	425
401(k)(8)(B)	425
401(k)(8)(D)	425
401(k)(11)	12
401(k)(11)(A)(iii)	427
401(k)(11)(B)(i)	427
401(k)(11)(B)(ii)	427
401(k)(11)(C)	427
401(k)(11)(D)(ii)	428
401(k)(12)(B)(i)	424
401(k)(12)(B)(ii)	424
401(k)(12)(B)(iii)	424
401(k)(12)(C)	424
401(k)(12)(D)	423
401(*l*)	385
401(*l*)	391
401(*l*)	397
401(*l*)	398
401(*l*)	399
401(*l*)	400
401(*l*)	401
401(*l*)	402
401(*l*)	403
401(*l*)	404
401(*l*)(2)	399
401(*l*)(3)(A)(i)	399
401(*l*)(3)(B)	401
401(*l*)(5)(A)	399
401(*l*)(5)(A)(ii)	398
401(m)	396

TABLE OF STATUTES AND REGULATIONS

UNITED STATES CODE ANNOTATED
26 U.S.C.A.—Internal Revenue Code

Sec.	This Work Page
401(m)	410
401(m)	418
401(m)(1)	422
401(m)(2)	422
401(m)(3)	422
401(m)(4)(A)	418
401(m)(4)(C)	419
401(m)(6)	425
402	156
402(a)(1)	150
402(c)	158
402(c)(1)	158
402(c)(2)	160
402(c)(2)(B)	160
402(c)(3)(A)	159
402(c)(3)(B)	159
402(c)(4)	159
402(c)(6)(A)	160
402(c)(6)(B)	160
402(c)(6)(D)	160
402(c)(8)(B)	159
402(c)(9)	160
402(e)(1)(B)	161
402(e)(3)	416
402(e)(4)(B)	156
402(e)(4)(B)	157
402(e)(4)(D)(i)	156
402(e)(4)(D)(ii)	156
402(e)(4)(E)	156
402(e)(6)	158
402(f)	162
402(g)(1)	418
402(g)(3)	359
402(g)(3)	368
402(g)(3)	450
403(a)	159
403(a)	244
403(b)	159
403(c)(2)	452
404(a)	449

L

UNITED STATES CODE ANNOTATED
26 U.S.C.A.—Internal Revenue Code

Sec.	This Work Page
404(a)(1)(A)	450
404(a)(1)(A)	451
404(a)(1)(D)(i)	451
404(a)(1)(D)(ii)	451
404(a)(1)(E)	451
404(a)(2)	244
404(a)(2)	450
404(a)(3)	450
404(a)(3)(A)(i)(I)	449
404(a)(3)(A)(i)(II)	449
404(a)(3)(A)(ii)	449
404(a)(3)(A)(iv)	449
404(a)(3)(A)(v)	451
404(a)(5)	32
404(a)(7)(A)	452
404(a)(7)(B)	452
404(a)(9)	308
404(j)(1)(A)	451
404(j)(1)(B)	449
404(k)	163
404(k)	315
404(k)(2)(A)(ii)	315
404(l)	450
404(n)	450
408	11
408(h)	244
408(k)	12
408(p)	12
408(p)(2)(C)(i)	427
408(p)(2)(E)(i)	427
408(p)(3)	427
409(a)(9)(B)(iii)	140
409(a)(9)(B)(iv)	141
409(e)	319
409(e)	320
409(e)(2)	311
409(e)(3)	312
409(e)(4)	312
409(e)(5)	312
409(h)(1)	312

TABLE OF STATUTES AND REGULATIONS

UNITED STATES CODE ANNOTATED
26 U.S.C.A.—Internal Revenue Code

Sec.	This Work Page
409(h)(1)(B)	313
409(h)(2)	313
409(h)(4)	313
409(*l*)(1)	306
409(*l*)(2)	307
409(*l*)(3)	307
409(n)	316
409(*o*)(1)(A)	313
409(*o*)(1)(B)	314
409(*o*)(1)(C)	314
409(p)	311
410(a)(26)(B)(ii)	379
410(b)	19
410(b)	362
410(b)	369
410(b)	370
410(b)	373
410(b)	379
410(b)	381
410(b)	383
410(b)	387
410(b)	392
410(b)	393
410(b)	396
410(b)	405
410(b)	410
410(b)	423
410(b)(1)	358
410(b)(1)(A)	363
410(b)(1)(A)	373
410(b)(1)(B)	363
410(b)(2)	363
410(b)(2)(B)	366
410(b)(2)(C)	366
410(b)(2)(C)(i)	368
410(b)(2)(D)	367
410(b)(3)(A)	371
410(b)(4)(A)	367
410(b)(4)(A)	372
410(b)(4)(B)	372

UNITED STATES CODE ANNOTATED
26 U.S.C.A.—Internal Revenue Code

Sec.	This Work Page
410(b)(5)	373
410(b)(5)(B)	373
410(b)(6)(B)	362
410(k)(3)(A)(i)	420
411(d)(3)	88
411(d)(3)	462
412(a)	437
412(a)	438
412(a)	439
412(a)(1)(A)	451
412(b)(1)	438
412(b)(2)	438
412(b)(2)(B)(ii)	434
412(b)(2)(D)	440
412(b)(3)	439
412(b)(3)(D)	440
412(c)(1)	441
412(c)(2)	442
412(c)(3)	441
412(c)(5)	446
412(c)(6)	443
412(c)(6)(B)	444
412(c)(7)	444
412(c)(7)(C)	444
412(c)(8)	109
412(c)(8)	447
412(c)(9)	441
412(c)(10)(A)	441
412(c)(10)(B)	441
412(d)	445
412(e)	445
412(f)(1)	446
412(f)(1)	447
412(f)(3)(B)	447
412(f)(4)	447
412(g)(1)	439
412(g)(2)	439
412(h)	437
412(i)	437
412(*l*)(1)	442

UNITED STATES CODE ANNOTATED
26 U.S.C.A.—Internal Revenue Code

Sec.	This Work Page
412(*l*)(2)—(*l*)(4)	443
412(*l*)(5)(A)	443
412(*l*)(7)	442
412(*l*)(7)(B)	443
412(*l*)(8)(A)	442
412(*l*)(8)(B)	442
412(*l*)(9)	442
412(*l*)(9)(C)	442
412(m)	441
412(n)	449
413(b)(6)	448
414	412
414(b)	369
414(c)	369
414(m)	369
414(m)(2)	370
414(m)(5)	370
414(n)(1)	370
414(n)(2)	370
414(n)(5)	370
414(q)(1)	358
414(q)(2)	359
414(q)(3)	359
414(q)(4)	359
414(q)(5)	359
414(q)(5)	376
414(q)(6)	360
414(q)(8)	359
414(r)(2)	376
414(r)(3)	376
414(s)	368
414(s)(2)	368
414(v)(1)	426
414(v)(2)(A)	426
414(v)(2)(B)(ii)	428
414(v)(2)(D)	426
414(v)(3)(A)	426
414(v)(3)(B)	426
414(v)(5)(B)	426
415	411

UNITED STATES CODE ANNOTATED
26 U.S.C.A.—Internal Revenue Code

Sec.	This Work Page
415	449
415	451
415(b)(1)	413
415(b)(2)(A)	414
415(b)(2)(C)	414
415(b)(2)(D)	414
415(b)(4)	413
415(b)(5)(A)	414
415(b)(5)(B)	414
415(b)(5)(C)	414
415(b)(7)	413
415(b)(8)	400
415(c)(1)	412
415(c)(3)	359
415(c)(3)	367
415(c)(3)	368
415(c)(3)(C)	413
415(c)(3)(D)	412
415(e)	415
415(f)(1)	412
415(g)	412
415(h)	412
415(k)(1)	412
416	90
416(b)(2)	91
416(c)(1)	107
416(c)(2)	107
416(g)	90
416(i)	136
416(i)(1)	90
416(i)(1)(B)	359
417	122
420	245
457	368
457(b)	159
503	282
1042	315
1042(a)	316
1042(a)(1)	316
1042(a)(2)	316

LV

UNITED STATES CODE ANNOTATED
26 U.S.C.A.—Internal Revenue Code

Sec.	This Work Page
1042(b)(2)	316
1042(b)(3)	316
1042(b)(4)	316
1042(c)(1)	315
1042(c)(3)	316
1042(c)(4)	316
1042(c)(7)	316
1042(d)	317
1042(e)	317
1563	369
3405(c)(1)	161
3405(c)(2)	161
4941	282
4971(a)	20
4971(a)	438
4971(a)	448
4971(b)	448
4971(c)(3)	448
4971(d)	448
4972(a)	452
4972(c)	452
4975(a)	298
4975(b)	299
4975(c)(1)(A)—(c)(1)(D)	288
4975(c)(1)(E)	288
4975(c)(1)(F)	291
4975(c)(2)	296
4975(d)(1)	148
4975(d)(3)	309
4975(e)(2)	15
4975(e)(2)	282
4975(e)(2)(H)	283
4975(e)(7)	6
4975(e)(7)	311
4975(e)(7)	312
4975(e)(7)	313
4975(e)(7)(A)	306
4975(e)(8)	306
4975(f)(2)	299
4975(f)(3)	285

UNITED STATES CODE ANNOTATED
26 U.S.C.A.—Internal Revenue Code

Sec.	This Work Page
4975(f)(4)	299
4975(f)(4)(B)	299
4975(f)(5)	299
4978	316
4979A	316
4980	20
4980(a)	479
4980(d)(1)	479
4980(d)(2)	480
4980(d)(3)	480
4980F(b)	111
4980F(c)	111
6057	199
6057(a)	202
6057(d)	202
6058	199
6652	210
6692	210

28 U.S.C.A.—Judiciary and Judicial Procedure

Sec.	This Work Page
1331	349
1391(b)	350
2412(d)(1)(A)	353

29 U.S.C.A.—Labor

Sec.	This Work Page
623(a)	80

TABLE OF STATUTES AND REGULATIONS

POPULAR NAME ACTS

CIVIL RIGHTS ACT OF 1964

Tit.	This Work Page
VII	115
VII	119

EMPLOYEE RETIREMENT INCOME SECURITY ACT

Tit.	This Work Page
I	6
I	7
I	9
I	10
I	11
I	12
I	15
I	16
I	17
I	18
I	19
I	20
I	21
I	77
I	144
I	194
I	208
I	210
I	267
I	273
I	281
I	282
I	288
I	301
I	303
I	306
I	319
I	326
I	333
I	348
I	351
I	352

TABLE OF STATUTES AND REGULATIONS

EMPLOYEE RETIREMENT INCOME SECURITY ACT

Tit.	This Work Page
I	437
I	454
I	462
I	463
I	467
I	481
I, Subt. A	16
I, Subt. B	16
I, Subt. B, Pt. 2	91
I, Subt. B, Pt. 2	244
I, Subt. B, Pt. 3	244
I, Subt. B, Pt. 4	351
II	6
II	10
II	11
II	12
II	15
II	19
II	20
II	21
III	16
IV	16
IV	20
IV	21
IV	194
IV	244
IV	454
IV	455
IV	456
IV	463
IV	475
IV	480
IV	482

Sec.	
2(b)	167
3(1)	3
3(1)—(3)	2
3(2)	3
3(2)(A)(ii)	45
3(7)	13

TABLE OF STATUTES AND REGULATIONS

EMPLOYEE RETIREMENT INCOME SECURITY ACT

Sec.	This Work Page
3(8)	13
3(14)	15
3(14)(A)	283
3(14)(B)	283
3(14)(C)	283
3(14)(D)	283
3(14)(E)	283
3(14)(F)	283
3(14)(G)	283
3(14)(H)	283
3(14)(I)	283
3(15)	283
3(16)	235
3(16)(A)	14
3(16)(A)	229
3(16)(B)	13
3(18)	305
3(20)	301
3(21)(A)	14
3(21)(A)	225
3(21)(A)	232
3(21)(A)	234
3(21)(A)(ii)	231
3(22)	80
3(23)	107
3(23)(A)	99
3(23)(A)	112
3(23)(B)	98
3(24)	80
3(28)	431
3(29)	443
3(31)	432
3(34)	4
3(35)	3
3(36)	11
3(37)(A)	8
3(38)	14
3(38)	230
4	326
4(a)(1)	9
4(b)(1)	9

TABLE OF STATUTES AND REGULATIONS

EMPLOYEE RETIREMENT INCOME SECURITY ACT

Sec.	This Work Page
4(b)(2)	10
4(b)(3)	10
4(b)(4)	10
4(b)(5)	10
101—111	16
101—111	194
101(c)	209
101(d)	447
102(a)	197
102(a)	199
102(b)	214
103	199
103(a)(3)(A)	200
103(a)(3)(D)	200
103(b)	200
103(c)(3)	201
103(c)(4)	201
103(d)	201
103(e)	201
104(a)(1)	203
104(a)(6)	203
104(b)(1)	205
104(b)(1)(B)	205
104(b)(2)	206
104(b)(3)	202
104(b)(3)	206
104(b)(4)	206
105(a)	207
105(b)	207
105(c)	206
106	203
107	208
201	92
201—211	16
201(1)	92
201(1)	107
202(a)(1)(A)	96
202(a)(1)(B)(i)	97
202(a)(1)(B)(ii)	97
202(a)(2)	97
202(a)(3)	96

TABLE OF STATUTES AND REGULATIONS

EMPLOYEE RETIREMENT INCOME SECURITY ACT

Sec.	This Work Page
202(a)(4)	97
202(b)	96
203(a)	81
203(a)(1)	83
203(a)(2)(A)	83
203(a)(2)(B)	83
203(a)(3)(A)	86
203(a)(3)(B)	86
203(a)(3)(D)	87
203(a)(4)	84
203(b)(1)	85
203(b)(2)	84
203(b)(3)(A)	85
203(b)(3)(B)	85
203(b)(3)(D)	86
203(b)(3)(E)	85
203(c)(1)	88
203(d)	84
203(e)(1)	129
203(e)(1)	139
204(b)(1)(A)	101
204(b)(1)(B)	102
204(b)(1)(B)(i)	103
204(b)(1)(B)(ii)	103
204(b)(1)(C)	104
204(b)(1)(F)	105
204(b)(1)(H)	106
204(b)(1)(H)(i)	112
204(b)(2)	106
204(c)(1)	99
204(c)(2)(A)	99
204(c)(3)	99
204(d)	129
204(g)	108
204(g)(1)	109
204(g)(1)	110
204(g)(2)	110
204(g)(2)	479
204(g)(2)(A)	108
204(g)(4)	110
204(g)(5)	110

TABLE OF STATUTES AND REGULATIONS

EMPLOYEE RETIREMENT INCOME SECURITY ACT

Sec.	This Work Page
204(h)	110
204(h)(2)	110
204(h)(3)	110
204(h)(6)	111
204(h)(9)	110
205	122
205	123
205(a)	123
205(b)(1)(C)	123
205(c)(1)	125
205(c)(2)	126
205(c)(3)	127
205(c)(5)	127
205(c)(7)	126
205(c)(8)	127
205(d)	123
205(e)(1)(A)	124
205(e)(1)(B)	124
205(e)(2)	124
205(f)	125
205(g)(1)	130
205(g)(2)	130
205(h)(1)	124
205(h)(2)(A)	125
206(a)	139
206(d)	148
206(d)(1)	141
206(d)(1)	142
206(d)(2)	148
206(d)(3)(A)	145
206(d)(3)(B)	145
206(d)(3)(C)	146
206(d)(3)(D)	146
206(d)(3)(E)	147
206(d)(3)(F)	147
206(d)(3)(G)	146
206(d)(3)(H)	147
206(d)(3)(K)	145
206(d)(4)	149
206(d)(5)	149
209	208

EMPLOYEE RETIREMENT INCOME SECURITY ACT

Sec.	This Work Page
209(a)	210
209(b)	210
301—308	17
301(a)	437
401—414	17
401(a)(1)	244
401(b)(1)	239
401(b)(2)	241
401(b)(2)	242
401(b)(2)(B)	241
401(c)	243
402	211
402(a)	14
402(a)	226
402(a)(1)	211
402(a)(2)	211
402(b)	211
402(c)(1)	229
402(c)(3)	228
403(a)	14
403(a)	227
403(a)	243
403(a)(1)	229
403(a)(1)	319
403(a)(2)	228
403(b)(1)	244
403(b)(2)	244
403(b)(3)	244
403(b)(4)	244
403(c)	245
403(c)	477
403(c)(2)	245
403(c)(3)	245
403(d)(2)	245
404	283
404	292
404—406	15
404(a)(1)	249
404(a)(1)	250
404(a)(1)	271
404(a)(1)(B)	263

EMPLOYEE RETIREMENT INCOME SECURITY ACT

Sec.	This Work Page
404(a)(1)(B)	305
404(a)(1)(C)	266
404(a)(1)(C)	305
404(a)(1)(D)	212
404(a)(1)(D)	267
404(a)(1)(D)	320
404(a)(2)	305
404(c)(1)	274
404(c)(1)	275
404(d)(1)	454
405	292
405(a)(1)	269
405(a)(2)	269
405(a)(3)	269
405(a)(3)	273
405(b)(1)(A)	271
405(b)(1)(B)	229
405(b)(1)(B)	271
405(b)(3)	271
405(b)(3)(B)	272
405(c)(1)	228
405(c)(2)(A)	271
405(c)(3)	228
405(d)(1)	271
406	292
406	297
406—407	15
406(a)	284
406(a)	285
406(a)	288
406(a)	293
406(a)	304
406(a)(1)(A)	285
406(a)(1)(B)	131
406(a)(1)(B)	286
406(a)(1)(B)	309
406(a)(1)(C)	286
406(a)(1)(D)	287
406(a)(1)(E)	287
406(a)(1)(E)	300
406(a)(2)	288

TABLE OF STATUTES AND REGULATIONS

EMPLOYEE RETIREMENT INCOME SECURITY ACT

Sec.	This Work Page
406(b)	284
406(b)	287
406(b)	288
406(b)	290
406(b)	291
406(b)(1)	288
406(b)(1)	289
406(b)(1)	304
406(b)(2)	287
406(b)(2)	288
406(b)(2)	289
406(b)(2)	290
406(b)(2)	291
406(b)(2)	304
406(b)(3)	291
406(b)(3)	293
406(c)	285
407(a)	287
407(a)	300
407(a)(1)(A)	303
407(a)(2)	303
407(b)(1)	304
407(d)(1)	301
407(d)(2)	302
407(d)(3)	303
407(d)(4)	302
407(d)(5)	301
407(d)(5)	302
407(e)	302
407(e)	304
407(f)(1)	302
408	2
408	292
408(a)	296
408(b)(1)	131
408(b)(1)	293
408(b)(2)	293
408(b)(3)	309
408(b)(4)	294
408(b)(5)	294
408(b)(6)	294

TABLE OF STATUTES AND REGULATIONS

EMPLOYEE RETIREMENT INCOME SECURITY ACT

Sec.	This Work Page
408(b)(8)	294
408(c)(1)	295
408(c)(2)	293
408(c)(2)	295
408(c)(3)	235
408(c)(3)	295
408(d)	292
408(e)	304
409	193
409	250
409	251
409	275
409	276
409	278
409	297
409(b)	270
410	274
410(a)	273
410(b)(1)	273
410(b)(2)	273
410(b)(3)	273
411(a)	248
411(b)	248
412	238
412(a)	246
412(a)(2)	246
412(b)	247
412(c)	247
413	351
501	210
501—515	18
502(a)	172
502(a)	178
502(a)	279
502(a)	331
502(a)	343
502(a)	344
502(a)	348
502(a)	349
502(a)(1)(B)	179
502(a)(1)(B)	181

TABLE OF STATUTES AND REGULATIONS

EMPLOYEE RETIREMENT INCOME SECURITY ACT

Sec.	This Work Page
502(a)(1)(B)	188
502(a)(1)(B)	190
502(a)(1)(B)	209
502(a)(1)(B)	219
502(a)(1)(B)	348
502(a)(1)(B)	350
502(a)(2)	193
502(a)(2)	250
502(a)(2)	251
502(a)(2)	275
502(a)(2)	297
502(a)(2)	344
502(a)(3)	191
502(a)(3)	193
502(a)(3)	209
502(a)(3)	250
502(a)(3)	251
502(a)(3)	270
502(a)(3)	278
502(a)(3)	279
502(a)(3)	280
502(a)(3)	281
502(a)(3)	297
502(a)(3)	298
502(a)(3)	344
502(a)(3)	345
502(a)(5)	281
502(a)(5)	297
502(a)(5)	298
502(a)(9)	482
502(c)(1)	209
502(c)(2)	210
502(c)(3)	252
502(d)	2
502(d)	275
502(d)	331
502(d)	332
502(d)(1)	350
502(e)(1)	348
502(e)(1)	349
502(e)(2)	350

TABLE OF STATUTES AND REGULATIONS

EMPLOYEE RETIREMENT INCOME SECURITY ACT

Sec.	This Work Page
502(g)(1)	352
502(g)(1)	353
502(h)	351
502(i)	298
502(l)	279
502(l)	280
502(l)	297
502(l)	298
502(l)(2)	298
502(l)(3)	298
502(l)(4)	298
503	165
503	166
503	167
503	169
503	177
503(a)(3)	280
510	114
510	115
510	116
510	117
510	351
514	326
514	329
514(a)	178
514(a)	326
514(a)	327
514(a)	329
514(a)	342
514(b)(2)(A)	326
514(b)(2)(A)	337
514(b)(2)(B)	327
514(b)(2)(B)	339
514(b)(2)(B)	341
514(c)	326
601—609	18
609(a)	143
701—734	18
3001	207
3001	208
3002(b)	448

TABLE OF STATUTES AND REGULATIONS

EMPLOYEE RETIREMENT INCOME SECURITY ACT

Sec.	This Work Page
3022	329
3041—3042	201
4001(a)(3)	456
4001(a)(8)	458
4001(a)(13)	457
4001(a)(14)	469
4001(a)(15)	456
4001(a)(16)	464
4001(a)(19)	472
4001ff	20
4002	21
4002	455
4005	20
4005(a)	457
4005(b)(1)	457
4005(b)(2)	457
4006	20
4006(a)(3)(A)(i)	458
4006(a)(3)(A)(iii)	458
4006(a)(3)(E)	458
4007(a)	457
4007(e)	457
4021(a)	456
4021(b)	456
4021(b)(12)	466
4022(a)	458
4022(b)(1)	459
4022(b)(3)	459
4022(b)(5)(A)	460
4022(b)(5)(B)	460
4022(b)(5)(C)	460
4022(b)(7)	459
4022(c)(1)	472
4022(c)(3)	472
4022A(a)	460
4022A(b)	460
4022A(c)	460
4022B(a)	459
4041	20
4041(a)(2)	464
4041(a)(3)	468

EMPLOYEE RETIREMENT INCOME SECURITY ACT

Sec.	This Work Page
4041(a)(3)	473
4041(b)(2)(A)	465
4041(b)(2)(B)	465
4041(b)(2)(C)	465
4041(b)(2)(D)	465
4041(b)(3)(A)	467
4041(b)(3)(B)	466
4041(c)(1)	468
4041(c)(2)(A)	469
4041(c)(2)(B)	469
4041(c)(2)(C)	469
4041(c)(3)(A)	470
4041(c)(3)(B)	470
4041(c)(3)(C)(ii)	470
4041(c)(3)(D)	471
4042	20
4042(a)	473
4042(b)(1)	473
4042(b)(3)	473
4042(c)	474
4042(d)(1)(A)	473
4042(d)(1)(B)	474
4042(d)(2)	474
4042(d)(3)	474
4042(e)	474
4042(f)	474
4043(a)	463
4043(b)	463
4043(c)	463
4043(d)	464
4043(e)	464
4044(a)	466
4044(d)	245
4044(d)	467
4044(d)	477
4044(d)(2)	479
4047	475
4062	21
4062(b)(1)	471
4062(b)(2)	471
4062(c)	475

TABLE OF STATUTES AND REGULATIONS

EMPLOYEE RETIREMENT INCOME SECURITY ACT

Sec.	This Work Page
4065	199
4067—4068	21
4068(a)	471
4068(c)	472
4068(d)(1)	472
4069(a)	471
4071	463
4201	483
4201—4303	21
4201(b)	483
4202	483
4203(a)	482
4204(a)(1)	483
4205(a)	483
4206	483
4211	483
4219(b)(1)	483
4219(b)(2)	483
4221(a)	483
4221(b)(1)	483
4221(b)(2)	483
4222	484
4281	110

LABOR MANAGEMENT RELATIONS ACT

Sec.	This Work Page
302(c)(5)	63
302(c)(5)	66

McCARRAN–FERGUSON ACT

Sec.	This Work Page
1	326

SECURITIES EXCHANGE ACT OF 1934

Sec.	This Work Page
12	312

TABLE OF STATUTES AND REGULATIONS

SECURITIES ACT OF 1933

	This Work
Sec.	**Page**
2(1)	301

STATE STATUTES

DELAWARE CODE

	This Work
Tit.	**Page**
8, § 203	325

TEMPORARY TREASURY REGULATIONS

	This Work
Sec.	**Page**
1.411(a)–3T(a)(2)	87
1.411(a)–4T	87
1.414(q)–1	359

PROPOSED TREASURY REGULATIONS

	This Work
Sec.	**Page**
1.401(a)(9)–2	138
1.412(b)–1(a)	444

TREASURY REGULATIONS

	This Work
Sec.	**Page**
1.72–2(a)(3)	154
1.72–2(a)(3)(iv)	155
1.72–2(b)(2)	151
1.72–4(b)(1)	151
1.72–5	152

TREASURY REGULATIONS

Sec.	This Work Page
1.72–9	152
1.401–1(b)(1)(i)	7
1.401–1(b)(1)(i)	135
1.401–1(b)(1)(ii)	7
1.401–1(b)(1)(ii)	135
1.401–1(b)(1)(iii)	6
1.401–1(b)(1)(iii)	7
1.401–1(b)(1)(iii)	135
1.401–1(b)(2)	454
1.401–2(b)(1)	478
1.401(a)–7(d)(4)(ii)	130
1.401(a)–7(d)(4)(iii)	130
1.401(a)–13(d)(2)	133
1.401(a)–14(a)	139
1.401(a)–14(b)	139
1.401(a)–20	123
1.401(a)–20	124
1.401(a)–20	126
1.401(a)–20	134
1.401(a)(4)–1 to 1.401(a)(4)–13	383
1.401(a)(4)–1(b)	383
1.401(a)(4)–1(b)(2)(ii)(B)	387
1.401(a)(4)–1(c)(4)	383
1.401(a)(4)–1(c)(5)	383
1.401(a)(4)–1(c)(6)	394
1.401(a)(4)–1(c)(7)	394
1.401(a)(4)–2(b)(2)	385
1.401(a)(4)–2(b)(2)(ii)	385
1.401(a)(4)–2(b)(2)(ii)	397
1.401(a)(4)–2(b)(3)	386
1.401(a)(4)–2(b)(4)	387
1.401(a)(4)–2(c)(1)	387
1.401(a)(4)–2(c)(2)	386
1.401(a)(4)–2(c)(3)	388
1.401(a)(4)–3(b)(2)	389
1.401(a)(4)–3(b)(3)	389
1.401(a)(4)–3(b)(4)(i)(A)	390
1.401(a)(4)–3(b)(4)(i)(A)	391
1.401(a)(4)–3(b)(4)(i)(B)	390
1.401(a)(4)–3(b)(4)(i)(B)	391
1.401(a)(4)–3(b)(4)(i)(C)(1)	390

TREASURY REGULATIONS

Sec.	This Work Page
1.401(a)(4)–3(b)(4)(i)(C)(2)	391
1.401(a)(4)–3(b)(4)(i)(C)(3)	391
1.401(a)(4)–3(b)(5)	391
1.401(a)(4)–3(b)(6)	391
1.401(a)(4)–3(b)(6)(ii)	391
1.401(a)(4)–3(b)(6)(ii)	397
1.401(a)(4)–3(c)(1)	392
1.401(a)(4)–3(c)(3)	392
1.401(a)(4)–3(d)(1)(i)	391
1.401(a)(4)–3(d)(1)(ii)	392
1.401(a)(4)–3(e)(2)	389
1.401(a)(4)–4(a)(1)	406
1.401(a)(4)–4(b)	407
1.401(a)(4)–4(c)	407
1.401(a)(4)–4(d)(4)	407
1.401(a)(4)–5(a)	408
1.401(a)(4)–5(a)(3)	408
1.401(a)(4)–5(b)	409
1.401(a)(4)–6	395
1.401(a)(4)–7(b)	404
1.401(a)(4)–7(c)	406
1.401(a)(4)–8(a)	393
1.401(a)(4)–8(b)(1)(i)(A)	393
1.401(a)(4)–8(b)(1)(i)(B)	393
1.401(a)(4)–8(b)(2)	393
1.401(a)(4)–8(b)(3)	393
1.401(a)(4)–8(c)	394
1.401(a)(4)–8(d)	393
1.401(a)(4)–9(b)	395
1.401(a)(4)–9(b)(2)(v)(A)	395
1.401(a)(4)–9(b)(2)(v)(B)	395
1.401(a)(4)–9(b)(2)(v)(C)	395
1.401(a)(4)–9(b)(2)(v)(D)	395
1.401(a)(4)–9(c)	423
1.401(a)(4)–9(c)(1)	396
1.401(a)(4)–9(c)(2)	396
1.401(a)(4)–9(c)(3)	396
1.401(a)(4)–9(c)(4)	396
1.401(a)(4)–10	394
1.401(a)(4)–11(c)	383
1.401(a)(4)–11(d)	383

TREASURY REGULATIONS

Sec.	This Work Page
1.401(a)(4)–11(g)(2)	410
1.401(a)(4)–12	384
1.401(a)(5)–1(e)(3)(ii)	406
1.401(a)(17)–1(c)(1)	422
1.401(a)(26)–1(b)(1)	381
1.401(a)(26)–1(b)(2)	381
1.401(a)(26)–2(c)	378
1.401(a)(26)–2(d)(1)	378
1.401(a)(26)–2(d)(2)	379
1.401(a)(26)–3	380
1.401(a)(26)–4	380
1.401(a)(26)–4(d)(2)	380
1.401(a)(26)–6(b)(8)	379
1.401(a)(31)–1	159
1.401(k)–1(a)(3)(vi)	418
1.401(k)–1(a)(4)(iv)	421
1.401(k)–1(b)(3)(i)	423
1.401(k)–1(b)(3)(ii)	423
1.401(k)–1(b)(5)	422
1.401(k)–1(e)(6)	419
1.401(k)–1(f)	425
1.401(k)–1(f)(6)(i)	425
1.401(k)–1(f)(6)(ii)	425
1.401(k)–1(g)(4)	420
1.401(k)–1(g)(13)(i)	418
1.401(k)–1(g)(13)(ii)	419
1.401(*l*)–1(c)(3)	399
1.401(*l*)–1(c)(4)	398
1.401(*l*)–1(c)(7)	400
1.401(*l*)–1(c)(10)(i)	398
1.401(*l*)–1(c)(10)(ii)	399
1.401(*l*)–1(c)(14)	399
1.401(*l*)–1(c)(15)	398
1.401(*l*)–1(c)(16)(i)	399
1.401(*l*)–1(c)(16)(ii)	398
1.401(*l*)–1(c)(17)	401
1.401(*l*)–1(c)(18)	401
1.401(*l*)–1(c)(25)	401
1.401(*l*)–2(b) to (d)	399
1.401(*l*)–3(b)(2)	400
1.401(*l*)–3(b)(3)	401

TABLE OF STATUTES AND REGULATIONS

TREASURY REGULATIONS

Sec.	This Work Page
1.401(*l*)–3(c)(1)	402
1.401(*l*)–3(d)	402
1.401(*l*)–3(d)(9)	400
1.401(*l*)–3(d)(9)	401
1.401(*l*)–3(e)(2)	400
1.401(*l*)–3(e)(2)	401
1.401(*l*)–5(b)(1)	402
1.401(*l*)–5(b)(2) to (b)(8)	403
1.401(*l*)–5(c)	403
1.402(a)–1(b)(2)(i)	156
1.402(c)–2	159
1.402(c)–2	160
1.402(f)	161
1.404(a)–9(b)	450
1.410(a)–7	86
1.410(a)(26)–6(c)	380
1.410(b)–2(b)(5)	368
1.410(b)–2(b)(6)	368
1.410(b)–2(b)(7)	368
1.410(b)–2(c)	369
1.410(b)–3(a)(1)	363
1.410(b)–3(b)(1)	363
1.410(b)–4(b)	364
1.410(b)–4(c)	374
1.410(b)–4(c)(2)	364
1.410(b)–4(c)(3)	365
1.410(b)–4(c)(3)(ii)	365
1.410(b)–4(c)(4)(i)	364
1.410(b)–4(c)(4)(ii)	365
1.410(b)–4(c)(4)(iii)	364
1.410(b)–4(c)(4)(iv)	364
1.410(b)–5	366
1.410(b)–5(f)	367
1.410(b)–6(b)(3)	372
1.410(b)–6(d)(1)	371
1.410(b)–6(d)(2)(iii)(B)	371
1.410(b)–6(h)	372
1.410(b)–7(a)	361
1.410(b)–7(b)	361
1.410(b)–7(c)	361
1.410(b)–7(c)(5)	367

TABLE OF STATUTES AND REGULATIONS

TREASURY REGULATIONS

Sec.	This Work Page
1.410(b)–7(d)	362
1.410(b)–7(e)	366
1.410(b)–9	363
1.411(a)–7(a)(1)	99
1.411(a)–7(d)(4)(i)	129
1.411(a)–11(c)	139
1.411(b)–1(a)	100
1.411(d)–2(b)(1)	89
1.411(d)–4	108
1.412(c)(1)–2	440
1.412(c)(1)–3	476
1.414(c)–1 to 1.414(c)–5	369
1.414(l)–1(b)(1)	361
1.414(r)–1(b)(1)	373
1.414(r)–1(c)(2)	373
1.414(r)–1(c)(2)(i)	373
1.414(r)–1(c)(3)(i)	373
1.414(r)–2	374
1.414(r)–3(b)	375
1.414(r)–5(c)	376
1.414(r)–5(d)	376
1.414(r)–5(e)	376
1.414(r)–5(f)	377
1.414(r)–5(g)	377
1.414(r)–6	377
1.414(r)–8(b)(2)	373
1.414(r)–8(b)(2)(ii)	374
1.414(r)–8(b)(3)	373
1.414(r)–8(c)(1)	373
1.414(r)–11(b)(2)	375
1.414(r)–11(b)(3)	375
1.414(s)–1(c)	368
1.415–1(d)	411
1.415–2(b)	412
1.415–3(b)	414
1.415–3(c)	414
1.415–6(b)(3)	412
1.416–1	91
1.416–1	107
1.7476–1	208
31.3405(c)–1	161

TREASURY REGULATIONS

Sec.	This Work Page
54.4975–7(b)(3)	309
54.4975–7(b)(4)	309
54.4975–7(b)(5)	310
54.4975–7(b)(6)	310
54.4975–7(b)(8)	310
54.4975–7(b)(13)	310
54.4975–11(a)(2)	311
54.4975–11(a)(7)(ii)	311
54.4975–11(c)	311
54.4975–11(d)(2)	311
54.4980F	110
54.4980F	111
301.6104(a)–2	208
301.6104–3	208

CODE OF FEDERAL REGULATIONS

Tit.	This Work Page
29, § 2509.75–4	274
29, § 2509.75–5	230
29, § 2509.75–5	234
29, § 2509.75–5	235
29, § 2509.75–5	247
29, § 2509.75–5	270
29, § 2509.75–8	225
29, § 2509.75–8	227
29, § 2509.75–8	230
29, § 2509.75–8	231
29, § 2509.75–8	233
29, § 2509.75–8	235
29, § 2509.75–8	263
29, § 2509.75–8	264
29, § 2509.75–8	271
29, § 2509.94–2	318
29, § 2510.3–1	7
29, § 2510.3–1(b)	47
29, § 2510.3–1(j)	336
29, § 2510.3–2(b)	92
29, § 2510.3–2(d)	12
29, § 2510.3–3(b)	11

TABLE OF STATUTES AND REGULATIONS

CODE OF FEDERAL REGULATIONS

Tit.	This Work Page
29, § 2510.3–18(b) (proposed)	305
29, § 2510.3–21(c)	231
29, § 2510.3–101(a)(2)	240
29, § 2510.3–101(h)	240
29, § 2510.3–101(i)	240
29, § 2510.3–102(a)	238
29, § 2510.3–102(b)	238
29, § 2520.102–2(a)	197
29, § 2520.102–2(b)	198
29, § 2520.102–2(c)	197
29, § 2520.102–3	198
29, § 2520.102–3	214
29, § 2520.102–3(t)(2)	198
29, § 2520.103–1(c)	202
29, § 2520.103–1(d)	202
29, § 2520.104–1(b)(1)	204
29, § 2520.104–20	204
29, § 2520.104–20	207
29, § 2520.104–21	204
29, § 2520.104–22	204
29, § 2520.104–23	204
29, § 2520.104–24	204
29, § 2520.104–25	204
29, § 2520.104–41	202
29, § 2520.104–46	200
29, § 2520.104(c)	205
29, § 2520.104b–1(b)(3)	205
29, § 2520.104b–2	205
29, § 2520.104b–3	205
29, § 2520.104b–3(d)	205
29, § 2520.104b–10	203
29, § 2520.104b–10(b)	206
29, § 2520.104b–10(g)	206
29, § 2530.200b–2	84
29, § 2550.401c–1	243
29, § 2550.404a–1	264
29, § 2550.404a–1(b)(3)	264
29, § 2550.404c–1(d)(2)(ii)	274
29, § 2550.408b–1(a)(2)	293
29, § 2550.408b–1(b)	131
29, § 2550.408b–1(c)	131

CODE OF FEDERAL REGULATIONS

Tit.	This Work Page
29, § 2550.408b–1(d)(2)	132
29, § 2550.408b–1(e)	132
29, § 2550.408b–1(f)(2)	132
29, § 2550.408b–2(a)	293
29, § 2550.408b–2(b)	293
29, § 2550.408b–2(c)	293
29, § 2550.408b–2(e)	293
29, § 2550.408c–2	293
29, § 2550.408e(d)	304
29, § 2560.503–1	170
29, § 2560.503–1(b)(2)	170
29, § 2560.503–1(b)(3)	170
29, § 2560.503–1(b)(4)	170
29, § 2560.503–1(b)(5)	171
29, § 2560.503–1(b)(6)	171
29, § 2560.503–1(c)(1)(i)	174
29, § 2560.503–1(c)(1)(ii)	174
29, § 2560.503–1(c)(2)	175
29, § 2560.503–1(c)(3)	175
29, § 2560.503–1(c)(4)	175
29, § 2560.503–1(e)	171
29, § 2560.503–1(f)(1)	171
29, § 2560.503–1(f)(2)(i)	174
29, § 2560.503–1(f)(2)(ii)	174
29, § 2560.503–1(f)(2)(iii)(A)	174
29, § 2560.503–1(f)(2)(iii)(B)	174
29, § 2560.503–1(g)(1)	171
29, § 2560.503–1(g)(1)(v)	175
29, § 2560.503–1(g)(2)	175
29, § 2560.503–1(h)(1)	172
29, § 2560.503–1(h)(2)	172
29, § 2560.503–1(h)(3)	176
29, § 2560.503–1(i)(1)	172
29, § 2560.503–1(i)(2)(i)	176
29, § 2560.503–1(i)(2)(ii)	177
29, § 2560.503–1(i)(2)(ii)(B)	177
29, § 2560.503–1(i)(2)(iii)(A)	177
29, § 2560.503–1(j)(1)—(j)(4)	172
29, § 2560.503–1(j)(5)	177
29, § 2560.503–1(k)(1)	177
29, § 2560.503–1(k)(2)(i)	177

CODE OF FEDERAL REGULATIONS

Tit.	This Work Page
29, § 2560.503–1(k)(2)(ii)	178
29, § 2560.503–1(k)(2)(ii)	191
29, § 2560.503–1(*l*)	169
29, § 2560.503–1(m)(1)	173
29, § 2560.503–1(m)(2)	173
29, § 2560.503–1(m)(3)	173
29, § 2560.503–1(m)(6)	170
29, §§ 2570.30—2570.52	296
29, § 2575.209b–1	210
29, § 2575.502c–1	209
29, § 2575.502c–2	210
29, § 2580.412–2	246
29, § 2580.412–4	238
29, § 2580.412–5	246
29, § 2580.412–5(a)	238
29, § 2580.412–5(b)(1)	239
29, § 2580.412–5(b)(2)	239
29, § 2580.412–6(a)	246
29, § 2580.412–6(b)	247
29, §§ 2580.412–7 to 2580.412–20	247
29, § 2580.412–9	247
29, § 4001.2	458
29, § 4022.2	458
29, § 4022.3(a)	458
29, § 4022.3(b)	458
29, § 4022.3(c)	458
29, § 4022.4	458
29, § 4022.25	460
29, § 4041.22	465
29, § 4041.23(a)	465
29, § 4041.23(b)(5)	481
29, § 4041.23(b)(9)	481
29, § 4041.24	465
29, § 4041.25	465
29, § 4041.26	465
29, § 4041.28(a)	466
29, § 4041.28(c)	465
29, § 4041.28(c)	467
29, § 4041.28(c)(3)	481
29, § 4041.28(c)(4)	468
29, § 4041.28(d)	467

TABLE OF STATUTES AND REGULATIONS

CODE OF FEDERAL REGULATIONS

Tit.	This Work Page
29, § 4041.28(d)	481
29, § 4041.31	464
29, § 4041.31	465
29, § 4041.41	468
29, § 4041.41(b)	464
29, § 4041.42	471
29, § 4041.44	468
29, § 4041.45	469
29, § 4041.46	469
29, § 4041.47(a)	470
29, § 4041.47(c)	470
29, §§ 4043.20—4043.35	463
29, §§ 4043.61—4043.68	463
29, § 4047.3	476
29, § 4047.5	476

REVENUE PROCEDURES

Rev.Proc.	This Work Page
81–44	448
91–64	376
95–51	446
97–6	207
98–10	446
99–45	446
2000–40	446

REVENUE RULINGS

Rev.Rul.	This Work Page
60–83	137
65–178	132
67–288	132
69–25	454
70–611	136
71–295	135
71–437	132
72–240	138
72–241	138

TABLE OF STATUTES AND REGULATIONS

REVENUE RULINGS

Rev.Rul.	This Work Page
74–307	137
83–52	478
85–6	479
85–15	138
85–31	87
87–77	160
91–4	452
95–57	320

SECURITIES EXCHANGE ACT RELEASE

No.	This Work Page
15230	317

IRS GENERAL COUNCIL MEMORANDA

No.	This Work Page
39870	318

IRS NOTICES

No.	This Work Page
87–13	154
97–2	425
98–2	152
99–44	415
2002–2	315
2002–3	162
2002–24	204

EMPLOYEE BENEFIT PLANS

IN A NUTSHELL

THIRD EDITION

*

CHAPTER 1

OVERVIEW AND BASIC CONCEPTS

The law of plans is a medley of diverse and often quite intricate topics. Books and courses on this body of law usually present it as a sequence of these varied topics. This mode of presentation is natural and straightforward, but it has several drawbacks. One is that the unifying themes tend to be obscured by details. Another is that many of the parts are inscrutable without at least a basic understanding of the whole. To avoid these pedagogic problems, this book gives the reader some important and useful background before it plunges into the details of the law. This chapter supplies an overview of ERISA. The next four introduce themes and concepts that are indispensable to a full understanding of the field.

A. PLANS AND THE SCOPE OF ERISA

1. WHAT IS A PLAN?

ERISA—the Employee Retirement Income Security Act of 1974, as amended—is the law of employee benefit plans; it is not the law of employee benefits. If pension or welfare benefits are provid-

1

ed through some means other than a plan, then, with few exceptions, ERISA does not apply. Hence, to begin to understand ERISA, one must understand what an *employee benefit plan* is.

Unfortunately, the statute is not very helpful. Unlike corporation law, for example, ERISA does not prescribe a method of forming its central concern, plans. Instead, it takes plans and their formation as given. Nor does it define "plan" or lay down criteria for plan existence. Instead, it takes for granted that we all know what a plan is.

The statutory provisions, though, reflect what plans are assumed to be. It is reasonably clear that ERISA conceives plans primarily as employer programs (although plans may also be established or maintained, in whole or in part, by unions). Specifically, sections 3(1)-(3), the closest approach to a statutory definition, indicate that a plan is a regularly conducted, employment-based program or practice, whose purpose is to afford certain kinds of benefits to employees. However, it is equally clear that a plan is not simply a part of an employer's business. One of ERISA's major innovations is to make a plan a legal entity distinct from the employer or other sponsor. A plan, like a corporation, may sue or be sued, have judgment entered against it, enter into contracts, own property, hire employees, and engage attorneys to represent it. ERISA §§ 408, 502(d). A plan is also an artificial individual.

This statutory sketch of the nature of plans clearly needs to be refined. We shall see later (Chapter 15) how this has been done.

2. VARIETIES OF PLANS

ERISA divides the universe of employee benefit plans into *pension benefit plans* (or *pension plans*) and *welfare benefit plans* (or *welfare plans*). Pension benefit plans either provide retirement income or provide for the deferral of income until the termination of employment or beyond. ERISA § 3(2). Welfare benefit plans provide medical and certain other non-pension benefits to employees and their beneficiaries. ERISA § 3(1).

a. Pension Plans

There are two categories of pension plans. One is the *defined benefit plan*, ERISA § 3(35), in which employees are promised a level of retirement income according to a formula. The formula might depend on the employee's years of service, in which case it is a *unit benefit plan*. For example, a plan's formula for the annual retirement benefit might be:

Years of service × final average salary × 1.5%.

(This is a *final average* formula; a *career average* formula credits a unit of benefit each year based on compensation for the year.) For this plan, an employee who retired after 30 years with a final average salary (over the specified averaging period) of $100,000 would receive 30 × $100,000 × 1.5%, or

$45,000, each year. By contrast, a defined benefit plan whose formula is independent of years of service is a *flat benefit* (or *fixed benefit*) *plan*. Such a plan might provide either a fixed dollar amount or a fixed percentage of final or average pay on retirement.

An employer who establishes a defined benefit plan must contribute, on an ongoing basis, funds to pay the promised benefits. The funds are invested, and investment gains and losses affect the employer's obligation. If a plan invests in common stocks, market gains may reduce, and market losses may increase, the employer's obligation to contribute in future years. Investment gains or losses, however, do not affect the level of benefits to which the participants are entitled.

The second category of pension plan is the *defined contribution plan* or *individual account plan*. ERISA § 3(34). In this kind of plan, participants are not promised a specified level of retirement benefits. Rather, each participant has an account in the plan, to which employer contributions are allocated. A participant's benefit is the value of this account at retirement, determined mainly by the history of contributions (possibly including those of the employee) and the investment experience of the funds contributed. In a defined contribution plan, the employer is not obligated to ensure that the plan has enough money to fund any specified benefit level. The employer's only obligation is to make the promised contributions, if any.

There are many kinds of defined contribution plan. The simplest, a *money purchase plan*, is one in which the employer is obligated to contribute a specified dollar amount each year to each participant's account. Typically, the specified amount is a percentage of the participant's compensation.

A *target benefit plan*, a kind of money purchase plan, is in some respects a cross between a defined benefit plan and defined contribution plan. The employer chooses a target level of benefits, and then determines a contribution level actuarially sufficient to fund those benefits. Once the contribution level is set, however, it is not necessarily changed to reflect investment experience or other developments. Unlike as in a defined benefit plan, the targeted level of benefits is a mere projection; it is not a promise or guarantee.

A *profit sharing plan*, the most common form of defined contribution plan, provides for annual employer contributions (which may be zero), and their allocation to participant accounts according to a formula. The amount of the employer's contribution may be specified by a formula or left to the employer's discretion (possibly within specified limits). Despite the name, contributions need not come from current or accumulated profits. Furthermore, it is permissible for tax-exempt organizations to establish profit sharing plans. IRC § 401(a)(27).

There are additional, more specialized types of defined contribution plans. A *stock bonus plan* is a profit-sharing plan that distributes benefits in the form of employer stock. Treas. Reg. § 1.401–1(b)(1)(iii). An *employee stock ownership plan*, or *ESOP*, is a stock bonus plan or combination stock bonus and money purchase plan, that is designed to invest primarily in stock of the employer. IRC § 4975(e)(7). ESOPS are examined in detail in Chapter 14. A *cash or deferred arrangement* (or *CODA*, or *401(k) plan*) is a profit sharing plan or stock bonus plan (or pre-ERISA money purchase plan) that gives participants the choice of having the employer contribute money to their accounts in the plan or pay the same amount to them as compensation. IRC § 401(k). The advantage to the participant is that money contributed to the plan is not included in taxable income for the year. CODAs are examined in detail in Chapter 20.

A type of defined benefit plan that resembles a defined contribution plan is the *cash balance plan*. In a cash balance plan, the benefit for each participant is calculated by reference to a hypothetical account, in which the participant is credited with hypothetical allocations plus interest on the hypothetical allocation at a rate determined by the plan. Unlike as in a defined contribution plan, the participant's ultimate benefit is not affected by investment gains or losses. Rather, the hypothetical allocations to the account and the interest rate are merely items in a formula used to calculate the benefit.

The reader should be aware that Title I of ERISA (the so-called labor provisions) and Title II (the tax-related provisions, codified in the Internal Revenue Code) use slightly different terminology to describe plans. The most important difference is that, under the Internal Revenue Code, a *pension plan* is defined as a retirement plan in which benefits are "definitely determinable." Treas. Reg. § 1.401–1(b)(1)(i). Benefits are definitely determinable if they are fixed by formula, or if contributions are "fixed without being geared to profits." Hence, this definition of pension plan includes defined benefit and money purchase plans, but excludes profit sharing and stock bonus plans. Treas. Reg. § 1.401–1(b)(1)(ii) & (iii). The Code, unlike Title I, distinguishes plans that provide pensions from those that defer income. We will use Title I terminology unless indicated otherwise.

b. Welfare Plans

ERISA deems a wide variety of benefit programs to be welfare benefit plans. For example, a plan that provides employees with hospital care, severance pay, prepaid legal services, or scholarship funds may be a welfare plan. With few exceptions, though, ERISA limits the category of welfare benefits (and thus welfare plans) to those in the form of money or services that are provided to employees on an individualized basis. It excludes programs offering workplace features such as company cafeterias (an exception to this exclusion is day-care centers) or non-compensatory benefits, such as seniority rights or the right not to be terminated without cause. 29 C.F.R. § 2510.3–1.

ERISA presumes that any covered plan can be categorized neatly as either a welfare plan or pension plan, and that there are no intermediate cases. (It does recognize, however, that a single plan may provide both pension and welfare benefits. Such a plan is treated as if the pension and welfare components were separate plans.) Yet experience has shown that welfare and pension plans are not always so clearly distinguishable as ERISA presumes. For example, a plan that provides medical benefits to retired employees straddles the line between categories. On the one hand, medical benefits are provided: a paradigm welfare benefit. Yet the benefits are provided to retirees, and arguably constitute a form of retirement income. Under current law, these plans are treated as welfare plans. However, they generate many problems that are handled only by ERISA's rules governing pension plans (Chapter 6). As this example points up, categorization of a plan as a welfare benefit plan or a pension plan may matter greatly, because ERISA regulates the two kinds differently.

c. Multiemployer Plans

Many plans are established pursuant to collective bargaining agreements. A *multiemployer plan* is a plan maintained pursuant to one or more collective bargaining agreements, to which more than one employer is required to contribute. ERISA § 3(37)(A). (A non-collectively bargained plan covering employees of more than one employer is a *multiple employer plan*.) Multiemployer plans are most common in industries, such as the garment trade, with many small companies, and industries, such as construction, where work is irregular and employees frequently move from employer to employer. A multiemployer plan may be either a welfare plan or a pension plan (usually defined benefit).

3. PENSION AND WELFARE PLANS COVERED BY ERISA

ERISA does not govern every plan that provides pension and welfare benefits. As already noted, some plans are excluded on the basis of benefits provided. There are, however, further limitations on coverage.

a. Title I

Title I of ERISA was enacted pursuant the Congress' power to regulate interstate commerce. Accordingly, Title I covers only plans established or maintained by: employers engaged in commerce or whose industry or activity affects commerce; unions representing employees engaged in commerce or in any industry or activity affecting commerce; or both. ERISA § 4(a)(1); *Sheffield v. Allstate Life Insurance Co.* (S.D.Tex.1991).

Title I also does not apply to any plan established by the United States or any state or local government. ERISA § 4(b)(1). This is a very significant exclusion since there are many such *governmental plans*. Some states have enacted statutes to protect employees covered by such plans. However, many state plans are underfunded, putting pensions at risk. In addition, some states have used or attempted to use their employees' pension funds for general state purposes, again threatening the security of the promised pensions. These are some of the kinds of conduct that ERISA was designed to halt in the case of private plans.

There are still other exclusions. Plans established by churches or church associations (*church plans*) are not subject to Title I (unless they elect coverage under Title II). ERISA § 4(b)(2). Also excluded are plans "maintained solely for the purpose of complying with applicable workmen's compensation laws or unemployment compensation laws or disability insurance laws." ERISA § 4(b)(3). In *Shaw v. Delta Air Lines, Inc.* (S.Ct. 1983), the Supreme Court gave this exclusion a narrow reading, limiting it, in the context of disability plans, to separately administered programs maintained solely to comply with a state law requiring such benefits. Yet another exclusion is for plans "maintained outside of the United States primarily for the benefit of persons substantially all of whom are nonresident aliens." ERISA § 4(b)(4).

Finally, Title I excludes unfunded *excess benefit plans*. ERISA § 4(b)(5). An excess benefit plan is a plan that provides a high level of benefits to highly compensated employees and that, because of the high level, is not entitled to the tax advantages generally given to pension plans. ERISA § 3(36). This exclusion reflects a theme of ERISA, that high-level or highly compensated employees can take care of themselves and do not need all the statutory protections.

b. Title II

In some respects, the coverage of Title II is more limited that that of Title I, for Title II is concerned almost exclusively with pension plans. Welfare plans receive little attention. On the other hand, Title II is broader, for it covers some arrangements that are not within the scope of Title I.

Title II covers *Keogh plans*—pension plans for self-employed persons—even where the plan does not include any common-law employees. IRC § 401(d). Title I, by contrast, with minor exceptions restricts the definition of "plan" to programs established by employers (or labor organizations) for employees, and excludes Keogh plans in which the only participants are owners of the business. 29 C.F.R. § 2510.3–3(b).

Title II also regulates *individual retirement accounts* (IRAs). IRC § 408. An IRA is a tax-favored savings or investment account, intended mainly to allow persons not covered by pension plans to save for retirement. (Title II also covers *individual retirement annuities*, which are certain tax-favored annuity contracts used as retirement savings vehicles.) IRAs are not considered plans and are generally excluded from Title I's coverage. 29 C.F.R. § 2510.3–2(d). Title II also covers *simplified employee pensions* (SEP's) and *savings incentive match plans for employees* (SIMPLE plans). SEPs are arrangements by which an employer directly funds individual retirement accounts or annuities established by or on behalf or its employees. IRC § 408(k). A SIMPLE plan may be in the form of either a SIMPLE IRA or a SIMPLE 401(k) plan. In either case, it is an arrangement by which employees make tax-deferred elective contributions and the employer makes either matching or nonelective contributions. SIMPLE plans can be established only by employers having 100 or fewer employees whose compensation is $5,000 or more. IRC §§ 401(k)(11), 408(p).

Finally, Title II permits state and local governments, churches and church organizations, and certain other tax-exempt entities to establish plans that are subject to its rules and that correspondingly receive favored tax treatment. We will not examine such plans and the rules governing them in this book.

B. PERSONS ASSOCIATED WITH PLANS

Plans may be complex enterprises, and persons can be associated with them in many ways. ERISA uses specialized terms and definitions to describe the roles people may have in plans.

A *participant* is the person ERISA is primarily concerned to protect. "Participant" is defined as "any employee or former employee ..., or any member or former member of an employee organization, who is or may become eligible to receive a benefit" from a plan, "or whose beneficiaries may be eligible to receive any such benefit." ERISA § 3(7). In this definition, *employee* has its common-law meaning. *Nationwide Mutual Insurance Co. v. Darden* (S.Ct.1992). A person *may become eligible* for a benefit if he has a colorable claim either that he will prevail in a suit for benefits or that he will fulfil benefit eligibility requirements in the future. *Firestone Tire & Rubber Co. v. Bruch* (S.Ct.1989). A *beneficiary* is an actual or potential recipient of plan benefits, other than a participant. The term is defined as a "person designated by a participant, or by the terms of an employee benefit plan, who is or may become entitled to a benefit thereunder." ERISA § 3(8).

If a plan is established or maintained by an individual employer or employee organization, that entity is the *plan sponsor*. For multiemployer plans and plans established or maintained by more than one employer, the plan sponsor is the committee, board or other group of representatives of the entities that establish or maintain the plan. ERISA § 3(16)(B).

Plans, like business organizations, may apportion managerial responsibility so that different managers have different duties. Under ERISA, the individuals responsible for the operation of a plan are called *fiduciaries*. The statute itself identifies some of the fiduciary offices in plans: *named fiduciaries*, *trustees*, *investment managers*, and *administrators*. Named fiduciaries are persons named in the plan document to have "authority to control and manage the operation and administration of the plan." ERISA § 402(a). A trustee is a person who holds the plan assets and has "authority and discretion to manage and control" those assets. ERISA § 403(a). An investment manager is a person, other than a trustee, "who has the power to manage, acquire or dispose of" plan assets. ERISA § 3(38). The administrator, ERISA § 3(16)(A), is the person who is responsible for plan administration. This includes recordkeeping and overseeing benefit payment.

These statutorily defined fiduciary roles are not exhaustive. ERISA § 3(21)(A) generally defines a plan fiduciary as any person:

[T]o the extent (i) he exercises any discretionary authority or discretionary control respecting management of such plan or exercises any authority or control respecting management or disposition of its assets, (ii) he renders investment advice for a fee or other compensation, direct or indirect, with respect to any moneys or other property of such plan, or has any authority or responsibility to do so, or (iii) he has any discretionary authority or discretionary responsibility in the administration of such plan.

Fiduciary status subjects a person to very stringent standards. ERISA §§ 404–06. We will examine fiduciary law in Chapter 12.

ERISA also identifies a class of persons called *parties in interest*. ERISA § 3(14). (The Code calls them *disqualified persons*. IRC § 4975(e)(2).) In general, a party in interest is a person who is or may be in a position to influence plan affairs or whose dealings with a plan may involve a conflict of interest. Parties in interest include plan fiduciaries; employees, officers, and counsel of the plan; service providers; the employer and employee organization of the covered employees; certain direct and indirect owners of the employer and employee organization; and certain relatives or affiliated enterprises of any of the above. The dealings of parties in interest with the plan are subject to careful scrutiny under the *prohibited transaction rules*. ERISA §§ 406–07. We examine these rules in Chapter 13.

C. OVERVIEW OF ERISA REGULATION

ERISA has three main substantive parts. The provisions of Title I apply to all pension and welfare plans not specifically excluded from coverage. The provisions of Title II deal mainly with tax aspects of pension plans. (This book, following practice in the field, will refer to Title II provisions as sections of the Internal Revenue Code.) The provisions of

Title IV, dealing with plan termination, apply only to defined benefit plans.

There is also a Title III, which contains miscellaneous administrative provisions. We will not be much concerned with it in this book.

1. THE STRUCTURE OF TITLE I

The subject of Title I is given by its caption: "Protection of Employee Benefit Rights." Title I is subdivided into two parts. Subtitle A, captioned "General Provisions," includes Congressional findings and declarations of policy, definitions, and descriptions of coverage. Subtitle B, captioned "Regulatory Provisions," is itself divided into parts, each of which deals with various aspects of plan regulation. The scope of regulation varies with plan type. Title I regulates defined benefit plans most thoroughly. By contrast, it regulates welfare benefit plans least; several important parts of Subtitle B are wholly inapplicable. Defined contribution plans receive an intermediate level of regulation.

The first part of Subtitle B (ERISA §§ 101–111) contains rules governing information that plans and administrators must supply to regulators and to participants and beneficiaries. This part applies, with few exceptions, to all employee benefit plans subject to ERISA. We will examine these provisions in Chapter 11.

The second part (ERISA §§ 201–211) deals with participant entitlement to pension benefits from a plan. It does not apply to welfare plans; unfunded, deferred-compensation plans for a select group of management or highly compensated employees (*top-hat plans*); excess benefit plans; and certain others. It imposes minimum standards for employee eligibility to participate in a plan, minimum periods within which benefits must become nonforfeitable, minimum rates at which benefits must accrue, restrictions on the alienability of benefits, and limitations on the form and payment of benefits. We will examine these provisions in Chapters 6–8.

The third part (ERISA §§ 301–308) deals with the funding of defined benefit plans. It does not apply to welfare benefit plans, defined contribution plans (other than money purchase plans), plans whose benefits are funded exclusively through insurance contracts, top-hat plans, excess benefit plans, and certain others. This part establishes the rates at which employers must fund plans to ensure that there are assets sufficient to meet benefit obligations. It also deals with problems generated by employers that are unable to meet their obligations. We examine these provisions in Chapter 21.

The fourth part (ERISA §§ 401–414) deals with fiduciary responsibility and related matters. With very minor exceptions, it applies to all plans subject to Title I. Its most important provisions are a general requirement that plan assets be held in trust or in the form of insurance contracts; a description of the duties imposed on fiduciaries to safeguard the plan and the integrity of its operation; rules for the allocation of fiduciary responsibility; a description of the liability imposed on fiduciaries for breaches; and a description of the limitations on plan-related business activity by parties in interest. The rules in this part are diverse, and will be dealt with at various places below. The primary treatment will be in Chapters 12–14.

The fifth part (ERISA §§ 501–515) applies to all plans subject to Title I. It includes criminal and civil enforcement provisions. It also contains a provision that preempts virtually all state laws that "relate to" employee benefit plans. This part, too, is quite eclectic. Chapter 10 examines benefit claims; Chapters 11–13 remedies; Chapter 15 preemption; and Chapter 16 procedure.

The sixth part (ERISA §§ 601–609) is applicable only to group health plans; it was added to ERISA through later amendments. It requires that group health coverage be made available to participants for specified periods, under certain circumstances, after their participation in the plan has ceased, and that plans provide benefits in accordance with qualified medical child support orders. We do not deal with its provisions in this book.

The seventh part (ERISA §§ 701–734) deals with group health plans and group health insurance coverage; it was added to ERISA through later amendments. It deals with preexisting condition exclusions, eligibility standards, benefits for mothers and newborns, mental health benefits, and other subjects. A major purpose of this part is to enable employees to continue with comparable health coverage when they change jobs. We do not deal with its provisions in this book.

2.   THE STRUCTURE OF TITLE II

Pension plans involve income and expenses: income to the participant (at retirement) and the plan (through investment), and expenses to the employer (in the form of contributions). The core concept of Title II is plan *qualification*. IRC § 401. If a plan is qualified, then the plan, the employer, and the employees all receive favorable tax treatment with respect to their plan-related income or expenses.

To be qualified, a plan must comply with an elaborate set of standards. Many are identical to standards found in Title I. For example, a plan is not qualified unless its participation, vesting, and accrual standards meet the requirements of Title I. However, qualification also requires compliance with rules not found in Title I. The most important are the nondiscrimination rules, which prohibit a plan from favoring highly paid employees and insiders of the business with respect to coverage and benefits. IRC §§ 401(a)(4)–(5), 410(b). The nondiscrimination rules are probably the most complex part of ERISA. They are explained in Chapters 17–18.

Title II also deals with matters other than qualification. There are rules for the tax treatment of plan-related income and expenses; in particular, the taxation of distributions to participants and beneficiaries, (Chapter 9), and the deductibility of contributions by the employer (Chapter 21). Title II also prescribes standards that are enforced through excise taxes. Many of these standards are also imposed by Title I. For example, Title II imposes a tax on an employer who fails to meet the minimum funding standards of Title I. IRC § 4971(a). But it also enforces in this way standards not found in Title I. For example, an employer who terminates an overfunded plan and retains the assets left over after satisfying benefit obligations may be required to pay a tax of up to 50% of the amount retained. IRC § 4980.

3. THE STRUCTURE OF TITLE IV

Title IV (ERISA § 4001 ff.) deals with problems relating to the termination of defined benefit plans having insufficient assets to pay all promised benefits. Title IV takes a four-part approach. First, it establishes a system of plan termination insurance for defined benefit plans. It sets up funds that may be used to help satisfy benefit obligations of underfunded plans, ERISA § 4005, and requires employers who maintain defined benefit plans to contribute to the funds. ERISA § 4006.

Second, Title IV regulates the voluntary termination of defined benefit plans, but especially underfunded ones, ERISA § 4041, and provides for the mandatory termination of financially troubled plans to prevent large future losses, ERISA § 4042. Title IV also makes the sponsor liable for funding deficiencies upon termination, and supplies procedural mechanisms (such as liens) to enforce that liability. ERISA §§ 4062, 4067–4068.

Third, Title IV regulates the withdrawal of employers from multiemployer plans, requiring a withdrawing employer to satisfy its proportionate share of the plan's underfunding. ERISA §§ 4201–4303. And fourth, it establishes a federally chartered corporation, the Pension Benefit Guaranty Corporation (PBGC), to collect information relating to plan terminations, oversee the plan termination insurance program, and supervise plan terminations. ERISA § 4002.

Title IV is examined in Chapter 22.

4. THE ALLOCATION OF REGULATORY AUTHORITY

ERISA is a potential regulatory nightmare. Three federal bodies have enforcement and oversight responsibility: the Department of Labor, the Department of the Treasury, and the PBGC. Exacerbating the problem is regulatory overlap: Title I, the bailiwick of the Labor Department, and Title II, the bailiwick of the Treasury Department, contain many identical provisions.

In general, though, conflicts are avoided by agreements to allocate regulatory authority. The ERISA Reorganization Plan of 1978 provides that the Treasury Department will have primary responsibility for participation, vesting and funding standards, the

Labor Department primary responsibility for fiduciary regulation and prohibited transactions, and that there shall be coordination in certain matters. The three ERISA regulators have further worked to avoid problems and reduce complexities by agreeing to the use of a single set of forms for plan reporting, and to the pooling of information received; by relying on each other's regulations; and by cooperating on policy statements concerning various important matters.

CHAPTER 2

BASIC PLAN FINANCE
AND TAXATION

Many features of pension plans, and much of their law and policy, cannot be understood without a grasp of some basic principles of finance and taxation. This chapter explains those principles.

A. PRESENT VALUE

If a person is to receive a sum of money—say $N—in Y years, he may wish to know how much that future $N is worth today. To ask this is to ask what amount must be invested today in order to have exactly $N in Y years. Clearly, the answer is not $N. If one is given $N today, he can put it in a bank and collect interest for Y years, and have more than $N in the future. It is better to have $100 today than $100 tomorrow.

To determine the worth today of the future $N, one calculates how much should be invested today, compounded at prevailing interest rates for Y years, to yield $N at the end of the period. This amount—call it $M—is the *present value* of $N. The formula to compute it, for prevailing interest rate r, is the following:

(1) $M = N(1+r)^{-Y}$ or, equivalently $M = N/(1+r)^{Y}$.

For example, if the interest rate is 10%, the present value of $100 to be paid one year from now is $100/(1.10) or $90.91. To be paid two years from now it is $100/(1.10)^{2}$ or $82.64.

We can also turn formula (1) around and calculate what $M invested today would be worth in Y years at r rate of interest:

(2) $N = M(1+r)^{Y}$

For example, $100 invested today at 10% interest will yield $110 in one year, and $121 in two years. Many books of mathematical and financial tables list values of $(1+r)^{Y}$ and $1/(1+r)^{Y}$ for a wide range of r and Y, and the computation can easily be performed with a financial calculator.

Usually, one is interested in determining the present value of a stream of future payments made over a certain period, rather than just one payment at one future date. For example, one might own a 30 year bond that pays $100 each year, and wish to know the present value of the total of 30 payments. To find it, one could add the results of 30 present value calculations: the value of $100 one year in the future, plus the value of $100 two years in the future, and so on. This would be very tedious. Happily, there is a simple formula that can be used instead. If the amount paid each year is $A, and the interest rate is r, and the number of years for which $A will be paid is Y (with the first payment

one year from now), then the present value of the
stream is given by:

(3) $M = A[1 - (1+r)^{-Y}]/r$.

Thus, in the 30 year bond example, if the prevailing
interest rate is 8%, the present value is $100 × [1
− (1.08)$^{-30}$]/.08, or $100 × [1 − .099]/.08, which is
about $1126.   Again, one can use tables or a finan-
cial calculator to determine $[1 - (1+r)^{-Y}]/r$ for giv-
en values of r and Y.

B. VALUING PENSIONS

These formulas can be used to value pensions
from defined benefit plans.   For example, suppose
that a defined benefit plan provides a yearly pension, starting at age 65, in an amount determined
by the formula: 1.5% × Years of Service × Final
pay.   Suppose that a participant retires at age 65,
with 30 years of service, at a final salary of $25,000.
He would be entitled to a yearly pension of 1.5% ×
30 years × $25,000/year = $11,250/year.   (For
simplicity, assume there is one payment per year, at
year end).   If the interest rate is 10%, and life
expectancy at age 65 is 13 years, then we can use
formula (3) to calculate the present value at age 65
of the expected thirteen year annuity:

(4) Present value = $11,250 × [1 − (1.10)$^{-13}$
]/.10.

which is about $79,913.   Thus, for this person, a
13–year, $11,250 yearly annuity commencing at age

65 has the same value as the lump sum, $79,913, paid at age 65.

We can use this equivalence to make a further calculation. Suppose that the individual is now only 55, with 20 years of service. If he expects to retire at age 65 with 30 years of service, at a salary of $25,000, then the present value to him now, at age 55, of the expected pension can be calculated. It is just the present value of the 13–year, $11,250 annual annuity commencing in 10 years; which is the same as the present value of the lump sum, $79,913, to be paid in 10 years. If we continue to assume a 10% rate of interest, we can calculate as follows:

(5) Present value of pension annuity = present value of $79,913 = $79,913 $\times$ $(1+.10)^{-10}$

which is about $30,810.

It is interesting to take this calculation one step further. If we compute the present value of the expected pension as of the day the individual begins employment, we find that:

(6) Present value at age 35 = $79,913 $\times$ $(1+.10)^{-30}$

which is about $4,580—much less than the present value at age 55 or 65. It is easy to understand why pensions may not seem important to younger workers, and why they might be more willing than workers closer to retirement to trade pensions for current income. The closer one comes to the time of receipt of the the pension, the greater is its present value.

C.   INDIVIDUAL TAX ADVANTAGES

If a plan is qualified, the participant is not subject to tax on the employer's contributions when they are made. Moreover, neither the plan nor the participant is subject to tax on the plan's investment gains. The participant is generally subject to tax with respect to his pension only when he receives it from the plan. This tax structure yields two advantages to the participant.

One results from the fact that marginal tax rates are progressive. To see this advantage, let us use a highly simplified example. Assume that a person works in year 1, and then is retired in year 2. Assume further that the marginal tax rate is 10% on the first $1000, 20% on the second $1000, 30% on the third $1000, and so on. Suppose now that the individual earns a total of $6000 in his two-year lifetime and can choose how to allocate it between year 1 and year 2. What allocation is best? If he takes all the money in year 1, he will pay taxes as follows:

Taxes in year 1	**Taxes in year 2**
$1000 × 10% = $100	$0
+ $1000 × 20% = $200	
+ $1000 × 30% = $300	
+ $1000 × 40% = $400	
+ $1000 × 50% = $500	
+ $1000 × 60% = $600	

Total tax: $2100 + $0 = $2100

He would thus net only $3900 for personal use. If he decides instead to defer $1000 to year 2, he would pay taxes as follows:

Taxes in year 1	**Taxes in year 2**
$1000 × 10% = $100	$1000 × 10% = $100
+ $1000 × 20% = $200	
+ $1000 × 30% = $300	
+ $1000 × 40% = $400	
+ $1000 × 50% = $500	

Total tax: $1500   + $100 = $1600

for a saving of $500 in taxes. This results from shifting the last $1000 earned from a 60% marginal rate to a 10% marginal rate. If he decides to defer an additional $1000 to year 2, he would pay tax on that $1000 of only 20% × $1000, or $200, in year 2 instead of 50% × $1000, or $500, in year 1, for an additional saving of $300. It is easy to see that he would pay the least taxes overall by splitting the $6000 evenly between year 1 and year 2. In that case, he would pay taxes of only $1200 ($600 each year), and net $4800 for his own use. The more progressive are marginal tax rates, the more pronounced is this effect.

There is a second tax effect, which results from investment gains not being taxed. To see it, let us suppose that there is a single tax rate, T. Suppose that a person earns \$N today, and wishes to put it in an account that pays r rate of interest (the prevailing rate), for Y years, after which he will retire and withdraw all the money for his use. If the \$N were treated as income, and subject to tax, the individual would actually have only $N(1-T)$ to invest. For example, if he earns \$100, and tax rates are 25%, he will have left only \$75 to place in the account. Interest income, too, will be reduced by 25% in the year earned. Thus, the real rate of interest net of taxes will be only $(1-T)r$. In other words, if the rate of interest is 10%, the individual earns \$10 on each \$100 invested; but since \$2.50 of that \$10 must be paid in taxes, the net rate of interest is only 7.5%. Using formula (2), with $N(1-T)$ as the investment and $(1-T)r$ as the net interest rate, we find that the individual, at retirement, will have accumulated:

(7) $V(\text{savings}) = N(1 - T)[1 + (1 - T)r]^Y$.

There is no additional tax when the individual withdraws the money at retirement. This calculation shows the result of placing part of one's salary into a conventional savings or investment account, and letting the return compound until retirement.

Suppose that the \$N is instead contributed by the employer to a qualified plan rather than paid as salary. The \$N is not taxed when contributed, and it accumulates interest in the plan without tax. It will be taxed to the individual only when it is withdrawn. Thus, if it is invested for Y years at interest rate r, at retirement the account balance will be $N(1+r)^Y$. When it is withdrawn, it will be subject to taxation at rate T, and so the individual will receive $N(1+r)^Y(1 - T)$. Rewriting this slightly, we find that the amount received at retirement is:

(8) $V(\text{pension}) = N(1 - T)(1+r)^Y$

This is more than the amount received from a taxable account.

Comparison of (7) and (8) shows the advantage to an individual of his retirement savings compounding at the pre-tax rate of interest, r. This advantage becomes greater as the tax rate increases. For example, if interest rates are 10% and the tax rate is 10%, $1000 placed in a taxable savings account for 20 years will yield $5044; but a qualified plan will yield $6055 after tax, which is 20% more. At a tax rate of 25%, a qualified plan will yield 58% more than a taxable account, and at at a tax rate of 33%, it will yield 84% more.

D. FIRM TAX ADVANTAGES

The tax advantages to participants that result from plan qualification can be captured, in whole or in part, by the employer in the form of lower salaries or wages. For example, suppose that an employee is paid a salary of $20,000, the prevailing interest rate is 10%, and there is a single tax rate of

25%. If the employee wishes to save half his salary
for retirement, he can place it in a savings account.
If he invests that $10,000 for 10 years, and then
retires, formula (7) shows that he will have accumulated $15,458. By contrast, the employer would
have to contribute only $7,946 to a qualified plan to
provide the same $15,458 to the employee at retire-
ment. From the employee's perspective, $7,946
contributed to the plan is equivalent to $10,000 in
salary, and he would treat the two as identical
compensation. From the employer's perspective,
however, the $7,946 contributed to the plan repre-
sents a savings of $2,054 over what would have
been paid in salary. Thus, through a qualified plan,
the employer can save $2,054 while still providing
the economic equivalent to the employee of what
was provided without a plan.

Whether or not an employer captures the tax
advantage this way, an employer who establishes a
qualified plan receives a further advantage in that
contributions to the plan are deductible when made,
rather than when the employee is subject to tax.
Because of the time value of money, this earlier,
rather than later, deductibility of pension expenses
is an economic benefit. It arguably constitutes
favored treatment, since general principles of taxation require that the year in which the employee
includes the employer's payment (i.e., as a pension)
in his taxable income, and the year in which the
employer deducts the corresponding payment from
its taxable income, be the same. For example, in
the case of nonqualified pension plans the Code

requires just this matching of the employer deduction and employee inclusion in taxable income. IRC § 404(a)(5).

CHAPTER 3

ECONOMIC ASPECTS OF PLANS

Different perspectives on plans highlight different plan features and uses. To the participant, a plan might be an arrangement for retirement security or non-cash compensation. To the employer, it might be an arrangement for managing the workforce or investing corporate assets. To public policymakers, plans are means to promote national goals of retirement security and health coverage, and are powerful forces in financial markets. One must understand these and other aspects of plans to appreciate the problems and policies that shape the law.

A. PLANS AS BUSINESS ACTIVITIES

Pension plans are modern innovations. They did not appear until the end of the nineteenth century and were not common until much later. The reason for their late appearance is that, until business enterprises and the economy had evolved to modern form, few individuals retired and few employers had any reason to establish them. These two factors are related.

Retirement is now taken for granted as a natural phase in the cycle of human life. Yet it is a very recent development, emerging as an institution only in the late nineteenth and early twentieth century. Before that time, America was predominantly agricultural. Business enterprises were small and few people worked for others in manufacturing or trade. Fewer still worked long enough in a job to have to leave it because of old age. Retirement, as a formal end to working life, could not emerge until individuals began to work long-term for others. Even then, it would not become important until demographics changed and a substantial number of people worked to retirement age and lived for many years after.

For similar reasons, until the end of the nineteenth century employers had no use for systematic pension programs. Where businesses were small, and long-term employees uncommon, the rare case of an employee who became too old for his job could be handled informally, for example by giving him lighter work. Systematic programs would not be needed until there were too many older workers to be accommodated by informal methods and discharge became the only practical option. Employers concerned that workers discharged because of age not face destitution could grant pensions, at least to those considered deserving. It is easy to see how this practice generated something resembling a plan.

Yet there were additional factors driving the development of systematic plans of the type known today. As large, professionally managed business enterprises evolved to modern form, their profitability depended on high-speed, high-volume, low-cost operation. This dependence of the success of the enterprise on operational efficiency transformed relationships between the enterprise and its employees. It increased demand for those who could work rapidly and efficiently, and who could adapt to new methods and new technologies. And it reduced the demand, indeed lessened tolerance, for those who did not possess, or who had lost, those highly valued characteristics. Older workers came to be considered, as a group, slow and inefficient, and less valuable to the enterprise than the younger workers. For the sake of profitability and efficiency, it was desirable to replace them with younger workers. It soon was taken as "common knowledge that there is an industrial old age ... an economic human obsolescence, entirely distinct from the evening of life," *Sigman v. Rudolph Wurlitzer Co.* (Ohio App.1937); and that, for the sake of the enterprise, employees who reached industrial old age must cease to work in the business. Plans could be used for the systematic and impersonal discharge of workers who had reached the business' designated retirement age.

This explains systematic retirement. Similar factors explain the emergence of the systematic promise of pensions. What is important is that plans were not only granting pensions; they were making promises and representations about them. Those promises and representations tended to create expectations, and those expectations could induce responsive conduct on the part of the employees. The prospect of old-age support could attract the younger and more efficient workers. And by making the pension conditional on long-term good behavior, employers could encourage dedicated service and reduce turnover. It was common before ERISA for pension rights to vest only after thirty or more years of continuous service. The prospect of a pension could thus serve as a complement to systematic retirement. While retirement would eliminate the undesirable workers, the prospect of a pension would attract, motivate and help retain the desirable ones. Thus emerged pension and retirement plans, not as vehicles for employer generosity, but as tools for business efficiency.

Workforce management and the promotion of efficiency remain important uses for plans today. Pension plans continue to serve as inducements to prospective employees and incentives for current employees to remain long-term. This is reflected in the continued use of defined benefit plans. By linking the pension amount to final salary levels, a plan may provide a strong incentive for employees to remain with the firm. To appreciate the value of this incentive, consider a plan that measures benefits by years of service multiplied by final salary multiplied by 1%, and an employee who leaves the employer's service after 10 years, at a salary of $10,000. This former employee would still be entitled to a retirement benefit from the plan at the stated retirement age. However, by leaving early, he loses not only credit for the years not worked for the employer; he loses the advantage of having the

10 years for which he does receive credit multiplied by the higher final salary he would have earned had he remained until retirement. If his final salary could reasonably be expected to be $35,000, by leaving early he gives up $2,500 per year in pension benefits simply as a result of using the lower final salary multiplier.

Yet ERISA and other developments have changed employer use of plans for workforce management. Most of the changes have involved restrictions. For example, ERISA requires that, after only a few years of employment, a pension become substantially nonforfeitable. This rule limits (but, as just noted, does not eliminate) use of the prospect of a pension to retain employees since, after a few years, an employee may leave and still have the right to at least some benefit. To take another example, the Age Discrimination in Employment Act (ADEA), as amended, has virtually outlawed employer-mandated retirement. As a result, pension plans cannot so directly be used to prune older employees from the workforce.

But not all changes have worked restrictions. Some statutory provisions have created new opportunities. For example, ERISA encourages the use of employee stock ownership plans, which give employees a financial stake in the enterprise. Many employers believe that this is an effective way to enhance productivity and morale, and to encourage employees to remain loyal to the business.

Economic and social changes have also affected this use of plans. For example, medical and hospital costs have increased to levels often unaffordable by lower- and middle-class individuals. The result has been to transform medical benefit plans into key attractions for new workers and powerful inducements for current employees to stay. Medical benefits may rival pensions in importance, and medical plans have come to fulfil many of the traditional functions of pension plans.

B. PLANS AS RETIREMENT SECURITY PROGRAMS

While the employer might be interested in a plan as a means to attract and retain employees, employees might be interested in it as a source of retirement financial security. This is a very different perspective with very different ramifications.

In retirement, individuals are not working, or are working substantially less, and must rely on other sources of income to satisfy wants and needs. Because employment-related expenses (e.g. clothing, transportation, meals out) are substantially reduced or eliminated, and because loans for major assets such as a house are likely to have been paid off, the income needed in retirement is probably less than that needed during working life. Yet income is still needed and there are three major sources. First, there are assets the individual may have accumulated over her working life: house, savings account, and investments, for example. Second, there is the

Old Age, Survivors and Disability Insurance (OAS-DI) Program—better known as Social Security. Third, there are pensions from employment-based plans. Pension plans, thus, are only one of several possible sources of retirement income. This circumstance affects both national policy and individual plan design.

1. NATIONAL POLICY

Since the Great Depression, an important national policy has been to promote financial security in retirement. The three sources of retirement income are viewed as forming an integrated system, the parts of which the federal government can influence to differing degrees.

Individual saving can be influenced the least, and the level of individual saving for retirement is strongly affected by personal preferences and individual circumstances. Moreover, higher income individuals are more responsive to inducements. Those individuals have proportionately more of their income available for discretionary use and, because they are taxed at higher marginal rates, benefit more from tax-based incentives. The disproportionate impact of tax incentives on the more affluent has generated fairness objections to IRAs and other such programs.

Social Security, by contrast, is a mandatory, federally administered system, designed to provide basic financial support in retirement. Revenues derive from a tax on both employers and employees (including the self-employed), based on a flat percentage of the employee's wages up to the *taxable wage base*, a statutory limit that increases from year to year. Benefits are paid to all individuals who have been employed for at least a specified period at a specified minimum earnings level.

Social Security benefits are not a simple function of the amounts paid by the covered employee and her employers. Rather, they are determined by age, years of employment, and average wages. The benefit structure is designed to help lower-earning employees the most, by providing replacement for a higher proportion of their pre-retirement income than it does for higher-earning employees. The reason for this partly redistributive character is that one of the system's purposes is to reduce old-age poverty. Thus, benefits are for life, are indexed to the cost of living, and are provided also to survivors of a covered worker. Because another of its original purposes was to open up jobs for younger workers, Social Security also contains disincentives to continued employment. Benefits are reduced, according to a complex formula, by an individual's current earnings.

Pension plan benefits are subject to less governmental control than Social Security, but receive more inducements than individual savings. From almost the beginning of the federal income tax system, the government has provided advantageous treatment for private pension plans. When tax rates were low, the inducement was weak. In the

1940's, however, marginal tax rates increased and long remained high. As a result, the tax-based encouragement of plans became more effective and led to a great increase in the rate of plan formation. Economists generally agree that the level of plan coverage today is substantially attributable to the tax advantages of qualified plans. Federal policy has continued to take the view that pension plans, as a source of retirement income, should be encouraged by the tax laws, but still left voluntary on the part of the employer. Proposals for mandatory pension plans have found little Congressional interest.

The use of tax incentives to promote pension plans raises important policy questions. The Treasury Department estimates that the tax expenditure (i.e. tax revenue lost due to preferential treatment) for fiscal year 2004, attributable to pension plans, is over $123 billion. (The estimated tax expenditure for employer contributions relating to employee health care is over $120 billion.) It has been one of the largest tax expenditures for many years, and its size prompts the question of whether it is economically and socially justified.

The question is difficult. On the one hand, there is economic evidence that, while pension plans draw some capital away from other savings vehicles, their net effect is still to raise total national saving. Thus, the tax inducement may produce real economic and social gains. But, on the other hand, the tax expenditure is arguably unfair because, as tax-driven, it benefits higher income individuals the most. Levels of pension plan coverage and participation are greater among the more highly paid employees. For example, in 2001, 76% of employees earning $50,000 or more per year worked for an employer that sponsored a retirement plan and 72% of employees earning $50,000 or more actually participated. By contrast, only 39% of employees earning $10,000 to $14,999 per year worked for an employer that sponsored a plan and only 21% participated. Thus, one can argue that tax benefits relating to plans go disproportionately to those who need them less. A response, however, is that if not for the tax incentives benefiting the higher income workers, and thereby raising overall demand for pension plans, there would be fewer plans that also cover the lower income employees. Thus the inducements and benefits to the more highly paid ultimately benefit the lower-paid.

Further complicating the debate over tax policy is the argument advanced by some that there really is no special tax treatment, and thus no tax expenditure. Proponents of this view argue that the tax laws relating to pension plans are precisely what ordinary principles of taxation require. On this account, it is nonqualified plans that are subject to special, but disadvantageous, tax treatment. This view of plan taxation, however, is a minority one.

Another policy question is that of the best mix of sources of retirement income in the economy and society as a whole. This question, too, is hard to answer.   One reason is that the economic interaction between the various sources is complex and uncertain.   As noted above, an increase in plan usage reduces saving through other vehicles, but still raises the overall amount.   Social Security has probably not reduced the national savings rate. However, increases in Social Security benefit levels very likely reduce plan coverage and plan benefit levels by lessening the need for plan benefits as a supplement to Social Security.   Because of these interactions, economic forecasting of the effects of changes in the law is difficult.

There are political factors, too, that bear on this policy question.   One consideration is the proper role of the government in providing retirement security.   Depending on outlook, one might prefer either public (Social Security) or private (plans and personal savings) sources of retirement income. Another consideration is the appropriate role of older individuals in society.   Current policy is expressed in a prohibition on age discrimination, which enables individuals to continue working until later in life than they had before.   This lessens the need for both Social Security and pension plans, although probably not to the same extent.   It may also affect the level of individual saving for retirement—on the one hand, by affording more time to accumulate it, but on the other hand by reducing the amount needed through reducing the total years of retirement.

2.　PLAN DESIGN

The role of plans as a source of retirement income, and as only one of several, affects individual plan design. For example, to the extent the function of a pension plan is to provide retirement security, it is arguably appropriate to *integrate* retirement benefits under the plan with Social Security, by adjusting plan benefits or employer contributions to take into account Social Security as an additional means to fulfil the retirement-security function. Pension plans have long been integrated with Social Security and ERISA permits them to continue to do so. IRC § 401(a)(5)(C) & (D).

That plans provide a source of retirement income may affect plan design in another way. Different individuals have different retirement needs and different preferences concerning the role of pension plans. For the risk-averse individual who wants assurance that she will have the means to live comfortably in retirement, a defined benefit plan, with its promise of a definite level of income, is safer than a defined contribution plan and thus preferable to it. On the other hand, a less risk-averse individual might prefer a defined contribution plan, and might also wish to be able to choose the investments made for her account. The extent of an individual's risk-averseness may depend on income level and alternative sources of retirement income.

C. PLANS AND COMPENSATION

There is another way of looking at pensions. Because pensions, in the end, are provided by the employer, they may be considered a form of delayed compensation for services rendered. This is especially plausible for defined contribution plans, which involve employer payments and employee accounts. But even for defined benefit plans the perspective has an economic basis. There is evidence that, in some cases, employers who establish pension plans pay lower salary and wages than employers who do not. Further evidence is the fact that unions often bargain for a package consisting of wages and benefits, and may trade current income for retirement benefits in negotiations.

The structure of legal regulation provides further support for this view of pensions, although the support is different for upper-level and for rank-and-file workers. With respect to the latter, the National Labor Relations Act treats plan benefits as "wages" or "other conditions of employment," and thus as mandatory subjects of collective bargaining. *Inland Steel Co. v. NLRB* (7th Cir.1948). With respect to upper-level employees, ERISA categorizes as pension plans those plans which result "in a deferral of income by employees for periods extending to the termination of covered employment or beyond." ERISA § 3(2)(A)(ii). ERISA thus acknowledges its overlap with the subject of executive compensation: the part of tax planning concerned with obtaining favorable tax treatment for the compensation of highly paid individuals, often through deferral of income until the individual's marginal tax rate is lower.

To the extent pensions are considered deferred compensation, the plan that provides them might be viewed as part of an individual's employment contract. If so, ERISA's mandatory provisions might be objected to as paternalistic legislation that, by imposing minimum standards and otherwise, interferes with the freedom of employers and employees to bargain over and agree to mutually advantageous contracts. Arguably this is bad for both philosophical reasons—as interfering with individual liberty—and economic reasons—as potentially reducing productivity and economic efficiency. The tax inducements for qualified plans might similarly be objected to, as interfering with individual preferences about how income should be consumed over the course of a lifetime, and in what form.

The force of such objections, however, is lessened by the fact that pension benefits differ in important ways from salary and wages, and cannot be treated simply as deferred compensation. For example, as noted above, pension benefits may be integrated with Social Security and thus reduced for non-employment reasons. There need not be any straightforward correlation between the amount of benefits and the amount of services rendered. Furthermore, an employee might not obtain a vested right to pension benefits until after several years of employment, and might even lose benefit rights through premature death or other circumstances. (See Chapter 6.) These factors limit the extent to which pensions can be treated as the equivalent of wages or salary.

In addition, plans themselves differ from individual employment contracts. A plan, unlike an employment contract, is not an arrangement between an employer and an individual employee; rather, it is an arrangement potentially involving a large and indefinite class of past, present and future employees. Plans, moreover, are not subject to the usual contract rules of formation, discharge, breach and the like. Arguably, they are not amenable to the kinds of policy arguments—such as the policy in favor of freedom of contract—commonly thought to apply to contracts.

On the other hand, welfare benefits do resemble compensation. They are usually paid to current employees and are commonly provided in cash, as periodic payments (e.g., disability benefits), or as reimbursement for a purchased services (e.g., medical benefits). DOL regulations address the problem of distinguishing many welfare benefits from analogous *payroll practices*, such as overtime pay, holiday gifts, and pay while on jury duty. 29 C.F.R. § 2510.3–1(b). The Supreme Court has held that whether a payment to an employee is a welfare benefit or current compensation may depend on whether the method used to provide the payment generates the kinds of problems ERISA was designed to regulate. *Massachusetts v. Morash* (S.Ct.

1989). Thus, whether vacation pay is treated as a plan-based benefit or as regular compensation may depend on whether payment is made from a fund or from general assets of the employer.

Benefits may be viewed as compensation in yet another respect. For the employer, the cost of benefits is a cost of doing business, in particular a cost of labor. The accounting treatment of benefit expenses supports this view. Indeed, the accounting standards for employer pension costs begin with the premise that pensions are deferred compensation, and that pension expenses should be treated as incurred when employee services are rendered.

The cost to employers of providing benefits has steadily grown over the past several decades as a proportion of the overall cost of labor. In 2001, employers expended $5.87 trillion on compensation; of this, $921 billion, or nearly 16%, consisted of employee benefits. In 1970, the comparable figures were $617 billion and $66 billion, or nearly 11%. A large part of the increase in benefits as a percentage of total compensation has been attributable to increases in medical benefits, rather than pensions.

D. PLANS AND CORPORATE FINANCE

Although plans legally are independent entities, their finances are intimately interconnected with those of the employer. This is especially so for defined benefit plans since, in the end, promised benefits are the responsibility of the employer. The employer funds pension liabilities on an ongoing basis; ultimately bears plan investment losses (through higher contributions in future years); and is liable for all or a substantial part of the plan's unfunded liabilities upon termination. For similar reasons plan assets might, in theory, be viewed as employer assets, albeit ones whose use is severely restricted. They are used to benefit the employer, and investment gains accrue to the employer by reducing the need for future contributions. Very commonly, the employer (or its agents) administers and manages the plan and its assets.

The financial interrelationship between the plan and the employer is closer still. If defined benefit plan assets consist of volatile or risky investments, the level of employer contributions may be volatile. This could have an adverse impact on the level and stability of employer profits. Conversely, if a plan holds safe, fixed-interest investments, the level of employer contributions may be stable and predictable, thereby making firm profits more stable and predictable. The character of a plan's assets can thus affect the financial condition of the employer; and thus the price and volatility of employer stock, the rating of employer bonds, and the general credit-worthiness of the company.

Plans are treated by ERISA as independent legal entities, in part to enforce a separation between plan assets and finances and employer assets and finances. Nonetheless, because the employer-plan financial interrelationship is unavoidable, important questions arise about its allowable scope. One question is the extent to which the employer should be able to use plan assets in the enterprise. For example, an employer in need of working capital might wish to use plan assets. It might wish to borrow money from the plan; issue treasury stock to the plan, either in exchange for cash or in satisfaction of current contribution obligations; or terminate the plan if it is overfunded, and keep the amount not needed to satisfy existing benefit obligations. (Similarly, a union-sponsored plan might wish to use plan assets for general union purposes.) These uses are generally prohibited or severely restricted by ERISA, except in special cases. (See Chapters 12–14, 22.)

A less direct use of plan assets by the employer is in contests for corporate control. Plan assets might be used either offensively or defensively. On the one hand, if the employer is seeking to acquire another corporation, the plan could purchase shares of the target. This would increase the amount of employer control, if the employer can direct the voting of shares. On the other hand, if an outsider is seeking to acquire control of the employer, the plan could purchase employer stock, either on the open market or from the employer, and make it more difficult for the acquiror to obtain control. Again, such conduct is severely restricted by ERISA.

Another, even more indirect, way for employers to use plan assets is by using the plan's tax-related

advantages. Since a plan is not taxed on its investment income, the return to it on bonds is higher
than the return to most investors, who are taxed on
interest income. An employer can capture some of
this excess return through arbitrage: by issuing
bonds, interest payments on which are deductible
from taxable income, to fund plan investment in
bonds. Sophisticated strategies have been designed
for maximizing the employer's tax advantage without significantly changing overall financial risk to
the plan and employer. It is doubtful that ERISA
permits plan investment strategies that are designed primarily to maximize employer tax advantages, but the issue has never been tested. One
reason is that relatively few pension plans invest
predominantly in bonds—a fact that has puzzled
some economists, who do not understand why the
tax advantages are foregone.

The interrelationship between plan and employer
finances has suggested to some that it might be
useful to consider the employer and plan as a single
financial unit. This unit would be described by
consolidated financial statements in which liabilities
are measured by conventional employer liabilities
plus benefit liabilities; assets are measured by conventional employer assets plus plan assets; net
worth is measured by difference between total assets and total liabilities; and employer contributions are simply intra-firm transfers. However,
present accounting rules and standards require the
employer and the plan to be treated as distinct legal
entities. In particular, plan assets and liabilities

are not included in the employer's financial statements.

Nonetheless, employer liability for pensions and other benefits, and the current costs to employers of benefits, must somehow be recognized on employer financial statements in order to completely describe the employer's financial condition. The Financial Accounting Standards Board has developed Standards (Statements No. 87 and 132) which require unfunded pension obligations to be reflected on the employer's balance sheet as a liability (and prepaid pension expenses as an asset). In addition, the Standards provide for the measurement of the employer's *net periodic pension cost*, which must be charged as an expense against income. The purpose of these rules is to standardize the measurement of pension liabilities, so that firm values can better be compared and markets can properly take pension liabilities into account when valuing the firm's financial instruments.

The Financial Accounting Standards Board has also adopted Standards (Statements No. 106 and 132) that require a company's unfunded liabilities for retiree health benefits to be reflected in the firm's financial statements. The motivation for the Standards is concern that accounting for these benefits merely as current period expenses severely understates true liabilities. Under the Standards, projected future liabilities must be accrued over the period between the beginning of the grant of credits and the date of eligibility for the benefits.

E. PLANS AND FINANCIAL MARKETS

Plans are extremely important financial intermediaries in investment markets and the national economy as a whole. Plans invest in equity securities, bonds, and commercial real estate. They also purchase financial instruments (including insurance contracts) that are based on underlying investments in stocks, bonds and real estate. In 2001, the total amount of assets in private and public pension plans and individual retirement accounts was $10.7 trillion. Pension plans own a large proportion of all publicly traded stock, corporate equity, and taxable bonds, and a substantial amount of real estate.

As a result of their holdings and investments, pension plans have an enormous impact on the economy. Every year, hundreds of billions of dollars of pension assets are invested, providing capital for economic growth. Conversely, the state of the economy has a profound influence on the financial health of pension plans and on sponsoring businesses and participants. Downturns in the stock market can reduce the the value of assets held in plans. Downturns in the real estate market can dangerously reduce the liquidity of plan investments.

The increasing concentration of stock in pension plans has been felt in financial markets. ERISA's fiduciary rules govern plan investment practices, and these rules arguably promote strategies of seeking short-term gains. Critics have charged that the short-term perspective of plans has harmed the ability of corporate managers to maximize long-term gains. In addition, plans with large holdings may trade frequently and use sophisticated strategies driven by continual analysis of market conditions. This arguably has contributed to volatility in the financial markets and has helped make financial markets too unstable for small investors.

Stock ownership involves the right to participate in decisions about corporate policies and control. Yet the economic power of plans has had minimal influence on corporate management and policies. In proxy contests, for example, plans usually vote in favor of management. Yet there is potential for great influence. In recent years, some plans have attempted to assert their voting power where they believed management not to be acting in the best interests of shareholders. However, it has mainly been public, rather than private, plans that have engaged in these efforts to affect corporate governance.

Some commentators have expressed concern that financial decisions of private plans are too responsive to the interests of the management of the sponsoring employer. The reason for such responsiveness is not hard to find: even an ostensibly independent fiduciary will be concerned to retain its fiduciary position—a paid one. The sensitivity of fiduciaries to employer management interests may explain, for example, the differences in proxy voting between public and private plans. Since, it is argued, managers of corporations tend to support each other, private plan fiduciaries would tend to vote in favor of management.

CHAPTER 4

TRADITIONAL FRAMEWORKS
FOR PLAN REGULATION

The enactment of ERISA was not the beginning of the law of plans. Plans had existed for nearly a century, and plan common law had been evolving for nearly as long. Statutory regulation existed as well. ERISA, however, was a response to the inadequacy of that prior law; in particular, its inability to deal with a few basic problems. To understand ERISA, one must understand the law it replaced and the problems that the prior law was unable to resolve.

A. THE PROBLEM OF EXPECTATIONS

As explained above, pension plans have long been valuable for workforce management. Plans have the capacity to induce employees to join the enterprise, work diligently, and remain long term. A plan induces this behavior, not so much through granting pensions as through holding out the prospect of pensions. This prospect may be systematically held out to the workforce as a whole, or a substantial part of it, through promises, representations, or consistent practice. These promises, representations or other actions create expectations that motivate the workers to behave in desired ways. The reliance induced can be reliance over a very long term; perhaps over an employee's entire working life.

This use of plans to create employee expectations generates a problem: the expectations might not be fulfilled. There are many possible threats. Before a worker retires, he might be fired, the company might go out of business, or the plan might be terminated. At the time of retirement, the worker might fail to satisfy possibly onerous prerequisites for a pension. Upon retirement, his request for a pension might be denied and the plan document might give the employer broad discretion to do this. At the time of retirement, the plan might not have sufficient funds to pay the promised pension. And even if payment does begin, it might later be terminated for any of the reasons that the pension might not be paid at all.

These threats to benefit expectations give rise to the historically central questions of benefit plan law: *When* should employee expectations of benefits be enforced? and *How* should employee expectations of benefits be protected?

B. THE COMMON LAW ANSWERS

Pre–ERISA common law took several different approaches to the problem of employee benefit expectations. In general, the approaches relied on analogies to more familiar concepts or areas of law.

One rather simplistic approach was to deem the employee expectations legally irrelevant. The approach emphasized that plans were unilaterally established by employers for their own purposes, and that pensions were unilaterally granted by employers from their own funds. Accordingly, plans could be viewed as the exclusive property of the employer, with which the employer could do as it pleased. Similarly, benefits could be viewed as gifts, which the employer could bestow or withhold as it saw fit. A few courts were receptive to this outlook. For example, in the very first reported case to deal with (and reject) an employee's assertion of pension rights under a plan, the court began its analysis as follows:

It must be conceded at the outset that a person or a corporation proposing to give a sum for the benefit of any person or any set of persons has the right to fix the terms of his bounty, and provide under what circumstances the gift shall become vested and absolute.

McNevin v. Solvay Process Co. (N.Y.1898).

Most courts, though, did not adopt this approach. The plain objection is that it disregards the character and purpose of plans; in particular, the fact that plans work by inducing employees to expect a pension and thereby alter their behavior, to their detriment and the employer's gain. As one court explained in rejecting this approach:

It is argued at considerable length by the [employer] that the profit-sharing plan ... was initi-

ated by means of the passage of a by-law, and
that by-laws are made for the internal government and regulation of the corporation and its
stockholders, and that third parties can assert no
rights thereunder.... If corporations desire to
have their so-called "by-laws" affect only the
corporation and its shareholders, then they
should refrain from exploiting them to third persons, for the purpose of inducing such persons to
act in reliance thereon.

Zwolanek v. Baker Manufacturing Co. (Wis.1912).

It was more common for courts to analogize plans
to contracts and treat the pension relationship between the employee and the employer or plan according to the regime of contract law. Under this
approach, courts, in determining whether an employee's claim to a pension should be enforced,
relied on conventional rules for consideration, offer
and acceptance. The issue of the enforceability of
employee expectations was translated into the issue
of whether the employer's promises regarding pensions were binding by virtue of employee acceptance
and bestowal of consideration in return. The prevailing rule was that the employee's continuation in
employment with knowledge of the plan served as
acceptance as well as consideration. Some courts,
though, took a slightly different approach. For
them, the pension plan was a unilateral contract,
and the employer was bound only when the employee had completely fulfilled the required term of
service and any other preconditions for the pension.

For still other courts, the employer was bound only when the committee that administered the plan had expressly determined that benefits should be paid.

There were serious problems with the contractual approach. Although a comprehensive plan document might resemble a negotiated deal, plans invariably were established, and their terms imposed, unilaterally by the employer. Some courts implicitly recognized this, calling plans "peculiar" contracts. But they nonetheless enforced plans according to their terms, and those terms were ones the employer had unilaterally chosen. In effect, courts accommodated plans to contract law by treating them as standardized contracts with employees, analogous, say, to form contracts for the purchase of an appliance. This approach to plan law simply evaded the problem of employee expectations. In particular, it provided no means to deal with reasonable employee expectations at variance with the terms of the plan document (which probably was never seen by the employees), or with onerous or illusory terms that gave employers the benefit of the employee expectations but imposed few obligations to fulfil them.

Some courts adopted an approach by which pension expectations would be enforced on grounds of fairness and public policy. For example, in *Sigman v. Rudolph Wurlitzer Co.* (Ohio App.1937), the court awarded a pension to an employee who, although only in his 50's, had been forced into retirement by the company. The employee handbook, which extolled the virtues of long and dedicated service to the company, set out a schedule of pensions to be paid "when old age overtakes you." The court explained that:

> [T]he particular business carried on by appellant was of such a nature that mature youth would be at a premium, and ... the appellee had reached a point where a younger man would serve the appellant much more satisfactorily. When it becomes apparent that longer employment will be a detriment to efficient service and that the alternative is a pension, a discharge is a most effective severance of the Gordian Knot. While effective and most serviceable to the appellant, it results in a complete abrogation of the security upon which appellee for twenty-seven and one-half years relied and had a right to rely.

* * *

> ... The appellant has made its election. It has concluded that he has reached the point of industrial old age. It is to its interest to discontinue the payment of the full wage. The employee must bow to the appellant's opinion and edict. He, however, cannot be in good faith and justice denied the alternative held out as an inducement, for more than a quarter of a century, to continue service with the appellant.

Such an approach dealt directly, rather than through analogies, with employee expectations and the reasons why the employer had created them. It was effective in protecting employee pension expectations but was not widely used.

Another possible approach was to treat pensions as deferred compensation. This view was adopted for a variety of purposes. It was used to legitimize grants of pensions by corporations (since payment of compensation is a proper use of corporate funds) and to validate public pensions under state constitutions (since public funds were then not being distributed gratuitously). It also underlay Internal Revenue Code rules for the deductibility of pension expenses. In principle, it could also have been used to protect employee interests in pensions by justifying restitutionary awards to employees who had been terminated without a pension. One late case did approve such an award. *Lucas v. Seagrave Corp.* (D.Minn.1967). However, the overwhelming majority of courts did not. The reason is that, for private plans, courts assimilated the treatment of pensions as deferred compensation to the view of plans as contracts. Plans were treated as express contracts for deferred compensation, to be enforced according to their terms. This generally precluded restitutionary awards that were arguably inconsistent with the terms of the plan. Some pre-ERISA cases, however, did approve restitutionary protection of welfare benefit entitlements, at least for collectively bargained plans. *E.g., Livestock Feeds, Inc. v. Local Union No. 1634* (Miss.1954).

Yet another approach was to treat plans as if they were trusts, and benefit entitlement as a matter governed by trust law. Although many plans used trusts to hold their assets, and thus lent themselves to such treatment, the approach was used primarily in connection with *Taft–Hartley plans*. Such plans are ones established pursuant to a collective bargaining agreement and jointly administered by a committee of management and union representatives. They are authorized by section 302(c)(5) of the Labor Management Relations Act of 1947. Because these plans are statutorily required to hold their assets in trust, many courts believed that the traditional law of trusts should govern them. In particular, courts applied trust law to the review of benefit determinations by the committee administering the plan, and ruled that courts must uphold the committee's decision to deny a pension unless the decision was was arbitrary or capricious. *Danti v. Lewis* (D.C.Cir.1962).

There were many problems with this approach; the fundamental one is that the analogy of a plan to a traditional trust is questionable. Testamentary and inter vivos trusts are vehicles designed primarily for bestowing gifts on, or transferring specific property to, a small number of identified individuals. The role of the traditional trustee is to carry out the intent of the settlor in his absence, and the rules of trust law constrain the power of the trustee to deviate from the settlor's intent. By contrast, plans are ongoing employment-based programs, designed to provide retirement income to a potentially large and indeterminate class according to definite rules. Plan participants have expectations regarding benefits, and it is these expectations, rather than settlor intent, that arguably give rise to the participant's claims. Rules concerned with implementation of settlor intent are irrelevant to plans and are not germane to problems of the enforceability and protection of employee expectations. Only by disregard of differences between plans and trusts could courts have developed the rule of deference to committee decisionmaking, which legally sanctions the defeat of employee benefit expectations.

C. STATUTORY REGULATION BEFORE ERISA

Most of benefit plan law before ERISA was judgemade. However, some statutory regulation existed, most of it federal.

The earliest statute to deal with issues concerning plans was the Internal Revenue Code, which expressly began to provide special tax treatment for certain plans in 1921. In time, the Code incorporated structural standards as requirements for qualification, the most important of which were nondiscrimination and exclusive benefit.

The nondiscrimination rules, first codified in 1942, limit the ability of plans to favor highly paid and managerial employees over lower-paid and rank and file workers. Although nondiscrimination rules are viewed today as rules to broaden plan coverage, their original purpose appears to have been preventing abuse of plan tax advantages. In any event, they are of limited value in protecting benefit expectations. Before ERISA, the Treasury Department imposed some very limited vesting requirements to implement the non-discrimination standard, and in 1942 proposed that pension benefits become nonforfeitable immediately upon participation in the plan. However, many businesses objected and Congress elected to impose no vesting requirements at all.

The exclusive benefit rule, which originally required that plan assets be held in trust for the exclusive benefit of "some or all" of the employees, also appears to have been directed primarily at preventing tax abuse. To implement the standard, the Treasury department developed rules for protecting plan investments, such as requirements that there be a fair return and that the investments be diversified and otherwise prudent. The sole remedy for violation, though, was disqualification. *See, e.g., Feroleto Steel Co. v. Commissioner* (Tax Ct.1977). This had a harsh effect on participants, and courts were not always willing to uphold disqualification orders. *See Time Oil Co. v. Commissioner* (9th Cir. 1958).

Although the Code encouraged plan formation and coverage of less highly compensated employees, the substantive protections for employees were quite limited. Moreover, they applied only to plans that voluntarily chose to be qualified. A further weakness was the nature of the enforcement authority. The mission of the IRS is to raise revenue and prevent tax evasion, and its main weapons are disqualification orders and tax penalties. It was not institutionally equipped to provide significant protection for employee benefit interests.

Another statute governing plans was section 302(c)(5) of the Labor Management Relations Act (also known as the Taft–Hartley Act). This section deals with collectively-bargained plans administered in part by employee representatives. It permits employers to contribute to plans established by unions, but imposes conditions designed to protect the integrity of plan funds and ensure that they will be used only for the purpose of paying pension and other specified forms of benefits. It requires, among other things, that plan funds be held in a "trust ... established for the sole and exclusive benefit of the employees ... and their families and dependents." In this way, section 302(c)(5) imports fiduciary law as a vehicle to protect employee benefit interests and expectations. *NLRB v. Amax Coal Co.* (S.Ct.1981).

These fiduciary protections proved insufficient by themselves. Thus, in 1958 Congress enacted the Welfare and Pension Plan Disclosure Act ("WPPDA"), primarily in response to evidence of union corruption in multiemployer plans. As a political compromise, though, the WPPDA was made applicable to both Taft–Hartley plans and plans established unilaterally by the employer, and was largely gutted of any substantive protections for benefit rights. It sought to protect participants entirely by requiring disclosure of information. It required plan administrators to publish a plan description and annual financial reports, to file them with the Secretary of Labor and to make them available for inspection by participants. The theory was that disclosure would deter wrongdoing, and that the information disclosed would enable participants to respond to any wrongdoing discovered.

The WPPDA was ineffective and widely viewed as such. The information it required to be disclosed was too general to be useful in monitoring the plan. It contained no civil enforcement provisions enabling participants to vindicate their rights or otherwise act on information they had obtained from the required disclosures. In 1962, the WPPDA was amended to impose criminal penalties for embezzlement, kickbacks, and certain forms of fraud, and to impose bonding requirements on persons who had positions of responsibility for plans and plan funds. However, the amendments failed to remedy the basic weaknesses and the WPPDA remained of little value for protecting benefit interests.

In theory, an additional source of federal statutory regulation for plans might have been the laws governing securities and securities markets. Because plans are, among other things, vehicles for investing money attributable to employees, those laws arguably apply to plans so long as a *security* is involved. The definition of "security" under the federal securities laws, 15 U.S.C. § 77b(1), includes *investment contracts*: arrangements for the investment of money in a common enterprise, the profits of which are to come solely from the efforts of others. *SEC v. W.J. Howey Co.* (S.Ct.1946). Whether the participant-plan relationship is governed by the securities laws is largely dependent on whether that relationship is considered an investment contract.

In *International Brotherhood of Teamsters v. Daniel* (S.Ct.1979), the Supreme Court unanimously held that the anti-fraud provisions of the federal securities laws, which might protect benefit expectations, do not apply to participants in a non-contributory defined benefit plan in which participation is mandatory. The stated rationale was that a participant's interest in such a plan is not an investment contract (or any other form of security). The Court reasoned that participants do not invest in such plans, viewing the underlying transaction as the exchange of labor for an "indivisible compensation package." It stated that "[o]nly in the most abstract sense may it be said that an employee 'exchanges' some portion of his labor in return for ... possible benefits." The Court also refused to accept the characterization of plans as common enterprises in which profits result from the efforts of others. It emphasized that plan assets derive mainly from employer contributions, and that the employee's profits—i.e. benefits—"depend primarily on the employee's efforts to meet the vesting requirements." This explanation of the financial characteristics of plans and pensions is far from compelling. An underlying reason for the decision may have been the then-recent enactment of ERISA and the Court's wish to avoid conflicts with ERISA's regulatory scheme.

Even if a plan does involve an investment contract, there are limitations to the applicability of the securities laws. The SEC long took the position that, even if participation in a voluntary, contributory pension plan involves a security, such plans generally need not be registered and need not comply with all the provisions of the Securities Act. In 1970 Congress amended the 1933 Securities Act to specifically exempt interests in certain qualified pension plans from its registration and other provisions. 15 U.S.C. § 77c(a)(2).

CHAPTER 5

THE LEGISLATIVE BACKGROUND TO ERISA

To complete our preliminary examination of the law of plans, we briefly examine the process of ERISA's enactment. ERISA was an ambitious effort to create a new and systematic body of law. What emerged was a compromise between competing goals. What emerged was also an incomplete statute, intended in large measure to be a starting point for judicial, administrative, and further legislative development. Full understanding of ERISA requires an appreciation of how it came to have the characteristics it does.

A. THE MOTIVATIONS FOR ERISA

ERISA was enacted because of concerns about the private pension system: that too few employees were receiving or would receive the pensions they had come to expect; that too many participants were being treated unfairly by plans and employers; and that existing law was inadequate to deal with the problems. These concerns, expressed by both members of Congress and private citizens, increased steadily throughout the 1960's and early 1970's.

An important catalyst for legislative action was the 1963 closing of the Studebaker manufacturing plant, which left thousands of workers stranded with a highly underfunded pension plan. In the end, the plan's assets were allocated so that retirees and fully vested individuals who had reached age 60 were given full pensions, while all other fully vested participants received payments of only 15% of the value of their pensions. The harsh and seemingly unfair results for the many employees who had worked decades for Studebaker, but who received only a pittance, incited public outcry and prompted Congressional hearings and legislative proposals.

The Studebaker incident, though, was only the most dramatic of the many factors that prompted plan-related legislation. Public and Congressional concern with problems of the private pension system was heightened by hearings replete with horror stories about unfair denials of pensions and resultant suffering in old age; by books and a television documentary detailing inequities and inadequacies in the system; and by studies showing that only a very small proportion of employees ever received pensions from a plan.

Yet legislation did not come easily. In the years before ERISA, bills repeatedly were introduced to deal with problems relating to plans. However, there was no consensus as to which problems should be addressed or how best to deal with them. Indeed, there was not even consensus that reform legislation was needed. Large businesses, small

businesses, unions, professionals and highly mobile
workers, the various administrations, the Treasury
Department, the Labor Department, Republicans
and Democrats all had different perspectives and
interests that were hard to reconcile. The political
obstacles to plan legislation were overcome only
because result of public and Congressional reaction
to heavy-handed, and temporarily successful, efforts
by some business interests to kill pension reform
legislation in 1972.

B. THE POLICY UNDERPINNINGS
OF ERISA

ERISA reflects a Congressional reconciliation of
two different kinds of reform proposals involving
two very different approaches: those treating plan
law as a matter for labor legislation and those
treating plan law as a matter for tax legislation. A
basis for reconciliation existed from the outset because there were a few core areas of agreement. All
major legislative proposals agreed that there should
be minimum vesting and funding standards for
pension plans and a system of plan termination
insurance. These common proposals responded to
the threats to employee interests that hearings and
studies had emphasized. Beyond this central area
of agreement, however, there were important differences.

The labor bills took the more comprehensive approach. They dealt with welfare plans as well as
pension plans, and defined a framework of manda-

tory protections that would systematically protect employee benefit expectations. They sought to impose on pension plans minimum standards for eligibility, vesting, and funding; establish a system of mandatory registration for pension plans; establish a program of plan termination insurance; establish a voluntary system for transfer of vested credits between registered pension plans; strengthen the reporting and disclosure obligations for all benefit plans; impose stringent fiduciary standards on persons responsible for benefit plans; provide a panoply of enforcement mechanisms; and confer substantial enforcement and regulatory authority on the Secretary of Labor.

The tax bills, by contrast, were more limited. They were concerned only with pension plans, proposed fewer protective standards, and sought to impose the standards as conditions for qualification. Qualification would remain voluntary. The bills also proposed to give primary authority for regulation and enforcement to the Treasury Department. The tax bills also emphasized the use of tax incentives to expand plan coverage and to encourage retirement savings by persons not covered by plans.

Ultimately, the more comprehensive labor approach prevailed and most, but not all, of the forms of protection the labor bills had proposed were adopted. However, the resulting legislation was strongly affected by the concern of the tax bills to encourage plan coverage. It was also shaped by Congress' intent that the private retirement plan system remain voluntary, and that employers have the flexibility to adopt or not adopt plans as they deemed best and to design plans that they believed would best serve the needs of themselves and their employees. Thus, while Congress wished to protect employees, it also wished to avoid undue burdens on employers. As one Senate Report explained [4904] (note: all citations in brackets are to 1974 U.S.C.C.A.N.):

> Generally, it would appear that the wider or more comprehensive the coverage, vesting, and funding, the more desirable it is from the standpoint of national policy. However, since these plans are voluntary on the part of the employer and both the institution of new pension plans and increases in benefits depend on employer willingness to participate or expand a plan, it is necessary to take into account additional costs from the standpoint of the employer. If employers respond to more comprehensive coverage, vesting and funding rules by decreasing benefits under existing plans or slowing the rate of formation of new plans, little if anything would be gained from the standpoint of securing broader use of employee pensions and related plans.

C. THE INCOMPLETENESS OF ERISA

Because ERISA was concerned mainly with protecting employee benefit interests and expectations and expanding plan coverage, there remained a large collection of plan-related subjects that the statute barely addressed, if at all. For example, ERISA does not directly treat the use of plans as employee-relation tools. It imposes rules (such as vesting standards) that indirectly restrict such use but otherwise seems to leave employers free to do as they wish. Nor is ERISA concerned with plans as financial intermediaries. Plan investment practice is subject to the fiduciary rules, but no rules treat plans as important sources of investment capital or as loci of financial power. And, as originally enacted, ERISA was not concerned with policy issues relating to welfare plans. For example, it dealt little with health plans as part a national system for delivering care.

But even within the domain of its primary concern, ERISA was and still is incomplete. For example, it fails to deal with the transferability of pension credits and rights from one employer to another, the impact of inflation on pensions, and problems of governmental plans. When enacted, ERISA constituted only an initial effort at comprehensive regulation. Like many initial efforts, it failed to address many issues and problems within its apparent scope. Some of those problems Congress just did not foresee. Others Congress was unable to reach agreement on. Many it preferred to leave for agencies and courts to work out details. Some it did not wish to regulate at all.

Congress was aware that ERISA could not plausibly be considered the last word on the subject of benefit plan regulation. It provided in the statute itself for several different groups to study ERISA's effects and to report to Congress for purposes of legislation. Statements by legislators in the final debate acknowledged that ERISA would have to be revised and amplified later.

And, in fact, ERISA has been much amended since 1974. A few of those amendments may be briefly noted. In 1978, legislation authorized SEPs and CODAs. In 1980, the Multiemployer Pension Plan Amendments Act (MPPAA) revised ERISA to deal with special problems of multiemployer plans. The Tax Equity and Fiscal Responsibility Act of 1982 (TEFRA) established the category of *top-heavy plan*—one in which the proportion of benefits or contributions for key employees is high—and imposed special rules for it. The Retirement Equity Act of 1984 (REA), amended ERISA, *inter alia*, to deal with special problems relating to women. The Tax Reform Act of 1986 (TRAC), amended ERISA, among other ways, to accelerate the statutory vesting schedules. The Single–Employer Pension Plan Amendments of 1986 (SEPPA) substantially revised the system of plan termination insurance to prevent perceived abuses. Legislation enacted in 1992 strongly discourages employees from cashing out plan interests when they leave employment before retirement. The Small Business Job Protection Act of 1996 (SBJPA) established SIMPLE plans, changed some rules regarding distributions, responded to a Supreme Court decision on the applicability of fiduciary law to insurance companies, and made a host of changes (many of them simplifying changes) throughout the statute. The Health Insurance Portability and Accountability Act of 1996 (HIPAA) amended Title I, among other ways, to enhance the portability of health coverage. The Taxpayer Relief Act of 1997 (TRA '97) made numerous changes concerning reporting, IRAs, plan distributions and other matters. The Economic Growth and Tax Relief Reconciliation Act of 2001 (EG-TRRA) made an array of changes concerning contributions, plan distributions, top-heavy plans, IRA's, and other matters. The subjects of these, and other amendments, will be discussed in later chapters.

CHAPTER 6

BENEFIT PROTECTION: VESTING

A. THE VESTING PROBLEM

One of the main purposes of ERISA is to promote the *vesting* of retirement benefits—their becoming *nonforfeitable*. Congress was deeply troubled by plans in which pension benefits never vested before retirement, or vested only after such a long period—perhaps 30 years—that few employees would ever become entitled to them. Congress' main objection to plans that made pre-retirement vesting difficult or impossible was the great potential for unfairness: an employee might lose all pension rights through discharge, plant shutdown or other termination of employment, after very long job tenure. A secondary objection was that lengthy vesting periods inhibited job mobility, especially for engineers and other professionals. Arguably, this was detrimental to the national economy. To redress these problems, ERISA ensures the vesting of all pension benefits within a reasonable time.

But merely to require vesting in a short period is not enough. Results comparable to long vesting periods can be achieved by adjusting other features of plans. For example, a plan might specify that a break in service would cause a forfeiture of all vesting credit to date. Or the plan could provide for slow growth in the value of the pension, so that participants would be entitled only to a low level of benefits until they neared retirement. Vested rights in such a case would be vested rights to very little for many years.

Clearly, to accomplish Congressional goals, features of plans beyond vesting had to be regulated. In this chapter we examine the vesting rules. In the next chapter we discuss the ancillary standards needed to make the vesting rules work.

B. VESTING STANDARDS

Requiring pension rights to vest from the first day of employment would afford maximal protection to employees. Congress, however, did not impose such a requirement. It recognized that to do so would increase costs, deter plan formation, and undermine the ability of employers to use plans for many traditional purposes. Thus, ERISA's vesting rules (and related standards) reflect compromises between the need of employees for protection and the need of employers for flexibility. They also reflect compromises between the competing needs of employees for broad plan coverage and for strong protection once a plan exists.

1. VESTING OF THE NORMAL RETIREMENT BENEFIT

Under the Age Discrimination in Employment Act, an employer cannot impose a mandatory retirement age on its employees. 29 U.S.C. § 623(a). Nonetheless, a plan may identify a *normal retirement age* as a standard for determinations relating to retirement benefits. Normal retirement age may vary from individual to individual, because it may be defined by reference to years of service in addition to a specified age. For example, normal retirement age might be defined as age 60 with at least 5 years of service.

ERISA restricts the choice of normal retirement age. ERISA § 3(24) provides that normal retirement age is the later of age 65 or the fifth anniversary of plan participation, or else any earlier normal retirement age specified in the plan. The most important use for normal retirement age is in determining the *normal retirement benefit*. Under ERISA § 3(22), an individual's normal retirement benefit is the greater of the benefit commencing at normal retirement age or the early retirement benefit under the plan. (In the determination, medical and certain disability benefits are excluded.) For most plans, the normal retirement benefit is the benefit commencing at normal retirement age. (Thus, the normal retirement age is generally the earliest age at which an employee may retire with full benefits.) This normal retirement benefit is a standard used to determine the benefits to which a participant is entitled if she retires at other ages, or chooses an alternative form for the payment of benefits (see Chapter 8).

One of ERISA's vesting rules is that a participant's right to her normal retirement benefit must become nonforfeitable upon her attaining normal retirement age. ERISA § 203(a). Thus, if a plan's normal retirement age is 65, a participant who reaches 65 becomes irrevocably entitled to her normal retirement benefit. This occurs even if, at normal retirement age, she has only a few years of service and would not be fully vested under the plan's schedule for the vesting of accrued benefits (a subject discussed below). This rule makes a difference only for participants who leave the employer's service at or after normal retirement age; i.e. who might be said to *retire*.

2. VESTING OF ACCRUED BENEFITS

A different vesting rule focuses on employees who separate from service before normal retirement age. The rule specifies the extent to which such employees must be vested in benefits that have accrued as of the time of separation. It requires that a plan's schedule for the vesting of accrued benefits be at least as rapid as one of two alternative schedules set out in the statute.

To understand the concept of a *vesting schedule*, one must understand the difference between the vesting of benefits and the *accrual* of benefits. The degree of vesting in a benefit measures the extent to which it is nonforfeitable, and is measured by a percentage ranging from 0%—no vesting, or complete forfeitability—to 100%—full vesting, or complete nonforfeitability. For example, 50% vesting in a benefit means that half the benefit, or half its value, is nonforfeitable. A vesting schedule specifies the rate at which the nonforfeitability of a participant's benefit increases with time. An accrual schedule or formula, on the other hand, specifies the rate at which a fully vested benefit increases over time. The value of a participant's nonforfeitable benefit at any time is equal to the accrued benefit at the time multiplied by the nonforfeitable percentage at the time.

A simple example will make this clear. Assume that under a vesting schedule the nonforfeitable percentage is 25% after 1 year of service, 50% after 2 years, 75% after 3 years, and 100%, or full vesting, after 4 years. If a defined benefit plan provides for a retirement annuity measured by $100 × years of service, then the participant's accrued benefit would be $100 after 1 year of service, $200 after 2 years of service, and so on. A participant's vested benefit would thus be $25 after 1 year (25% × $100), $100 after 2 years (50% × $200), $225 after 3 years (75% × $300), $400 after 4 years (100% × $400), and the amount of the accrued benefit for all years thereafter. Hence, if the participant leaves the employer after 3 years of service, she would be entitled to a $225 retirement annuity (commencing at normal retirement age). A similar calculation can be made for a defined contribution plan.

With this in mind, let us turn to ERISA's basic vesting schedules. Under one schedule, accrued benefits derived from employer contributions become completely nonforfeitable—100% vested—no later than the end of five years of service; they may be completely forfeitable—0% vested—at any time before. ERISA § 203(a)(2)(A). (An employee is always fully vested in benefits derived from her own contributions. ERISA § 203(a)(1).) A schedule under which benefits jump from full forfeitability to full nonforfeitability is called *cliff vesting*.

Under the alternative, a plan may provide that the extent of nonforfeitability of accrued benefits attributable to employer contributions increases steadily over time. ERISA § 203(a)(2)(B). Specifically, the percentage of nonforfeitability at any time must be at least as great as in the following:

Years of service	Nonforfeitable percentage
3	20%
4	40%
5	60%
6	80%
7	100%

This form of vesting is called *graded vesting*.

There is a special rule for the vesting of employer matching contributions to a cash or deferred arrangement (discussed in Chapter 20). These contributions must vest according to one of two schedules: either 3–year cliff vesting, or else graded vesting as follows:

Years of service	Nonforfeitable percentage
2	20%
3	40%
4	60%
5	80%
6	100%

ERISA § 203(a)(4).

These schedules are only minima: a plan's vesting schedule may be more generous. ERISA § 203(d). For example, a plan's schedule may provide for cliff vesting upon three years of service. Or it may provide for graded vesting, with 30% nonforfeitability after 3 years of service, 40% after 4 years, 60% after 5 years, and full vesting after 6 years.

ERISA includes detailed rules for calculating years of service for purposes of the vesting schedules. Except in the case of certain industries subject to special rules, a year of service means any consecutive 12–month period designated by the plan (for example, the calendar year, or a year beginning June 1) during which the participant has completed 1,000 hours of service. ERISA § 203(b)(2). The term "hour of service" is defined by regulations. 29 C.F.R. § 2530.200b–2. Any year of service with the employer must be counted toward vesting unless ERISA permits it to be disregarded. Among those that need not be counted are years of service before the employee attains age 18, years of service before the employer maintained the plan (or a predecessor plan), and, in certain cases, years of service before the enactment of ERISA. ERISA § 203(b)(1). All of these time-counting rules are minimum standards: again, a plan may count time in a way that is more generous. For example, a plan might define a year of service as any consecutive 12–month period in which an employee works at least 800 hours, or count years of service before age 18.

One complication in determining years of service is the *break in service*—a period in which employment with the employer is interrupted. ERISA treats this subject in detail, because service breaks had traditionally been a major obstacle to vesting, especially in industries where work is cyclic or layoffs common. A *1–year break in service* is statutorily defined as a calendar year or other 12–month period designated by the plan, during which the participant has not completed more than 500 hours of service. ERISA § 203(b)(3)(A). (However, time off for pregnancy or for maternity or paternity leave must be counted as hours of service, up to 501 hours per year. ERISA § 203(b)(3)(E).) The basic rule is that years of service before a 1–year break in service must be counted for vesting purposes, but not until the completion of a year of service after the employee's return. ERISA § 203(b)(3)(B). However, a participant with no vested rights can irrevocably lose credit for years before a break in service if the length of the break exceeds 5 years or the total number of years of service before the break, whichever is greater. ERISA § 203(b)(3)(D).

The standard method for calculating years of service requires substantial recordkeeping by the employer. This can be burdensome and expensive, since it requires counting actual hours. To ease the burden, Treas. Reg. § 1.410(a)–7 allows plans to use the *elapsed time method*. This method is based on the concept of a *period of service*, rather than a year of service. A period of service is the period from the employment commencement date to the severance date; its calculation does not require counting actual hours of employment. The regulation describes how period of service is calculated and applied.

3.   FORFEITURES

ERISA permits otherwise nonforfeitable benefit rights, attributable to employer contributions, to become forfeitable on the employee's death. The rationale is that death eliminates the need for retirement income. ERISA § 203(a)(3)(A). However, to protect surviving spouses, such forfeiture is limited if the right to a survivor annuity has not been waived (see Chapter 8).

ERISA permits forfeitures in a few other instances. A plan may provide for the suspension of benefits during a period of reemployment with the sponsor after benefit payment commences. ERISA § 203(a)(3)(B). It may also provide for the forfeiture of accrued benefits attributable to employer contributions, where an employee who is less than 50% vested withdraws amounts attributable to her mandatory contributions. However, the plan must provide for the reinstatement of forfeited benefits if the employee repays (with interest) the withdrawn amount in a specified period. ERISA § 203(a)(3)(D).

Another kind of forfeiture provision is the so-called *bad-boy clause*: a provision for the loss of benefits by reason of prohibited conduct, such as the employee's engaging in illegal acts or competing with the employer after separation from service. Some such clauses are permitted. A plan may provide one vesting schedule for employees who engage in the prohibited conduct, and another schedule for other employees, so long as each schedule satisfies the cliff or graded vesting standard. Temp. Treas. Reg. §§ 1.411(a)–3T(a)(2) & 1.411(a)–4T; Rev. Rul. 85–31. Some cases have held that both schedules must satisfy either ERISA's 5–year cliff vesting standard or its 7–year graded vesting standard: that it is impermissible for one schedule to satisfy 5–year cliff vesting and the other to satisfy 7–year graded vesting. *See Hummell v. S.E. Rykoff & Co.* (9th Cir.1980).

Forfeiture problems may arise in the context of plan amendments. An amendment changing a vesting schedule cannot have the effect of reducing the nonforfeitable percentage of any employee's accrued benefits. In addition, where a plan's vesting schedule is amended, every participant with 3 or more years of service must be permitted to elect to have her nonforfeitable percentage determined under the old schedule. ERISA § 203(c)(1).

4. VESTING UPON PLAN TERMINATION

The Internal Revenue Code imposes an additional vesting requirement as a qualification rule. Under the Code, a plan must provide that, upon its termination or partial termination, the rights of affected employees to all their accrued benefits become nonforfeitable to the extent funded or credited to their accounts. In addition, a plan to which minimum funding standards (see Chapter 21) do not apply must provide for the vesting of all accrued benefits of affected employees, to the extent funded or credited, upon the complete discontinuation of contributions. IRC § 411(d)(3). The purpose of these requirements is to prevent discrimination; for example, through the termination of a plan for a small business at a time when the president has just retired and most other employees are only partially vested.

A termination or partial termination must be distinguished from a mere preservation of the status quo (sometimes called *freezing the plan*), where no additional employees are allowed to participate and no further contributions are made, but the plan is continued in order to distribute vested benefits upon retirement. Similarly, a complete discontinuance of contributions must be distinguished from a temporary cessation of contributions. Whether a termination, partial termination, or complete discontinuance of contributions has occurred is a question of fact for which it is difficult to lay down anything resembling black-letter rules.

Partial terminations may occur in many ways. One is through amendments to or replacements of the plan that either exclude covered employees or adversely affect the rights of participants to vest in their benefits. In addition, partial terminations may occur in connection with plant closings and other reductions in the workforce. Treas. Reg. § 1.411(d)–2(b)(1). In determining whether there has been a partial termination, a dispositive factor is often whether a "significant percentage" of the plan's participants have been affected. *Ehm v. Phillips Petroleum Co.* (D.Kan.1984). In general, though, a reduction of 20% or less in the number of plan participants is not sufficient by itself for a finding of partial termination. *Halliburton Co. v. Commissioner* (Tax Ct.1993).

In calculating percentage reductions, it appears that only non-vested participants are counted in the numerator and denominator. *Matz v. Household International Tax Reduction Inv. Plan* (7th Cir. 2001). The law on this issue, however, is not entirely settled. It is also unsettled whether courts can aggregate a series of reductions that occur over a period of years and consider them to form a single reduction. *See id.*; *Administrative Committee of the*

Sea Ray Employees' Stock Ownership and Profit Sharing Plan v. Robinson (6th Cir.1999).

Other considerations may also be important in determining whether a partial termination has occurred. These include disproportionate impact on lower-paid employees, impact on the plan, or intent of the employer to profit from forfeitures. *Kreis v. Charles O. Townley, M.D. & Associates, P.C.* (6th Cir.1987). Voluntary employee departures generally do not give rise to partial terminations. *Sage v. Automation, Inc. Pension Plan & Trust* (10th Cir. 1988).

5. VESTING RULES FOR TOP–HEAVY PLANS

The Code contains additional vesting provisions designed to prevent discrimination. IRC § 416 contains special rules for *top-heavy plans*. A plan is top heavy for a given year if the present value of accrued benefits for *key employees*, or in the case of defined contribution plans the total value of the accounts for key employees, exceeds 60% of the respective value of accrued benefits or accounts for all employees. IRC § 416(g). A key employee is a 5% owner, or one of certain other highly paid officers or other owners. IRC § 416(i)(1).

One of the qualification rules for top-heavy plans is a set of special vesting schedules. For plans that are top-heavy, the 5–year cliff vesting standard is replaced with 3–year cliff vesting and the 7–year graded vesting standard is replaced with the following:

Years of service	Nonforfeitable percentage
2	20%
3	40%
4	60%
5	80%
6 or more	100%

To the extent consistent with these requirements, all other vesting rules continue to apply. IRC § 416(b)(2).

The top-heavy schedules apply only for years in which a plan is top-heavy. If a top-heavy plan reverts to non-top heavy status in a subsequent year, the vesting schedule may (but need not) revert to one that satisfies 5–year cliff or 7–year graded vesting. However, no participant's nonforfeitable percentage may be reduced. In addition, any participant with 3 or more years of service may elect to have her vested interest continue to be determined under the plan's top-heavy schedule. Treas. Reg. § 1.416–1, at V–7.

C. WHAT BENEFITS ARE NONFORFEITABLE?

ERISA's statutory vesting standards apply only to pension plans. The statute excludes from the coverage of the vesting rules (indeed from all of Part 2 of Subtitle B) top-hat plans (not to be confused with top-heavy plans); plans established by labor organizations which do not provide for employer contributions; excess benefit plans; and certain other retirement or deferred-compensation arrangements. ERISA § 201.

Welfare benefit plans are specifically excluded from coverage. ERISA § 201(1). However, some welfare benefit plans have important features in common with pension plans, and this has prompted arguments that benefit rights under them should vest. The argument has been advanced for severance plans and retiree medical plans. Courts have largely rejected such arguments, holding benefit rights under those kinds of plans to be forfeitable absent special circumstances.

Severance benefits are benefits paid on account of an employee's separation from the employer's service. They may be provided either to assist the employee through a period of unemployment while searching for a new job, or to reward past service (or for both reasons). *Bennett v. Gill & Duffus Chemicals, Inc.* (S.D.N.Y.1988). The material characteristic severance plans share with pension plans is that of providing benefits upon separation from service. This similarity has led the DOL to issue regulations providing criteria for distinguishing the two kinds of plans. 29 C.F.R. § 2510.3–2(b).

Severance benefits are welfare benefits and thus do not vest under ERISA. *Sutton v. Weirton Steel Division of National Steel Corp.* (4th Cir.1983). In general, they may be eliminated by the employer, through plan amendment or plan termination, at any time, so long as the plan document (or a collective bargaining agreement) does not prohibit their elimination under the circumstances. The modification or elimination of severance and other welfare benefits ordinarily is not governed by ERISA's fiduciary rules. *Id.* (See Chapter 12.)

Retiree medical benefits are materially similar to pension benefits in that they are provided to retirees as forms of retirement financial support. Since they are welfare benefits, however, they are forfeitable under ERISA. The rising cost of health care coverage in the recent past has led many employers to modify or eliminate retiree health benefits that had previously been granted. This has produced a great deal of litigation.

Courts have rejected arguments that retiree health benefits should become nonforfeitable under federal common law. *Alday v. Container Corp. of America* (11th Cir.1990); *Hansen v. White Farm Equipment Co. (In re White Farm Equipment Co.)* (6th Cir.1986). However, retiree medical benefits under a given plan may be nonforfeitable under the terms of the plan document or collective bargaining agreement, or because of special factors.

Most non-collectively bargained plans contain provisions allowing the benefits to be changed or eliminated at will, and this language is usually dispositive. *E.g.*, *Howe v. Varity Corp.* (8th Cir. 1990). The failure of a summary plan description to include a statement to that effect, however, does not preclude the provision's enforceability. *Sprague v. General Motors Corp.* (6th Cir.1998).

For collectively bargained plans, the bargaining agreement is likely to be the more important document. If it permits the employer to change or eliminate retiree health benefits, that language is usually dispositive. *E.g., Anderson v. Alpha Portland Industries, Inc.* (8th Cir.1988). Where the agreement is silent or ambiguous, courts make use of various tools of contract interpretation to determine whether the employer and union intended the benefits to be vested (or, at least, to continue beyond the expiration of the collective bargaining agreement).

However, courts differ in their approaches to finding ambiguity. For example, one court held there to be a presumption that retiree welfare benefits do not survive the expiration of the collective bargaining agreement, and that silence on the subject does not create an ambiguity. *Senn v. United Dominion Industries, Inc.* (7th Cir.1992). This position, however, is not widely accepted and most courts are more willing to find ambiguity in the collective bargaining agreement. Courts also differ in their treatment of ambiguity once found. Some courts recognize a modest presumption in favor of nonforfeitability, reasoning that retiree health benefits are *status benefits*, which "continue so long as the prerequisite status is maintained." *International Union, United Automobile Workers v. Yard–Man, Inc.* (6th Cir.1983). Other courts, however, recognize a presumption to some degree against nonforfeitability. *See Bidlack v. Wheelabrator Corp.* (7th Cir.1993)(en banc); *Int'l Union, United Automobile, Aerospace & Agricultural Implement Workers of America, U.A.W. v. Skinner Engine Company* (3d Cir.1999).

Some plaintiffs have argued that a term of the plan reserving to the employer the right to modify or terminate retiree health benefits can itself be modified or amended through oral, and usually informal, communications, of the employer or a plan fiduciary. Courts have generally rejected such arguments. *Alday v. Container Corp. of America* (11th Cir.1990); *Moore v. Metropolitan Life Insurance Co.* (2d Cir.1988). The subject of benefit rights based on oral representations is discussed below in Chapter 11.

When an employer seeks protection of a bankruptcy court, it may petition to modify or terminate payment of retiree health benefits. Section 1114 of the Bankruptcy Code provides that, in a Chapter 11 proceeding, retiree health benefits shall continue to be paid unless the trustee and the authorized representative of the employees agree to a modification, or the court orders such a modification. 11 U.S.C. § 1114(e)(1). A court may order a modification if it is necessary for the reorganization of the company, assures that all interested parties are treated fairly and equitably, and is "clearly favored by the balance of the equities." 11 U.S.C. § 1114(g).

CHAPTER 7

BENEFIT PROTECTION: PARTICIPATION, ACCRUAL AND NON-INTERFERENCE

To advance the purposes of the vesting rules, ERISA limits the time an employee must wait before participating in a pension plan; sets standards for the accrual of benefits; and protects benefit rights against threats and harms in the workplace. This chapter examines those protective rules.

A. PARTICIPATION

A pension plan cannot restrict an employee's eligibility to participate beyond the later of her becoming 21 years old or completing 1 year of service. ERISA § 202(a)(1)(A). A year of service is determined substantially as under the vesting rules. ERISA § 202(a)(3). However, all years of service with the employer, except those excludable under service break rules (which differ somewhat from the service break rules for vesting), must be counted toward fulfillment of a plan's eligibility standard. ERISA § 202(b).

There are a few variations on the basic eligibility standard. Plans that provide 100% vesting after no more than two years of service may condition eligibility on the later of the employee's becoming 21 years old or completing 2 years of service. ERISA § 202(a)(1)(B)(i). (An exception to this exception is that a 401(k) plan may not require more than 1 year of service or the attainment of age 21 for participation. IRC § 401(k)(2)(D).) In addition, plans for employees of tax-exempt educational institutions, which provide for 100% vesting after one year, may condition eligibility on the later of the employee's becoming 26 years old or completing one year of service. ERISA § 202(a)(1)(B)(ii).

ERISA does not require that employees be allowed to participate as of the very day they satisfy the plan's eligibility criteria. For the administrative convenience of the plan, it is generally sufficient that an employee's participation begin no later than the earlier of the first day of the plan year beginning after the satisfaction of the eligibility standards, or 6 months after the date of satisfaction of the standards. ERISA § 202(a)(4).

In addition to these standards complementing the vesting rules, there is a standard designed to prevent age discrimination: a pension plan may not exclude employees from participation on the basis of their having attained a specified age. ERISA § 202(a)(2). In addition, the Code contains a complex set of rules to govern a plan's overall coverage of the workforce. These rules, part of the standards for nondiscrimination, are discussed in Chapter 17.

B. ACCRUAL OF BENEFITS

The main purpose of the accrual rules is to limit *backloading*—an arrangement by which the level of a participant's benefit grows disproportionately in later years. Limiting backloading is a necessary adjunct to the vesting rules. If a plan were to provide for benefit accrual thus:

Years of service	Total benefit to be paid at retirement
1	$1
2	$2
3	$3
* * *	* * *
19	$19
20 and more	Final pay × years of service × 1.5%

then even 100% vesting immediately upon participation would have only trivial value for the first nineteen years. A secondary purpose of the accrual rules is to prevent discrimination on the basis of age.

1. ACCRUED BENEFITS IN GENERAL

ERISA defines *accrued benefit* differently for defined contribution and defined benefit plans.

For a defined contribution plan, an employee's accrued benefit is the balance in her account. ERISA § 3(23)(B). However, employees often contribute to such plans and, when they do, it may be important (e.g. for purposes of the vesting rules) to distinguish the accrued benefit attributable to employee contributions from the accrued benefit attributable to employer contributions. If employer and employee contributions are kept in separate accounts, the accrued benefit attributable to employee contributions is just the balance of the employee-contribution account. If separate accounts are not maintained, then the accrued benefit attributable to employee contributions is equal to: total accrued benefit $\times$ [(employee contributions – withdrawals)/(total   contributions – withdrawals)]. ERISA § 204(c)(2)(A). The accrued benefit attributable to employer contributions is the remainder. ERISA § 204(c)(1).

For a defined benefit plan, the accrued benefit is "the individual's accrued benefit determined under the plan ... expressed in the form of an annual benefit commencing at normal retirement age." ERISA § 3(23)(A). In other words, the accrued benefit at any given time is the benefit the employee would be entitled to receive at normal retirement age under the plan's benefit formula if the employee left the employer's service at that time. If the plan does not specify the retirement benefit as an annual benefit commencing at normal retirement age (for example, if it specifies benefits as monthly annuities), the actuarial equivalent must be computed. ERISA § 204(c)(3); Treas. Reg. § 1.411(a)–7(a)(1).

2. DEFINED BENEFIT PLANS: ANTI-BACKLOADING RULES

The anti-backloading rules for defined benefit plans are conceptually simple but mathematically a bit complex. They fix minimum standards for the rate of accrual and require that a plan's benefit formula satisfy at least one of them. The standards focus on years of participation, rather than of service (as in the vesting and participation standards).

A plan may have different benefit formulas for different classes of participants so long as the combined effect is not to circumvent ERISA's accrual standards. In such case, the formula for each classification must satisfy at least one of the accrual standards. Treas. Reg. § 1.411(b)–1(a).

a. The 3 Percent Rule

The three percent rule compares the accrued benefit at any time with a steadily increasing proportion of the plan's maximum normal retirement benefit. To apply the rule, one first calculates a hypothetical normal retirement benefit to which a participant would be entitled if she commenced participation at the earliest possible entry age, and worked continuously until the earlier of age 65 or the normal retirement age specified in the plan. One then takes 3% of this amount; the resulting figure becomes the measuring stick for the test. One multiplies this 3% figure by the number of years of a participant's actual participation in the plan, up to a maximum of 33–1/3. If her actual accrued benefit is greater than or equal to this sum, the test is satisfied. ERISA § 204(b)(1)(A).

Consider a simple example. Suppose that a plan allows participation at age 21 and sets normal retirement age as 65. If the benefit formula is $100 × years of service, the maximum normal retirement benefit is $4400. 3% of this amount is $132. For this plan, the 3% rule is never satisfied: a participant's accrued benefit at any time will be years of participation times $100, while the 3% rule requires that accrued benefits at that time be at least years of participation times $132.

From the perspective of the 3% rule, the problem with the plan's benefit formula is that, for long-term employees, too little of the normal retirement benefit accumulates in early years of service. If the goal is to provide up to $4400 in retirement benefits, it could be achieved through a more rapid formula: for example, $200 × years of service up to a maximum of 22. Since the normal retirement age and the earliest participation age remain the same, so does the 3% factor: $132 per year. However, since benefits are now accruing at the faster rate of $200 per year, the 3% rule is satisfied.

The 3% rule may be used where the benefit formula relies on compensation over a period of N years. In such cases, the hypothetical normal retirement benefit is determined as if the participant continued to earn until normal retirement age the average rate of compensation during the N consecutive years (up to 10) in which her compensation was highest. For example, suppose that a plan's normal retirement age is 65 and that there is no minimum entry age. The benefit formula provides for 2% of average compensation for the highest 3 consecutive years of service, for each year of participation up to 25 years. Suppose that an employee, at age 40, has 10 years of participation. Call C the average compensation for her highest 3 consecutive years of service as of that time. Then the maximum normal retirement benefit is 50% of C, and 3% of that is 1.5% of C. Thus, for the 3% test to be satisfied at the time, the accrued benefit must be at least 15% of C. In fact, the accrued benefit is 20% of C, and the test is satisfied. (This benefit formula always satisfies the 3% rule.)

b. The 133–1/3% Rule

The second rule examines the plan's rate of accrual rather than amounts accrued. It requires that, at any time, say $Y(1)$, the rate of accrual for any subsequent year, say $Y(2)$, not be more than 133–1/3% of the rate of accrual for years between $Y(1)$ and $Y(2)$. ERISA § 204(b)(1)(B). This rule is designed to prevent a large acceleration in the rate of benefit growth for later years of participation. Some examples make clear how it works.

Consider the first example given above, of the plan in which benefits accrue steadily at the rate of $100 per year. This plan's formula satisfies the test, since the rate of accrual in any year is 100% of the rate in any prior year. Similarly, the plan in which benefits accrue at the rate of 2% of highest average compensation per year also satisfies the test.

It is easy to construct examples of accrual rules that fail. Suppose that a plan provides for accrual at the rate of 1% of final salary for the first 5 years, 1.25% for the next 5 years, and 1.5% for all years thereafter. The rate of accrual in years 11 and following is 150% of the rate in years 1–5, and so the test is not satisfied. It makes no difference that the accrual rate increases only 25% from year 5 to 6 and from year 10 to 11.

Plan amendments increasing the rate of benefit accrual can complicate application of the test. To deal with this situation, ERISA provides that an amendment in effect for a given year is treated as if it were in effect for all other years. ERISA § 204(b)(1)(B)(i). Thus, if a plan originally provided for a single accrual rate of 1% of final pay per year, but was amended to provide for an accrual of 1.5% per year, the plan will not be deemed to provide for an increase of 150% in the accrual rate for its first year of amended operation; for purpose of application of the 133–1/3% rule, it will be treated as if the accrual rate were always 1.5% per year. Correspondingly, in the year before the amendment went in to effect, the plan will not be considered to provide for a 150% increase in the accrual rate for subsequent years. ERISA § 204(b)(1)(B)(ii).

The 133–1/3% rule contains one more requirement: the accrued benefit payable at normal retirement age must be equal to the normal retirement benefit. This prohibits a plan from, for example, specifying that the normal retirement benefit is $10,000 per year, while the rate of accrual of benefits is only $100 per year. Under such a plan, an employee who left the company before retirement, even a year before, would receive a benefit very substantially less than the normal retirement benefit.

c. The Fractional Rule

The third rule compares a hypothetical normal retirement benefit to actual benefits accrued at the time of separation from service. ERISA § 204(b)(1)(C). Here, one first calculates the *fractional rule benefit* : the retirement benefit, R, to which the employee would be entitled were she to continue to work until normal retirement age. In this calculation, one presumes that the employee would continue to earn until normal retirement age the relevant salary (e.g., final or average over 3 years) used in computing the normal retirement benefit, determined as if she had attained normal retirement age on the date of separation from service. (For example, if the benefit formula is 1% × years of service × final pay, then, in calculating the hypothetical normal retirement benefit, one assumes that the employee would continue to earn until normal retirement age the salary at separation from service.) One then forms a fraction, F, equal to the years of actual participation at separation divided by the total number of years the employee would have participated had she retired at the normal retirement age. If actual accrued benefit is at least equal to R × F, then the test is satisfied.

An example may help. Suppose that a plan provides for benefit accrual at the rate of $1000 per year and a normal retirement age of 65. If an employee terminates employment X years before age 65, with N years of service, then we can calculate as follows: (a) the accrued benefit at separation from service is N × $1000; (b) the projected normal retirement benefit is (N+X) × $1000; (c) the fraction, F, is N/(N+X). The plan's benefit formula satisfies the fractional rule, since the accrued benefit, N × $1000, is equal to [(N+X) × $1000] × [N/(N+X)].

d. Insurance Plans

There is a special accrual rule for defined benefit plans funded exclusively through insurance contracts. If the contracts provide for level annual premiums commencing with participation, benefits under the plan are equal to benefits under that contracts at normal retirement age, and benefits are guaranteed by the insurance company to the extent premiums have been paid, then the anti-backloading standard is met so long as the accrued benefit is no less than cash surrender value (calculated under certain assumptions). ERISA § 204(b)(1)(F).

3. DEFINED BENEFIT PLANS: AGE DISCRIMINATION RULES

To promote the goal of preventing age discrimination, ERISA prohibits defined benefit plans from ceasing accruals, or reducing the rate of accrual, on account of the employee's age. (There is an exception for highly compensated employees.) A defined benefit plan, though, may limit the amount of benefit, or the years of participation taken into account by the benefit formula, so long as this is not done on the basis of age. ERISA § 204(b)(1)(H).

4. DEFINED CONTRIBUTION PLANS

Backloading is not a significant problem with defined contribution plans. The general accrual rules for such plans, thus, respond only to age-discrimination concerns and provide that contributions to an employee's account may not cease, and that the rate of contribution to the employee's account not be reduced, on account of age. ERISA § 204(b)(2).

5. TOP–HEAVY PLANS

In years that a plan is top-heavy, it is subject to special accrual rules. For participants in top-heavy defined benefit plans who are not key employees, the accrued benefit (expressed in the form of a single-life annuity) attributable to employer contributions may not be less than the following percentage of average compensation for years in the *testing*

period : the lesser of (a) 2% times years of service
with the employer, or (b) 20%. The testing period
is determined by the period of consecutive plan
years (disregarding years in which the plan was not
top-heavy), up to 5, in which the participant had the
greatest aggregate compensation. IRC § 416(c)(1);
Treas. Reg. § 1.416–1, at M–2.

For participants in top-heavy defined contribution plans who are not key employees, the employer
contribution must be at least 3% of the participant's
compensation, unless 3% is greater than the highest
percentage rate at which contributions are made for
key employees. In such case, the contribution percentage for non-key employees must equal the maximum contribution percentage for key employees.
IRC § 416(c)(2).

6. PLAN AMENDMENTS AND ACCRUED BENEFITS

Welfare benefits do not accrue in any meaningful
sense: the term "accrued benefit" is defined only
with respect to benefits from defined benefit and
defined contribution plans, ERISA § 3(23), and the
accrual rules apply only to those kinds of plans,
ERISA § 201(1). However, not every benefit from
a pension plan is an accrued benefit. For a defined
benefit plan, an accrued benefit is a benefit equivalent to "an annual benefit commencing at retirement age," and for a defined contribution plan an
accrued benefit is "the balance of the individual's
account." ERISA § 3(23). But a plan might also

offer other benefits as well, such as life insurance or alternative forms for the distribution of pension benefits. A plan might also offer an early retirement subsidy. This is an amount paid at early retirement greater than the actuarial equivalent of a pension commencing at normal retirement age. Whether a benefit or optional form of benefit is an accrued benefit is important for application of certain rules.

One, the *anti-cutback rule*, prohibits plan amendments that reduce accrued benefits. ERISA § 204(g); Treas. Reg. § 1.411(d)–4. Courts have held that an automatic cost-of-living adjustment, and like provisions for automatic benefit increases, may be an accrued benefit protected against elimination or decrease. *Hickey v. Chicago Truck Drivers, Helpers & Warehouse Workers Union* (7th Cir. 1992).

Section 204(g) also specifies that a plan amendment which eliminates or reduces "an early retirement benefit" is deemed to reduce accrued benefits to the extent it reduces benefits attributable to service before the plan amendment. ERISA § 204(g)(2)(A). The meaning of this restriction can be illustrated as follows. Suppose that a plan's normal retirement age is 65, its benefit formula is 1% × years of service × final pay, and early retirement benefits are provided at age 55 based on a formula for the actuarial equivalent of the normal retirement benefit. If the formula is changed so as to reduce the age 55 early retirement benefit from

60% of the normal retirement benefit to 50%, then an individual's early retirement benefit cannot be reduced to less than what she had accrued under the old formula. Thus, if, at the time of the amendment, an individual, aged 45, with salary of $30,000, had worked for 20 years, her early retirement benefit could not be reduced below 20 years $\times$ 1% $\times$ $30,000 $\times$ 60% = $3,600.

In the case of retirement-type subsidies, the rule is a little more complicated. Benefits attributable to service before the amendment still cannot be reduced or eliminated, but only for those participants who actually satisfy the preamendment conditions for the subsidy, either before or after the amendment. Thus, if a plan provides an early retirement subsidy for participants who retire at age 55 with 30 years of service, only those participants who actually meet the age and service condition at some time will be entitled to the subsidy after the plan is amended to eliminate it. If a 45 year-old participant has 20 years of service at the time of the amendment, she loses her right to the subsidy if she leaves the employer within the next ten years.

There are several exceptions to the anti-cutback rule. Amendments reducing accrued benefits are permitted, if approved by the Secretary of the Treasury, in certain cases where a waiver of the applicable plan funding rules (see Chapter 21) is inadequate or unavailable. ERISA § 204(g)(1); IRC § 412(c)(8). The anti-cutback rule also does not apply where the relevant benefits or subsidies create significant burdens or complexities for the plan and its participants and the amendment has no more than a *de minimis* impact on the rights of the participants. ERISA § 204(g)(2). It also does not apply in certain cases involving the termination of multiemployer plans. ERISA §§ 204(g)(1) & 4281. Finally, there are several exceptions that relate to the elimination of forms of benefit distribution from defined contribution plans. ERISA §§ 204(g)(4) & (5).

ERISA does not prohibit amendments that reduce future rates of accrual. It does, however, provide that in case of a "significant reduction" in the rate of future accrual, participants and certain other parties likely to be affected must be timely notified of the amendment. ERISA § 204(h). For purposes of this rule, an amendment eliminating or reducing an early retirement benefit or early retirement subsidy is treated as having the effect of reducing the rate of future benefit accrual. ERISA § 204(h)(9).

The notice under this rule must be written in a manner calculated to be understood by the average plan participant, must allow the participant or beneficiary to understand the effect of the amendment, and must be provided within a reasonable time before the amendment's effective date. ERISA §§ 204(h)(2) & (3). Generally, 45 day notice is required unless the regulations specify otherwise. Treas. Reg. § 54.4980F, at A–9. Failure to meet these notice requirements can subject the author to an excise tax of $100 per day per affected participant or beneficiary, subject to certain limitations in cases of reasonable diligence. IRC §§ 4980F(b) & (c). In the case of an "egregious failure" to meet the notice standards, the affected participants and beneficiaries may receive whichever benefits (before or after the amendment) are greater. An "egregious failure" in one that is within the control of the sponsor, and that is either an intentional failure, or a failure to provide most of the individuals with most of the information they are entitled to receive, or otherwise egregious under the applicable regulations. ERISA § 204(h)(6); Treas. Reg. § 54.4980F, at A–14.

7. CASH BALANCE PLANS

In recent years, the case balance plan has become an increasingly popular type of defined benefit plan. The principal difference between a cash balance plan and the more common types of defined benefit plan is in the way benefits accrue.

Traditional defined benefit plans are generally somewhat backloaded, notwithstanding ERISA's accrual rules. This is because benefits under a traditional plan ordinarily depend on the product of years of service and final (average) pay, both of which increase over time. This combination of increasing factors can cause the value of the accrued benefit to grow at an accelerating pace as the participant approaches normal retirement age. By contrast, in a cash balance plan, benefits accrue more steadily. As a result, the accrual rate for participant in their early years of service generally will be greater under a cash balance plan than they would be under a comparable traditional defined benefit plan.

Some litigants and scholars have challenged cash balance plans as violating ERISA's prohibition on ceasing or reducing the rate of benefit accrual on account of age, ERISA § 204(b)(1)(H)(i). The argument is based on the reading of ERISA § 3(23)(A) as requiring that the rate of benefit accrual under a defined benefit plan be measured in terms of an annuity commencing at normal retirement age. The argument is that the annual rate of increase in value of the annuity at normal retirement age, resulting from each year's addition to the hypothetical account, decreases as the participant gets older. One court has accepted this argument. *Cooper v. IBM Personal Pension Plan* (S.D.Ill.2003). Others have rejected it. *Eaton v. Onan Corp.* (S.D.Ind. 2000). *See Campbell v. BankBoston, N.A.* (1st Cir. 2003).

Cash balance plans are rarely started anew. Instead, they usually result from the amendment of existing, traditional defined benefit plans to change the accrual formula. When a plan is converted, it must deal with prior accruals under the old formula. There are two principal ways that this can be done. On the one hand, the plan can provide that every participant immediately begins accruing benefits under the new cash balance formula, and that

these benefits are added the benefits accrued under
the old formula. Alternatively, the plan can provide
for *wear away*. In this case, a participant does not
begin to accrue additional benefits under the new
cash balance formula until the amount of benefit
that the new formula yield exceeds the accrued
benefit under the old formula. For example, if participant P has accrued a benefit with a present
value of $100,000 under the old formula, she would
not begin to accrue additional benefits under the
plan until the balance of her hypothetical account
exceeded $100,000. There are, moreover, tow main
variants on wear away. Under one, the plan can
retroactively credit P's hypothetical account with
the amount it would have had, were the plan to
have used the cash balance formula from the beginning. Under this option, P's hypothetical account
might well start with a substantial balance and the
period in which there are no accruals would correspondingly be shortened. Alternatively, the plan
might fix P's new hypothetical account at zero.
Under this option, it could be a very long time
before P's benefits resumed their accrual.

In a cash balance plan conversion, participants
nearing normal retirement age may experience a
lower accrual rate than they would have had under
the old plan, and when there is wear away there
may be a period in which the participant sees no
further accruals. Because of these consequences,
conversions tend to defeat the expectations of participants, especially those nearing normal retirement age. The anti-cutback rule does not protect

these expectations. *Campbell v. BankBoston, N.A.* (1st Cir.2003). Accordingly, conversions have been challenged on a variety of other legal and policy grounds. Congress and the Treasury Department (which has primary responsibility for accrual regulations) have been considering legislative and regulatory standards to govern cash balance plans and plan conversions.

C. PROTECTION OF BENEFIT RIGHTS IN THE WORKPLACE

ERISA protects benefits against some threats emanating from the workplace. The potential for such threats is easy to understand. If a plan provides for 5–year cliff vesting, the employer might be tempted to fire the employee after 4 years and 11 months in order to save pension costs. Such practice is forbidden by ERISA § 510.

ERISA § 510 prohibits an employer from discharging or disciplining an employee, or discriminating against her, *inter alia* "for the purpose of interfering with the attainment of any right to which such participant might become entitled under the plan." It prohibits, for example, discharging an employee to prevent vesting or further accruals of pension benefits. The provision, in effect, constitutes a prohibition on employment discrimination for reasons relating to plan rights. State laws on the subject are preempted, leaving this area of employment discrimination law wholly governed by

ERISA. In particular, state law claims for wrongful discharge, where the wrong is interference with benefit rights, are displaced by claims under ERISA § 510. *Ingersoll–Rand Co. v. McClendon* (S.Ct. 1990).

To establish a violation of § 510, an employee must show that the employer had the specific intent to violate her rights. Impact on benefit rights alone is insufficient. The employee need not show that interference with benefit rights was the sole reason for the employer's action; it is enough to show that the discriminatory reason was a determining factor of the conduct. By analogy to the law developed under Title VII of the Civil Rights Act, courts have held that the plaintiff initially may establish a *prima facie* case of prohibited discrimination by a preponderance of the evidence, after which a presumption of discrimination arises and the burden shifts to the employer to show a legitimate, nondiscriminatory reason for the the challenged actions. If the employer meets its burden, the employee may attempt to show that the employer's proffered reason is pretextual. It is not necessary that the challenged conduct result in actual discrimination against or interference with benefit rights. It is enough for liability that the employer specifically intended to do so and engaged in conduct in furtherance of that intent. *Gavalik v. Continental Can Co.* (3d Cir.1987).

Section 510 generates several interesting problems. First, although the language seems to be concerned mainly with discrimination against individuals, it also applies to conduct directed against a group of employees. Thus, it may protect one group of workers at the expense of another. In the context of reductions in force, the question arises of the extent to which an employer can choose, in deciding which employees to discharge, to reduce pension costs rather than current wage costs. A critical factor is whether the desire to reduce pension costs is a causally determinative factor; that is to say, whether it makes a difference to the employer's choice. *Nemeth v. Clark Equipment Co.* (W.D.Mich.1987).

The second problem area is that of medical and disability plans. If an employee contracts a disease that is very expensive to treat—for example, AIDS or cancer—or is at risk of contracting an expensive illness—for example, the employee smokes heavily—the employer may be tempted to discharge the employee or otherwise avoid plan coverage for her. Section 510 protects rights in benefits, even though such benefits do not vest. *Inter–Modal Rail Employees Ass'n v. Atchison, Topeka & Santa Fe Railway Co.* (S.Ct.1997). Thus, section 510 may offer some protection for employees in such cases. *See Folz v. Marriott Corp.* (W.D.Mo.1984). However, courts generally permit employers to terminate or amend a welfare benefit plan to eliminate coverage of an expensive illness, even after a participant has contracted it. *See McGann v. H & H Music Co.* (5th Cir.1991). The reason is the strong policy of non-interference with employer decisions regarding welfare plans. Some courts have held that section 510 governs only the employment relationship, and imposes no constraints on amendments to plans. *Deeming v. American Standard, Inc.* (7th Cir.1990).

CHAPTER 8

BENEFIT DISTRIBUTION: SUBSTANTIVE STANDARDS

In this chapter we examine rules governing the form of distributions from pension plans, their timing, and allowable benefits and recipients. (There are no corresponding standards for welfare plans.) These rules deal almost exclusively with distributions to participants and beneficiaries. ERISA generally prohibits the distribution of pension plan benefits to anyone else.

A. ANNUITIES

An *annuity* is a commitment to make periodic payments in a determinate amount over a specified period. The period may be measured in years or in lives, or in some combination. An annuity is one of the two principal forms by which plans pay benefits; the other is the lump sum payment. If a plan distributes benefits in the form of an annuity, it likely will purchase an annuity contract from an insurance company. However, if a defined benefit plan has sufficiently large assets, it might instead make annuity payments directly from plan funds.

1. ANNUITIES AND ACTUARIAL PRINCIPLES

There are many forms of annuity, characterized by how the duration is fixed, whether there is a guaranteed minimum period, and whether there is a refund feature. The two basic forms offered by plans are *single life* annuities and *joint life* annuities. The single life annuity is for the life of a single individual, such as the participant, terminating on his death. The joint life annuity is for the life of two (or more) persons, usually the participant and his spouse, terminating on the death of the later of them. Either form may provide for a minimum number of periodic payments. Either form may also guarantee the return of all or part of the participant's contributions. The return may be in the form of a lump sum payment or periodic payments to a beneficiary.

The actuarial value of an annuity is determined by calculating the present value of all the periodic payments (see Chapter 2) over the expected duration of the annuity. In the case of an annuity measured by one or more lives, expected duration is given by a *mortality table*. A mortality table is a listing of average remaining lifetimes for given ages, based on current demographic data. Mortality tables may list life expectancies not just by age, but by other characteristics as well. Title VII of the Civil Rights Act prohibits the use of sex-based mortality tables in connection with annuities from plans. *Arizona Governing Committee for Tax De-*

ferred Annuity and Deferred Compensation Plans v. Norris (S.Ct.1983).

A plan will typically select one annuity form as the *normal annuity form* and use it in calculating the normal retirement benefit. A common choice, and the simplest, is the *straight-life* annuity—a single life annuity with no minimum duration and no refund feature. Typically (and in many cases necessarily—see below), the plan will offer alternative annuity forms, involving joint lives or minimum payment periods. In most cases, the actuarial value of the alternatives will be the same as the actuarial value of the normal form. Thus, if the straight-life annuity is the normal form, periodic payments under the alternatives will be lower. The reason is that joint life annuities and guaranteed payment annuities will have a longer expected payout period than a single life annuity and thus require smaller payments to yield the same present value. Some plans offer alternative annuity forms with greater actuarial value than the normal form. In such case the alternative form is said to be *subsidized*.

Another payment option may be an *early retirement benefit*—an annuity that commences before normal retirement age. Usually, to achieve actuarial equivalence, early retirement payments are smaller than payments under an annuity commencing at normal retirement age. (Note that what is actuarially reduced is the accrued benefit as of the date of early retirement, not a hypothetical benefit that would be paid had the employee continued to work until the normal retirement age.) The reduction is based on two factors. One is the likelihood of a longer payout period, since payments begin at a younger age. Another is the lower reserves available to pay the benefit, as compared to what there would have been at normal retirement age, since there has been less time for investment gains and forfeitures to build up the reserves. Just as with alternative forms of annuity, a plan may subsidize an early retirement benefit by paying more than the actuarially reduced value of a benefit that would be paid at normal retirement age.

2. ANNUITIES AND SPOUSAL PROTECTION

a. The Need for Spousal Protection

ERISA, as originally enacted, was primarily concerned with protecting the interests of participants, especially male participants. Yet participants commonly have spouses and dependents. A spouse or dependent may have an interest in receiving benefits from the plan, even if the participant does not— for example, after his death. Indeed, a spouse or dependent may have such an interest even when the participant is hostile—for example, after a divorce.

The threats to spousal and dependent interests in benefits are obvious. Some derive from the plan. To reduce costs, a plan might wish to terminate benefit payments on the death of the participant, or make benefit rights forfeitable if the participant dies before retirement. Other threats derive from the participant himself. For example, although a plan might offer a joint and survivor annuity, a participant might decline it in favor of a single life annuity or even a lump sum payment and thereby threaten the spouse's financial security after the participant's death. Where the spouse is a non-working wife with no independent source of retirement support, these threats may be severe.

ERISA § 205, along with the corresponding qualification rules of IRC §§ 401(a)(11) & 417, were substantially amended by the Retirement Equity Act of 1984 (and further amended by the Tax Reform Act of 1986) to protect surviving spouses of participants—in particular, wives—from both sources of threat, and to increase the likelihood that they would receive benefits after the death of a participant. They afford protection in the event of the participant's death by requiring most plans to provide joint and survivor annuities as the default form of benefit payment, and a survivor annuity to the spouse on the participant's death before retirement. They require express consent from the spouse to waive her rights to these protections. (Protection relating to divorce is discussed below.) The surviving spouse's right to such an annuity cannot be defeated by a claim to an interest in the participant's pension, by or through a prior spouse of the participant, under state community property law. *Boggs v. Boggs* (S.Ct.1997).

b. Required Forms for Annuities

ERISA § 205(a) requires every defined benefit plan and every money purchase plan to provide that accrued benefits payable to a *vested participant* who lives until the *annuity starting* date shall be in the form of a *qualified joint and survivor annuity* ("QJSA"). It also requires every such plan to provide a *qualified preretirement survivor annuity* ("QPSA") to the surviving spouse of a vested participant who dies before the annuity starting date. These, and the other, mandates of section 205 apply also to participants in other plans (except portions of accounts in ESOPs) unless, *inter alia*, the plan provides that nonforfeitable accrued benefits are payable in full to the surviving spouse (or other beneficiary under certain conditions) on the participant's death. ERISA § 205(b)(1)(C).

A qualified joint and survivor annuity is an annuity for the life of the participant, coupled with a survivor annuity for the life of the surviving spouse that is at least 50% (but no more than 100%) of the annuity amount payable during the life of the participant; which together are the actuarial equivalent of a single life annuity for the life of the participant. ERISA § 205(d). (A QJSA for an unmarried participant is just a single life annuity. Treas. Reg. § 1.401(a)–20, at A–25.) The most common form of QJSA is the *50 percent survivor annuity*, in which the survivor receives benefits at 50% of the level paid during the participant's life. A participant must be able to receive a distribution in the form of a QJSA as of the earliest retirement age under the plan. Treas. Reg. § 1.401(a)–20, at A–17.

A qualified preretirement survivor annuity is a pure survivor annuity for the life of the surviving spouse. For a defined benefit plan, the amount of the QPSA must be at least the amount that would have been paid as a QJSA-type survivor annuity (or the actuarial equivalent), calculated as if the participant had retired on the later of the attainment of the earliest retirement age or the day before the date of death. ERISA § 205(e)(1)(A). The QPSA must commence no later than the month in which the participant would have reached the earliest retirement age under the plan. ERISA § 205(e)(1)(B). It may be forfeited if the spouse does not survive to the date of commencement. Treas. Reg. § 1.401(a)–20, at A–19.

For a defined contribution plan, the amount of the QPSA must be actuarially equivalent to at least 50% of vested account balance at the time of the participant's death. ERISA § 205(e)(2). The surviving spouse must be able to direct commencement of the QPSA within a reasonable time after the participant's death. Treas. Reg. § 1.401(a)–20, at A–22(b). The account balance is not forfeitable, even if the spouse does not survive to the commencement of the QPSA. *Id*. at A–19.

A vested participant is one who has a nonforfeitable right to any part of his accrued benefit. ERISA § 205(h)(1). The annuity starting date is the first day of the first period for which an amount is paid as an annuity (or, if the benefit is not in annuity form, the first day on which all events have occurred entitling the participant to the benefit.) ERISA § 205(h)(2)(A). It is not necessarily the date of first payment.

c. Who is a Spouse?

A plan may specify that a QJSA will not be provided unless the participant and spouse have been married throughout the one-year period ending on the the annuity starting date. However, a plan must treat a participant and spouse as having been married for that period (even if they were in fact not), if they were married for at least a one year period ending on or before the participant's death. Thus, if a participant marries at age 64–1/2, has an annuity starting date of his 65th birthday, and dies at age 67, the spouse must be entitled a survivor annuity (unless there has been a waiver). A plan may also specify that a QPSA will not be provided unless the participant and spouse have been married throughout the one-year period ending on the date of the participant's death. ERISA § 205(f).

d. Waiver and Election

A participant and spouse must be allowed to waive, and revoke the waiver, of the QJSA and QPSA. ERISA § 205(c)(1). However, ERISA lays down strict requirements governing waiver and revocation.

One rule sets timing standards. Any waiver of the QJSA (and any revocation of such waiver) must be made within the 90 day period ending on the annuity starting date. Any waiver of the QPSA (and any revocation) must be made between the first day of the plan year in which the participant turns 35 and the date of the participant's death. ERISA § 205(c)(7). The purpose of this requirement is to ensure that any waiver is made at a time when the spouse is most likely to fully understand her financial needs.

Another requirement is that the spouse consent to the waiver, and acknowledge the effect of the consent, in writing, before a notary or plan representative. The consent must designate a new beneficiary or new form of benefits, which may not be changed without the spouse's consent (unless she expressly permits such designations without further consent). This requirement of consent is inapplicable if there is no spouse, if she cannot be found, or in other special circumstances. ERISA § 205(c)(2). An antenuptial agreement does not satisfy the consent requirements. Treas. Reg. § 1.401(a)–20, at A–28. A consent executed by one spouse does not bind a subsequent one. *Id.* at A–29. A consent may be irrevocable after expiration of the statutory election period. *Id.* at A–30.

Yet another requirement is that the plan provide to each participant (including unmarried participants), within a reasonable period before the annuity starting date, a written explanation of the participant's and spouse's rights with respect to the QJSA; and within a statutorily specified period a comparable written explanation concerning the QPSA. ERISA § 205(c)(3). In certain cases, the written explanation may be provided after the annuity starting date; in such cases, absent waiver, the election period may not end before the 30th day after the explanation is provided. ERISA § 205(c)(8).

ERISA does not always require a plan to permit waiver of the QJSA or the QPSA. A plan might *fully subsidize* such an annuity, in the sense that a failure to waive it would not decrease benefits for, or increase contributions from, the participant. For example, a plan might provide a QJSA whose periodic payments to both participant and surviving spouse are the same as periodic payments under a single life annuity. In such a case, a participant would have no economic reason to waive the survivor annuity form. A plan that offers a fully subsidized QJSA or QPSA may prohibit waiver of that benefit form or selection of a different beneficiary. If it does, the consent rules are inapplicable. ERISA § 205(c)(5).

B.   NON–ANNUITY PAYMENTS

1.   LUMP SUM PAYMENTS OF BENEFITS

A plan may allow a participant to elect lump sum payment of the actuarial value of an annuity instead of periodic payments. However, there is nothing in ERISA to require this. Whether a plan does so is a matter for the employer (and union, for collectively bargained plans) to determine. A plan may give a fiduciary discretion to decide whether to pay benefits in lump sum form. *See, e.g., Pompano v. Michael Schiavone & Sons, Inc.* (2d Cir.1982).

The advantages of a lump sum option to employees are increased flexibility in financial planning and the potential for maximizing benefits if the employee believes his life expectancy to be less than average. Of course the latter point suggests a disadvantage to the plan, in that a lump sum option could yield adverse selection—short-lived employees choosing lump sum payment, long-lived employees choosing annuities—thereby increasing funding costs. This problem can be controlled by requiring election of lump sum payment substantially before retirement. Other disadvantages to a plan may be reduced liquidity or the need to sell assets to make the distribution.

Other disadvantages are societal. Lump sum payment creates a risk that plan-based retirement support will run out before death, since participants can squander it or lose it to creditors. A lump sum distribution option, thus, is not wholly consistent with ERISA's purpose of protecting retirement financial security.

2. CASH OUTS

If an employee terminates employment substantially before normal retirement age, his vested interest in the employer's plan may be small.   It would be administratively burdensome for the plan to have to maintain records for many years and, in a defined benefit plan, expensive to provide funding for the possibility of the employee's subsequent return to service.   ERISA permits plans under some circumstances to *cash out* participants and then disregard, for purposes of future accruals, service with respect to which the distribution was made. ERISA § 204(d).   A cash out is a special form of lump sum payment; it may be involuntary or voluntary on the part of the employee.

A plan may involuntarily cash out only those employees who terminate participation with a nonforfeitable benefit having a present value less than or equal to $5,000. ERISA § 203(e)(1).   The plan must have a repayment provision for employees who return to covered service, with restoration of the non-vested portion of the benefit.   An involuntarily cashed-out employee must receive the entire amount of his nonforfeitable benefit.   Treas. Reg. § 1.411(a)–7(d)(4)(i).

A voluntary cash out is governed by the same rules, except that the employee elects to receive the distribution and the present value of the nonforfeitable benefit may exceed $5,000.   In addition, the distribution may be of only part of the value of the nonforfeitable benefit. Treas. Reg. § 1.401(a)–7(d)(4)(ii) & (iii).

3. SPOUSAL CONSENT

Distribution of the present value of an annuity generates spousal consent issues because the distribution is not in the form of a survivor annuity. If the present value of a QJSA or QPSA is no greater than $5,000, it may be distributed before the annuity starting date without the consent of the spouse (and participant). ERISA § 205(g)(1). Spousal consent (and that of the participant, if alive) is required, however, for distribution of the present value of a QJSA or QPSA if either the value exceeds $5,000 or the distribution takes place after the annuity starting date. ERISA § 205(g)(1) & (2).

4. PLAN LOANS

Plan assets must be invested; one way is to loan them to others. Plan participants and beneficiaries, as consumers, often need to borrow money. It would thus seem advantageous to both plans and participants if plans could make loans to participants.

There are risks to such loans, however. One is that, through a loan, a participant reaches money intended as retirement support; he might be tempted to use the loan as, in effect, a pre-retirement distribution by failing to repay it. Another is that a fiduciary-participant might be tempted to use the plan as a private bank with very favorable loan terms. Accordingly, plans may make loans to participants and beneficiaries only under conditions designed to prevent abuse and safeguard assets.

There are four sets of standards for plan loans to participants and beneficiaries. To begin, there are the prohibited transaction rules (discussed more fully in Chapter 13). ERISA § 406(a)(1)(B) generally prohibits loans from a plan to a party in interest. However, section 408(b)(1) provides that a loan to a party in interest who is also a participant or beneficiary is not a prohibited transaction if five conditions are met.

First, loans must be available to all participants and beneficiaries on a reasonably equivalent basis, with consideration given only to factors, such as creditworthiness and financial need, that would be considered in a normal commercial setting. 29 C.F.R. § 2550.408b–1(b). Second, loans must not be made available to highly compensated employees in an amount greater than the amount made available to other employees. However, consistent with this standard, a plan may fix the maximum individual loan amount to be a percentage of the vested interest. In such case, individuals with larger vested interests will be able to borrow greater dollar amounts. 29 C.F.R. § 2550.408b–1(c). Third, loans must be made in accordance with specific provisions in the plan. The plan must specify who administers the loan program and describe the procedure for applying for loans, the basis on which loans will be approved or denied, any limitations on the type or amount of loans, the procedure for determining interest rates, the allowable types of collateral, the events constituting default and the steps to be taken to preserve plan assets in the event of default. 29 C.F.R. § 2550.408b–1(d)(2). Fourth, loans must bear a reasonable rate of interest. Regulations interpret this to be a rate that provides a return "commensurate with the interest rates charged by persons in the business of lending money for loans which would be made under similar circumstances." 29 C.F.R. § 2550.408b–1(e). Finally, loans must be adequately secured. A participant's vested benefit may be used as security, but no more than 50% of the present value of the vested benefit may be used to secure all loans from the plan to that participant. 29 C.F.R. § 2550.408b–1(f)(2).

The second set of standards derive from the basic qualification rules. A loan must be genuine: there may not be a tacit understanding that the plan will not seek collection, or anything else to prevent the creation of a true debtor-creditor relationship. Rev. Rul. 71–437. Loans must be made available pursuant to uniform rules consistently followed, Rev. Rul. 65–178, and must be adequately secured, bear a reasonable rate of interest, and provide for repayment within a specified period, Rev. Rul. 67–288. The qualification rules generally prohibit assignments of plan interests (see below). However, the pledge of a participant's interest as security for a loan from the plan will not violate this prohibition, so long as the loan meets the requirements of the prohibited transaction rules (even in cases where the borrower is not a disqualified person). Treas. Reg. § 1.401(a)–13(d)(2).

The third set of standards relates to the taxability of distributions (a subject examined in the next chapter). An ordinary loan from a plan should not be deemed a distribution—the trigger for taxation—since it is only a temporary payout. Thus, IRC § 72(p) provides that a loan from a qualified plan to a participant or beneficiary (or an assignment or pledge of any part of his interest) does not constitute a taxable distribution, provided that certain criteria are met.

First, the amount of the loan plus the outstanding balance of other loans from the plan to the participant and his beneficiaries may not exceed the lesser of the following: $50,000, reduced by the excess (if any) of the highest outstanding balance of loans from the plan during the prior one-year period (not including the loan date) over the outstanding balance of loans from the plan on the date of the loan; or the greater of $10,000 or one-half of the present value of the participant's nonforfeitable accrued benefit. IRC § 72(p)(2)(A). (The nonforfeitable accrued benefit does not include accumulated deductible employee contributions, as defined in IRC § 72(*o*)(5)(B).) For purposes of this rule, all plans of an employer and related enterprises are treated as a single plan. IRC § 72(p)(2)(D).

Second, the loan must, by its terms, be repayable within five years (unless it is used to acquire the participant's principal dwelling). IRC § 72(p)(2)(B). And third, the loan must, by its terms, be amortizable in substantially level payments at least quarterly. IRC § 72(p)(2)(C). The Conference Report to TEFRA (which added section 72(p)) states that, if a loan to a beneficiary is subject to tax under these rules, the tax is imposed on the participant, rather than the beneficiary, if the participant is alive at the time the loan is treated as a distribution.

The final set of standards are the rules governing survivor annuities. Since the foreclosure of a security interest in a benefit reduces the spouse's interest, a plan must provide for spousal consent to the use of the participant's accrued benefit as security for a loan in any case where spousal consent would be required for a waiver of the QJSA or QPSA. No consent is required if the total accrued benefit secured does not exceed $5,000. The consent must be obtained no earlier than the beginning of the 90–day period that ends on the date on which the loan is to be secured. The consent is subject to the formal requirements for waiver of the QJSA or QPSA. Treas. Reg. § 1.401(a)–20, A–24.

C. NON–RETIREMENT BENEFITS

As the spousal annuity rules demonstrate, a pension plan may furnish more than just retirement benefits. Special rules govern these other benefits to ensure that the tax advantages for qualified plans are not abused.

1. ALLOWABLE BENEFITS

A profit-sharing or stock bonus plan is "primarily a plan of deferred compensation"; thus, it may offer a wide range of non-retirement benefits. Under Treas. Reg. § 1.401–1(b)(1)(ii), a qualified profit-sharing plan may provide for the distribution of funds, not only "after a fixed number of years [or] the attainment of a stated age," but also "upon the prior occurrence of some event such as layoff, illness, disability, retirement, death, or severance of employment." ("Fixed number of years" means at least two. Rev. Rul. 71–295.) Funds allocated to a participant's account may also be used to provide him or his family with "incidental life or accident or health insurance." The same rules hold for stock bonus plans. Treas. Reg. § 1.401–1(b)(1)(iii).

Defined benefit and money purchase plans are more restricted because they must be established and maintained "primarily to provide systematically for the payment of definitely determinable benefits ... after retirement." They may, however, provide "for the payment of a pension due to disability [or] the payment of incidental death benefits through insurance or otherwise." Treas. Reg. § 1.401–1(b)(1)(i).

In addition, IRC § 401(h) allows defined benefit and money purchase plans to provide medical-related benefits to retired employees and their spouses and dependents, if six conditions are met. The medical benefits must be "subordinate to" the retirement benefits provided; a separate account must be maintained for the benefits; employer contributions must be "reasonable and ascertainable"; the funds in the account cannot be divertible to other purposes before satisfaction of all obligations to provide the medical benefits; any residual sums in the account after satisfaction of liabilities must be returned to the employer; and separate accounts must be maintained for the payment of benefits to key employees (as defined in section 416(i)). The "subordinate to" requirement is violated if, after the date on which the account is established, contributions for retiree medical benefits, when added to contributions for life insurance under the plan, exceed 25% of total contributions to the plan (other than contributions to fund past service credits).

2. DEATH BENEFITS

A non-retirement benefit commonly offered by qualified plans is a pre-retirement death benefit, often in the form of life insurance. Such a benefit, though, must be "incidental," in accordance with the standards discussed above. The IRS has established guidelines to clarify when this requirement is met.

In general, the cost of the death benefit for a participant may not exceed 25% of the total cost of all plan benefits for him. Rev. Rul. 70–611. However, where the death benefit is funded through whole life insurance, the 25% limitation rises to 50%, since one-half of the premium is deemed to be allocated to pure insurance and one-half to investment. Rev. Rul. 74–307. A defined benefit plan or money purchase plan will also satisfy the incidental benefit restriction if the policy does not provide a death benefit greater than 100 times the anticipated normal retirement benefit. Rev. Rul. 60–83.

There is an additional requirement for profit-sharing and stock bonus plans. At or before retirement, the trustee must either cash in the insurance contract and credit the proceeds to the employee's account, convert it to periodic payments to the employee so that life insurance protection is discontinued, or distribute the contract to the employee. *Id.*

Profit-sharing and stock bonus plans risk disqualification for failure to comply with the incidental benefit rule only if the limitations are exceeded with premiums paid out of funds contributed less than two years before. In such a case there is insufficient deferral of income before its distribution (i.e. through the purchase of insurance for the benefit of the participant). Rev. Rul. 60–83. After that time plan funds may be used to purchase insurance. For defined benefit plans, failure to meet the incidental benefit standard always risks disqualification.

A QPSA must be taken into account in determining whether death benefits satisfy the incidental benefit rule. A QPSA by itself satisfies it. However, a QPSA and a death benefit equal to 100 times the anticipated monthly pension does not.   Rev. Rul. 85–15.

3. PAYMENTS OF ACCRUED BENEFITS TO BENEFICIARIES

A plan might provide for part of an accrued benefit to be distributed to a beneficiary (e.g., through a QJSA). Such payment must satisfy the requirement that it be incidental to the payment of benefits to the participant. This requirement was codified at IRC § 401(a)(9)(G) by the Tax Reform Act of 1986.

Section 401(a)(9)(G), however, does not prescribe standards. Under pre-TRA standards, the incidental benefit rule is satisfied if, at the commencement of distribution, more than 50% of the present value of the nonforfeitable accrued benefit is payable to the participant. Rev. Rul. 72–241. It is also satisfied by a joint and survivor annuity in which the amount of the periodic payment to the surviving beneficiary (over the life of the surviving spouse, whether or not she is the beneficiary) does not exceed the amount of the periodic payment to the participant. Rev. Rul. 72–240. The IRS has proposed detailed standards for compliance with section 401(a)(9)(G). Treas. Reg. § 1.401(a)(9)–2.

D. TIMING OF DISTRIBUTIONS

1. CONSENT

If the present value of a participant's vested benefit is greater than $5,000, a plan must obtain his written consent to distribute any part of it before he has reached the later of normal retirement age or age 62. After that time, a plan may distribute benefits in the appropriate form (such as a QJSA) without the participant's consent. Consent is not required for the distribution of benefits payable on the participant's death. ERISA § 203(e)(1); Treas. Reg. § 1.411(a)–11(c).

2. REQUIRED BEGINNING

A plan may allow a participant to delay the commencement of benefit payments, Treas. Reg. § 1.401(a)–14(b), but unless he does a plan must begin payment no later than the 60th day after the latest of the close of the plan year in which the participant: attains the earlier of age 65 or normal retirement age under the plan; completes ten years of participation; or terminates service with the employer. ERISA § 206(a). A plan may require a participant to file a claim in order for payment to commence. Treas. Reg. § 1.401(a)–14(a).

3. LIMITS ON PARTICIPANT DELAY

The plan qualification rules limit a participant's right to delay the receipt of benefits. A qualified plan must provide for the distribution of a participant's entire interest: (a) by the *required beginning date*; or (b) commencing by the required beginning date and extending over the life of the participant (or a period of years not greater than his life expectancy) or the lives of the participant and a designated beneficiary (or a period of years not greater than their life expectancies). IRC § 401(a)(9)(A). The required beginning date is generally April 1 of the calendar year following the calendar year in which the participant attains age 70–1/2 or retires. IRC § 401(a)(9)(C). The purpose of these rules is to limit the use of plan-related tax deferral for estate planning purposes rather than retirement saving purposes.

4. DEATH DISTRIBUTIONS

If the participant dies after benefit payments have commenced but before his entire interest has been distributed, the remaining portion must be distributed at least as rapidly as under the method of distribution that was being used at the time of his death. IRC § 401(a)(9)(B)(i). If the participant dies before distribution has begun, his entire interest must be distributed within five years. IRC § 401(a)(9)(B)(ii). However, there are exceptions to this five-year rule. First, any amount payable to a designated beneficiary may be paid over the life or life expectancy of that beneficiary, beginning no later than one year after the participant's death. IRC § 409(a)(9)(B)(iii). Second, if the designated beneficiary is the surviving spouse, commencement of distribution need not begin until the date on which the participant would have reached age 70–1/2. IRC § 409(a)(9)(B)(iv). Third, if the surviving spouse dies before distribution to her begins, the five-year rule and the first exception are applied as if the spouse were the participant. *Id.*

E. ANTI–ALIENATION RULES

1. THE BASIC PROVISION

ERISA § 206(d)(1) requires every pension plan to provide that benefits under it may not be assigned or alienated. There is an identical requirement for qualification. IRC § 401(a)(13). The purpose is to protect pension benefits from dissipation. The prohibition does not extend to benefits that have already been paid out. *Guidry v. Sheet Metal Workers International Ass'n, Local No. 9* (10th Cir.1994) (en banc); *Tenneco Inc. v. First Virginia Bank of Tidewater* (4th Cir.1983).

The provision unambiguously governs voluntary assignments by a participant or beneficiary and requires plan fiduciaries not to give them any effect. The language has been construed to govern involuntary assignments as well. Although section 206(d)(1) is written only so as to require pension plans to contain an anti-alienation clause, it must be understood as implicitly providing that federal law will give that term effect. *See Patterson v. Shumate* (S.Ct.1992).

Section 206(d)(1) generates the question of when, if ever, third parties may obtain interests in plans. State law cannot provide an answer: ERISA's preemption provision (see Chapter 15) generally invalidates state laws to the extent they purport to allow anyone to acquire rights in a plan. Thus the answer is largely one of federal statutory and common law.

2. WELFARE BENEFIT PLANS

Section 206(d)(1) on its face does not apply to welfare plans. This makes sense as a matter of balancing interests of creditors and participants. Welfare benefits arguably are less vital to a participant's long-term economic well-being than pension benefits and do not have to be protected over long periods. Arguably, there is less harm to participants if welfare benefits are used to satisfy creditors. In addition, many welfare benefits—such as medical and hospital benefits—are intended to be paid to third parties. Convenience results if they can be assigned in advance.

In light of these considerations, courts have routinely upheld the assignability of medical benefits to health care providers. *E.g., Misic v. Building Service Employees Health & Welfare Trust* (9th Cir. 1986). The assignee has standing to sue for the benefits. *Tango Transport v. Healthcare Financial Services LLC* (5th Cir.2003). A health care provider can subsequently assign its rights to a collection agency. *Id.*

On the other hand, courts have also held that ERISA does not bar welfare plans from prohibiting such assignment. *Davidowitz v. Delta Dental Plan of California* (9th Cir.1991). This, however, can yield inequitable results for providers who rely on a participant's coverage under a plan in rendering treatment. Thus, some courts have been willing to construe a general anti-alienation provision in a medical and hospital plan as applying only to unrelated assignees and not to providers of the medical or hospital care for which the benefits are paid. *See Dallas County Hospital District v. Associates' Health & Welfare Plan* (5th Cir.2002); *University of Tennessee William F. Bowld Hospital v. Wal–Mart Stores, Inc.* (W.D.Tenn.1996).

ERISA requires group health plans to comply with certain orders of state courts and state administrative agencies that provide for continuing health benefit coverage for the child of a participant (for example, in connection with divorce proceedings). The relevant statutory standards, ERISA § 609(a), are modeled on the standards governing qualified domestic relations orders, described below.

3.   PERSONAL BANKRUPTCY

Under the Bankruptcy Code, the commencement of a case creates an estate comprising all the legal and equitable interests of the debtor. 11 U.S.C. § 541(a). The assets of this estate are used to satisfy the creditors' claims. However, the Bankruptcy Code excludes from the estate any "beneficial interest of the debtor in a trust [subject to a restriction on transfer] that is enforceable under applicable nonbankruptcy law." 11 U.S.C. § 541(c)(2). For many years, federal courts were divided over when, if ever, the debtor's interest in a qualified pension plan was excludable from the bankruptcy estate because of the plan's anti-alienation provision. In *Patterson v. Shumate* (S.Ct. 1992), the Supreme Court held that section 541(c)(2) excludes all participant interests in "ERISA-qualified" plans from the participant's bankruptcy estate. Most courts have construed the cryptic term "ERISA-qualified" plan to mean a plan subject to Title I. *E.g., In re Baker* (7th Cir.1998).

Patterson does not resolve the underlying tension between the Bankruptcy Code and ERISA: the former is mainly designed to permit the orderly payment of an individual's assets to creditors, while the latter is designed mainly to ensure that assets are preserved for individuals until retirement. *Patterson* merely concluded that Congress had chosen ERISA's policy to have priority. Problems still remain. One, which had motivated some lower courts to include plan interests in the estate, is the practice of individuals making substantial contributions to plans shortly before filing a petition in bankruptcy, to shield the assets from creditors. Arguably this is an abusive practice. If so, legislation may still be needed to deal with it.

4. QUALIFIED DOMESTIC RELATIONS ORDERS

The anti-alienation provision can interfere with state efforts to arrange support for a participant's (ex-)spouse or dependents after a divorce or other family-related proceeding. The REA thus amended ERISA to create the category of *qualified domestic relations order* ("QDRO") and require plans to pay benefits in accordance with them.   ERISA § 206(d)(3)(A).

A *domestic relations order* is a state court decree or order, made pursuant to state domestic relations law, that deals with child support, alimony, or marital property rights. A QDRO is a domestic relations order that provides for an *alternate payee's* right to receive all or part of the benefits payable with respect to a participant, and that meets procedural requirements discussed below.   ERISA § 206(d)(3)(B). An alternate payee is a spouse, former spouse, child or other dependent of the participant who has rights to benefits under the domestic relations order.   ERISA § 206(d)(3)(K).

The procedural requirements for a QDRO are designed to ease the administrative burden on the plan and to protect it from litigation. There are two sets of requirements. First, the order must contain the name and address of the participant and alternate payees, the amount or percentage of the participant's benefits to be paid to each alternate payee (or the manner of determination), the number of payments or period to which the order applies, and the plans to which the order applies. ERISA § 206(d)(3)(C). Second, a QDRO may not require the plan to provide any form of benefits not otherwise available under the plan, may not require the plan to provide actuarially increased benefits, and may not require the payment of benefits that are already required to be paid to a different alternate payee under a prior QDRO. ERISA § 206(d)(3)(D).

A plan is required to establish reasonable procedures for determining whether a domestic relations order is a QDRO and for administering distributions under QDROs. Whenever a plan receives a domestic relations order, the administrator must promptly notify the participant and alternate payees of such receipt and of the procedures for determining whether the order is qualified; and then determine whether the order is a QDRO and notify the participant and alternate payees, both within a reasonable time. ERISA § 206(d)(3)(G). A plan may not impose a fee for determining the status of the order on the participant or alternate payee, either directly or as a charge against the participant's account. DOL Advisory Opinion 94–32A. While the status of a domestic relations order is being determined—if necessary, by a court—the plan must separately account for sums that would be payable under the order during that period. (One case held that state courts have jurisdiction to determine whether an order is a QDRO. *Oddino v. Oddino* (Cal.1997).) If the order is determined to be a QDRO within 18 months of the date on which the first payment under it would be required, the segregated amounts are to be paid to the persons entitled to them under the order. Otherwise the sums are to be paid to the persons who would be entitled to them in the absence of the order. A determination after the 18–month period that the order is a QDRO will have prospective effect only. ERISA § 206(d)(3)(H).

A QDRO may require payment of benefits in any form permitted under the plan to the participant (except a QJSA with respect to the alternate payee and subsequent spouse). It may also require payment before the participant has separated from service, provided that the participant has reached the earlier of: the date on which he is entitled to a distribution under the plan, or the later of age 50 and the earliest date on which he could begin to receive benefits upon separation from service. In such cases a QDRO may require payment as if the participant had retired on the date on which payments are to begin under the order, but only taking into account the present value of benefits actually accrued and not taking into account the value of any early retirement subsidies. ERISA § 206(d)(3)(E). A QDRO may provide that the alternate payee, if a former spouse, shall be treated as the surviving spouse for purposes of the QJSA and QPSA rules (and that any subsequent spouse of the participant shall not be so treated). ERISA § 206(d)(3)(F).

5. OTHER STATUTORY EXCEPTIONS

ERISA § 206(d) contains two express exceptions in addition to the one for QDROs. First, once a benefit is in pay status, a participant may make a voluntary and revocable assignment of up to 10% of any benefit payment, provided that the assignment is not for purposes of defraying plan administration costs. A garnishment or levy is not considered a voluntary assignment. Second, a plan loan to a participant, secured by his accrued vested benefit, is not treated as an assignment, provided that the loan satisfies the prohibited transaction exemption contained in IRC § 4975(d)(1). ERISA § 206(d)(2).

6. BENEFIT OFFSETS

In *Guidry v. Sheet Metal Workers National Pension Fund* (S.Ct.1990), the Supreme Court held that, because section 206(d) "reflects a considered congressional policy choice ... to safeguard a stream of income for pensioners (and for their dependents, who may be, and perhaps usually are, blameless)," courts should be very reluctant to create equitable exceptions to it. In *Guidry*, the Court held it improper for the lower court to have imposed a constructive trust on pension benefits payable to a participant, in favor of the union from whom the participant had admittedly embezzled funds.

In the Taxpayer Relief Act of 1997, Congress provided for a limited exception to *Guidry*. ERISA

§ 206(d)(4) provides that a participant's benefits may be offset by the amount he is required to pay to the plan under a conviction for a crime involving the plan, a civil judgment involving a violation of a fiduciary rule, or a settlement with the Secretary or the Pension Benefit Guaranty Corporation involving a violation or alleged violation of a fiduciary rule; so long as the judgment or agreement expressly provides for such offset. Where the survivor annuity requirements apply to the distribution, and the spouse herself is not required to pay an amount to the plan for the violation, either the spouse must consent in writing to the offset (or have properly waived the right to the annuity or be unable to give consent), or else the judgment or agreement must provide for the spouse to retain the survivor annuity, subject to a statutory calculation of its amount. ERISA § 206(d)(5).

CHAPTER 9

TAXATION OF DISTRIBUTIONS

Participants in a qualified plan are generally exempt from tax on their plan interests until those interests are distributed. In this chapter we examine the taxation of the three main forms of distribution: annuities, lump sum distributions, and rollovers.

A. ANNUITIES

IRC § 402(a)(1) specifies that distributions from a qualified plan (other than rollovers and certain lump sum distributions) are taxable in the year in which they are made, in accordance with IRC § 72. Section 72 deals with the taxation of annuities, including annuities from plans, and certain other distributions. Its basic rule is that amounts received in the form of annuity payments are taxed as ordinary income. IRC § 72(a).

Section 72 is complex. Its complexities, though, result mainly from the need to exclude portions of annuity payments on which the participant has already been taxed—for example, portions attributable to her own after-tax contributions. Of course, where only non-taxable employer contributions were made on behalf of the participant, the rule is very simple: the annuity payments are taxable in full.

1. AMOUNTS RECEIVED AS AN ANNUITY—BASIC RULES

The basic exclusion rule deals with *amounts received as an annuity*. These are annuity payments proper. They are defined as amounts payable at regular intervals, over a period of more than one full year from the *annuity starting date*, for which the total amount payable can be determined as of the annuity starting date, either from the terms of the annuity contract or from actuarial tables. Treas. Reg. § 1.72–2(b)(2). The annuity starting date is the later of the date on which the obligations become fixed and the first day of the payment period that ends on the date of first payment. Treas. Reg. § 1.72–4(b)(1).

For amounts received as an annuity, the following proportion—the *exclusion ratio*—is excluded from gross income: *investment in the contract* as of the annuity starting date/*expected return* under the contract as of that date. IRC § 72(b)(1). Thus, if an annuity pays $500 per month, and the exclusion ratio is 10%, $50 of each monthly payment is excluded from gross income.

The investment in the contract is the total of the employee's after-tax contributions plus any amount of employer contributions that were includible in the employee's gross income, less the amount received to date under the annuity contract to the extent it was excludible from gross income. IRC §§ 72(c)(1) & (f). It is essentially the undistributed amount that has already been taxed. The expected return is the total amount expected to be received under the annuity contract, either as fixed by the terms of the contract or from actuarial tables. IRC § 72(c)(3). The actuarial tables to be used are contained in regulations. Treas. Reg. §§ 1.72–5 & –9.

The exclusion continues until the participant's investment in the contract has been distributed to her. IRC § 72(b)(2) & (4). After that time, the entire amount of the annuity payment is subject to tax. On the other hand, if annuity payments cease because of death before the full investment in the contract is recovered, the unrecovered portion is allowed as a deduction in the participant's final taxable year. IRC § 72(b)(3).

2.   SIMPLIFIED EXCLUSION METHOD

IRC § 72(d) provides a simplified method of calculating the amount excluded from gross income for most single life and joint and survivor annuities from qualified plans. See also Notice 98–2. The method applies to distributees who are less than 75 years old when payments begin or, if 75 or older, where there are fewer than five years of guaranteed payments. For single life annuities, section 72(d) establishes five groups distinguished by age at annuity starting date (55 and under, 56–60, 61–65, 66–70, and 71 and over), and an expected number of monthly annuity payments for each such group (respectively, 360, 310, 260, 210, and 160). For joint and survivor annuities, section 72(d) establishes five groups distinguished by combined ages at annuity starting date (110 or less, 111–120, 121–130, 131–140, more than 140) and an expected number of monthly payments for each such group (respectively 410, 360, 310, 260, 210).

To calculate the income exclusion, one divides the investment in the contract by the expected number of payments for the applicable age group. The resulting dollar amount is the portion of the monthly annuity payment excludable from gross income. The exclusion continues until the investment in the contract has been recovered.

3. AMOUNTS NOT RECEIVED AS AN ANNUITY

Somewhat confusingly, the Code deals with *amounts not received as an annuity* under an annuity arrangement. IRC § 72(e). These are not the same as lump sum distributions, described below, though they may well be lump sum payments in a non-technical sense. Among the amounts not received as an annuity are payments before the annuity starting date, dividends, amounts in the nature of refunds, and other non-periodic distributions.

There are two basic rules for amounts not received as an annuity. First, all such amounts received on or after the annuity starting date are included in gross income. IRC § 72(e)(2)(A). Second, amounts received before the annuity starting date are excludable to the extent *allocable to the investment in the contract*. IRC §§ 72(e)(2)(B) & (8)(A). (A lump sum payment from a qualified plan, made in connection with the commencement of annuity payments, is treated as if received before the annuity starting date. IRC § 72(d)(1)(D).) The amount allocable to investment in the contract is the amount received multiplied by the following ratio: investment in the contract/nonforfeitable account balance (computed as of the date of distribution or another date permitted by regulation). IRC § 72(e)(8)(B)-(C). For defined benefit plans the present value of the vested portion of the accrued benefit is the account balance. IRS Notice 87–13, at A–11. Special rules deal with investment in the contract before 1987. IRC § 72(e)(8)(D).

4. SEPARATE CONTRACTS

The rules of section 72 are applied separately to each distribution with respect to a *separate contract*—that is, to each distribution under a separate program of the employer "consisting of interrelated contributions and benefits." Treas. Reg. § 1.72–2(a)(3). Thus, the excludible portion of a distribution is the sum of the exclusions for each separate contract that contributes to the distribution as a whole.

A "separate contract" is not necessarily a separate plan, although it may be one. A single plan may have two or more separate contracts and two plans may constitute a single contract. Whether separate contracts are involved in a distribution of benefits is a fact-specific inquiry. A profit-sharing plan and a defined benefit plan of an employer constitute separate contracts. Treas. Reg. § 1.72–2(a)(3)(iv).

IRC § 72(d)(2) provides that employee contributions under a defined contribution plan (and income attributable thereto) may be treated as a separate contract. This is advantageous to a participant who can treat a distribution from a defined contribution plan as a distribution with respect to that separate contract. For example, suppose that a participant in a defined contribution plan contributed $10,000, and that the account balance is $100,000, of which 25% is attributable to the separate contract for participant contributions. If the participant receives a $1,000 distribution before the annuity starting date, then, under section 72(e), she could exclude from gross income only $10,000/$100,000, or 10%, of the distribution, were separate contract treatment unavailable. Treating the distribution as one entirely from her employee contribution contract, however, she would be able to exclude $10,000/$25,000, or 40% of the distribution.

B. LUMP SUM DISTRIBUTIONS

Not every lump sum payment from a qualified plan constitutes a lump sum distribution under the Code. A lump sum distribution is here defined as a distribution from a qualified plan of the balance to the credit of an employee, within a single taxable year, on account of any of the following: the death of the employee; the employee's reaching age 59–1/2; the employee's separating from service; or, for self-employed individuals within the meaning of IRC § 401(c)(1), the employee's becoming disabled. IRC § 402(e)(4)(D)(i). The distribution need not be to the employee. In determining the balance to the credit of an employee, all pension plans (in the Code sense) of the employer are treated as a single plan, all profit-sharing plans of the employer are treated as a single plan, and all stock bonus plans of the employer are treated as a single plan. IRC § 402(e)(4)(D)(ii). A cash out may be a lump sum distribution.

A lump sum distribution (less investment in the contract) is generally subject to ordinary income taxation. However, the Code provides some limited forms of relief from this potentially heavy tax burden.

If a lump sum distribution includes securities of the employer (as defined in IRC § 402(e)(4)(E)), then, for purposes of IRC §§ 72 & 402, gross income does not include net unrealized appreciation of those securities. IRC § 402(e)(4)(B). Net unrealized appreciation is the excess of the market value of the security at the time of distribution over its cost or basis to the plan. Treas. Reg. § 1.402(a)–1(b)(2)(i). Hence, the amount of a lump sum distribution attributable to employer securities that is taxed at the time of distribution is the amount of the original employer contribution. Net unrealized appreciation is subject to tax later, when the securities are sold.

The exclusion of net unrealized appreciation from gross income is optional. A taxpayer may elect to waive it. IRC § 402(e)(4)(B).

For lump-sum distributions in plan years beginning on or before December 31, 1999, the Code allows a 5–year averaging method for determining the amount of tax. The 5–year averaging method has been eliminated, largely because of the rollover rules, described below, which give the taxpayer flexibility to plan the time in which a lump-sum distribution will be taxed. However, a 10–year averaging method remains available, through a grandfather clause, for certain individuals who had attained age 50 before January 1, 1986.

C. ROLLOVERS AND TRUSTEE–TO–TRUSTEE TRANSFERS

An individual who leaves an employer's service might wish to take her plan interests with her, and move it either to an IRA or the plan of a new employer. There are two ways this may be done: a *trustee-to-trustee transfer* (or *direct transfer of rollover distribution*), by which the interest is directly transferred from the old plan to a new plan or an IRA, and a *rollover distribution*, in which the participant's interest is first distributed to her so that she can contribute it to a new plan or an IRA. An advantage of a trustee-to-trustee transfer is that it removes the temptation for the participant to use the amounts distributed for current consumption. ERISA now strongly encourages this method.

A trustee-to-trustee transfer or a rollover distribution is a distribution, potentially subject to tax. Yet to tax it would undermine the general policy of deferring tax on qualified plan interests until retirement. Thus, trustee-to-trustee transfers are not taxed, IRC § 402(e)(6), and rollovers are exempt from tax in appropriate cases. IRC § 402(c).

1.   ROLLOVER DISTRIBUTIONS

A distribution to an employee of all or part of the balance to her credit in a qualified plan may be excluded from gross income if three conditions are met. First, the distribution must be an *eligible rollover distribution*. Second, the distributee must timely transfer any part of the distribution to an *eligible retirement plan*. And third, to the extent property is distributed, the property or its equivalent must be transferred to the new plan. If these conditions are met, the amount transferred to the new plan is excluded from gross income. IRC § 402(c)(1).

a.   Eligible Rollover Distributions

In general, an eligible rollover distribution is a distribution to an employee of any portion of the balance to her credit in a qualified plan, with three exceptions. One is for a distribution that is part of a series of substantially equal periodic payments, annually or more frequent, made for: the life (or life expectancy) or the employee or the joint lives (or life expectancies) of the employee and her designated beneficiary; or a specified period of 10 years or more. The second is for required minimum distributions under section 401(a)(9). The third is for certain hardship distributions. IRC § 402(c)(4). An eligible rollover distribution of part of an employee's interest may be coupled with an annuity distribution of the remainder. Treas. Reg. § 1.402(c)–2, at A–6.

b. Transfer to the New Plan

To be excluded from gross income, the distribution must be transferred to an eligible retirement plan within 60 days of receipt. IRC § 402(c)(3)(A). However, the Secretary of the Treasury may waive the 60–day requirement where called for by "equity and good conscience." IRC § 402(c)(3)(B). An eligible retirement plan is either a qualified trusteed plan, an annuity plan governed by IRC § 403(a), an individual retirement account or annuity, certain deferred compensation plans of state and local governments that are subject to IRC § 457(b), and certain annuity contracts governed by IRC § 403(b). IRC § 402(c)(8)(B). There is no requirement that a qualified plan accept rollover contributions, Treas. Reg. § 1.401(a)(31)–1, at A–13.

The maximum amount that may be excluded from income is the portion of the distribution that would be includible in gross income if the rollover exclusion rules were disregarded. IRC § 402(c)(2). Thus, after-tax employee contributions may not be rolled over. Treas. Reg. § 1.402(c)–2, at A–3(b)(3). There is an exception for rollovers to individual retirement accounts and annuities. IRC § 402(c)(2)(B).

Where property has been distributed from a plan, only a transfer of the property itself or any part of the proceeds from its sale is considered a transfer of the property for purpose of the rollover rules. IRC § 402(c)(6)(A). Retention of the property and transfer of its fair market value to the eligible plan does not satisfy the rules. Rev. Rul. 87–77. The excess of fair market value on sale of the property over its fair market value on distribution is treated as property received in the distribution. IRC § 402(c)(6)(B). No gain or loss is recognized on the sale to the extent an amount equal to the proceeds is transferred to the new plan. IRC § 402(c)(6)(D).

c. Distributions to Spouses

A distribution after an employee's death to her surviving spouse may be rolled over, provided that the statutory criteria would be met by treating the spouse as the employee. IRC § 402(c)(9). A distribution from a qualified plan to a spouse or former spouse, under a qualified domestic relations order, is eligible for rollover treatment if the statutory criteria would be met by treating the alternate payee as the employee.   IRC § 402(e)(1)(B).

d. Withholding Tax

Although an eligible rollover distribution is excluded from gross income, it is subject to a withholding tax of 20%. IRC § 3405(c)(1).   The withholding tax may not be waived.   Treas. Reg. § 31.3405(c)–1, at A–2.   A recipient who wishes to roll over the entire amount of a distribution must contribute the whole amount to the new plan within 60 days; she cannot contribute 80%, wait for a refund and then contribute the remaining 20% the next year.   By contrast, there is no withholding if the amount is transferred directly to the new plan. IRC § 3405(c)(2).   Thus there is a strong incentive for participants and beneficiaries to use trustee-to-trustee transfer.

e. Notice

No earlier than 90 days and no later than 30 days before making an eligible rollover distribution, the plan administrator must provide the recipient with a written explanation of the applicable rules. Treas. Reg. § 1.402(f).   In particular, the administrator must provide an explanation of plan provisions for trustee-to-trustee transfer, withholding rules, rules for exclusion of eligible rollover distributions from gross income, if applicable, rules regarding lump sum distributions and certain other matters, and certain differences between distributions under the two plans. IRC § 402(f). The IRS has prepared a model notice for plan administrators. IRS Notice 2002–3.

2.   DIRECT TRANSFER OF ROLLOVER DISTRIBUTIONS

Every qualified plan must provide that the distributee of an eligible rollover distribution may elect to have the distribution directly transferred to an eligible retirement plan specified by the distributee. IRC § 401(a)(31)(A). For purpose of this rule, the only trusteed plans deemed eligible retirement plans are defined contribution plans that permit acceptance of rollover distributions. IRC § 401(a)(31)(E). After-tax amounts may be transferred to either a defined contribution plan that separately accounts for the after-tax amounts, or to an individual retirement account or annuity. IRC § 401(a)(31)(C).

A qualified plan that provides for involuntary cash outs must provide that, unless the distributee elects otherwise, any involuntary distribution in excess of $1,000 shall be transferred directly to a designated individual retirement account or annuity. IRC § 401(a)(31)(B).

D.   ADDITIONAL TAX ON EARLY DISTRIBUTIONS

Qualified defined benefit plans generally may not distribute participant interests before retirement, and profit sharing and stock-bonus plans are not obligated to do so. Early distributions are inconsistent with ERISA's purpose of promoting retirement security and inconsistent with some of the purposes for which tax benefits are granted. To promote retirement saving, and to recapture tax benefits unnecessarily provided, a tax is imposed on premature distributions from qualified plans. IRC § 72(t).

The tax is imposed on distributions made before the date on which the employee turns 59–1/2, and is equal to 10% of the amount of the distribution includible in gross income. However, there are numerous exceptions. Among them are the following distributions: those made upon the death of the employee; those attributable to the employee's becoming disabled; those part of a series of substantially equal periodic payments (annually or more frequently), beginning after separation from service and made for life (or life expectancy) of the employee or the joint lives (or life expectancies) or the employee and designated beneficiary; those made to an employee after separation from service after attaining age 55; and those constituting dividends on employer stock for which a deduction to the employer is available under section 404(k). IRC § 72(t)(2)(A). There are also exceptions for distributions to an alternate payee pursuant to a qualified domestic relations order, distributions for medical expenses to the extent allowable as a deduction under section 213, distributions to unemployed individuals for health insurance premiums, and certain

distributions from individual retirement plans for
higher education expenses or first home purchases.
IRC § 72(t)(2)(B)–(F).

CHAPTER 10

BENEFIT PAYMENT: PROCEDURE

ERISA provides for two different methods by which a participant or beneficiary can obtain payment of benefits. One is the internal claims procedure that ERISA requires every plan to establish. The other is the suit for benefits. Despite the importance of these methods, ERISA deals with them only in barest outline. As a result, this area of ERISA has generated much disagreement and much caselaw. Benefit procedures and their interpretive problems are the focus of this chapter.

A. PLAN CLAIMS PROCEDURES

1. THE MEANING AND PURPOSE OF THE REQUIREMENT

ERISA § 503 requires every plan to have a claims procedure, but announces only two specifications. First, any participant or beneficiary whose claim is denied must be given written notice of the denial and the reasons for it. Second, the plan must "afford a reasonable opportunity" for a "full and fair" review of a claim denial by the appropriate fiduciary. Further detail is left to regulations and caselaw.

Congress' primary, if not exclusive, reason for requiring a claims procedure was to ensure that participants and beneficiaries have a quick and inexpensive means to challenge denials of benefits. The statutory sketchiness may result from Congressional uncertainty (and disagreement) over the form claims procedures should take and the role they should play. Faced with a variety of proposals, Congress opted for a simple, bare-boned provision.

Section 503 speaks only of plans "afford[ing]" participants and beneficiaries a reasonable opportunity for full and fair review of a claim denial. Nonetheless, courts have generally held that participants and beneficiaries must avail themselves of the full range of plan procedures before they can sue for benefits. A leading case establishing this requirement of *exhaustion of plan claims procedures* is *Amato v. Bernard* (9th Cir.1980).

In reaching its conclusion, the court in *Amato* relied in part on labor law policy, which promotes arbitration and correspondingly restricts judicial resolution of disputes. There are, however, objections to relying on labor law for this purpose. Labor law reflects a deliberate sacrifice of individual rights and interests to the interests of the group in order to promote the fundamental goal of industrial peace. Labor law policy also reflects a concern that too-extensive judicial involvement in the collective bargaining process would upset the balance of power between labor and management and threaten industrial peace. *Emporium Capwell Co. v. Western*

Addition   Community   Organization   (S.Ct.1975);
*United Steelworkers v. Warrior & Gulf Navigation
Co.* (S.Ct.1960). But ERISA, by contrast, is central-
ly concerned to vindicate individual rights, by litigation if need be. One of its stated policies is to
afford "ready access to the Federal courts." ERISA
§ 2(b). Hence, although ERISA presupposes a
background of labor law and must coexist with it,
the importation of labor law's preference for arbitration is questionable. *See Schneider Moving &
Storage Co. v. Robbins* (S.Ct.1984); *Anderson v.
Alpha Portland Industries, Inc.* (8th Cir.1985).

The *Amato* court also based its requirement of
exhaustion on other considerations. Most important was its belief that among the purposes of
ERISA § 503 were those of reducing the number of
"frivolous lawsuits" and minimizing the costs to
"all concerned." This belief, however, is also questionable. It is difficult to find in the legislative
history any rationale for the requirement of a
claims procedure other than the need of participants and beneficiaries for simple and inexpensive
claims resolution.

Yet another basis for the court's conclusion was
that requiring plan fiduciaries to review benefit
claims in all cases would improve their "ability to
expertly and efficiently" make decisions. This is an
odd consideration. It suggests that benefit rights
may be sacrificed for the sake of improving fiduciary skill—a proposition inconsistent with ERISA's

policy of protecting benefit interests, and not obviously justified by anything in the statute.

At bottom, the exhaustion requirement is probably based on a felt need to protect federal courts from inundation with benefit suits. This concern over allocation of scarce judicial resources may be well founded. But it arguably should not be central in this context because it is unlikely Congress intended the requirement of a claims procedure to be a means for restricting participant access to court. To the contrary, Congress wished to increase such access.

Right or wrong, *Amato* has been widely followed. Exhaustion is treated as a jurisdictional requirement. *Graham v. Federal Express Corp.* (W.D.Ark. 1989). Failure to exhaust is grounds for dismissal, *Scheider v. U.S. Steel Corp.* (W.D.Pa.1980), or summary judgment, *Weldon v. Kraft, Inc.* (3d Cir.1990). In appropriate cases, however, a court might stay proceedings until the claimant has exhausted plan remedies. *Evans v. Midland Enterprises, Inc.* (M.D.La.1989).

Exhaustion has been required even if the plan language appears to make it permissive. *Baxter v. C.A. Muer Corp.* (6th Cir.1991). Other courts, though, have held otherwise, excusing a participant from the exhaustion requirement if she reasonably interpreted the summary plan description as permitting her to file a lawsuit without availing herself of all of the plan's appeal procedures. *Watts v. BellSouth Telecommunications, Inc.* (11th Cir. 2003).

There are exceptions to the exhaustion requirement. The Department of Labor has adopted regulations to implement ERISA § 503 (see the following section). Those regulations provide that, in the event of the failure of a plan to establish or follow claims procedures with the required characteristics, a claimant is deemed to have exhausted his remedies under the plan and may bring suit for benefits. 29 C.F.R. § 2560.503–1(*l*).

There are also judicial exceptions. A court may decline to require exhaustion where pursuing plan claim procedures would be futile or where the remedy would be inadequate. *E.g., Fallick v. Nationwide Mutual Insurance Co.* (6th Cir.1998); *Berger v. Edgewater Steel Co.* (3d Cir.1990). The claimant, however, must make a "clear and positive" showing of futility or other excuse; conclusory allegations are not enough. *Harrow v. Prudential Insurance Co. of America* (3d Cir.2002); *Makar v. Health Care Corp. of Mid–Atlantic* (4th Cir.1989). The decision to excuse exhaustion is committed to the discretion of the district court; it will not be overturned on appeal unless it constitutes an abuse of discretion. *Springer v. Wal–Mart Associates' Group Health Plan* (11th Cir.1990).

2. STANDARDS FOR A REASONABLE CLAIMS PROCEDURE

ERISA § 503 directs the Department of Labor to set detailed guidelines for plan claims procedures. The DOL has issued a regulation establishing minimum standards. 29 C.F.R. § 2560.503–1. The regulations contain special rules for *group health plans* (and for disability plans), and make important distinctions among various types of medical care claims. (A group health plan is a welfare benefit plan to the extent it provides medical care. 29 C.F.R. § 2560.503–1(m)(6).) For convenience of exposition, one can divide the standards into two broad classes—basic standards, and standards governing the process of claim determination—and within the latter one can distinguish standards applicable to all plans from special standards applicable to group health plans. (Special rules for disability plans are not discussed here.)

a. Basic Standards

The regulations set out four basic standards that all plans must satisfy. First, the summary plan description must contain a description of the plan's claims procedures. 29 C.F.R. § 2560.503–1(b)(2). Second, the procedures must neither contain any provision nor be administered in such a way that "unduly inhibits or hampers the initiation or processing of claims for benefits." 29 C.F.R. § 2560.503–1(b)(3). For example, no fee can be required for pursuing a claim. Third, the procedures may not prevent an authorized representative from acting on behalf of a claimant. 29 C.F.R. § 2560.503–1(b)(4). And fourth, the procedures must contain safeguards designed to ensure that benefit determinations are made in accordance with plan documents and that plan provisions are applied consistently. 29 C.F.R. § 2560.503–1(b)(5). Collectively bargained plans (other than Taft–Hartley plans) are granted alternative means of compliance with these general standards. 29 C.F.R. § 2560.503–1(b)(6).

b. Claim Determination—All Plans

Under the regulations, a *claim for benefits* is a request for plan benefits made by a claimant in accordance with a plan's reasonable procedures for filing a claim. 29 C.F.R. § 2560.503–1(e). The basic standard governing claim determination is that a plan administrator must notify a claimant of the denial of a claim within 90 days of receipt of the claim, unless the administrator determines that special circumstances require an extension of time and notifies the claimant in writing. An extension cannot exceed an additional 90 days. 29 C.F.R. § 2560.503–1(f)(1).

The notice of denial must be in written or electronic form, and must set forth in an understandable fashion the reasons for the denial, the relevant plan provisions, a description of additional information needed to perfect the claim, a description of the plan's review procedure, and a statement of the claimant's right to bring a civil action following an adverse decision on review. 29 C.F.R. § 2560.503–1(g)(1).

A plan must establish and maintain a procedure for full and fair review of an adverse claim determination by an appropriate named fiduciary. 29 C.F.R. § 2560.503–1(h)(1). Full and fair review involves providing the claimant, at a minimum: at least 60 days to appeal after receipt of the notice of denial; an opportunity for the claimant to submit relevant information relating to the claim; reasonable access to records and information relevant to the claim; and a process of review that takes into account information submitted by the claimant. 29 C.F.R. § 2560.503–1(h)(2).

In general, the administrator must notify the claimant of the decision on review within 60 days after receipt of request for review unless the administrator determines that special circumstances (such as the need to hold a hearing) require an extension of time, and so notifies the claimant in writing. An extension cannot exceed an additional 60 days. Where the appropriate named fiduciary is a committee that meets at least quarterly, an alternative schedule for notification applies. 29 C.F.R. § 2560.503–1(i)(1). The notice of denial must be in written or electronic form, and must set forth in an understandable fashion the reasons for the denial, the relevant plan provisions, a statement that the claimant is entitled to receive upon request, free of charge, access to and copies of relevant records and information, a description of any voluntary appeal procedures available under the plan, and a statement of the claimant's right to bring an action under ERISA § 502(a). 29 C.F.R. § 2560.503–1(j)(1)-(4).

c. Claim Determination—Group Health Plans—Initial Determination

The special claim determination rules for group health plans distinguish between various types of claims, and provide somewhat different rules for each. A *pre-service claim* is a claim as to which the plan requires prior approval. 29 C.F.R. § 2560.503–1(m)(2). A *post-service claim* is a claim that is not a pre-service claim. 29 C.F.R. § 2560.503–1(m)(3). An *urgent care claim* is a claim for medical care as to which application of the time periods for non-urgent care determinations could seriously jeopardize the life or health of the claimant or her ability to regain maximum function or, in the opinion of a physician with knowledge of the claimant's condition, would subject the claimant to severe pain that cannot adequately be managed without the treatment involved in the claim. The determination of whether a claim involves urgent care is to be determined by a person acting on behalf of the plan, exercising the judgment of a prudent layperson with average knowledge of health and medicine. However, if a physician with knowledge of the claimant's condition determines that the claim involves urgent care, it must be treated as such. 29 C.F.R. § 2560.503–1(m)(1).

For an urgent care claim, the initial determination by the plan and notice to the claimant must take place as soon as possible, but no later than 72 hours after receipt of the claim. The regulations provide for extensions of time in the event the

claimant fails to provide sufficient information. 29
C.F.R. § 2560.503–1(f)(2)(i). For pre-service claims,
the determination and notice to the claimant must
take place within 15 days after receipt of the claim;
there are provisions for extensions of time because
of a claimant's failure to provide necessary information and for other reasons. 29 C.F.R. § 2560.503–
1(f)(2)(iii)(A). For post-service claims, the determination and notice must take place within 30 days,
again with provisions for extensions of time. 29
C.F.R. § 2560.503–1(f)(2)(iii)(B). The regulations
also deal with cases where a plan reduces or terminates a course of ongoing treatment (considered an
adverse benefit determination) or is requested to
extend such ongoing treatment. 29 C.F.R.
§ 2560.503–1(f)(2)(ii).

Where a claimant has failed to follow the procedures for filing a pre-service claim, the claimant
must be notified of the failure and informed of the
proper procedures to be followed. 29 C.F.R.
§ 2560.503–1(c)(1)(i). This requirement applies only
to claims properly communicated to the plan and
containing appropriate specificity. 29 C.F.R.
§ 2560.503–1(c)(1)(ii).

Group health plans must provide specific kinds of
information in a claim denial. A denial must refer to
and describe any internal rule, protocol or criterion
relied on in denying the claim. In the case of denials
on the basis of medical necessity or experimental
treatment, the denial must explain or offer to explain the scientific or clinical basis for the judg-

ment. 29 C.F.R. § 2560.503–1(g)(1)(v). In the case of urgent care claim denials, the initial notice of denial may be oral, so long as it is followed with written or electronic notice within three days. 29 C.F.R. § 2560.503–1(g)(2).

d. Claim Determinations—Group Health Plans—Review

There are three structural requirements governing review of claim denials by group health plans. First, the plan may not require a claimant to file more than two appeals of an adverse determination prior to bringing suit. 29 C.F.R. § 2560.503–1(c)(2). Second, the plan may provide for voluntary levels of appeal, in addition to the required ones, so long as there are safeguards to the claimant, such as the tolling of any relevant statute of limitations during the pendency of the voluntary appeal. 29 C.F.R. § 2560.503–1(c)(3). Third, the plan may not require arbitration of adverse determinations, except to the extent that the arbitration is one of the permitted stages of required appeal, and so long as the claimant is not precluded from challenging the decision in court. 29 C.F.R. § 2560.503–1(c)(4).

There are six special requirements that a group health plan must satisfy in order to provide full and fair review of an adverse determination, in addition to (or in variance from) the provisions applicable to all plans. First, claimants must have at least 180 days in which to appeal an initial adverse determination. Second, the review must not accord deference to the initial adverse determination and must be conducted by an appropriate named fiduciary who is neither the individual who made the initial determination nor one of her subordinates. Third, where the initial adverse determination was made on the basis of a medical judgment (such as that the treatment was experimental or not medically necessary), the fiduciary must consult with a health care professional who has experience in the relevant medical field. Fourth, the plan must identify the experts whose advice was obtained (whether or not relied on) in connection with the initial adverse determination. Fifth, the plan must provide that the expert consulted for purposes of review is neither a person who was consulted in the initial adverse determination nor a subordinate of such a person. Sixth, in the case of an urgent care claim, the plan must provide for expedited review involving expedited means of communicating notice and relevant information. 29 C.F.R. § 2560.503–1(h)(3).

The notice requirements for the determination on review vary with the type of claim. The plan administrator must provide notice of the determination on review of an urgent care claim as soon as possible, but in no case later than 72 hours after receipt of the request for review. 29 C.F.R. § 2560.503–1(i)(2)(i). For pre-service claims and post-service claims, the notice must be given within a reasonable period; where the plan provides for only one appeal, notice must be given within 30 days after receipt of the request for review in the case of pre-service claims and 60 days in the case of post-service claims. 29 C.F.R. § 2560.503–1(i)(2)(ii) & (iii)(A). Other timing rules apply to multiemployer plans with review committees that meet at least quarterly. 29 C.F.R. § 2560.503–1(i)(2)(ii)(B).

The notice of an adverse determination on review must contain the same explanation regarding internal rules and the basis for medical determinations as must a notice of initial denial. It must also contain prescribed language regarding other voluntary forms of alternative dispute resolution that might be available. 29 C.F.R. § 2560.503–1(j)(5).

e. State Law

The regulations also deal with the interrelationship between plan claims procedures and state law. First, the regulations shall not be construed to preempt any state law that regulates insurance, except to the extent that such a law prevents application of one of the regulations. 29 C.F.R. § 2560.503–1(k)(1). Second, the regulations address state laws establishing review procedures to resolve benefit disputes under group health plans. Where the state law review procedure is conducted by a person other than the insurer, plan, plan fiduciary, or employer (or employee or agent of any of them), that procedure is not by itself deemed to prevent application of any of the regulations. 29 C.F.R. § 2560.503–1(k)(2)(i). However, such a procedure is not considered part of a plan's required "full and fair review" under ERISA § 503 and a claimant

need not exhaust it prior to bringing suit under
ERISA § 502(a). 29 C.F.R. § 2560.503–1(k)(2)(ii).

B. SUITS FOR BENEFITS

1. POLICY CONSIDERATIONS

Prior to ERISA, suits by participants seeking plan
benefits faced many obstacles. These suits generally
were brought under state contract law and, as explained in Chapter 4, courts usually applied contract law to enforce plan documents as written.
Since plan documents generally were drafted to
limit, or even eliminate, the participants' benefit
rights, participants had little success. Federal law
suits for benefits from Taft–Hartley plans met other
obstacles, mainly in the form of judicial deference to
the decisions of plan decisionmakers. The legislative history of ERISA criticizes the then-prevailing
law, charging that "courts strictly interpret the
plan indenture and are reluctant to apply concepts
of equitable relief or to disregard technical document wording." [4842.] Congress clearly intended
to change the law governing benefit suits.

Congress took two steps to rectify the problems.
First, through the preemption provision it swept
away the state law of benefit suits.   ERISA
§ 514(a); *Pilot Life Insurance Co. v. Dedeaux* (S.Ct.
1987). Second, it gave participants and beneficiaries access to federal courts through a provision
allowing them to bring a civil action in district
court (or in state court) "to recover benefits due to

him under the terms of his plan." ERISA § 502(a)(1)(B).

Congress also made it clear that federal courts should develop a federal common law of benefit suits to replace the ousted state law. *Firestone Tire & Rubber Co. v. Bruch* (S.Ct.1989). However, it gave almost no guidance concerning the law to be developed. With only one Supreme Court decision on the law governing benefit suits, *Firestone Tire & Rubber Co. v. Bruch* (S.Ct.1989), and a not carefully reasoned one at that, the law remains unsettled in many important respects and its foundations unclear.

2. THE CHARACTER OF THE SUIT FOR BENEFITS

a. The Labor–Law Model

In developing the law of benefit suits, courts have been reluctant to start from scratch. Rather, they prefer to use familiar types of suits as models, adapting them to accommodate ERISA's policies as the need arises.

The simple language of section 502(a)(1)(B) naturally suggests that the model chosen should be one that keeps the suit for benefits relatively simple, perhaps like an action on a note. Courts, however, have declined to do this. Instead, they have drawn on labor law and trust law as sources for guidance and have developed the law governing benefit suits in more complex and less intuitive ways.

Until the Supreme Court's decision in *Firestone Tire & Rubber Co. v. Bruch* (S.Ct.1989), the prevailing model for the ERISA benefit suit was the labor-law suit for benefits from a Taft–Hartley plan. Under this model, a suit for benefits was treated as an appeal from a fiduciary's adverse decision, rather than as an original proceeding. The model presupposed that a participant had fully availed herself of plan procedures for seeking benefits, and the basic rule was that a determination by the plan fiduciary would be upheld unless it was arbitrary and capricious.

This "arbitrary and capricious" standard was extraordinarily deferential. One court noted that, "[a]lthough it is an overstatement to say that a decision is not arbitrary or capricious whenever a court can review the reasons stated ... without a loud guffaw, it is not much of an overstatement." *Pokratz v. Jones Dairy Farm* (7th Cir.1985). The problem with the standard is obvious: it sanctions fiduciary errors and it disregards conflicts of interest that might lead decisionmakers to deny claims improperly. The standard is at odds with ERISA's policy of protecting benefit rights and expectations. Recognizing this, some courts began to modify the standard by decreasing or even eliminating judicial deference when conflicts of interest or other factors seemed to make deference inappropriate. *Van Boxel v. Journal Co. Employees' Pension Trust* (7th Cir.1987); *Bruch v. Firestone Tire & Rubber Co.* (3d Cir.1987).

b. The Trust–Law Model

In *Firestone Tire & Rubber Co. v. Bruch,* the Supreme Court took a different approach. It completely rejected the labor-law model on which the arbitrary and capricious standard was based. The Court observed that the standard had been developed primarily as a device to overcome jurisdictional obstacles under the LMRA, which contains no express provision allowing participant suits. (The theory was that an arbitrary and capricious claim denial violated the LMRA requirement that plans be "for the sole and exclusive benefit of the employees"—an actionable wrong over which federal courts had jurisdiction.) The Court reasoned that, since there were no jurisdictional impediments to benefit suits under ERISA, the LMRA justification for the arbitrary and capricious standard was inapropos.

The Court instead adopted a trust-law model. It noted that "ERISA abounds with the language and terminology of trust law." It then concluded that the "standard of review" for actions under section 502(a)(1)(B) should be clarified in light of trust law principles. Significantly, the Court continued to assume that a suit for benefits under ERISA was suit for review of a fiduciary's decision, rather than an original proceeding.

To develop an appropriate standard the Court noted that, in trust law, a trustee's actions are subject to review under an abuse of discretion standard whenever she exercises discretionary powers.

(The Court then tacitly assumed that deference to a plan fiduciary's decisionmaking was proper.)   On this basis it suggested that an abuse of discretion standard for review of plan benefit decisions would be appropriate when the plan fiduciary exercises discretionary authority over benefit claims.

However, the Court rejected any presumption that the fiduciary, merely because she necessarily has some discretion, automatically has the kind of discretion needed to invoke the abuse of discretion standard.   It concluded that there could be such discretion only when the plan document confers on the fiduciary discretion to determine benefit eligibility and construe the terms of the plan.   In all other cases, review was to be *de novo*.   Finally, the Court noted that, even where the abuse of discretion standard applies, a conflict of interest on the part of the fiduciary should be a factor in determining whether there has been an abuse of discretion.

c.   Caselaw Development

The main significance of *Bruch* is its rejection of deference as the default standard of review.   Apart from that, however, it neither clarifies nor radically changes the law.   *Bruch* retains the model of benefit suits as review proceedings for which a standard of deference is appropriate in some cases, and identifies trust law as the primary source of standards; but it offers no principled rationale to guide caselaw development.   *Bruch* provides very little guidance as to when deference is appropriate and how review, whether deferential or not, should be carried out. In the years since the decision was handed down, lower courts have struggled to deal with those questions.

Under trust law, discretionary power is frequently conferred on a trustee through language specifying that her decisions shall be "final" or "conclusive" or "binding on all parties," or through like terminology. The same terms may be used to confer on a plan fiduciary discretion regarding benefit claims. However, discretion is not conferred by a general grant of authority to manage the operation and administration of the plan. *Michael Reese Hospital & Medical Center v. Solo Cup Employee Health Benefit Plan* (7th Cir.1990). The majority of courts have held that language requiring satisfactory proof of the claim is not sufficient to grant discretion, either, *see Herzberger v. Standard Insurance Co.* (7th Cir.2000); *Kearney v. Standard Insurance Co.* (9th Cir.1999); although language requiring proof satisfactory to the plan administrator may be, *see Nance v. Sun Life Assurance Co. of Canada* (10th Cir.2002).

In general, courts demand no special form of words to invoke the abuse of discretion standard, and rely on conventional principles of construction to determine whether the plan document demonstrates intent to confer the requisite discretion. *Baxter v. Lynn* (8th Cir.1989). One court, though, has announced that the language, "Benefits under this plan will be paid only if the plan administrator decides in his discretion that the applicant is entitled to them," constitutes a safe harbor conferring the requisite discretion. *Herzberger v. Standard Insurance Co.* (7th Cir.2000).

A basic question concerning *de novo* review is whether courts may receive evidence that was not before the plan fiduciary. One Court of Appeals has held that review must be limited to the record that was before the plan fiduciary, else the proceeding would not be a review. *Perry v. Simplicity Engineering* (6th Cir.1990). Most circuits, however, hold that a district court may, in its discretion, receive new evidence in appropriate circumstances. *Hall v. Unum Life Insurance Co. of America* (10th Cir. 2002); *Quesinberry v. Life Insurance Co. of North America* (4th Cir.1993). The rationale is that allowing courts the discretion to receive new evidence appropriately balances ERISA's purposes of protecting participant interests and promptly resolving benefit claims. One circuit has gone farther still, and generally allows new evidence to be introduced in suits for benefits. *Moon v. American Home Assurance Co.* (11th Cir.1989).

In cases of *de novo* review, some courts will apply the rule of *contra proferentum*—that documents are to be construed against their drafters—to resolve ambiguities, *Kunin v. Benefit Trust Life Insurance Co.* (9th Cir.1990), at least where the relevant plan document is an insurance policy, *Eley v. Boeing Co.* (9th Cir.1991). Others have held that documents should be construed without favoring either party's interpretation. *Brewer v. Lincoln National Life Insurance Co.* (8th Cir.1990).

Many courts applying the rule of *contra proferentum* have further held that an ambiguous plan term should be construed in accordance with the reasonable expectations of the participant. *Wheeler v. Dynamic Engineering, Inc.*, (4th Cir.1995). The rule of *contra proferentum* has generally been held inapplicable in cases of abuse of discretion review. *Winters v. Costco Wholesale Corp.* (9th Cir.1995).

Bruch itself involved review of a fiduciary's interpretation of plan provisions. Most courts have concluded that review of factual determinations is also presumptively *de novo*. They have read the *Bruch* rationale as extending to purely factual determinations and have been persuaded that *de novo* review better promotes ERISA's protective purposes. *E.g., Rowan v. Unum Life Insurance Co. of America* (6th Cir.1997); *Luby v. Teamsters Health, Welfare & Pension Trust Funds* (3d Cir.1991). One court, though, holds the abuse of discretion standard to be the default standard for review of factual determinations by plan fiduciaries. *Pierre v. Connecticut General Life Insurance Co.* (5th Cir.1991). That court reads *Bruch's* holding as limited to plan interpretation. The court also maintains that this application of the abuse of discretion standard is consistent with trust law and with federal appellate standards and would have the effect, believed salutary, of reducing the amount of benefit litigation.

Consistent with the Supreme Court's opinion in *Bruch*, courts have developed law to deal with cases in which the decisionmaking fiduciary operates under a conflict of interest: a state of affairs in which the fiduciary could benefit financially from the denial of a claim. Important cases of potential conflict include those in which the plan is funded through the purchase of insurance and the same insurance company (or a related entity) makes benefit determinations. Most courts hold that this state of affairs inherently creates a conflict of interest. *E.g., Pinto v. Reliance Standard Life Insurance Co.* (3d Cir. 2000); *Brown v. Blue Cross and Blue Shield of Alabama, Inc.* (11th Cir.1990). Some courts, however, require greater factual showing of conflict before they will alter the standard of review. *E.g., Mers v. Marriott Intern. Group Accidental Death and Dismemberment Plan* (7th Cir.1998). Courts generally decline to find an inherent conflict where the plan is self-funded and the decisionmaking fiduciary is an employee or committee of the employer. *See, e.g., Jones v. Kodak Medical Assistance Plan* (10th Cir. 1999); *Friedrich v. Intel Corp.* (9th Cir.1999).

To deal with conflicts of interest, most courts apply a sliding scale, by which they reduce the deference accorded the plan fiduciary's decision. The degree to which deference is reduced is a function of the seriousness of the conflict. *E.g., Pinto v. Reliance Standard Life Insurance Co.* (3d Cir.2000); *Woo v. Deluxe Corp.* (8th Cir.1998). Other courts have held that a substantial conflict of interest shifts to the fiduciary the burden of showing that the decision to deny benefits was not "tainted by self-interest." *Brown v. Blue Cross and Blue Shield of Alabama* (11th Cir.1990).

The character of abuse of discretion review varies from court to court. For some, the proper approach is to determine whether the fiduciary's interpretation of the plan is reasonable. *Ellis v. Metropolitan Life Insurance Co.* (4th Cir.1997); *Pagan v. NYNEX Pension Plan* (2d Cir.1995). Unreasonableness can be substantive or procedural. An interpretation inconsistent with the plain language of the plan is substantively unreasonable. *Dewitt v. Penn–Del Directory Corp.* (3d Cir.1997). A failure of the plan fiduciary to consider relevant evidence might show the procedural unreasonableness of her decision. *Miller v. United Welfare Fund* (2d Cir.1995).

Other courts take more complex approaches to the determination of whether there has been an abuse of discretion. For example, in *Chalmers v. Quaker Oats Co.* (7th Cir.1995), the Seventh Circuit held that the reviewing court should consider "the impartiality of the decisionmaking body, the complexity of the issues, the process afforded the parties, the extent to which the decisionmakers utilized the assistance of experts where necessary, and finally the soundness of the fiduciary's ratiocination."

A different approach has been taken by the Fifth Circuit, which requires a two-step process to review a plan fiduciary's benefit determination. First, a court must determine the "legally correct" interpretation of the plan. To do so, it may consider whether a uniform construction has hitherto been given to the relevant provisions, whether the fiduciary's interpretation is fair and reasonable, and whether a given interpretation would result in substantial unanticipated costs to the plan. *Kennedy v. Electricians Pension Plan* (5th Cir.1992). If the fiduciary adopted a different interpretation, the court must then determine whether it was an abuse of discretion for the fiduciary to do so. In this assessment, the court must examine the internal consistency of the plan under the fiduciary's interpretation, the existence of any relevant administrative regulations, and the factual background of the determination with special reference to issues of good faith. *Batchelor v. International Brotherhood of Electrical Workers Local 861 Pension & Retirement Fund* (5th Cir.1989).

3.   THE PROPER DEFENDANT

ERISA § 502(a)(1)(B) provides that a participant or beneficiary may bring suit to recover benefits, but does not specify the parties against whom suit may be brought. Courts are in agreement that the plan is a proper defendant. Some hold that only the plan may be sued for benefits. *Jass v. Prudential Health Care Plan, Inc.* (7th Cir.1996); *Guiles v. Metropolitan Life Ins. Co.* (E.D. Pa. 2002). Some courts also permit suits against the plan administrator. *Hamilton v. Allen–Bradley Co.* (11th Cir. 2001); *Carducci v. Aetna U.S. Healthcare* (D.N.J. 2003). The law is sufficiently unclear that one can find appellate decisions on both sides of the issue in the same circuit. *Compare Gelardi v. Pertec Computer Corp.* (9th Cir.1985)(per curiam)(only plan can be sued) *with Taft v. Equitable Life Assurance Soc'y* (9th Cir.1993)(administrator may be sued).

4.   THE AVAILABILITY OF JURY TRIAL

Congress, in drafting ERISA, failed to identify when, if ever, there is a right to jury trial under the statute and, in particular, whether there is a right to a jury trial in a suit for benefits. The legislative history is unilluminating. Since there is no statutory guidance, courts rely directly on the Seventh Amendment to the Constitution, which provides that in "Suits at common law, . . . the right of trial by jury shall be preserved."

A suit for benefits under ERISA is not literally a suit at common law. It is statutory. However, the Seventh Amendment is construed to extend the right of jury trial to statutory actions that are sufficiently like traditional common-law actions. *Curtis v. Loether* (S.Ct.1974).   In determining whether there is a constitutional right to jury trial for a statutory action, courts focus on the nature of the relief sought and on the similarity of the action to traditional legal or equitable ones. *Chauffeurs, Teamsters & Helpers Local No. 391 v. Terry* (S.Ct. 1990).

Beginning with the court of appeals' decision in *Wardle v. Central States, Southeast & Southwest Areas Pension Fund* (7th Cir.1980), courts have regularly concluded that there is no constitutional right to jury trial in suits under section 502(a)(1)(B). They have reasoned that ERISA is based on trust law and that all suits under it seek fundamentally equitable relief. This reasoning appears consistent with *Bruch 's* trust-law approach to the law benefit suits. Yet *Bruch 's* holding that *de novo* review is the default standard arguably makes benefit suits more strongly resemble legal suits for money damages. This, plus *Bruch 's* suggestion that pre-ERISA suits for benefits were contract suits, initially led some district courts to hold that there is a right to jury trial in at least some cases. However, every court of appeals that has considered the issue has held that there is no right to jury trial under ERISA § 502(a)(1)(B). *See, e.g., Thomas v. Oregon Fruit Products Co.* (9th Cir.2000). Most courts base this holding on the conclusion that a suit under ERISA § 502(a)(1)(B) is inherently equitable in character. *E.g., Adams v. Cyprus Amax Minerals Co.* (10th Cir.1998). Some courts have also held that a suit for benefits, since a type of review proceeding, is more appropriately tried to a court than to a jury. *Thomas v. Oregon Fruit Products Co.* (9th Cir. 2000).

C. LIABILITIES INCIDENTAL TO BENEFIT PAYMENTS

If a plan has failed to establish a claims procedure, or persistently fails to follow one, the Secretary of Labor, any participant or beneficiary, or any fiduciary may bring suit under ERISA § 502(a)(3) to compel correction of the deficiency. *See, e.g., Schwartz v. Interfaith Medical Center* (E.D.N.Y. 1989).

The more complex question is what remedies are available to a participant or beneficiary when a plan or plan fiduciary fails to maintain or follow reasonable claims procedures in an individual instance. As noted above, the regulations provide that in such a case the claimant is deemed to have exhausted the remedies available under the plan. 29 C.F.R. § 2560.503–1(k)(2)(ii). But there are other consequences as well.

Courts have generally held that substantial compliance with the regulations and a plan's own procedures is sufficient. *Gilbertson v. Allied Signal, Inc.* (10th Cir.2003); *Brown v. Retirement Committee of Briggs & Stratton Retirement Plan* (7th Cir.1986). Deficiencies that commonly give rise to claims of substantial procedural fault include use of an unauthorized decisionmaker, *e.g., Sanford v. Harvard Industries* (6th Cir.2001); failure to comply with time limits for rendering a decision, *e.g., Gilbertson v. Allied Signal, Inc.* (10th Cir.2003); and failure to give sufficient reasons for denying a claim, *e.g., Hackett v. Xerox Corp. Long–Term Disability Income Plan* (7th Cir.2003). Where there has not been substantial compliance, the two principal issues are how a court should procedurally handle the denial of the claim and, if the court decides to proceed with review of the claim, what the standard of review should be.

Where there has been a substantial procedural fault, a court might remand the claim to the plan for a new determination, summarily award benefits, or proceed to review the denial under an appropriate standard. Factors taken into account in deciding how to proceed include: whether the plan fiduciary denied an initial request for benefits or terminated the ongoing payment of benefits, *Hackett v. Xerox Corp. Long–Term Disability Income Plan* (7th Cir. 2003); whether the outcome is clear-cut or the record sufficiently complete, *Weaver v. Phoenix Home Life Mutual Insurance Co.* (4th Cir.1993); *Quinn v. Blue Cross and Blue Shield Ass'n* (7th Cir.1998); the nature of the procedural deficiency; and considerations that might suggest remand to the plan would be unnecessary or futile. Most courts that proceed to review the denial of benefits apply a *de novo* standard. *E.g.*, *Gilbertson v. Allied Signal, Inc.* (10th Cir.2003); *Jebian v. Hewlett–Packard Co. Employee Benefits Organization Income Protection Plan* (9th Cir.2002). Some, however, apply an abuse of discretion standard if the language of the plan document calls for deference, at least in non-egregious cases. *See, e.g.*, *McGarrah v. Hartford Life Insurance Co.* (8th Cir.2000). Some courts treat the effect of a serious procedural irregularity in the same way that they treat a conflict of interest. *E.g.*, *Morgan v. Contractors, Laborers, Teamsters and Engineers Pension Plan* (8th Cir.2002).

A participant or beneficiary has no right to damages for the mere failure to maintain or follow a reasonable claims procedure. *Sedlack v. Braswell Services Group* (4th Cir.1998). Nor does a participant or beneficiary have a right to damages under ERISA § 502(a)(2) and § 409 for individual losses caused by fiduciary malfeasance relating to benefit claims. In *Massachusetts Mutual Life Insurance Co. v. Russell* (S.Ct. 1985), the Supreme Court construed those sections to redress only breaches of duty to the plan and to supply a remedy only to the plan. It denied compensatory and punitive damages where a plan improperly discontinued a participant's disability benefits for several months. However, in *Varity Corp. v. Howe* (S.Ct. 1996), the Supreme Court held that participants and beneficiaries have standing to sue for equitable relief under ERISA § 502(a)(3) to redress breaches of fiduciary duty. The breaches so redressable include those relating to benefit claims and denials, but the scope of monetary relief in such cases is limited. *E.g., Dobson v. Hartford Financial Services* (D.Conn. 2002).

CHAPTER 11

PLAN INFORMATION

ERISA seeks to ensure that information about the plan is made available to participants, beneficiaries, regulators, and others who might be concerned and contains a host of rules to this end. Two broad categories of plan information must be disseminated: information about individual rights and interests, and information about plan financial condition and operations. Provisions throughout the statute require a filing or disclosure in connection with specific events or transactions—for example, a reduction of benefit accruals (Chapter 7) or a rollover distribution (Chapter 9). However, the most important information rules are contained in reporting and disclosure provisions of Title I (and allied provisions of the Internal Revenue Code), the fiduciary provisions of Title I, and the plan termination rules of Title IV. The rules are very detailed; this chapter can review only the highlights.

A. REPORTING AND DISCLOSURE

The main reporting and disclosure rules are contained in ERISA §§ 101–111. Their importance in the statute's protective scheme is evidenced by the fact that they apply, with only minor exceptions, to all plans subject to ERISA.

1.   THE RATIONALE FOR THE REQUIREMENTS

ERISA's reporting and disclosure requirements derive from, but greatly improve on, the Welfare and Pension Plans Disclosure Act ("WPPDA"). The WPPDA was the first federal statute to be concerned exclusively with plan regulation. It gave limited protection to employee benefit interests by requiring administrators to prepare plan descriptions and annual plan financial reports, file them with the Secretary of Labor, and make them available for inspection by participants.

Congress found the WPPDA to be very weak and designed ERISA in part to overcome its deficiencies. Through ERISA, Congress intended to make the reporting and disclosure obligations of plans more stringent, and in so doing strengthen the fiduciary and civil enforcement provisions. A congressional report explained that:

The underlying theory of the Welfare and Pension Plans Disclosure Act to date has been that reporting of generalized information concerning plan operations to plan participants and beneficiaries would, by subjecting the dealings of persons controlling employee benefit plans to the light of public scrutiny, insure that the plan would be operated according to instructions and in the best interests of participants and beneficiaries.... But experience has shown that the limited data available under the present Act is insufficient. Changes are therefore required to increase the information and data required in the reports both in scope and detail. Experience has also demonstrated a need for a more particularized form of reporting so that the individual participant knows exactly where he stands with respect to the plan—what benefits he may be entitled to, what circumstances may preclude him from obtaining benefits, what procedures he must follow to obtain benefits, and who are the persons to whom the management and investment of his plan funds have been entrusted. At the same time, the safeguarding effect of the fiduciary responsibility section will operate efficiently only if fiduciaries are aware that the details of their dealings will be open to inspection, and that individual participants and beneficiaries will be armed with enough information to enforce their own rights as well as the obligations owed by the fiduciary to the plan in general.

[4863.] Accordingly, the reporting and disclosure rules must be understood as adjuncts to the fiduciary and enforcement schemes.

2. THE REQUIRED REPORTS AND DOCUMENTS

Unless exempted by regulation, every plan must prepare specified documents and reports, and file them with governmental agencies or provide them to participants, or both. The most important documents and reports are the following.

a. Summary Plan Description

The summary plan description ("SPD") is intended to be the primary source of information for participants and beneficiaries. It must be a straightforward, non-technical explanation of the plan—of what the plan is, how it works and how benefits can be obtained. It must be "written in a manner calculated to be understood by the average plan participant." Not entirely consistently, it must also be "sufficiently accurate and comprehensive to reasonably apprise such participants and beneficiaries of their rights and obligations under the plan." ERISA § 102(a). Regulations direct the administrator to strive for intelligibility, advising her to "exercise considered judgment and discretion by taking into account such factors as the level of comprehension and education of typical participants ... and the complexity of the terms of the plan"; avoid "technical jargon and ... long, complex sentences"; and use "clarifying examples." 29 C.F.R. § 2520.102–2(a). Under some circumstances, non-English language assistance must be made available. 29 C.F.R. § 2520.102–2(c).

The SPD must contain basic information about the plan, accurate as of no more than 120 days before the date of disclosure. The information to be disclosed varies somewhat with type of plan but includes, as appropriate, the name of the plan; the type of pension or welfare plan; the identification of the administrator, trustees, and agent for service of process; participation requirements; normal retirement age; vesting and accrual rules; health benefit coverage and limitations; joint and survivor benefits and related election requirements; schedules of benefits (e.g., medical benefits); circumstances causing loss of benefits; sources of contributions; funding medium; termination insurance or its absence; and claims procedures. 29 C.F.R. § 2520.102–3. The SPD must also contain a statement of participant rights under ERISA. A model statement is contained in the regulations. 29 C.F.R. § 2520.102–3(t)(2).

Since the SPD is written for the employees, there is a risk that the sponsor might emphasize the more attractive features of the plan and deemphasize the less attractive ones. Regulations prohibit this, specifically requiring that the SPD not have "the effect of misleading, misinforming or failing to inform participants and beneficiaries." Exceptions, limitations, and restrictions may not be minimized or made obscure, and must be described or summarized no less prominently than the descriptions or summaries of plan benefits. In general, the description of plan provisions must be fair and balanced. 29 C.F.R. § 2520.102–2(b).

b. Summary of Material Modifications and Changes

The administrator must also prepare, when appropriate, a summary of material modifications in the terms of the plan and of changes in the information required to be contained in the SPD (the "SMM"). The SMM, in effect, is a supplement to the SPD. Like the SPD, it must be "written in a manner calculated to be understood by the average plan participant." ERISA § 102(a).

c. Annual Report

Plans must file with the Secretary of Labor an annual report containing detailed information on plan finances and operation. ERISA § 103. In addition, IRC § 6058 requires the employer or administrator for every qualified plan to file an annual information return with the Secretary of the Treasury and IRC § 6057 requires every plan (whether or not qualified) to which the vesting standards apply to file an annual registration statement. Furthermore, ERISA § 4065 requires most defined benefit plans to file an annual report with the PBGC. There is substantial overlap among these requirements. Plans may satisfy them all through a single filing, using IRS Form 5500 or one of its variants. The report is filed with the IRS; the IRS forwards copies to the DOL and the PBGC.

The annual report is intended to be a comprehensive source of information about the plan, primarily for regulators. It has several components, each completed by different persons with different areas of expertise.

The report contains statements of assets and liabilities. For welfare plans, it also contains statements of changes in fund balance and changes in financial position; for pension plans, statements of changes in net assets available for benefits. In both cases extensive notes to the financial statements are required. In addition, various schedules to the financial statements must be supplied, with details about the plan's assets, liabilities, receipts and disbursements. The schedules also provide information about potential violations of ERISA and other problems, such as party in interest transactions, loans in default, leases in default, and certain transactions involving more than 3% of the plan's assets. ERISA § 103(b). Except in the case of plans covering fewer than 100 participants at the beginning of the plan year, 29 C.F.R. § 2520.104–46, the report must include an opinion by a *qualified certified public accountant* (as defined by ERISA § 103(a)(3)(D)) that the statements are in conformity with generally accepted accounting principles applied on a consistent basis and that the schedules and addenda fairly present their contents. ERISA § 103(a)(3)(A). The purpose of these requirements is to allow monitoring of the fiduciaries' handling of plan assets, so as to facilitate action in cases of wrongdoing or questionable conduct.

The annual report must be accompanied by a form (Schedule C) containing information about service providers and other persons who entered into transactions with the plan; trustees; and changes in the appointment of persons involved in the ongoing activity of the plan. ERISA § 103(c)(3) & (4).

Except for plans not subject to the funding and termination rules (see Chapters 21–22), the annual report must also include an actuarial statement (Schedule B) prepared by an *enrolled actuary* (as defined in ERISA §§ 3041–3042 and accompanying regulations). This document contains information underlying plan actuarial calculations as well as some of the important calculations themselves. It must be accompanied by a statement of the enrolled actuary that, to the best of her information, the report is complete and accurate and the actuarial assumptions reasonable; that, in her opinion, the matters reported are reasonably related to plan experience and to reasonable expectations, and represent her best estimate; and describing any events and assumptions she has not taken into account. ERISA § 103(d).

If some or all plan benefits are purchased from or guaranteed by an insurance company or similar organization, the annual report must also include a statement of the insurer or other organization (Schedule A). This document identifies, among other things, premium rates, premiums received, claims paid, administrative and other fees, and commissions paid. ERISA § 103(e).

Every plan to which ERISA's vesting rules apply must also include a form (Schedule SSA) identifying those participants who, during the year, separated from service with a deferred vested benefit and to whom retirement benefits were not paid. The document must also describe the benefit to which each such participant is entitled. IRC § 6057(a). This form is transmitted to the Commissioner of Social Security; its information is included in Social Security records. IRC § 6057(d).

ERISA provides for a few exceptions and alternatives to the annual report requirements. Plans with fewer than 100 participants at the beginning of the plan year may prepare a simpler annual report (Form 5500–C/R). 29 C.F.R. §§ 2520.103–1(c) & 2520.104–41. The full version of this simpler report is filed initially and then every third year; only the first two pages are filed in the intervening years. Plans with 80–120 participants may file the same category of form (i.e., 5500 or 5500–C/R) filed the previous year. 29 C.F.R. § 2520.103–1(d). An even simpler form, the 5500–EZ, may be filed by certain plans covering only individual or married-couple sole owners, or only partners and their spouses.

d.　Summary Annual Report

The summary annual report ("SAR") is a document that "fairly summarize[s] the latest annual report." ERISA § 104(b)(3). The DOL has prescribed two fill-in-the-blanks forms that must be used by pension plans and welfare plans respectively. Each form consists of a brief explanation of plan financial information, a description of other information to which participants and beneficiaries are entitled, and a statement that participants and beneficiaries may examine the entire annual report. For plans filing Form 5500–C/R, the first two pages of that form and a notice specified by regulation may serve as the SAR. In some cases, a non-English language SAR must be made available. 29 C.F.R. § 2520.104b–10.

3. REPORTING TO GOVERNMENT AGENCIES

The plan administrator is responsible for filing reports and other documents with governmental agencies. The annual report must be filed within 210 days after the close of the plan year (or such other time required by regulation). ERISA § 104(a)(1). The administrator must also file the SPD, or any other document relating to the plan, at the request of the Secretary. ERISA § 104(a)(6). All documents filed with the DOL become public and are available for inspection and copying, except for certain information about individuals' benefits. ERISA §§ 104(a)(1) & 106.

Pursuant to statutory authority, the Secretary of Labor has granted limited exemptions from the reporting requirements. One important exemption is for small unfunded welfare plans: they need not file annual reports. The exemption applies only to plans with fewer than 100 participants at the beginning of the plan year, for which benefits are paid either as needed from general assets of the employer (or employee organization) maintaining the plan; through insurance contracts or a health maintenance organization, the premiums for which are paid, at least in part, directly by the employer (or employee organization) from general assets; or through both means. (In the case of insured plans, there are additional requirements.) 29 C.F.R. § 2520.104–20.

There are other exceptions for group insurance arrangements, 29 C.F.R. § 2520.104–21; apprenticeship plans, 29 C.F.R. § 2520.104–22; top hat plans and analogous welfare plans, 29 C.F.R. § 2520.104–23 & 2520.104–24; day care centers, 29 C.F.R. § 2520.104–25; and certain other plans, IRS Notice 2002–24.

4. DISCLOSURE TO PARTICIPANTS

There are three categories of documents and reports that must be disclosed to participants and beneficiaries. Some are required to be disclosed by the administrator at particular times or on particular occasions; some must be disclosed at the participant's or beneficiary's request; and some need only be made available for inspection. For items in the first two categories, the administrator must use measures reasonably calculated to ensure actual receipt by the participants and beneficiaries. 29 C.F.R. § 2520.104–1(b)(1). Disclosure through electronic means is permitted under prescribed standards. 29 C.F.R. § 2520.104(c). Materials in the third category must be made available at the administrator's principal office, and at employer establishments and union facilities under conditions specified in the regulations. 29 C.F.R. § 2520.104b–1(b)(3).

The SPD must be furnished to participants and to beneficiaries receiving benefits on several occasions. First, the SPD and a statement of ERISA rights must be provided within 120 days after the plan becomes subject to ERISA. Second, the SPD and statement of rights must be furnished to any new participant within 90 days after she becomes a participant and to a beneficiary within 90 days after she first receives benefits. Third, an updated SPD must be furnished, except to beneficiaries under welfare plans, within 210 days after the end of the fifth year after a material amendment of the plan. If there has been no intervening amendment, a copy of the SPD must be furnished within 210 days after the end of the tenth year after the last such change. ERISA § 104(b)(1); 29 C.F.R. § 2520.104b–2.

An SMM must be furnished within 210 days after the end of the plan year in which the change is adopted. This requirement may be satisfied by incorporating the changes in an updated SPD. 29 C.F.R. § 2520.104b–3. Shorter disclosure periods apply in the case of a *material reduction in covered services or benefits* under a group health plan. ERISA § 104(b)(1)(B); 29 C.F.R. § 2520.104b–3(d).

The administrator must also furnish a copy of the SAR within nine months of the close of the plan or fiscal year to participants and to beneficiaries receiving benefits. ERISA § 104(b)(3); 29 C.F.R. § 2520.104b–10(b). Totally unfunded welfare plans, and plans that are exempt from the requirement of filing the annual report (except for welfare plans forming part of a group insurance arrangement), are also exempt from the requirement of preparing and distributing an SAR. 29 C.F.R. § 2520.104b–10(g).

The administrator must make available for examination by participants and beneficiaries copies of the latest updated SPD, the latest annual report, and the documents under which the plan is established and maintained. ERISA § 104(b)(2). In addition, upon written request of any participant or beneficiary, the administrator must furnish a copy (at a reasonable charge) of the latest updated SPD, the latest annual report, or any document under which the plan is established or maintained. ERISA § 104(b)(4).

An administrator who must file a Schedule SSA for a given year must provide each participant identified in it with an individual statement containing the same information about her. The statement must notify the participant if any benefits are forfeitable upon death before a certain date. ERISA § 105(c).

In addition to these requirements, the administrator must furnish to a participant or beneficiary who so requests in writing a statement of her total accrued benefits and either her nonforfeitable accrued benefits or the earliest date on which benefits will become nonforfeitable. ERISA § 105(a). Such statement need not be furnished more frequently than once every 12 months. ERISA § 105(b).

There are a few exemptions from these disclosure requirements. A small unfunded welfare plan (as described above) is not required to furnish or make available annual reports or SAR's. 29 C.F.R. § 2520.104–20. Other exemptions exist for plans exempt from some or all of the reporting requirements.

5. DETERMINATION OF QUALIFIED STATUS

Although an employer is not required to secure a determination from the IRS that a plan meets the IRC § 401 qualification criteria, most employers do. (However, a favorable determination letter is not conclusive evidence of qualified status.) A determination letter may be sought when a plan is established, amended, or terminated. The IRS has a procedure for issuing such letters. ERISA § 3001; Rev. Proc. 97–6.

The application for a determination letter is an occasion for the filing of a substantial amount of general information about the plan and the benefits it provides (especially about its compliance with nondiscrimination standards). The application procedure also requires the disclosure of substantial information to *interested parties* (i.e., employees identified in Treas. Reg. § 1.7476–1), the DOL, and the PBGC. ERISA § 3001. Except for plans with 25 or fewer participants, the application for a determination letter, any supporting documents, and any related IRS letters and documents are generally open to the public for inspection. Treas. Reg. § 301.6104(a)–2 & 301.6104–3.

6.   ADDITIONAL REQUIREMENTS

Title I contains several other provisions governing reporting and disclosure that warrant brief description here.

ERISA § 209 requires employers to maintain employee records sufficient to determine their employees' benefits. It also requires administrators to provide a statement of accrued and nonforfeitable benefits to any employee who properly requests one, terminates service, or has a one-year break in service. The employer must furnish the administrator with information sufficient to prepare the report. No more than one report need be provided to an employee in any 12–month period.

ERISA § 107 requires every person subject to a reporting or certification requirement under Title I to maintain records on the matters for which she is responsible, sufficient to allow the necessary basic information to be verified, explained or clarified. The records must be kept for six years after the relevant filing date (or date on which the relevant document would have been filed but for an exemption or other special provision).

ERISA § 101(c) requires the administrator of a pension plan that is winding up its affairs to file a *terminal report* in accordance with any DOL regulations. There are no current regulations. However, plans winding up their affairs are required to continue to file annual reports while distributing assets. For the final year of distribution, the administrator complies with the terminal report requirement by checking a box on the Form 5500 indicating that it is the final return.

7.   REMEDIES AND SANCTIONS

ERISA's civil enforcement provisions themselves include a disclosure rule. ERISA § 502(a)(1)(B), the provision that allows suits for benefits, also allows a participant or beneficiary to bring suit to "clarify his rights to benefits under the terms of the plan," and thereby obtain needed information.

Remedies are available for violations of the reporting and disclosure rules. ERISA § 502(a)(3) generally permits a participant or beneficiary, fiduciary, or the Secretary of Labor to obtain equitable relief to redress a violation of the statute. There are also special remedies. ERISA § 502(c)(1) (as adjusted by regulation, 29 C.F.R. § 2575.502c–1) provides that an administrator who fails to comply with a participant's or beneficiary's request for information to which she is entitled, by mailing the

material requested to the last known address of the
requestor within 30 days, may be held personally
liable, in the court's discretion, for an amount of up
to $110 per day from the date of the failure or
refusal, and be subjected to any other relief the
court deems appropriate (unless noncompliance results from matters beyond the administrator's control). The purpose of such harsh penalties is to
negate the incentives for an administrator to delay
or avoid compliance with the disclosure rules. *Winchester v. Pension Committee of Michael Reese
Health Plan, Inc. Pension Plan* (7th Cir.1991). A
corresponding provision, ERISA § 502(c)(2), permits the Secretary of Labor to impose a penalty of
up to $1,100 a day on an administrator who fails to
file the annual report on time. See 29 C.F.R.
§ 2575.502c–2.

Another sanction is included in ERISA § 209(b),
which imposes a civil penalty of $11 per employee
on any person who fails to comply with the recordkeeping and report-providing rules of ERISA
§ 209(a). See 29 C.F.R. § 2575.209b–1. The Internal Revenue Code also contains provisions imposing
civil penalties for non-compliance with reporting
rules, some of which overlap with the civil penalties
imposed under Title I. IRC §§ 6652 & 6692.

There are also criminal penalties for violations of
reporting and disclosure rules. ERISA § 501 specifies that any person who wilfully violates any provision of Title I, including reporting and disclosure
rules and regulations, may be convicted for such

violation. Penalties include up to 10 years of imprisonment and a fine of up to $100,000 for individ-
uals, and a fine of up to $500,000 for corporations
and other entities. The United States Criminal
Code, in 18 U.S.C. § 1027, also provides criminal
sanctions for false statements and knowing nondisclosure in connection with plan-related documents
that are required to be published, kept as records,
or certified. Penalties for violation are fines and
imprisonment for up to five years. Liability does
not require specific intent. *United States v. S &
Vee Cartage Co.* (6th Cir.1983). Nor is liability
limited to individuals expressly regulated by
ERISA's reporting and disclosure rules. The sanction applies, for example, to health care providers,
United States v. Martorano (3d Cir.1985); to attorneys, *United States v. Sarault* (9th Cir.1988); and
even to participants, *United States v. Bartkus* (6th
Cir.1987), who submit false information to plans.

B. THE WRITING REQUIREMENT

Another set of rules governing another aspect of
plan information may be found in section 402, one
of ERISA's fiduciary provisions. ERISA § 402(a)(1)
announces the *writing requirement* : that every
benefit plan must "be established and maintained
pursuant to a written instrument." Section
402(a)(2) also requires the plan instrument to identify the named fiduciaries, who have "authority to
control and manage the operation and administration of the plan." Section 402(b) requires the in-

strument to contain a description of the procedures for establishing and carrying out the plan's funding policy, allocating responsibility for plan operation and administration, and amending the plan; and the basis on which payments are made to and from the plan. To further reinforce the writing requirement, section 404(a)(1)(D) obligates every fiduciary to carry out his duties "in accordance with the documents and instruments governing the plan insofar as such documents and instruments are consistent with the provisions of [ERISA]."

ERISA's requirement of a written plan—and, by implication, written amendments to it—has generated interpretive difficulties. Some result from unclarity over the purpose of the requirement. Others result from judicial efforts to reconcile the requirement with other policies and rules.

1. THE RATIONALE FOR THE WRITING REQUIREMENT

The Joint Explanatory Statement to ERISA (i.e., the Conference Report) explains that the writing requirement is for the protection of participants and beneficiaries. It states that "[a] written plan is to be required in order that every employee may, on examining the plan document, determine exactly what his rights and obligations are under the plan. Also, a written plan is required so the employees may know who is responsible for operating the plan." [5077–78.] This suggests that the requirement should be interpreted and applied primarily, if not exclusively, for the protection of individual participants and beneficiaries. Courts, however, have inferred additional purposes.

Probably the most important of the inferred additional purposes is that of protecting the "actuarial soundness" of plans. The underlying concern is that, if written plan terms are ignored, a plan may have to pay out more funds than anticipated and risk having insufficient assets to pay benefits due. *Cefalu v. B.F. Goodrich Co.* (5th Cir.1989). Another inferred purpose is that of preventing "collusive or fraudulent side agreements" between employers or fiduciaries and employees, with resulting discrimination among participants. *Id.* Yet another is eliminating disputes over the substance of an oral communication that occurred many years before the effort to enforce benefit rights based on it. *Nachwalter v. Christie* (11th Cir.1986).

These additional considerations are commonly invoked to defeat participant and beneficiary claims based outside the written terms of the plan. Such claims may be based on the SPD, oral plans, or oral representations to an individual. The analysis is different for each of the three kinds of claim.

2. CONFLICTS BETWEEN THE PLAN DOCUMENT AND THE SPD

The SPD presents the central facts about a plan briefly and in easily understood language. The plan document, by contrast, is the complete statement of all rights and responsibilities with respect to a plan. Because they have different purposes, there is a significant chance of inconsistencies between the two documents. It is an important question which should prevail in cases of conflict.

The law is fairly clear that, where the SPD and the plan document make inconsistent statements about a matter affecting a participant, the SPD generally controls. *Hansen v. Continental Insurance Co.* (5th Cir.1991). A rule to the contrary would defeat the purpose of the SPD. It would prevent participants from safely relying on the SPD and force them to consult the plan document to be sure of their rights. On the other hand, some courts have held that the plan document controls where it is more favorable to the participant's interest than the SPD. *Bergt v. Retirement Plan for Pilots Employed by Markair, Inc.* (9th Cir.2002).

Since the rule that the SPD takes priority in case of conflict is based on the purposes and special character of that document, it is important to determine whether a writing is an SPD in the event it does not fully comply with ERISA § 102(b) and 29 C.F.R. § 2520.102–3. Some courts hold that a document is not an SPD unless it complies with substantially all of the requirements appropriate to the type of plan and benefits in question; in particular, unless it is sufficient for filing and other statutory purposes. *E.g., Hicks v. Fleming Companies, Inc.* (5th Cir.1992); *Rubio v. Chock Full O'Nuts Corp.* (S.D.N.Y. 2003). Other courts focus on the participant, and hold that a document is an SPD if it "contains all or substantially all of the information the average participant would deem crucial to a knowledgeable understanding of his benefits under the plan." *Kochendorfer v. Rockdale Sash and Trim Co., Inc. Profit Sharing Plan* (N.D.Ill.1987). One court has also held that only a document prepared by the plan can be an SPD, and that a descriptive document prepared by the employer cannot. *Helfrich v. Carle Clinic Ass'n* (7th Cir.2003).

A recurring issue is the effect of disclaimer clauses. Many SPD's contains statements to the effect that all participant and beneficiary rights are governed by the plan document and that the latter's terms always control. Some courts have held these provisions ineffective on the ground that they would defeat the purpose of the SPD and allow evasion of the obligation of drafting a clear, accurate and comprehensive summary. *Hansen v. Continental Insurance Co.* (5th Cir.1991). A few courts have held such disclaimers effective. *Kolentus v. Avco Corp.* (7th Cir.1986). In one case, the court held the disclaimer effective only as a basis for rejecting the insurer-administrator's argument that language in the SPD should limit the participant's benefit rights under the plan. *McGee v. Equicor–Equitable HCA Corp.* (10th Cir.1992).

A second issue is the extent, if any, to which a participant must rely on the language of the SPD to obtain the benefit of it. Some courts do not require individual reliance. *E.g., Edwards v. State Farm Mutual Auto Insurance Co.* (6th Cir.1988); *Lancas-*

ter v. United States Shoe Corp. (N.D.Cal.1996). Most courts, however, do require reliance on or prejudice from the relevant terms of the summary plan description. *E.g., Chiles v. Ceridian Corp.* (10th Cir. 1996). Yet reliance is sometimes irrelevant to the issues and in such circumstances a court may either dispense with the requirement of reliance or else demand proof of little beyond the participant's having read the relevant language. *E.g., Williams v. Midwest Operating Engineers Welfare Fund* (7th Cir.1997); *Hansen v. Continental Insurance Co.* (5th Cir.1991).

The above issues arise only where the SPD and the plan are inconsistent. The silence of the SPD on a matter does not alone create a conflict. *Charter Canyon Treatment Center v. Pool Co.* (10th Cir. 1998). In the absence of conflict, the plan document may be used, if appropriate, to clarify the SPD. *Senkier v. Hartford Life & Accident Insurance Co.* (7th Cir.1991). In some cases, a provision in the SPD can establish a new plan term. *White v. Jacobs Engineering Group Long Term Disability Benefit Plan* (9th Cir.1989). Where there is an SPD but no plan document, the SPD will supply the terms of the plan, even if they differ from the actual practice followed by the employer. *Hamilton v. Air Jamaica, Ltd.* (3d Cir.1991).

3.   THE STATUS OF ORAL PLANS

When the writing requirement collides with a putative oral plan, two issues arise: the legal status of the supposed plan and its amendability.

a.   The Existence of Oral Plans

If a purported benefit plan is implemented through employer conduct without a plan document, there are two choices for describing what results. Either there is no plan because of the lack of a writing, or there is a plan in violation of ERISA. Courts have unanimously agreed that the lack of a written document does not negate the existence of a plan subject to ERISA. Any other rule would allow plan sponsors to circumvent obligations under ERISA simply by ignoring the writing requirement. *Donovan v. Dillingham* (11th Cir. 1982).

b.   The Amendability of Oral Plans

If a plan is oral, it almost certainly contains no term describing a procedure for amending it. Nonetheless, amendments to oral plans have been allowed. *Adams v. Avondale Industries, Inc.* (6th Cir.1990); *Whitfield v. Torch Operating Co.* (E.D.La. 1996). The conclusion seems right. It would be arbitrary to hold that oral plans may exist, but once initiated cannot be amended. The real issues are when and how such plans can be amended. One court has suggested that participant expectations and reliance must be taken into account in determining amendability. *Adams v. Avondale Industries, Inc.* (6th Cir.1990).

4. ORAL REPRESENTATIONS AT VARIANCE WITH PLAN TERMS

The caselaw on oral representations that purport to vary written plan terms is complicated and still evolving. In theory, many factors could affect the enforceability of such a statement: whether it is a purported amendment to the plan or an isolated representation to an individual; whether the plan is multiemployer or single employer; whether the plan is a pension plan or welfare plan and, if the latter, whether it is funded; who made the representation (employer, fiduciary, insurer); to whom the representation was made (officer or rank-and-file employee); who seeks to enforce the oral statement (participant, beneficiary, employer, insurer); and the basis on which suit is brought (ERISA or federal common law). The law of oral representations about plan terms has been marked by increasing judicial recognition of the need to take these factors into account.

a. Purported Oral Amendments

Oral amendments to plans contradict the writing requirement. Thus, courts have invariably rejected claims that a plan has been amended this way. Courts have rejected both claims for benefits based on purported oral terms of plans, *e.g., Straub v. Western Union Telegraph Co.* (10th Cir.1988); as well as defenses that a claim should be denied on such a basis, *Confer v. Custom Engineering Co.* (3d Cir.1991).

b. Individualized Oral Representations

Even if suits under ERISA, based on oral amendments, are impermissible, it does not necessarily follow that suits under federal common law, based on individualized oral representations about benefits, are also impermissible. An individualized oral representation is not a plan amendment, and a suit based on it is not a suit under section 502(a)(1)(B). Nevertheless, courts initially failed to distinguish between the two kinds of suits and flatly rejected all estoppel-type claims based on oral representations. *E.g., Cefalu v. B.F. Goodrich Co.* (5th Cir.1989); *Nachwalter v. Christie* (11th Cir.1986). They did so even where the representations were made by an employer concerning a welfare plan in which benefits were paid directly from employer assets. *Saret v. Triform Corp.* (N.D.Ill.1986). In effect, the writing requirement became a statute of frauds. *Frahm v. Equitable Life Insurance Society of the United States* (7th Cir.1998). A substantial number of courts take this position. *E.g., Rodrigue v. Western & Southern Life Insurance Co.* (5th Cir.1991); *Hansen v. Western Greyhound Retirement Plan* (9th Cir.1988).

Courts that broadly reject estoppel claims often rely on the "actuarial soundness" consideration. Yet its force is questionable. Actuarial soundness is irrelevant to welfare plans funded from general employer assets or through insurance: there is no fund to deplete. *See Black v. TIC Investment Corp.* (7th Cir.1990). But even for pension plans it may be a weak consideration. In defined contribution plans, every participant has her own account, the balance in which determines the benefits to be paid. Defined contribution plans are always fully funded by definition, and so there are no actuarial risks created by allowing estoppel claims. *See Lockrey v. Leavitt Tube Employees' Profit Sharing Plan* (N.D.Ill.1990). Even for defined benefit plans, the impact of estoppel liability on plan assets would be offset by the resulting obligation of the employer to fund the outlay as an experience loss. (See Chapter 21.) Furthermore, the impact of estoppel liability on any plan's funds may be offset by the liability to the plan of the individual who made the representation, either for breach of fiduciary duty (Chapter 12) or for indemnity (Chapter 15).

Perhaps in light of these considerations, some courts have come to emphasize different bases. One court has emphasized that plans can be complex and have many participants. Many are administered by the employer (see Chapter 12). As a result, there will be many communications between the employer and the employees regarding benefits, and errors and misunderstandings will be inevitable. It would be very difficult for the employer to administer the plan if the terms could easily be varied, depending on what a participant believed from statements made years before. To protect the employer-administrator under such circumstances, to encourage its staff to provide advice to participants, and to encourage employers to offer plans, the written terms must be enforced and estoppel claims limited. *Frahm v. Equitable Life Assurance Society of the United States* (7th Cir.1998).

Notwithstanding the professed judicial reluctance to permit estoppel claims, a significant number of decisions have approved suits based on oral representations in particular circumstances. Some courts allow them where the oral representation can be treated as a clarification or interpretation of an ambiguous plan document. *Sprague v. General Motors Corp.* (6th Cir.1998); *Kane v. Aetna Life Insurance* (11th Cir.1990). Some courts permit estoppel claims where there are "extraordinary circumstances." *Curcio v. John Hancock Mutual Life Insurance Co.* (3d Cir.1994); *Brant v. Principal Life and Disability Insurance Co.* (N.D. Iowa 2002).

Other exceptions, some broad, can also be found in the case law. For example, estoppel claims have been allowed generally where the plan is an unfunded, single-employer welfare plan, *Black v. TIC Investment Corp.* (7th Cir.1990); or a welfare plan in which benefits are paid under an insurance policy, *Armistead v. Vernitron Corp.* (6th Cir.1991). Other courts have held that an employer can be individually liable, since recovery would not affect plan funds. *Smith v. Hartford Insurance Group* (3d Cir. 1993); *Bogue v. Ampex Corp.* (N.D.Cal.1990).

Several policy justifications for estoppel derive from the opinion in *Black v. TIC Investment Corp.* One is to reject the writing requirement as a starting point and begin instead with a presumption in favor of the availability of estoppel. As the court in *Black* noted, "estoppel principles generally apply to all legal actions. It is an exception to that general rule to deny use of the doctrine." On this basis, estoppel claims have even been upheld in connection with misrepresentations concerning profit sharing plans. *Lockrey v. Leavitt Tube Employees' Profit Sharing Plan* (N.D.Ill.1991).

A second approach focuses on the risks created by individual authority to bind the plan through representations. The *Black* court noted that judicial rejection of estoppel was most common in multiemployer plan cases, where one employer's representation could bind an entire plan to the detriment of other employers and their employees. But "where there is no danger that others associated with the Plan can be hurt, there is no good reason to breach the general rule that misrepresentations can give rise to an estoppel." Based on this consideration, a later decision suggested that estoppel might be recognized even in a multiemployer plan where administration is so centralized as to reduce the risk of stray misrepresentations. *Russo v. Health, Welfare & Pension Fund, Local 705, International Brotherhood of Teamsters* (N.D.Ill.1991).

Where estoppel is allowed, the elements of the action are conventional. While there is some variation from court to court in the statement of requirements, the basic elements are that there must be a misrepresentation of material fact by a person who was aware of the truth and who intended that the misrepresentation be acted on (or had reason to believe that the misrepresentation would be acted on). The misrepresentation must be made to a person who did not know or have reason to know the truth, and cause reasonable and detrimental reliance. *E.g., National Companies Health Benefit Plan v. St. Joseph's Hospital of Atlanta, Inc.* (11th Cir.1991); *Ellenburg v. Brockway, Inc.* (9th Cir. 1985). Finally, the representations must be made by a person with authority to bind the person sought to be bound. *Cleary v. Graphic Communications International Union Supplemental Retirement & Disability Fund* (1st Cir.1988).

CHAPTER 12

FIDUCIARY REGULATION

"Fiduciary" and "fiduciary duty" are concepts used in trust law and in other legal domains where one individual assumes special responsibility for another. There is much in common among the various uses. All fiduciaries owe a duty of loyalty, virtually as a matter of definition, to the persons for whom they are specially responsible. All fiduciaries similarly owe a duty of care. Yet there are differences resulting from the need to adjust fiduciary concepts to special features and concerns. Fiduciary law is adaptable, not monolithic. In this chapter we examine how fiduciary law has been adapted to the needs and characteristics of plans.

A. PLAN FIDUCIARIES

1. BASIC CHARACTERISTICS OF PLAN FIDUCIARIES

ERISA characterizes the persons responsible for the management and operation of a plan as "fiduciaries." What does this mean?

For several reasons, a strict trust-law model for plan fiduciaries would not work. One reason is that trust law takes a "one size fits all" approach.

It acknowledges only one kind of fiduciary, the trustee, who (perhaps along with co-trustees) has all significant responsibility for administering the trust. The trustee, in fact, is under a duty to avoid delegating responsibility. This approach ill-suits plans, which are ongoing and often complex activities: they may have up to tens of thousands of participants and beneficiaries and billions of dollars in assets. As a result of their size and complexity, plans often need to divide managerial, financial and administrative responsibility.

ERISA recognizes this. It treats responsibility for plan management and operation as divisible and allows for the possibility of many plan fiduciaries, each with his own area of specialization: "A plan may have as few or as many fiduciaries as are necessary for its operation and administration." 29 C.F.R. § 2509.75–8, at FR–12. It also permits extensive delegation of fiduciary responsibility, making the delegatees fiduciaries as well. Most significantly, it provides a highly functional, general definition of "fiduciary" that permits adjustment for the individual circumstances of each plan. ERISA § 3(21)(A).

A second reason that a trust-law model would be inappropriate is that traditional trustees and plan fiduciaries have very different reasons for their existence. Traditional trustees exist to carry out the aims of the settlor. To that end, they are endowed with powers used to implement the settlor's intent. Traditional trustees, indeed, may be viewed primarily as bearers of powers, the exercise of which it is the function of trust law to oversee and control. Plan fiduciaries, however, do not exist to carry out a settlor's intent. They exist to implement an ongoing program of providing benefits and to safeguard benefit interests. ERISA does not view plan fiduciaries as bearers of powers so much as bearers of duties: to the plan and to participants and beneficiaries. It is the purpose of ERISA's fiduciary rules, as we shall see, to regulate the fulfillment of those duties.

2. DENOMINATED FIDUCIARY ROLES

Certain plan fiduciaries have roles that are defined by ERISA. Some of these statutorily defined fiduciaries are ones every plan must have; others are optional.

a. Named Fiduciary

Every plan must have one or more named fiduciaries. The named fiduciary is an invention of ERISA. Named fiduciaries must be named in the plan document (or named by the employer, employee organization, or the two acting jointly, pursuant to a procedure specified in the plan). They must also, either jointly or severally, "have authority to control and manage the operation and administration of the plan." ERISA § 402(a). Often a committee, called the "Administrative Committee" or the like, is identified as the named fiduciary and has employer officers as its members.

Named fiduciaries have two salient features. First, they can easily be identified by participants, beneficiaries, and other interested persons. Second, they are *prima facie* responsible for all phases of plan operation. *Arakelian v. National Western Life Insurance Co.* (D.D.C.1987). In this respect they are somewhat like traditional trustees. But in this same respect they are unlike all other plan fiduciaries, whose responsibilities are limited by their specific functions in a plan. 29 C.F.R. § 2509.75–8, at FR–16. The responsibility of a named fiduciary is narrowed only through the allocation or delegation of portions of his responsibility, a matter discussed below.

b. Trustee

Subject to exceptions discussed below, plan assets must be held in trust by one or more trustees. ERISA § 403(a). The trustee, like the named fiduciary, must be identifiable: he must be named in the trust instrument or plan document, or else be appointed by a named fiduciary. A trustee must expressly accept the appointment. *Id.* However, as the court held in *Donovan v. Mercer* (5th Cir.1984), one who exercises discretionary authority respecting management of the plan and its assets ("If it Talks Like a Duck ..."), and who is identified in plan documents as trustee and signs documents as trustee ("... and Walks Like a Duck ..."), *is* a fiduciary with trustee responsibilities, despite the lack of express appointment or acceptance ("... It is a Duck").

c.   Allocation of Fiduciary Responsibility

ERISA allows a plan document to describe procedures for the allocation of fiduciary responsibilities,
other than *trustee responsibilities*, among named
fiduciaries. It also allows a plan document to describe procedures for named fiduciaries to designate
persons other than named fiduciaries to carry out
fiduciary responsibilities other than trustee responsibilities. ERISA § 405(c)(1). The plan document
must provide expressly for such allocation or delegation; otherwise any purported allocation or delegation will be ineffective.

Trustee responsibilities are the responsibilities
provided in the plan's trust instrument (if there is
one) to manage or control the assets of the plan.
ERISA § 405(c)(3). The limited delegability of
trustee responsibility reflects ERISA's extreme concern to safeguard plan assets.

ERISA's handling of trustee responsibility is curi-
ous. Although there is a flat prohibition on its
delegation, the statute permits substantial limitations to be placed on a trustee's authority and
discretion. A trustee's authority over plan assets
may be reduced or eliminated through a named
fiduciary's delegating authority to manage, acquire,
or dispose of some or all of the assets to an investment manager. ERISA §§ 402(c)(3) & 403(a)(2).
In such a case, the trustee may be relegated to the
status of little more than a custodian of plan assets
with fiduciary responsibility reduced accordingly.
E.g., *Beddall v. State Street Bank and Trust Co.* (1st

Cir.1998). In addition, a trustee's responsibility may be limited through an express plan provision that he is subject to the proper directions of a named fiduciary who is not a trustee. ERISA § 403(a)(1). In such cases the trustee is called a *directed trustee*.

Where there are two or more trustees, they are presumed to manage and control the assets of the plan jointly. However, if the trust instrument so permits, the trustees may agree to allocate specific responsibilities among themselves. ERISA § 405(b)(1)(B).

In addition to the foregoing, ERISA deals with the reverse of delegation: concentration of fiduciary responsibility. It makes clear that any person or group of persons may serve in more than one fiduciary capacity. ERISA § 402(c)(1).

d. Administrator

The administrator is a fiduciary found in every plan. If the plan document fails to name the administrator, it is the plan sponsor by default. ERISA § 3(16)(A). Obligations imposed on the administrator are scattered throughout the statute. Most relate to plan information and benefit payment.

The administrator is necessarily a fiduciary because he must have discretionary authority or discretionary responsibility in the administration of the plan (see below). However, not every person who performs plan administrative tasks is an administrator, or even a fiduciary. Individuals who perform purely ministerial functions relating to reports, recordkeeping, benefit payments and benefit claims, all "within a framework of policies, interpretations, rules, practices and procedures made by other persons," are not fiduciaries since they do not have the discretion in plan administration that would be needed for fiduciary status. 29 C.F.R. § 2509.75–8, at D–2. Thus, establishing the presence or absence of an individual's discretion in plan administration is often important. *See, e.g., Harold Ives Trucking Co. v. Spradley & Coker, Inc.* (8th Cir.1999); *Chambers v. Kaleidoscope, Inc. Profit Sharing Plan and Trust* (N.D.Ga.1986).

e. Investment Manager

An investment manager is a fiduciary, other than a trustee or named fiduciary, who has the power to manage, acquire or dispose of any plan asset; is either an investment advisor registered under the Investment Advisors Act, a bank, or an insurance company qualified under the laws of more than one state; and has acknowledged in writing that it is a fiduciary with respect to the plan. ERISA § 3(38). The definition is strict. An investment advisor (other than a bank or insurance company) that has not registered under the Investment Advisors Act because exempt from registration may not serve as an investment manager. 29 C.F.R. § 2509.75–5, at FR–6. In addition, if the putative investment manager has not acknowledged its fiduciary status, it is not an investment manager and any delegation of fiduciary authority to it is ineffective. *Whitfield v. Cohen* (S.D.N.Y.1988); 29 C.F.R. § 2509.75–8, at FR–15.

f. Investment Advisor

Providers of investment advice to plans are the only advisors who are fiduciaries solely by virtue of their advice-giving role. ERISA § 3(21)(A)(ii), part of ERISA's general statement of criteria for fiduciary status, provides that anyone is a fiduciary to the extent "he renders investment advice for a fee or other compensation, direct or indirect, with respect to any moneys or other property of [a] plan, or has any authority or responsibility to do so." *Investment advice* is advice as to the value of securities or other property or recommendations concerning investment in, or purchase or sale of them. The advice must be given on a regular basis, pursuant to an agreement or understanding that the advice will serve as the primary basis for plan investment decisions, and with the understanding that particularized advice will be given responsive to the needs of the plan. 29 C.F.R. § 2510.3–21(c). The mere giving of investment advice, *Brown v. Roth* (D.N.J. 1990), even a substantial amount by a brokerage firm, *Farm King Supply, Inc. Integrated Profit Sharing Plan & Trust v. Edward D. Jones & Co.* (7th Cir.1989), does not make one a fiduciary if the statutory and regulatory criteria are not satisfied.

3. OTHER FIDUCIARIES

a. The Function and Discretion Standard

The fiduciary roles described above are not the only ones. Fiduciary status attaches to any person who, as a matter of fact, has or exercises certain forms of discretion, authority or control. ERISA § 3(21)(A) provides in relevant part that:

> [A] person is a fiduciary with respect to a plan to the extent (i) he exercises any discretionary authority or discretionary control respecting management of such plan or exercises any authority or control respecting management or disposition of its assets, . . . or (iii) he has any discretionary authority or discretionary responsibility in the administration of such plan.

(The language of subpart (ii), concerning investment advice for a fee, is quoted above.) Note that *any* authority or control with respect to management of plan assets serves as the predicate for fiduciary status; discretion is not required (although one can argue that authority or control over assets is inherently discretionary). This extra breadth to an already sweeping definition reflects ERISA's extraordinary concern with safeguarding plan assets.

Several features of this definition are noteworthy. First, the emphasis is on the actual role and conduct of an individual, rather than on title. Courts

have held individuals to be fiduciaries notwithstanding clever plan draftsmanship or avoidance of
title. *E.g., Pension Benefit Guaranty Corp. v. Solmsen* (E.D.N.Y.1987). Correspondingly, they have
held individuals not to be fiduciaries despite their
title—for example, "trustee." *Richardson v. U.S.
News & World Report, Inc.* (D.D.C.1985).

Second, those who are plan fiduciaries by virtue
of this definition are limited fiduciaries: they are
fiduciaries only *to the extent* they satisfy a condition
of fiduciary status. (An individual can satisfy more
than one.) Thus, a person who is a fiduciary with
respect to, say, the determination of benefit entitlement is not necessarily a fiduciary with respect to
plan investments, too. *See* 29 C.F.R. § 2509.75–8,
at FR–16.

Third, whether a person is a fiduciary is not
always clear-cut. The determination of fiduciary
status may call for judgment. "Discretion" is a
flexible term. In a sense, anyone who provides a
service to a plan which requires him to act as a
thinking agent must exercise some discretion. Yet,
as a practical matter, there is a minimal level below
which it makes little sense to impose fiduciary status. There is little point in making a secretary to
the administrator a fiduciary with respect to administration simply because he has discretion to schedule the administrator's appointments. Similar considerations apply to "control" of plan assets. There
is little point in imposing fiduciary responsibility for
plan assets on a janitor, even though his job, in

part, is to dispose of them. *Nieto v. Ecker* (9th Cir.1988). Inevitably, there is a pragmatic element to a court's determination of fiduciary status. The ultimate question may the appropriateness of subjecting a person to the duties that accompany that status.

b. Attorneys and Other Professionals

Plans and plan fiduciaries engage attorneys for guidance and assistance. The mere rendering of legal advice or legal services to a plan or a fiduciary does not make an attorney a fiduciary under ERISA. 29 C.F.R. § 2509.75–5, at D–1. A similar rule applies to auditors, *Painters of Philadelphia District Council No. 21 Welfare Fund v. Price Waterhouse* (3d Cir.1989), other accountants, *Brown v. Roth* (D.N.J.1990), and actuaries, *Pappas v. Buck Consultants, Inc.* (7th Cir.1991). For such a professional to be a fiduciary, the standards of section 3(21)(A) must be independently satisfied.

Courts have been reluctant to find that attorneys for plans or for fiduciaries have sufficient discretion, authority or control to justify imposing fiduciary status under ERISA. *E.g., Useden v. Acker* (11th Cir.1991). Of course, an attorney may have other kinds of fiduciary responsibility to his client under the relevant law governing the attorney-client relationship. But that is different from fiduciary responsibility under ERISA.

4. THE EMPLOYER AS FIDUCIARY

ERISA § 408(c)(3) expressly permits a plan fiduciary to be the employer (or union) of the participants, or one of its officers, employees, agents or other representatives. Other rules and regulations expand on the employer's role as fiduciary. ERISA § 3(16) specifies that the employer (or a union) is the default plan administrator. 29 C.F.R. § 2509.75–5, at FR–3 makes it clear that a corporate employer may even be the named fiduciary. Another regulation, 29 C.F.R. § 2509.75–8, at D–4 explains that a board of directors may be a fiduciary, for example with respect to the selection and retention of other plan fiduciaries. (On the other hand, an officer or employee of the plan sponsor is not a fiduciary solely because of his position with the employer. 29 C.F.R. § 2509.75–8, at D–5.)

Since an overriding purpose of ERISA is to safeguard employee expectations created by the employer, allowing the employer and its representatives to be fiduciaries might seem a case of allowing the wolf to guard the sheep. But matters are not so simple. In the language of one Congressional report, there is a "symbiotic relationship existing between the employer and the plan covering his employees." [4869.] This means two things.

First, most employers who implement benefit plans surely want them managed properly and want the plan purposes fulfilled. After all, the plan likely was established, at least in part, to serve the employer's own business purposes; and those purposes commonly involve the creation or maintenance of good relations with employees. It can be argued that, although some employers may misuse their position as fiduciaries, most will not wish to alienate employees by mismanaging or abusing the plan. *See Van Boxel v. Journal Co. Employees' Pension Trust* (7th Cir.1987).

Second, in the end it is the employer's money that is used to pay benefits and expenses. An employer will legitimately want to maintain oversight of plan funds (particularly in defined benefit plans), both to ensure that they are managed properly (for example, that they are soundly invested and that excessive benefits are not paid out) and to control administrative costs. If ERISA did not permit employers and their representatives to serve as fiduciaries, employers might be less willing to establish plans, thereby defeating a different purpose of the statute.

5. TERM OF FIDUCIARY OFFICE

The Department of Labor has taken the position, DOL Opinion Letter No. 85–41A, and the few courts to consider the question have agreed, *e.g.*, *Mobile, Alabama–Pensacola, Florida Building & Construction Trades Council v. Daugherty* (S.D.Ala. 1988), that a trustee may not be appointed for life or for an indefinite term subject to removal only for malfeasance or incapacity. A plan provision specifying such a term would be inconsistent with the fiduciary duties of loyalty and prudence and thus ineffective. Other provisions insulating trustees from oversight or removal have similarly been invalidated. *E.g., Levy v. Local Union No. 810* (2d Cir.1994). On the other hand, a trustee may be appointed for a specified term that is reasonable under the circumstances. Presumably the same conclusions hold for other appointed fiduciaries.

B. TRUST AND RELATED REQUIREMENTS

In addition to the general fiduciary standards discussed below, ERISA contains special rules for the safeguarding of plan assets. One set, the prohibited transaction rules, are examined in the next chapter. Others are described in this section.

1. PLAN ASSETS

Although ERISA's fiduciary rules are substantially concerned with protecting plan assets, the statute contains no general criteria for identifying them and distinguishing them from other items. However, it does address specific cases and issues.

a. Plan Assets vs. Funds or Other Property

The assets that the fiduciary rules are principally designed to safeguard are contributions, investments, insurance contracts and other funds available for the payment of benefits. However, the notion of "plan asset" in the fiduciary rules probably encompasses all plan assets, whether or not used directly to pay benefits. That, at any rate, is the more straightforward interpretation. Another indication is found in the bonding rules (discussed below), which apply to fiduciaries and persons who handle "funds or other property" of the plan. ERISA § 412. Regulations explain that "funds or other property" include only those assets that are or may be used as a source of benefit payments, and exclude permanent assets and other assets used in the operation of the plan. 29 C.F.R. § 2580.412–4.

b. Time of Asset Acquisition

Contributions to a plan are the ultimate source of its assets. For purposes of the fiduciary rules, participant and beneficiary contributions that are paid to the employer or withheld from wages become plan assets as of the earliest date on which they can reasonably be segregated from general employer assets. For pension plans, the date generally may not be later than the 15th business day of the month following the month in which the contributions are received by the employer or in which the amounts withheld would have been paid to the employee. 29 C.F.R. § 2510.3–102(a) & (b).

There is no corresponding rule for employer contributions. However, under the bonding rules, employer contributions generally become funds or other property of a plan when the plan administrator receives them. 29 C.F.R. § 2580.412–5(a). When the employer is the administrator, such contributions become plan funds or other property when the earliest of the following occurs. They are: taken out of the general assets of the employer and placed in a separate account; identified on a separate set of books or records; paid over to a corporate trustee or used to purchase benefits from an insurer or other organization; or otherwise segregated, paid out or used for plan purposes. 29 C.F.R. § 2580.412–5(b)(2). (There are corresponding standards for when participant and beneficiary contributions become plan funds or other property; however, they differ from the standards specifying when such contributions become plan assets. 29 C.F.R. § 2580.412–5(b)(1).)

c. Mutual Fund Interests

When a plan invests in shares of a mutual fund issued by an investment company registered under the Investment Company Act of 1940, only the mutual fund shares are plan assets. The underlying securities and other assets of the investment company are not. ERISA § 401(b)(1). The rationale is that mutual funds are already regulated by federal law and their assets made secure through diversification.

d. Other Investments

The mutual-fund rule prompts a broader question. Where a plan invests in other entities, to what extent do the other entities' assets constitute plan assets? If the definition of "plan asset" were broad enough to include the assets of those entities, their managers would be subjected to ERISA's fiduciary standards—usually an untenable result, since ERISA requires fiduciaries to act solely in the interest of plan participants and beneficiaries. To deal with this question, the DOL has issued a regulation stating, as a general rule, that plan assets include the investment in the entity but not the assets underlying the investment. 29 C.F.R. § 2510.3–101(a)(2).

The rule, however, has a complex set of qualifications and exceptions. They can only be sketched here. The major exception is for an *equity interest* that is neither a *publicly offered security* nor a security issued by an investment company registered under the Investment Company Act. For such investments, plan assets include both the equity interest and an undivided interest in each of the underlying assets of the entity, unless the entity is an *operating company* or the equity participation in it by *benefit plan investors* is not *significant*. 29 C.F.R. § 2510.3–101(a)(2). Each of the italicized terms is defined in the regulation, generally in a conventional way. The regulation also lays down rules for interests in trusts and certain other entities, 29 C.F.R. § 2510.3–101(h), and in government mortgage pools, 29 C.F.R. § 2510.3–101(i).

e. Guaranteed Benefit Policies

If a plan purchases a *guaranteed benefit policy* from an insurer qualified to do business in a state, only the policy is a plan asset; not the underlying assets of the insurer. ERISA § 401(b)(2). This rule, too, limits the scope of ERISA's fiduciary rules. Behind it is the policy, expressed in the McCarran–Ferguson Act and elsewhere, of leaving the regulation of insurers to the states.

The key term "guaranteed benefit policy" (not a technical insurance term) is defined by ERISA as an insurance contract or policy to the extent it provides for benefits in an amount guaranteed by the insurer. ERISA § 401(b)(2)(B). It clearly encompasses annuity contracts that provide fixed benefits.

Yet many insurance contracts that fund plan benefits do not involve the simple purchase of an annuity. Rather, they have two features. First, the insurer collects payments from many contractholders, puts them in an unallocated fund, and invests them. These funds may be used later to purchase annuities for retired employees. Second, when an employee is to receive benefits, the insurer issues an annuity and deducts the cost from the fund, or else turns over an equivalent amount to the plan so that the plan can purchase an annuity elsewhere.

For many years it was unclear whether insurance arrangements of this kind, or any parts of them, were guaranteed benefit policies so that the underlying assets would not be considered plan assets. The analytic difficulty resulted from the presence of two parts to the arrangement: the accumulation and investment of premiums in the unallocated fund, and the payment under annuities to retirees.

The insurer's funds underlying the annuities are not plan assets, but what of the assets in the unallocated fund? Some courts viewed the insurer, in managing the portion of those funds not supporting fixed annuity payments, as no different from an investment manager hired to manage plan assets. Thus, they deemed the portion of the insurance contract with respect to these funds as something other than a guaranteed benefit policy and categorize the underlying assets as plan assets. Other courts viewed the segregation of the insurance contract into two parts as artificial. To them, since the contract as a whole provided for annuities, the contract as a whole is a guaranteed benefit policy and the underlying assets excluded.

In *John Hancock Mutual Life Insurance Co. v. Harris Trust & Savings Bank* (S.Ct.1993), the Supreme Court adopted the former view. The Court held that in determining whether an insurance contract is a guaranteed benefit policy, each component of the contract must be examined. A component falls under the section 401(b)(2) exclusion only if it allocates investment risk to the insurer by providing a genuine guarantee of an aggregate amount of benefits payable to participants and beneficiaries. Thus, assets in the unallocated fund are plan assets to the extent they are attributable to the nonguaranteed portion of a contract issued to a plan.

Because the *John Hancock* decision upset the understanding of the insurance industry, the Secretary and Congress moved to minimize the potential disruption and to reduce unanticipated liability. The DOL issued a prohibited transaction exemption exempting a range of activities from the prohibited transaction rules (see Chapter 13). PTE 95–60. In addition, Congress amended ERISA to direct the Secretary to issue regulations applicable to policies issued on or before December 31, 1998, clarifying which assets held by the insurer are plan assets and providing guidance as to the application of ERISA with respect to such assets. ERISA § 401(c). The regulations were issued as prescribed, and contain standards for avoiding treatment of assets in an insurer's general account as plan assets, as well as a limitation on fiduciary liability for certain conduct relating to assets in the general account. 29 C.F.R. § 2550.401c–1. Policies issued on or after January 1, 1999 are not governed by the regulations and remain fully subject to ERISA's fiduciary standards in accordance with the rule of *John Hancock*.

2.   THE TRUST REQUIREMENT

Subject to a few exceptions, all assets of an employee benefit plan must be held in trust. ERISA § 403(a); IRC § 401(a). This rule expands the limited pre-ERISA trust requirements (under the Internal Revenue Code and the Labor Management Relations Act, respectively) for qualified plans and Taft–Hartley plans. Its purpose is to enforce the separation of plan assets from employer (and union) assets, and invoke the protections of the law of trusts.

The more significant exceptions are the following. Top-hat plans are exempt from all of ERISA fiduciary rules, including the trust requirement. ERISA § 401(a)(1). Plan assets that consist of insurance contracts issued by an insurance company qualified to do business in a state need not be held in trust— doing so would provide no added protection. ERISA § 403(b)(1). (Under the Code, a qualified pension plan funded through annuity contracts, rather than a trust, is called an *annuity plan*. IRC §§ 403(a), 404(a)(2).) Plan assets held by a qualified insurance company need not be held in trust; state regulation is presumed adequate. ERISA § 403(b)(2). Plans covering self-employed individuals and plans consisting of individual retirement accounts need not hold assets in trust, to the extent the assets are held in custodial accounts qualified under either IRC § 401(f) or § 408(h). ERISA § 403(b)(3).

In addition, the Secretary of Labor is authorized to exempt plans that are not subject to any of the following: Title I, parts 2 (relating to vesting and allied matters) and 3 (relating to funding); and Title IV (relating to plan termination). ERISA § 403(b)(4). To date, no regulations have been issued pursuant to this authority.

3. NON–INUREMENT

Whether or not plan assets are held in trust, ERISA directs that they "shall never inure to the benefit of any employer and shall be held for the exclusive purposes of providing benefits to participants in the plan and their beneficiaries and defraying reasonable expenses of administering the plan." ERISA § 403(c). This, like the trust requirement, derives from labor and tax law. It is substantially restated in ERISA's general fiduciary rules. Again, the purpose is to segregate plan assets and ensure that they are used only to provide benefits.

The exceptions to the non-inurement rule are very few. In limited circumstances, surplus assets may revert to the employer on plan termination. ERISA § 4044(d). (See Chapter 22.) In addition, IRC § 420 permits certain transfers of excess pension assets in a defined benefit plan to an account in the same plan for retiree health benefits. ERISA §§ 403(c)(2) & (3) permit the return of employer contributions or withdrawal payments in cases of mistake and in cases of certain conditional payments for which the condition (e.g., initial qualification) was not fulfilled. Finally, ERISA § 403(d)(2) provides that on termination of a welfare plan, the assets may be distributed however the plan specifies.

4. BONDING REQUIREMENTS

Another set of rules to protect plan assets are the bonding rules. The statutory standards derive from the WPPDA and the temporary regulations in force are in fact the WPPDA regulations. The rules generally require every fiduciary and every person who *handles* funds or other property of a plan (a so-

called *plan official*) to be bonded in an amount
fixed yearly at no less than 10% of the funds handled (but in no case for less than $1,000 and not
necessarily for more than $500,000). The bonds
must protect the plan against loss from acts of
fraud or dishonesty, and must have an acceptable
corporate surety. ERISA § 412(a). Bonding is not
required for completely unfunded plans in which
plan assets are not segregated in any way and
benefits are paid solely from the general assets of
the employer or employee organization. 29 C.F.R.
§ 2580.412–2. Nor is bonding required for property that has not yet become funds or other property
of the plan. 29 C.F.R. § 2580.412–5. Nor are
bonds required for certain corporate fiduciaries that
have large capital and surplus and that are regulated by federal or state authorities. ERISA
§ 412(a)(2).

For purposes of the bonding rules, a person handles plan funds or property whenever his duties
present a risk that funds or property could be lost
in the event of his fraud or dishonesty. The definition is intended to be very broad. There is no
minimum amount of handled plan funds to which
the definition applies. However, it does not apply
where the risk of loss is negligible (e.g., because of
the nature of the funds handled or because the
relevant duties are clerical and closely supervised).
29 C.F.R. § 2580.412–6(a). Criteria for handling
include physical contact (except for closely supervised clerical work), power to exercise contact or
control (e.g., access to depositories or power over

accounts), power to transfer or negotiate the property, disbursement, endorsement of checks or other negotiable instruments, and supervisory or decision-making authority involving any of the above. 29 C.F.R. § 2580.412–6(b). A person who is a fiduciary solely by virtue of giving investment advice for a fee does not handle funds and need not be bonded. 29 C.F.R. § 2509.75–5, at FR–8.

ERISA not only prohibits the handling of plan funds and property without a bond; it makes it unlawful for any plan official or other person with authority to permit such handling by an unbonded person who is required to be bonded. ERISA § 412(b). It is also unlawful to procure a bond from a surety or through an agent in which the plan or a party in interest has any control or significant financial interest. ERISA § 412(c).

Regulations prescribe in detail the acceptable form and content of bonds. 29 C.F.R. §§ 2580.412–7 to –20. The bonds must protect against all risks of loss that might arise from the dishonest or fraudulent handling of plan funds, whether or not the wrongdoer personally gained and whether or not the wrongful act is criminal (so long as state law would allow recovery on a comparable bond for such a wrongful act). 29 C.F.R. § 2580.412–9.

5.   PROHIBITED PERSONS

A person who has been convicted of any of a large number of crimes (both state and federal) is prohibited from serving in any of a wide variety of capacities with respect to any plan. The period of disqualification is 13 years after the conviction or the end of imprisonment, whichever is later. The period may be shortened by the sentencing court, or, after sentencing, by an appropriate district court in accordance with U.S. Sentencing Commission guidelines, or upon the full restoration of citizenship rights if they had been revoked. A person subject to the prohibition may not serve as fiduciary or other representative of a plan, consultant or advisor to a plan, or in any other capacity involving decisionmaking authority or custody or control of assets. No person may place another person in a position for which he is disqualified under this prohibition. However, no corporation or partnership will be disqualified from serving as fiduciary, officer, custodian, agent, counsel, or consultant for a plan unless the sentencing court determines after notice and hearing that the entity's serving in such role would be inconsistent with the intention of the provision. ERISA § 411(a). Violation of these prohibitions are punishable by fine of up to $10,000 and imprisonment for up to 5 years. ERISA § 411(b).

C. **FIDUCIARY STANDARDS**

ERISA prescribes basic standards to govern all plan fiduciaries. Some standards resemble ones found in trust law; others are clearly different. Even where the standards appear to be the same, important differences may lurk. As the Joint Explanatory Statement advises, Congress "expect[s] that the courts will interpret th[e] prudent man rule (and the other fiduciary standards) bearing in mind the special nature and purpose of employee benefit plans." [5083.]

1. THE STRUCTURAL CHARACTER OF ERISA FIDUCIARY DUTIES

ERISA's fiduciary standards specify how a "fiduciary shall discharge his duties with respect to a plan." ERISA § 404(a)(1). The standards, thus, are framed as second-order duties, regulating the way a fiduciary must carry out his specific obligations, e.g., to pay benefits or invest funds. It is not clear why Congress chose this formulation. Surely a plan fiduciary ought to be required to act with loyalty and prudence throughout his assigned domain, whether or not the conduct is viewed as the discharge of a duty. In fact, courts have construed ERISA's fiduciary obligations in this broader way. The statutory language may simply emphasize ERISA's conception of plan fiduciaries as primarily bearers of duties rather than (as in trust law) of powers.

As the formulation highlights, ERISA imposes two very different kinds of duties on plan fiduciaries. First, there are primary duties, such as the duty to pay benefits, hold assets, or file annual reports. Second, there are fiduciary duties, which govern the way in which the primary duties are carried out. The two species differ in a number of respects. For example, there are different remedies for violations. ERISA §§ 409 and 502(a)(2) afford a panoply of legal and equitable remedies for breach of fiduciary duty; ERISA § 502(a)(3), on the other hand, supplies only equitable remedies for breach of the underlying duties.

The statutory formulation emphasizes another distinctive feature of ERISA's fiduciary duties, namely that they are limited fiduciary duties. They govern only conduct with respect to which an individual has fiduciary status. Thus, for example, if a plan administrator is a fiduciary only with respect to plan administration, he has not violated a fiduciary duty if he gratuitously gives poor investment advice which the trustee follows to the plan's detriment. *Brandt v. Grounds* (7th Cir.1982).

2. THE DUTY OF LOYALTY

ERISA § 404(a)(1) requires a fiduciary, *inter alia*, to "discharge his duties with respect to a plan solely in the interest of the participants and beneficiaries and—(A) for the exclusive purpose of: (i) providing benefits to participants and their beneficiaries; and (ii) defraying reasonable expenses of administering the plan...." This is ERISA's statement of the duty of loyalty, arguably the central duty of any fiduciary. It is often called the *exclusive benefit rule*.

On its surface, the ERISA duty of loyalty is straightforward. A fiduciary must act with one and only one purpose and must act to further one and only one interest. However, there are subtle difficulties for interpretation and application.

a.   To Whom Is The Duty Owed?

Although the duty is to act solely in the interest of participants and beneficiaries, the focus of the obligation is the plan as a whole, rather than the individual participants and beneficiaries. This interpretation is based on two considerations.

First, the Supreme Court has held that any damage remedy for breach of fiduciary duty inures to the benefit of the plan as a whole. Individual participants and beneficiaries may not recover under ERISA §§ 409 & 502(a)(2) for injuries to themselves. *Massachusetts Mutual Life Insurance Co. v. Russell* (S.Ct.1985). The basis for the holding is the language of section 409. That provision allows redress only of "losses to the plan" resulting from breaches of fiduciary duty and provides only for remedies that make the plan whole or otherwise serve its needs. It does not allow redress of losses to individuals.

Yet, this consideration has its limits, for in *Varity Corp. v. Howe* (S.Ct.1996), the Supreme Court held that participants and beneficiaries can obtain equitable relief on their own behalf for certain breaches of fiduciary duty under ERISA § 502(a)(3). Still, in *Mertens v. Hewitt Associates* (S.Ct.1993) the Court had held that participants and beneficiaries could not recover damages under section 502(a)(3), and in both *Varity* and the later case of *Great–West Life & Annuity Insurance Co. v. Knudson* (S.Ct.2002), the Court construed the scope of equitable relief available under section 502(c)(3) narrowly (see below). Thus, even after *Varity* the plan as a whole remains the primary focus and beneficiary (in the non-technical sense) of ERISA's fiduciary duties.

Second, situations may arise where different participants or groups of participants have conflicting interests concerning some aspect or activity of the plan. For example, if a plan is seriously underfunded, the payment of benefits to one participant may deplete the resources available to pay benefits to others. Or, for another example, current employees, concerned more about their jobs than about retirement income, might want the plan to make a sizeable loan to the employer's largest customer that would help keep it afloat and thus maintain levels of their own employment. Retirees, on the other hand, concerned only about their retirement benefits, might object to a large loan to a financially troubled enterprise. Other conflicts can easily be imagined. Both the legislative history and the case law make it clear that a fiduciary cannot favor individual participants or beneficiaries or groups of them. *See Varity Corp. v. Howe* (S.Ct.1996). Where there are conflicts among such interests, the fiduciary must determine which course best serves the purpose of the plan in providing benefits to the participants and beneficiaries as a whole. *See Morse v. Stanley* (2d Cir.1984); *Winpisinger v. Aurora Corp. of Illinois* (N.D.Ohio 1978). ERISA's duty of loyalty implicitly includes a duty of impartiality which prevents fiduciaries from favoring individual interests over the interest of the plan.

b. What Employer Conduct Is Subject to the Duty?

The fact that the employer of the participants (or its representative) may serve as a fiduciary creates complexities for the principled application of the exclusive benefit rule. A recurring and often difficult problem is that of determining which conduct by the employer (or its representative) is fiduciary conduct subject to ERISA's fiduciary duties, and which is not. The problem arises because, in acting with respect to a plan, the employer-fiduciary may be carrying out either a settlor function or a fiduciary function (or both). *Lockheed Corp. v. Spink* (S.Ct.1996). In general, for it to be fiduciary conduct, the employer conduct must involve plan management or administration (the problem rarely arises with respect to investment advice or asset management). One thus needs criteria for identifying the kinds of conduct that amount to plan management or administration.

It is clear that the establishment of a plan is not a fiduciary function. *Berlin v. Michigan Bell Telephone Co.* (6th Cir.1988). Nor is termination or amendment. *Lockheed Corp. v. Spink* (S.Ct.1996); *Curtiss-Wright Corp. v. Schoonejongen* (S.Ct.1995). Nor are the personnel activities of the employer. *Hickman v. Tosco Corp.* (8th Cir.1988). Similar conclusions apply to union activity. For example, negotiation of plan terms is not ERISA fiduciary conduct of either the employer or the union. *United Independent Flight Officers, Inc. v. United Air Lines, Inc.* (7th Cir.1985).

The more difficult cases are those where an employer's conduct could plausibly be considered as *either* settlor conduct or fiduciary conduct; and those where an employer's conduct appears to involve *both* settlor and fiduciary conduct. An example of the former is a severance plan administered by the employer, which provided that severance pay would be granted to an employee when his manager determined that severance pay is appropriate. In *Noorily v. Thomas & Betts Corp.* (3d Cir.1999), the Court of Appeals held (contrary to the District Court's determination) that the decision to grant or not grant severance pay was settlor, rather than fiduciary, conduct, and that the employer's decision not to grant benefits to certain individuals who refused to relocate was not a breach of fiduciary duty.

An example of the latter case is the circumstance where the employer-administrator makes representations to employees about the future status of a plan (e.g., plan termination) or future benefits that might be offered (e.g., early retirement benefits). In these communications, the employer might be considered to be acting as a settlor, or administrator, or both. In *Varity Corp. v. Howe* (S.Ct.1996), the Supreme Court held that these communications can involve fiduciary conduct, potentially subjecting the employer to fiduciary liability if they involve misrepresentations.

However, the Court emphasized the fact-dependent nature of any such determination. In *Varity*, for example, the employer made misrepresentations about the security of future benefits at large, official meetings; the (misleading) representations were designed to encourage employees of failing divisions to accept transfer of employment to a newly created subsidiary, with concomitant coverage under a newly established benefit plan. The Court upheld the district court's determination that the employer had acted in its fiduciary capacity.

c. *Pegram* and the Functional Approach

The difficulty in borderline cases results from ERISA's failure to define "plan administration" or "plan management." Ultimately, the question is whether the employer conduct involved is conduct of the type Congress would have intended be governed by the exclusive benefit and other fiduciary rules. On this issue, the common law of trusts is an important guide. *Varity Corp. v. Howe* (S.Ct. 1996). But a functional approach is also appropriate. *Id.* In *Hozier v. Midwest Fasteners, Inc.* (3d Cir.1990), for example, a court of appeals concluded that the fiduciary standards did not apply to an employer's decision to amend an unfunded severance plan, because a contrary rule would be inconsistent with Congress' determination not to subject such plans to vesting rules and because Congress was concerned to limit employer costs with respect to welfare benefit plans. The advantage of a functional approach is that it focuses on the underlying question. For most often the reason it matters whether an employer has acted as a fiduciary is that, if it has, the employer arguably breached a fiduciary duty.

A good example of the functional approach is the Supreme Court's opinion in *Pegram v. Herdrich* (S.Ct.2000), which dealt with the analogous question of which conduct by an HMO that provides benefits under a plan is fiduciary conduct subject to ERISA. The question arises because, like an employer, an HMO can perform two different functions. A medical benefit plan might contract for an HMO to provide medical services covered by the plan to participants and beneficiaries. In such circumstances, the HMO and its representatives (including physicians) perform both fiduciary functions—determining eligibility for treatment—as well as nonfiduciary functions—diagnosing and treating medical problems. As the Supreme Court observed, however, a great many decisions the HMO physicians make are mixed, involving both eligibility and treatment issues. For example, in *Pegram,* the challenged decision was one to delay a diagnostic ultrasound so that it could be performed several days later at an HMO-operated facility, rather than immediately at a local hospital. (The participant suffered a ruptured appendix and peritonitis in the interim.) The Court deemed this a mixed eligibility and treatment decision, and held that decisions of this type do not constitute fiduciary conduct subject to ERISA's fiduciary standards.

In reaching its decision, the Court was influenced by three principal considerations. First, it concluded from an examination of the statute that Congress was unlikely to have intended decisions of this type to be subject to ERISA's fiduciary rules. The fiduciary rules are primarily concerned to safeguard plan assets and the payment of them to beneficiaries. Mixed eligibility and treatment decisions only faintly resemble this paradigmatic conduct. Second, the Court noted that to subject decisions of this type to ERISA's fiduciary duties would create conflicts of interest in nearly every case, and that this might effectively put HMO's (or, at least, for-profit HMO's) out of business—a result contrary to Congress' encouragement of HMO's in other legislation. Third, the Court emphasized that the upshot of deeming mixed eligibility and treatment decisions to be fiduciary decisions would be the federalization of medical malpractice law, a result Congress surely did not intend in enacting ERISA.

d. Employer Conflicts of Interest

An employer-fiduciary, in the course of acting as a fiduciary, may be faced with a situation in which its conduct might affect, even necessarily will affect, its business interests. Good examples come from the domain of corporate takeover activity. A recurring issue has been whether an employer-fiduciary breached the duty of loyalty by investing plan funds in a way that advanced its own business interest, through pursuing or resisting a takeover. The two leading cases are *Donovan v. Bierwirth* (2d Cir. 1982) and *Leigh v. Engle* (7th Cir.1984), which take similar, yet different approaches.

Bierwirth involved a hostile tender offer for a majority of common stock of the employer. The same persons who, as corporate officers, were fighting the tender offer had responsibility, as plan fiduciaries, to decide whether the plan should tender its shares of employer stock. The virtual impossibility of their ignoring the employer's interest was obvious. The fiduciaries decided, not only not to tender, but to purchase more shares of employer stock. The court found this conduct to violate ERISA's duties of loyalty and prudence.

The court rejected two rules that might have simplified the analysis. First, the court held that it was not a *per se* breach for the fiduciaries' decision to have advanced the employer's interest. In the court's analysis, a fiduciary's decision might be solely in the interests of the participants and beneficiaries and for the exclusive purpose of providing benefits, yet still *incidentally benefit* the employer. Second, the Department of Labor had argued that the only proper course for the fiduciaries was to have resigned, so that neutral fiduciaries could be appointed to decide what the plan should do. The court was receptive to the argument. However, it found it unnecessary to impose such a strict requirement because there were other reasons to find a breach of fiduciary duty in the case.

The court's rejection of bright-line tests demanded that it find some way to distinguish illegitimate conduct that advances the employer's interest from legitimate conduct that does so. The court rested the distinction on procedural grounds. It focused on the extent to which the fiduciaries followed procedures designed to ensure that whatever decision they reached would be in the participants' and beneficiaries' best interest and would not be tainted by consideration of the employer's interest. Here, serious and obvious irregularities undermined the decisionmaking process, including the failure promptly to convene a meeting of plan trustees, the failure to solicit the advice of independent counsel, and the swift and superficial decisionmaking regarding the purchase of additional shares. Thus it was easy to find liability.

It is not clear why the court chose a wholly procedural approach. The problem with such an approach is that it virtually conflates the duty of loyalty with the duty of prudent decisionmaking (discussed below). In fact, despite the court's repeated reference to the duty of loyalty, it could have decided the case on prudence grounds alone. The question the court left open is what the result would have been had the fiduciaries acted prudently but still decided to purchase additional shares. Would there be any basis for finding a breach of the duty of loyalty?

Leigh goes some way toward answering that question. There, the plan fiduciaries were employees or agents of the plan sponsor, which was controlled by an individual financier. The fiduciaries' positions in both the company and the plan were dependent on the financier. The fiduciaries consistently invested plan funds in corporations that the financier was trying to acquire. The question was whether this conduct violated the duty of loyalty. Prudence was not explicitly in issue.

The court, like the one in *Bierwirth*, agreed that for employer-fiduciaries to invest plan assets in a way that advances the employer's interest is not a *per se* violation of ERISA. It also agreed with the Department of Labor's suggestion that the preferred course in cases like the one at hand is for interested fiduciaries to resign in favor of neutral ones. Such a course would reduce the risk of improper decisionmaking, simplify review by courts, and "calm the fears of plan beneficiaries who might otherwise perceive the need to resort to the courts in order to ensure the safety of their entitlements." However, as in *Bierwirth*, the court opted for an approach requiring examination of the facts.

Yet the approach differed in that it was not wholly procedural. Instead, the court took the fundamental issue to be that of the actual independence of the fiduciaries' decisionmaking. The court held that, to evaluate independence, it had to closely examine the facts surrounding an alleged violation. Such facts include (but are not necessarily limited to) the risks of conflicts of interest, the nature of the investigation made by the fiduciaries, and the extent of congruence between the fiduciaries' decisions for the plan and the employer's interest. In *Leigh*, a telling factor in the court's finding of liability was the long-term congruence between fiduciary and employer decisionmaking, despite the divergence of plan and employer interests. Thus, unlike as in *Bierwirth*, the court was concerned to find the fiduciaries' true motive. The problem, however, is that motives are inevitably mixed and complex.

So long as persons who represent interests different from those of participants and beneficiaries can be fiduciaries, there will be a problem of distinguishing legitimate from illegitimate decisionmaking. But the problem does not result solely, or even primarily, from the fact that the fiduciary represents those other interests. *Every* fiduciary is a person with a complex set of personal interests and relationships that he will never be able to put entirely out of mind. Instead, the problem results from ERISA's extreme requirement that fiduciaries act *solely* in the interest of participants and beneficiaries. If taken literally, this requirement is probably impossible to meet in any situation calling for judgment. Where a fiduciary has a choice between several courses of action, all of which arguably would be in the interest of participants and beneficiaries, he must rely on other considerations to break the tie and decide what to do. Motives for decisionmaking are inescapably complex. Where a fiduciary also represents the employer, the problem is simply exacerbated. It is exacerbated by the importance of the employer interest to the fiduciary (the fiduciary's livelihood may be involved), its pervasiveness, and the significant chance for divergence of employer and plan interest (especially in defined benefit plans). The risk is not so much that the fiduciary will take the employer's interest into account at all—that may be inevitable—but that he will treat it as a primary consideration rather than, say, as a tie-breaker between two legitimate choices.

Where a controversial choice by an employer-fiduciary would advance the employer's interest, a literal application of the exclusive benefit rule does appear to mandate resignation of the fiduciary. Sometimes this is appropriate. *See Schwartz v. Interfaith Medical Center* (E.D.N.Y.1989). But courts understandably conclude that such an extreme requirement often amounts to overkill and is not always appropriate. Any workable rule must take into account the nature of decisionmaking and the virtual inevitability of complex motives. The first step is to decide when fiduciary action on mixed motives (whether or not by an employer-fiduciary) should be treated as wrong. On that basis pragmatic standards may be developed for identifying violations.

3. OTHER FIDUCIARY DUTIES

a. Prudence

Plan fiduciaries are required to act "with the care, skill, prudence, and diligence under the circumstances then prevailing that a prudent man acting in like capacity and familiar with such matters would use in the conduct of an enterprise of a like character and with like aims." ERISA § 404(a)(1)(B). This requirement derives from the trust law duty of prudence, another basic obligation of traditional trustees.

The standard of prudence is objective, *Katsaros v. Cody* (2d Cir.1984), and it applies mainly to deliberative conduct such as investment decisions, employment decisions, and delegations of responsibility. The standard is generally understood as that of a prudent expert. It may also require a fiduciary to obtain expert advice, *id.*, and heed it when given, *Brock v. Self* (W.D.La.1986). The duty is mainly procedural; the chief consideration is the steps taken before acting. "A court's task is to inquire whether the trustees, at the time they engaged in the challenged transaction, employed the appropriate methods.... The analysis considers the trustees' *conduct* and not ... success or failure." *Donovan v. Walton* (S.D.Fla.1985).

DOL regulations have provided some clarifications for the duty. A fiduciary who has appointed other fiduciaries has an obligation periodically to monitor their performance. 29 C.F.R. § 2509.75–8, at FR–17. A fiduciary may rely on information from and work of non-fiduciaries who perform services for the plan, provided he has exercised prudence in their selection and retention (i.e., if in the exercise of ordinary care he has no reason to doubt their competence, integrity or responsibility). 29 C.F.R. § 2509.75–8, at FR–11. In making investments, an investment manager appointed by a named fiduciary may rely on information provided by the latter, if the information is provided for the stated purpose of assisting the investment manager and he has no reason to know that the information is incorrect. 29 C.F.R. § 2550.404a–1(b)(3).

Other clarifications deal with plan investment. In an important regulation, the DOL has endorsed modern portfolio theory as a basis for assessing prudence. Under this approach, one examines the prudence of an investment, not in isolation (as under trust law), but by reference to its place in the plan's investment portfolio (specifically, the part with respect to which the fiduciary has investment duties). A fiduciary considering an investment will satisfy the prudence standard if he acts after determining that the investment is reasonably designed to further the purposes of the plan, taking into consideration the risk of loss and opportunity for gain; and taking into account the composition of the portfolio with respect to diversification, the liquidity and return relative to anticipated cash needs, and the projected return of the portfolio relative to funding objectives. 29 C.F.R. § 2550.404a–1.

Another area that has been addressed is tender offers. The DOL and the Treasury Department, in a joint statement, have advised fiduciaries responsible for plan investments that they need not automatically tender shares when the offer represents a premium over market price. A fiduciary might properly consider, among other factors, the "intrinsic value" of the target, the likelihood of that value's being realized by present management, the likelihood of subsequent tender offers, the long-term value of the company, the ability to invest proceeds from the tender, and the long-term business plans of the target's management. A similar approach may be taken in assessing a proposed merger. The Departments explained that they issued the clarification to help ensure that "government policies and actions do not prevent the huge pools of capital represented by private pension plans from being invested in manners that will facilitate our continued economic growth, provide corporate accountability, and enhance our nation's competitiveness." Joint Department of Labor/Department of Treasury Statement on Pension Investments (1989).

b. Diversification

Another investment-related fiduciary duty is diversification. A fiduciary who has investment responsibility must "diversify[ ] the investments of the plan so as to minimize the risk of large losses, unless under the circumstances it is clearly prudent not to do so." ERISA § 404(a)(1)(C). This duty is generally considered a specific application of the prudence standard and on its face provides that general prudence concerns will trump. For example, in *Davidson v. Cook* (E.D.Va.1983), a plan had substantially all of its funds invested in an under-collateralized loan to a financially unsound borrower. The trustees decided not to divest the plan of the loan. This was held not to violate the duty of diversification. It would have been imprudent for the plan to dispose of the loan and suffer a large loss rather than to work with the borrower.

The diversification requirement is concerned with a wide variety of investment characteristics. The Joint Explanatory Statement advises that fiduciaries should take into account the purposes of the plan, the amount of plan assets, the general economic conditions, and the breakdown of plan investments by type, geography, industry, and dates of maturity. [5084–85.] An interesting application of the standard is *GIW Industries, Inc. v. Trevor, Stewart, Burton & Jacobsen, Inc.* (11th Cir.1990). There, an investment manager was held to have violated the diversification requirement by investing plan assets primarily in long-term government bonds. Although the bonds were very safe and very marketable, the plan's liquidity needs made a large investment in bonds with distant maturity dates inappropriate. Some of the bonds had to be sold at a loss to satisfy the plan's immediate cash needs.

c. Non–Deviation

ERISA requires fiduciaries to act "in accordance with the documents and instruments governing the plan insofar as such documents and instruments are consistent with the provisions of [Title I] or Title IV." ERISA § 404(a)(1)(D). This rule dovetails with the writing requirement and furthers its policies. In addition, the "insofar" clause reinforces the mandatory character of ERISA's standards by prohibiting deviations from them by plans. This is a change from trust law, which did permit modification of legal standards through the trust document.

The requirement that plan documents be strictly followed also marks a change from trust law; trust law permits departures from the terms of the trust instrument with the permission of a court. By contrast, courts may not sanction deviations from the terms of the plan. However, fiduciaries who are in genuine doubt as to how to proceed may be able to petition a court for instructions. *See* Joint Explanatory Statement [5080].

d. Truthfulness and Information

A core principle in the law of plans is that participants and beneficiaries should have access to relevant information about the plan, their benefits, and their rights. We have seen this principle expressed in many statutory provisions and regulations (see Chapters 8, 10, and 11), as well as in judicial rules such as those of estoppel (Chapter 10). In *Varity Corp. v. Howe* (S.Ct.1996), the Supreme Court recognized a fiduciary duty, grounded in both ERISA and the common law of trusts, not to make intentional misrepresentations about future benefits. Through other cases, both before and after *Varity*, federal courts have been developing a more general duty on the part of fiduciaries to disclose, to inform, and to be truthful. The scope and contours of the duty are still in the process of being worked out.

The law is being developed in a broad array of contexts. One important context is that of future benefit changes, such as early retirement incentives. Some courts hold that an employer-fiduciary has a duty not to misrepresent prospective changes in a benefit plan, if the changes have been adopted or are under serious consideration; and that changes are under serious consideration where "(1) a specific proposal (2) is being discussed for purposes of implementation (3) by senior management with the authority to implement the change." *Fischer v. Philadelphia Electric Co.* (3d Cir.1996). The "serious consideration" test is essentially a test of materiality, and a growing number of courts take a broader view, holding that the degree to which changes are being considered is one factor bearing on materiality. *See Martinez v. Schlumberger, Ltd.* (5th Cir.2003); *Ballone v. Eastman Kodak Co.* (2d Cir.1997).

Other areas in which the scope of the duty is being developed include individualized statements about individual benefits, *e.g., Daniels v. Thomas & Betts Corp.* (3d Cir.2001); failure to provide information about benefits, *e.g., Farr v. U.S. West Communications, Inc.* (9th Cir.1998); and nondisclosure of information about HMO business and financial practices, *e.g., Horvath v. Keystone Health Plan East, Inc.* (3d Cir.2003); *Shea v. Esensten* (8th Cir. 1997).

4. COFIDUCIARY RESPONSIBILITY

ERISA imposes on plan fiduciaries *cofiduciary duties*, which relate to the conduct of other fiduciaries. ERISA announces three such duties, framed as rules of liability for breaches by others. First, a fiduciary is liable for a breach of fiduciary duty by another fiduciary if he knowingly participates in, or knowingly undertakes to conceal, an act or omission of the other, knowing that act or omission to constitute a breach. ERISA § 405(a)(1). Second, a fiduciary is liable if, by the failure to comply with his own fiduciary duties, he has enabled another fiduciary to commit a breach. ERISA § 405(a)(2). Third, a fiduciary is liable if he has knowledge of a breach by another fiduciary and fails to make reasonable efforts under the circumstances to remedy it. ERISA § 405(a)(3). For those cofiduciary liabilities dependent on knowledge, constructive knowledge is enough.

Where a fiduciary must take reasonable steps to remedy a breach by another, he is not liable merely because the efforts fail. However, he is required to take "all reasonable and legal steps to prevent the action." 29 C.F.R. § 2509.75–5, at FR–10. Such steps might include undoing the action if it is within his power, bringing the breach to the attention of another person who might be able to rectify it, notifying the Department of Labor, or bringing suit under section 502(a)(3). A fiduciary who has knowledge of a breach by another fiduciary may not simply resign. Indeed, attempted resignation under such circumstances might itself be grounds for imposition of cofiduciary liability. *Freund v. Marshall & Ilsley Bank* (W.D.Wis.1979).

A fiduciary is responsible for correcting any breach of which he learns, even if it was committed before he became a fiduciary. *Successor Trust Committee of Permian Distributing, Inc. Employees' Profit Sharing Plan & Trust v. First State Bank of Odessa, N.A.* (W.D.Tex.1990). However, the fiduciary will be liable only for losses that occurred while he was a fiduciary. ERISA § 409(b).

D. LIMITATIONS ON FIDUCIARY RESPONSIBILITY

1. LIMITATIONS RESULTING FROM ALLOCATION RULES

If fiduciary responsibility of a named fiduciary is properly allocated to another named fiduciary or delegated to someone other than a named fiduciary, the first fiduciary has only limited direct liability for an act or omission of the other. His liability under section 404(a)(1) for acts or omissions of the other fiduciary is limited to liability with respect to the original allocation or delegation (e.g., as imprudent); the continuation of the allocation or delegation; or the establishment or implementation of the procedure for allocation or delegation. ERISA § 405(c)(2)(A). A caveat, however, is that the plan document must provide for an allocation or delegation procedure. Otherwise, any attempted allocation or delegation will be ineffective and the named fiduciary will not be relieved of responsibility. 29 C.F.R. § 2509.75–8, at FR–13 & –14.

Delegations and allocations with respect to trustees are governed by the same principles. No trustee of one trust is liable for the conduct of a trustee of another trust, except under the general cofiduciary rules. ERISA § 405(b)(3). However, every trustee must use reasonable care to prevent a cotrustee of the same trust from committing a breach. ERISA § 405(b)(1)(A). If trustee responsibility with respect to a trust has properly been allocated among cotrustees, then one trustee is not liable (except under the general cofiduciary provisions) for another trustee's breach of duty with respect to responsibilities that have not been allocated to the first. ERISA § 405(b)(1)(B). When an investment manager has been appointed, no trustee is liable for an act or omission of such a manager unless he knowingly participates in or undertakes to conceal it. ERISA § 405(d)(1).

2. DIRECTED TRUSTEES

When a plan provides that a trustee is subject to
the *proper directions* of a named fiduciary, ERISA
relieves the directed trustee from liability for following such directions.   ERISA § 405(b)(3)(B).
Proper directions are those in accordance with the
plan and with ERISA. The question then arises of
what the directed trustee's responsibility is where
he has reason to believe that directions of the
named fiduciary are not proper.   (This question
may arise in other circumstances, such as where the
plan administrator makes determinations of benefit
entitlements and then directs the trustee that benefits should be paid.)   In such cases, the duty to
follow plan documents and the duty of prudence are
in tension.   There is little law to guide their resolution.

The Joint Explanatory Statement suggests that
there is no direct liability unless it is "clear on their
face" that the directions are improper.   [5079.]
However, it is arguable that the purposes of ERISA
are best served by treating the duty of prudence as
overriding and imposing an obligation on the trustee to take some steps to ascertain the propriety of
suspect instructions. *See Lodge v. Shell Oil Co.*
(1st Cir.1984).   The extent of this duty to investi-
gate might depend on the amount of discretion
allowed the trustee by the relevant plan instrument.   For example, the trust instrument might
specify that the trustee can consult with counsel
concerning its responsibilities, thereby contemplat-

ing the trustee's discretion to make a limited inquiry. In any event, a duty to make inquiry or take action might be triggered by the cofiduciary rules, in particular section 405(a)(3), which imposes a duty to act in light of actual or constructive knowledge of a breach.

3. EXCULPATORY PROVISIONS, INSURANCE AND INDEMNIFICATION

ERISA invalidates any provision in any document that purports to relieve a fiduciary of responsibility or liability for a duty imposed by Title I. The only exception is for provisions relieving a trustee of liability for acts of other trustees, acts of investment managers, or proper directions of others. ERISA § 410(a).

A plan may purchase insurance for its fiduciaries or to cover losses or liability for fiduciary breaches. However, the policy must permit the insurer recourse against a fiduciary who breaches his fiduciary duty, thus maintaining the fiduciary's ultimate responsibility. ERISA § 410(b)(1). This rule is partially undercut by other provisions which permit a fiduciary to purchase insurance to cover his own liability and permit an employer or employee organization to purchase insurance (without a right of recourse) to cover potential liability of plan fiduciaries. ERISA § 410(b)(2) & (3). The rationale for this differential treatment appears to be that, since the responsibility and liability of a fiduciary is to the plan, the purchase of insurance by the plan effectively constitutes exculpation, while the purchase of insurance by others does not.

Section 410 implicitly forbids arrangements for the indemnification of a breaching fiduciary by the plan. Such arrangement in effect would be exculpatory. On the other hand, agreements for indemnification by others are allowed, again since they do not relieve a fiduciary of responsibility or liability. 29 C.F.R. § 2509.75–4.

4. PARTICIPANT–DIRECTED ACCOUNTS

Many defined contribution plans allow participants to make investment decisions for their accounts. Typically, the participant is limited to a defined group of investment choices and may also be limited in the timing of investment decisions. The participant exercising such control is not deemed a plan fiduciary and no plan fiduciary is liable for losses or breaches that "result from" such control. ERISA § 404(c)(1). Thus plan fiduciaries are absolved of liability for imprudent investment decisions by participants.

A danger of participant-directed accounts is that a participant's investment decision might violate terms of the plan, jeopardize the qualified status of the plan, or constitute a prohibited transaction. Regulations clarify that a fiduciary is not relieved from liability for a participant's instructions that would result in such a wrong. 29 C.F.R. § 2550.404c–1(d)(2)(ii). Regulations also clarify other details of section 404(c)(1), such as what constitutes participant exercise of control over assets in his account.

The rule of section 404(c)(1), limiting fiduciary liability for participant-directed accounts, limits liability only for losses or breaches *resulting from* the participant's exercise of control. Thus, if a fiduciary otherwise breaches a duty, for example by imprudently or negligently executing instructions of a participant, the fiduciary might still be liable for any losses.

E. REMEDIES FOR BREACH OF DUTY

1. SUITS AGAINST FIDUCIARIES

a. ERISA § 409

As already noted, ERISA § 409 provides the plan with a remedy for breach of fiduciary duty. Curiously though, ERISA § 502(a)(2), the corresponding enforcement provision, confers standing to sue only on participants, beneficiaries, fiduciaries, and the Secretary of Labor. It omits plans. Most courts thus take the position that plans have no standing to sue for breach of fiduciary duty. *E.g., Pressroom Unions–Printers League Income Security Fund v. Continental Assurance Co.* (2d Cir.1983). However, a minority have allowed plans to do so, at least in some circumstances, reasoning that section 502(d), which generally allows plans to "sue ... as an entity," itself confers the requisite standing. *E.g., Coleman Clinic, Ltd. v. Massachusetts Mutual Life Insurance Co.* (C.D.Ill.1988).

Circumstances at times make it impossible or impractical to adhere to the general limitation that relief under section 409 must be for the benefit of the plan. In such cases, alternative forms of relief may be allowed. For example, in *Gruber v. Hubbard Bert Karle Weber, Inc.* (W.D.Pa.1987), the plan had ceased to exist, mainly because of the wrongful acts of the defendants. Thus, there was no plan for money damages to be paid to. The court granted relief directly to the class of participants, who ultimately would have benefited from relief provided to a plan. In another case, *Amalgamated Clothing & Textile Workers Union v. Murdock* (9th Cir.1988), the court imposed a constructive trust for the benefit of participants and beneficiaries on the profits realized by the employer-fiduciary through risky and self-serving investments of plan funds. An award to the plan would have been self-defeating because the employer could have terminated it and recovered what he had paid.

The remedies available under section 409 are extremely broad. They include monetary relief, equitable relief, and removal of the breaching fiduciary. Monetary relief may include restitution, disgorgement of profits, and consequential damages. Equitable relief may include injunctions, rescission and constructive trusts. Most courts hold that punitive damages are not available. *E.g., International Ass'n of Heat and Frost Insulators Local 17 Pension Fund v. American National Bank and Trust Co. of Chicago* (N.D.Ill. 1998); *Scardelletti v. Bobo* (D.Md. 1995).

Measuring plan losses in connection with investment malfeasance sometimes causes difficulties. Because ERISA recognizes the applicability of portfolio theory, the court may have to decide whether losses should be measured by reference to the plan's investment portfolio or by reference to individual investments. The choice made affects the amount of the loss, and may even affect the question of whether there was any loss at all. *See Leigh v. Engle* (7th Cir.1988). Of course, if purchases and sales were made for purposes other than investment, there is no meaningful investment portfolio. In such case, losses should be measured for each transaction separately, and then aggregated, without any offset for transactional gains. *Id.*

Measuring the actual loss presents other problems. Where a fiduciary causes a plan improperly to expend funds to purchase assets, losses are measurable by the difference between the actual value of the assets and the value they would have had were the funds used for proper investments. Similar rules apply to improper sales of, and failures to purchase or sell, plan assets. The choice of hypothetical alternative investments and the time for measuring the difference in value will affect the calculation of the loss. In *Donovan v. Bierwirth* (2d Cir.1985), the court of appeals held that the trial court had discretion to fix a reasonable time for determining difference in value. It also held that the alternative uses for the plan funds should be determined by reference to actual uses at the time of the improper transaction. In *Call v. Sumitomo*

Bank (9th Cir.1989), however, the court accepted the argument that a diminution of plan assets might diminish available investment alternatives, thus creating additional losses that might have to be taken into account.

Section 409 is extremely broad in that it provides a remedy even where the plan has sustained no monetary loss. Fiduciary duties may be breached through a fiduciary's improperly putting the plan's funds or the integrity of its operations at risk. *Leigh v. Engle* (7th Cir.1984). The injury to the plan in such cases is the increased risk to participant interests—risk that it is the purpose of ERISA to reduce. In such cases, equitable relief is appropriate to remove the risk. *Brock v. Robbins* (7th Cir.1987).

b. ERISA § 502(a)(3)

ERISA § 502(a)(3) confers standing on participants, beneficiaries, and fiduciaries to bring suit for violations of ERISA, including fiduciary violations, and for violations of the terms of the plan. *Varity Corp. v. Howe* (S.Ct.1996). However, it authorizes only injunctive and other appropriate equitable relief; not damages. *Mertens v. Hewitt Associates* (S.Ct.1993). In *Great–West Life & Annuity Insurance Co. v. Knudson* (S.Ct.2002), the Supreme Court held that the statutory reference to "equitable relief" should be construed narrowly, in particular to the relief typically available in courts of equity. Thus, in *Knudson*, the Court distinguished between two types of restitution: restitution that would have been available in a court of law, and restitution that would have been available in a court of equity. Only the latter can be awarded under ERISA § 502(a)(3).

Whether relief sought is "appropriate" must be determined in light of the nature and purposes of plans and the policy choices reflected in ERISA § 502(a). Where adequate relief is available under another provision, further relief under ERISA § 502(a)(3) normally would not be appropriate. *Varity Corp. v. Howe* (S.Ct.1996); *Forsyth v. Humana, Inc.* (9th Cir.1997).

2. CIVIL PENALTIES

ERISA § 502(*l*) provides for the assessment by the Secretary of Labor of civil penalties for breaches of fiduciary duty and participation in any such breach. The amount of the penalty is 20% of the amount recovered from the person to be penalized, either pursuant to settlement agreement with the Secretary of Labor or as award in a remedial suit brought by the Secretary. The penalty against a person, however, may be waived in the Secretary's discretion if he determines in writing that the person acted reasonably and in good faith, or that a waiver appears necessary to permit the person to restore all losses to the plan without severe hardship. In addition, the penalty is to be reduced by the amount of any penalty or tax imposed for engaging in a prohibited transaction (see Chapter 13).

3. SUITS AGAINST NON-FIDUCIARIES

Prior to the Supreme Court's decision in *Mertens v. Hewitt Associates* (S.Ct.1993), several courts had held that non-fiduciaries who participate in a fiduciary's breach of duty could themselves be held liable to the plan. *E.g., Brock v. Hendershott* (6th Cir.1988). Often it was an attorney who was subjected to liability on this basis. *E.g., Whitfield v. Lindemann* (5th Cir.1988). Although *Mertens* did not reach the general issue of nonfiduciary liability for participation in a fiduciary breach (because of the way the issue had been presented to the Court), most lower courts have read the decision as suggesting that the Court would reject such liability. A compensating trend, however, has been for lower courts to hold state law claims for professional malpractice not to be preempted. *E.g., Custer v. Sweeney* (4th Cir.1996); *Airparts Co. v. Custom Benefit Services of Austin, Inc.* (10th Cir.1994).

Notwithstanding the general limits on nonfiduciary liability suggested by *Mertens*, the Supreme Court held in *Harris Trust and Savings Bank v. Salomon Smith Barney, Inc.* (S.Ct.2000), that a party in interest who participates in a prohibited transaction may be held liable under ERISA § 503(a)(3). The Court held that, although ERISA's prohibited transaction rules (Chapter 13) do not impose a duty on parties in interest, the remedial provisions of ERISA § 502(a)(3) do. The Court further noted that ERISA § 502(*l*) provides for a civil penalty against a party in interest (indeed, appar-

.ently against any nonfiduciary) who participates in a breach of fiduciary duty, measured by the amount recovered under ERISA § 502(a)(5). Since ERISA § 502(a)(3) and (a)(5) are similarly worded, relief against a party in interest must be available under the former provision, too.

The rationale of *Harris Trust* could be extended to impose liability on persons other than parties in interest, and for violations of Title I other than violations of the prohibited transaction rules. *See LeBlanc v. Cahill* (4th Cir.2001); *L.I. Head Start Child Development Services, Inc. v. Frank* (E.D.N.Y. 2001). The full scope of *Harris Trust* remains to be clarified through caselaw.

CHAPTER 13

PROHIBITED TRANSACTIONS

ERISA's prohibited transaction rules supplement the exclusive benefit requirement. With narrow exceptions, the rules strictly prohibit fiduciaries from causing plans to engage in transactions that involve or create a risk of self-dealing. The self-dealing of concern is not only that of fiduciaries, but also of parties in interest: persons who stand in a position to profit in some way from the plan. The rules are modeled on pre-ERISA restrictions on non-arm's length transactions involving plans, *see* IRC § 503, and on self-dealing in private foundations, *see* IRC § 4941.

A. PARTIES IN INTEREST

Parties in interest are persons whose financial dealings with plans are put under special scrutiny. The definition of party in interest is sweeping, so that rules governing transactions with them will have maximum prophylactic effect. The Internal Revenue Code uses substantially the same definition as Title I, but labels the parties *disqualified persons*. IRC § 4975(e)(2).

There are four main categories of parties in interest. First are fiduciaries, counsel, and employees of a plan. ERISA § 3(14)(A). Second are service providers to a plan. ERISA § 3(14)(B). Third is the employer of the covered employees. ERISA § 3(14)(C). Fourth is the employee organization of the covered employees. ERISA § 3(14)(D).

Also included within the definition are persons in close or controlling relationships to parties in the first four categories. Thus, a fifth category consists of owners of 50% interest or more of the employer or employee organization. ERISA § 3(14)(E). A sixth category consists of relatives (spouses, ancestors, descendants, and spouses of descendants) of anyone in categories one, two, three or five. ERISA §§ 3(14)(F) & (15). A seventh category consists of enterprises or trusts of which 50% interest or more is owned by a person in the first five categories. ERISA § 3(14)(G). An eighth category consists of officers, employees, directors, 10% shareholders, and 10% partners or joint venturers, of anyone in categories two, three, four, five or seven. ERISA § 3(14)(H) & (I). Note that this last category encompasses plan participants, as employees of the employer. The Code, by contrast, includes only employees who earn 10% or more of the yearly wages of the employer. IRC § 4975(e)(2)(H).

B. PROHIBITED FIDUCIARY CONDUCT

There are two sets of prohibited transaction rules. Both, like the provisions of section 404, govern fiduciary conduct. One set focuses on a plan's commercial and financial dealings with parties in interest. ERISA § 406(a). The other set broadly prohibits self-dealing by fiduciaries. ERISA § 406(b).

1. THE PARTY IN INTEREST RULES

There are five rules governing transactions with parties in interest. ERISA § 406(a). Each prohibits a fiduciary from causing the plan to engage in a financial transaction of a specified kind where she knows or should know that it would be a transaction with a party in interest. The fairness of the transaction is irrelevant (unless an exemption specifically takes fairness into account) and there is little play in the language for judicial discretion.

Because of these prohibitions a fiduciary must always make a prudent investigation to ensure that a party in interest is not involved in a transaction. *Marshall v. Kelly* (W.D.Okl.1978). For substantial transactions, the fiduciary must make a thorough investigation of any other party's relationships to the plan. For day-to-day transactions, a check of a current list of parties in interest may be enough. Joint Explanatory Statement [5087].

The prohibitions are very strict. A violation does not depend on whether the plan sustained monetary loss, *Marshall v. Kelly* (W.D.Okl.1978), and there is liability unless some exemption (discussed below) applies. The specific prohibitions are as follows.

a.   Property Transactions

A fiduciary may not cause a plan to engage in a direct or indirect sale, exchange, or lease of property with a party in interest.   ERISA § 406(a)(1)(A). The aim of the rule is to ensure that property transactions are at arm's-length.   "Sale or exchange" includes a transfer by a party in interest of property subject to a mortgage or lien, if either the plan assumes the lien or the party in interest placed it on the property within ten years before the transfer.   ERISA § 406(c).   Note that the prohibition (like all others in section 406(a)) extends to "indirect" transactions with parties in interest. Thus, it was a prohibited transaction for a union to trade in its old airplane to the manufacturer, where the plan covering the union's members simultaneously purchased the plane from the manufacturer.   *McDougall v. Donovan* (N.D.Ill.1982).

In *Commissioner v. Keystone Consolidated Industries, Inc.* (S.Ct.1993), the Supreme Court held that an employer's transfer of unencumbered property to a plan in satisfaction of its funding obligation is a prohibited transaction.   The Court observed that, under tax law, it is well settled that a transfer of property in satisfaction of a monetary obligation is ordinarily a "sale or exchange."   The Court further emphasized that contributions of property involve a danger of overvaluation to the detriment of the plan.   Finally, the Court rejected the argument that the definition of "sale or exchange" in the corresponding tax provision, IRC § 4975(f)(3), excludes transfers of unencumbered property. The court read the provision as simply expanding the definition of "sale or exchange" to include transfers of encumbered property.

b. Loans

A fiduciary may not cause a plan to engage in a direct or indirect loan of money or extension of credit with a party in interest. ERISA § 406(a)(1)(B). This provision is especially important in barring loans to the employer, a common practice before ERISA. Note, however, that it bars loans no matter which way the money flows. Thus, it was a prohibited transaction for a bank's pension plan to borrow money from the bank. *Brock v. Citizens Bank of Clovis* (10th Cir.1988). The rule, through the "indirect" language, also prohibits loan guarantees by a party in interest.

c. Goods and Services

Another type of prohibited transaction is the furnishing of goods, services or facilities between the plan and a party in interest (again, no matter who does the furnishing). ERISA § 406(a)(1)(C). Because all suppliers of services are parties in interest, this rule has the effect of prohibiting the rendition of services to a plan. Obviously, there must be exceptions so that the plan can obtain what it needs to operate. The exceptions are discussed below.

d. Asset Transfer

The direct or indirect transfer of plan assets to, or the use of them by or for, a party in interest, is also prohibited. ERISA § 406(a)(1)(D). "Assets," here, includes income. However, "transfer" of plan assets does not encompass the payment of benefits under the terms of the plan. Thus, the payment of benefits conditioned on a release of employment-related claims against the employer is not prohibited by ERISA § 406(a)(1)(D). *Lockheed Corp. v. Spink* (S.Ct.1996).

This prohibition takes in some of the prior ones, but sweeps more broadly. For example, the investment of plan assets in a takeover target of the employer has been held to be a violation, *Leigh v. Engle* (7th Cir.1984), a conclusion also suggested by the Joint Explanatory Statement [5089]. In barring the use of plan assets indirectly for the benefit of a party in interest, the rule potentially overlaps the prohibition of section 406(b)(2) (discussed below). It is subject to the same disagreements over interpretation (see below) as is section 406(b).

e. Employer Stock and Employer Real Property

The last of the party in interest rules is a prohibition of the plan's acquisition of an employer security or employer real property. ERISA §§ 406(a)(1)(E) & 407(a). A comparable rule prohibits fiduciaries who have responsibility for management of plan assets from knowingly permitting a plan to hold employer securities or employer real property. ERISA § 406(a)(2). Discussion of these rules is deferred to Chapter 14.

f. Corresponding Code Provisions

The prohibited transaction provisions of the Code impose taxes on disqualified persons; they do not expressly prohibit any fiduciary conduct. The standards of IRC § 4975(c)(1)(A)-(D) are essentially the same as those in ERISA § 406(a). There is no counterpart, however, to the Title I prohibition on the acquisition and holding of employer stock and real property.

2. THE SELF–DEALING RULES

Section 406(b) prohibits three categories of fiduciary self-dealing and conflict of interest. Because of the open-ended language of these prohibitions, important questions have arisen about their interpretation.

a. Self–Dealing and Adverse Interest

Section 406(b) prohibits fiduciaries from acting other than on behalf of the plan. ERISA § 406(b)(1) states that a fiduciary shall not "deal with the assets of the plan in his own interest or for his own account." (*See also* IRC § 4975(c)(1)(E).) And ERISA § 406(b)(2) correspondingly requires a fiduciary not to act "in any transaction involving the plan on behalf of a party (or represent a party) whose interests are adverse to the interests of the plan or the interests of its participants and beneficiaries." The questions that arise are how far the prohibitions extend and what, if anything, they add to the exclusive benefit rule.

The problematic cases are those in which the fiduciary, on behalf of the plan, deals with a third party under circumstances where the fiduciary might obtain some benefit or suffer some detriment as a result of the dealing. The danger, which results from divided loyalty, is much the same as that arising when employer-fiduciaries participate in hostile takeovers, discussed in Chapter 12. The DOL has taken a very expansive view of section 406, reading it as "impos[ing] on fiduciaries the duty of undivided loyalty to the plans for which they act. When fiduciaries exercise the authority, control or responsibility which makes them plan fiduciaries in transactions in which they have other business or personal interests, or represent parties who have such interests, the fiduciaries have engaged in [prohibited] transactions." Exemption Application No. D–7257. The DOL position rejects the possibility of weighing interests and loyalties; fiduciary action that is subject to competing interests or loyalties is enough for violation. To avoid liability where some action is required, a fiduciary subject to competing loyalties or interests would have to step aside. While some courts have taken a relatively expansive view of ERISA § 406(b)(1) & (2), none have been willing to go as far as the DOL.

A few courts have taken a crabbed view of the scope of these provisions. In *Donovan v. Bierwirth* (2d Cir.1982), the facts of which are described in Chapter 12, the court brushed aside section 406(b), construing it narrowly. The discussion was condensed, but the court appeared to believe that only section 406(b)(2) was even arguably applicable, and that the section proscribed only direct dealings between the plan and a party having an adverse interest, in which the fiduciaries acted on behalf of that other party. Another restricted interpretation was given in *Brock v. Citizens Bank of Clovis* (10th Cir.1988). There, the trustees of a pension plan for a bank's employees, who were also bank officers, caused the plan to loan money to unrelated persons who used the proceeds to pay off loans to the bank. The court held that, so long as the loans were not sham transactions, nothing in section 406(b) prohibited them.

In contrast to these cases, *Leigh v. Engle* (7th Cir.1984) approved an expansive interpretation, concluding that the provisions "should be read broadly in light of Congress' concern with the welfare of plan beneficiaries." Thus, it interpreted "interest" in section 406(b) to include both financial and nonfinancial interests. Accordingly, because in a contest for corporate control, an officer of the acquiror who is also a plan fiduciary might find it in her interest to assist the corporation, the prohibitions of section 406(b) would be triggered. The court, however, declined to hold that such a conflict amounted to a *per se* violation. In *Sando-*

val v. Simmons (C.D.Ill.1985), a district court, following *Leigh*, held that, for interests to be "adverse" for purposes of section 406(b)(2), it is enough that they be different. And in *Lowen v. Tower Asset Management, Inc.* (2d Cir.1987), the court that decided *Bierwirth* moved substantially towards the DOL's position in dictum and explained that the prohibitions of section 406(b):

> [G]ive[ ] notice to fiduciaries that they must either avoid the transactions described ... or cease serving in their capacity as fiduciaries, no matter how sincerely they may believe that such transactions will benefit the plan. Such protection of beneficiaries and notice to fiduciaries requires that Section 406(b) be broadly construed, ... and that liability be imposed even where there is "no taint of scandal, no hint of self-dealing, no trace of bad faith"....

b. Kickbacks

Section 406(b)(3) prohibits a fiduciary from receiving any personal consideration "from any party dealing with [the] plan in connection with a transaction involving the assets of the plan." (*See also* IRC § 4975(c)(1)(F).) The evident purpose is to prevent kickbacks.

The provision is violated whether or not the fiduciary is influenced or the plan sustains harm. *Brink v. DaLesio* (D.Md.1980). The "in connection with" language reflects a modification of the stricter trust law standard. The change is necessary in light of the complex interests of investment advisors and investment managers who serve as plan fiduciaries. They may well have independent financial dealings with parties who deal with the plan. One court has held that the burden is on the fiduciary to show, through clear and convincing evidence, that a payment to her by a party dealing with the plan was not in connection with the plan transaction. *Lowen v. Tower Asset Management, Inc.* (2d Cir. 1987).

C. EXEMPTIONS

The breadth and stringency of the section 406 prohibitions make exceptions necessary. Otherwise, for example, a plan would be unable to pay its accountants and other service providers, making its operation virtually impossible. Hence, there are statutory exemptions, ERISA § 408, supplemented by administrative ones. These exemptions are from section 406 only; they are not exemptions from sections 404 or 405. Many of the exceptions are not available for transactions involving an *owner-employee* (as defined in the statute). ERISA § 408(d).

1. STATUTORY EXEMPTIONS

Of the many statutory exemptions, only some of the more important ones can be discussed here.

a. Participant Loans

ERISA § 408(b)(1) permits loans to parties in interest who are also participants or beneficiaries, so long as strict conditions are met. The conditions were described in Chapter 8. This statutory exemption is not an exemption from section 406(b)(3). 29 C.F.R. § 2550.408b–1(a)(2).

b. Operating Contracts

ERISA § 408(b)(2) permits contracts with parties in interest that make *reasonable arrangements* for office space and for services *necessary* to the establishment or operation of the plan, so long as no more than *reasonable compensation* is paid. The exemption is only from section 406(a). 29 C.F.R. § 2550.408b–2(a) & (e).

No contract or arrangement is reasonable unless the plan may, without penalty, terminate it on reasonably short notice, so as to avoid being locked into a disadvantageous long-term relationship. 29 C.F.R. § 2550.408b–2(c). A service is necessary if it is appropriate and helpful to the plan in carrying out its purposes. Goods necessary for the establishment or operation of the plan may be furnished incidentally. 29 C.F.R. § 2550.408b–2(b). Whether compensation is reasonable depends on the facts. However, compensation to a fiduciary who is already receiving full-time pay from an employer or union is never reasonable, except for reimbursement of expenses actually and properly incurred. ERISA § 408(c)(2); 29 C.F.R. § 2550.408c–2.

c. Banks and Insurers

Two provisions allow banks and insurers to provide services to their own plans. ERISA § 408(b)(4) permits a plan covering employees of a bank or similar institution (or of an affiliate of one), in some circumstances to invest plan assets in deposits with the institution that bear a reasonable rate of interest. Similarly, section 408(b)(5) permits a plan to purchase insurance or annuities from a qualified insurer who is the employer maintaining the plan. A plan may also purchase insurance, in some circumstances, from a party in interest wholly owned (directly or indirectly) by either the employer maintaining the plan or some other party in interest.

Several other exemptions relate to banks and insurance companies. ERISA § 408(b)(8) provides an exemption for certain plan investments in common or collective trust funds, or pooled investment funds, maintained by a party in interest that is a bank or trust company; and for investments in a pooled investment fund of a qualified insurance company. ERISA § 408(b)(6) permits a bank that is a fiduciary to offer ancillary services, such as maintenance of a non-interest bearing checking account to pay plan expenses, provided that certain internal safeguards are met.

2. STATUTORY CLARIFICATIONS

In addition to the exemptions, ERISA contains three clarifications of the scope of the prohibited transaction rules. First, a fiduciary may receive a benefit to which she is entitled as a participant or beneficiary, so long it is computed and paid consistently with the plan terms as they are applied to all other participants and beneficiaries. ERISA § 408(c)(1). Second, a fiduciary may receive reasonable compensation for services rendered and reimbursement for expenses incurred. ERISA § 408(c)(2). Third, already discussed in Chapter 12, a fiduciary may be an officer, employee, agent or representative of a party in interest. ERISA § 408(c)(3).

3. ADMINISTRATIVE EXEMPTIONS

When enacting the prohibited transaction rules, Congress recognized that "some transactions which are prohibited (and for which there are no statutory exemptions) nevertheless should be allowed in order not to disrupt the established business practices of financial institutions which often perform[ ] fiduciary functions in connection with these plans consistent with adequate safeguards to protect employee benefit plans." It also recognized that exemptions might be appropriate in connection with individual transactions that provide "substantial independent safeguards for the plan participants and beneficiaries." Joint Explanatory Statement [5089–90]. To deal with these cases, it delegated to the Secretaries of Labor and Treasury the authority to grant exemptions from the prohibited transaction rules.

ERISA § 408(a) directs the Secretary of Labor to establish a procedure for doing this, and sets general standards. The exemptions may be conditional or unconditional, fiduciary- or transaction-based, and applicable only to specific individuals or to an entire class. Any such exemption must be administratively feasible, in the interests of the plan and its participants and beneficiaries, and protective of the rights of participants and beneficiaries. A similar directive applies to the Secretary of the Treasury. IRC § 4975(c)(2). However, under the ERISA Reorganization Plan most authority to grant prohibited transaction exemptions has been allocated to the Department of Labor. Pursuant to this authority, the DOL has issued a regulation prescribing the procedure for obtaining exemptions. 29 C.F.R. §§ 2570.30 to .52.

The DOL has issued a substantial number of class exemptions since 1975, announcing categories of transactions that are exempt from some or all prohibited transaction rules. The first one (PTE 75–1) responded to a pointed suggestion in the Joint Explanatory Statement and granted exemptions for various securities-related transactions and services involving broker-dealers, reporting dealers, and banks. Another important exemption (PTE 84–14) is the qualified professional asset manager, or "QPAM," exemption. This one allows otherwise prohibited transactions in plan assets, so long as the assets are managed by a *qualified professional asset manager* who is independent of the parties in interest and who meets other standards. A QPAM may be a bank, insurance company or registered investment advisor. Yet another class exemption (PTE 79–15) exempts transactions authorized or required by judicial decree in cases where the DOL or IRS has been a party.

The DOL has also granted many individual exemptions. Unlike class exemptions, these are limited to specific parties and transactions. The exemptions have covered a wide variety of transactions. Common subjects include the sale of real property (which usually must be approved by an independent fiduciary), leasing arrangements, stock purchases, and loans (for example to the employer).

D. REMEDIES

1. FIDUCIARIES

A civil action may be brought under ERISA §§ 409 & 502(a)(2) on behalf of the plan against fiduciaries who violate section 406. Suits under these provisions were discussed in Chapter 12. A suit for equitable relief may also be brought by a participant, beneficiary or other fiduciary under ERISA § 502(a)(3), or by the Secretary of Labor under ERISA § 502(a)(5). In addition, civil penalties may be imposed pursuant to ERISA § 502(l). These penalties were discussed in Chapter 12.

2. PARTIES IN INTEREST

Parties in interest who participate in a violation of section 406 may be subject to a suit for equitable relief under ERISA § 502(a)(3) or (a)(5). *Harris Trust & Savings Bank v. Salomon Smith Barney* (S.Ct.2000). They may also be liable to pay a civil penalty under ERISA § 502(*l*). The amount of the penalty is 20% of the amount recovered by the Secretary, through a judicial proceeding or settlement, reduced by the amount of other penalties or taxes (described below). ERISA § 502(*l*)(2) & (4). The Secretary has discretion to reduce or waive the penalty in appropriate cases. ERISA § 502(*l*)(3).

ERISA § 502(i) provides for the imposition of a civil penalty on parties in interest who engage in a prohibited transaction with any plan other than a qualified plan. The amount of the penalty is up to 5% of the amount involved in the transaction for each year in which the transaction continues. If the prohibited transaction is not corrected within 90 days after notice from the Secretary of Labor, the penalty may increase to up to 100% of the amount involved.

The Internal Revenue Code imposes special taxes on prohibited transactions involving qualified plans and IRAs, which correspond to the civil penalties of ERISA § 502(i). The tax is owed by any disqualified person who participates except a fiduciary acting only as such. The initial tax is 15% of the *amount involved* in the transaction. IRC § 4975(a). The amount involved is the greater of the amount of money and fair market value of property given, and the amount received. Fair market value is determined as of the date of the transaction. In certain cases involving services, the amount involved is the compensation in excess of what is reasonable or otherwise permitted. IRC § 4975(f)(4).

Each participating disqualified person is jointly and severally liable for the tax. If the transaction extends over several years—for example, a lease— the tax is cumulative. Thus, a four-year lease will subject a disqualified person to a tax for the first year measured by the entire value of the lease; plus a tax for the second year measured by the value of the last three years of the lease; and so forth. *Lambos v. Commissioner* (Tax Ct.1987).

If the tax is not paid within the *taxable period*, an additional tax of 100% of the amount involved is imposed. IRC § 4975(b). Here, the amount involved is determined by the money and highest fair market value of the property given or received during the taxable period. IRC § 4975(f)(4)(B). The taxable period begins with the date of the prohibited transaction and ends on the earliest of the date of mailing of a notice of deficiency by the IRS; the date of assessment of the 15% tax; or the date on which *correction* of the prohibited transaction is completed. IRC § 4975(f)(2). Correction means undoing the transaction to the extent possible, and, in any event, placing the plan in a financial position no worse than it would be had the disqualified person been acting under the highest fiduciary standards. IRC § 4975(f)(5).

CHAPTER 14

EMPLOYER SECURITIES AND EMPLOYEE STOCK OWN-ERSHIP PLANS

A plan's investment in securities of the employer creates several threats to participants. First, it presents opportunities for self-dealing by the employer and others. Second, it reduces the participants' economic diversification: if the employer fails, they lose not only their jobs but part of their retirement security as well. Unsurprisingly, such an investment is a prohibited transaction. ERISA §§ 406(a)(1)(E) & 407(a).

Yet there are countervailing considerations. Plan investment in stock of the employer gives employees an ownership stake in the enterprise. Employee ownership can benefit employers by providing an incentive for productivity and commitment. It can benefit employees as well, by enabling them to reap in capital what they sow in labor. Because of these countervailing considerations, ERISA treats plan transactions in employer stock very differently than other prohibited transactions. In fact, ERISA strongly encourages *employee stock ownership plans*, or ESOPs, which are designed to invest primarily in employer stock.

ESOPs are unique in the extent to which they financially integrate the employer and the plan. They are also unique in the the extent to which ERISA encourages employer usage of them: ESOPs are treated not only as plans but as legitimate devices for generating equity and debt financing. Yet at the same time ERISA continues to demand with respect to ESOPs the same stringent protection of participants and beneficiaries that it demands with respect to all other plans. The need to protect employee benefit interests in the context of employer financial uses generates a controversial and complex body of law.

A. EMPLOYER SECURITIES

1. DEFINITIONS

For purposes of Title I, an *employer security* with respect to a plan is a security issued by the employer of the participants, or by an affiliate. ERISA § 407(d)(1). *Security* here has the meaning given to it under section 2(1) of the Securities Act of 1933. ERISA § 3(20). A *qualifying employer security* is an employer security that is either stock, a *marketable obligation*, or certain publicly traded partnership interests. ERISA § 407(d)(5). The concept of qualifying employer security is important because it is the only kind of employer security that plans are allowed to hold.

A marketable obligation is a bond, debenture, note or other evidence of indebtedness that meets two criteria. First, it is acquired either in the market, or from an underwriter or issuer, at a fair price (under statutory criteria). Second, the plan investment in the given obligation and in other employer obligations is not excessive (again, under standards set down in the statute). ERISA § 407(e).

For plans other than eligible individual account plans (explained below), stock is a qualifying employer security only if two additional standards are met. First, immediately following the acquisition of the stock, no more than 25% of the outstanding stock of the same class is owned by the plan. Second, at least 50% of the outstanding stock of the same class is owned by persons independent of the issuer. ERISA § 407(d)(5) & (f)(1).

There are concepts analogous to employer securities involving real property. *Employer real property* means real property leased by the plan to the employer or an affiliate. ERISA § 407(d)(2). *Qualifying employer real property* means parcels of employer real property of which a substantial number are geographically dispersed; each parcel and its improvements can be adapted, without excessive cost, to more than one use; and their acquisition and retention do not violate any fiduciary standards. ERISA § 407(d)(4).

Another important concept is the *eligible individual account plan*. This is a profit-sharing plan, stock bonus plan or employee stock ownership plan (or one of a few other varieties of plan), that expressly provides for the acquisition and holding of qualifying employer securities or qualifying employer real property, and the benefits from which do not reduce benefits payable under any defined benefit plan.   ERISA § 407(d)(3).   Eligible individual account plans are subject to special treatment with respect to the holding of employer securities.

2.   PROHIBITED TRANSACTIONS AND EXEMPTIONS

Two types of plan dealings in employer securities are governed by detailed sets of prohibited transaction rules: acquiring and holding the securities, and borrowing the funds to acquire them.   Title I is the primary source of rules to govern the former and the Code is the primary source of rules to govern the latter.   We deal with the Title I rules here; the Code provisions concerning loans are treated below, in the discussion of ESOPs.

ERISA lays down two basic rules governing employer securities.   First, a plan may not acquire or hold any employer securities that are not qualifying employer securities.   ERISA § 407(a)(1)(A).   Second, a plan may not acquire qualifying employer securities (or qualifying employer real property) if, immediately after the acquisition, the fair market value of employer securities and real property held by the plan exceeds 10% of the fair market value of its total assets.   ERISA § 407(a)(2).

There is an important exception to the second rule. The 10% limitation does not apply to the acquisition or holding of qualifying employer securities (or qualifying employer real property) by eligible individual account plans. ERISA § 407(b)(1). An eligible individual account plan may hold as much of its assets in qualifying employer securities as the fiduciaries choose, consistently with the terms of the plan and other provisions of ERISA.

The acquisition or sale of qualifying employer securities is a prima facie violation of the prohibited transaction rule governing sales or exchanges of plan property if the transaction is with a party in interest. ERISA § 408(e) provides an exemption for eligible individual account plans (and for other plans that comply with the 10% limitation). Under it, the acquisition or sale of qualifying employer securities is exempt from ERISA §§ 406(a), (b)(1) & (2), if no commission is charged and the acquisition or sale is for *adequate consideration*.

In the case of a marketable obligation, adequate consideration means a price no less favorable than the price required under ERISA § 407(e). Otherwise, ERISA's general definition applies. 29 C.F.R. § 2550.408e(d). Under that definition, adequate consideration means the following. If there is a generally recognized market for the securities, adequate consideration is either the prevailing price on a national securities exchange (if there is one) or the offering price quoted by persons independent of the issuer or any party in interest. Where there is no generally recognized market, adequate consideration is fair market value determined in good faith by the trustee or named fiduciary pursuant to the terms of the plan. ERISA § 3(18). The DOL has proposed a regulation to further clarify the meaning of adequate consideration. Under it, "fair market value" is defined as the price at which the asset would change hands between willing, informed buyers and sellers under no compulsion; "good faith" is defined as objective good faith. Criteria for good faith include a prudent inquiry and a written valuation by an independent person (who may be a fiduciary). When the price involves a control premium, actual control must pass to the plan; it must be reasonable to assume that control will not be dissipated shortly after the acquisition; and the seller must be able to have obtained a control premium in a sale to an unrelated third party. Prop. Reg. 29 C.F.R. § 2510.3–18(b).

3. EXCEPTIONS TO FIDUCIARY REQUIREMENTS

ERISA exempts eligible individual account plans from the diversification requirements of ERISA § 404(a)(1)(B) & (C) with respect to the acquisition or holding and qualifying employer securities and real property. ERISA § 404(a)(2). Other fiduciary standards, though, continue to apply. Thus, for example, changed circumstances may render it imprudent for an ESOP fiduciary to continue to invest in employer stock, even if the plan instrument permits it to do so. *Moench v. Robertson* (3d Cir. 1995).

There is no exemption from the fiduciary standards for any other plan's transactions in employer securities. Hence, even where a plan holds less than 10% of the value of its assets in qualifying employer securities, the fiduciaries may still have violated the standards of prudence and diversification.

B. ESOPS

1. ESOPS IN GENERAL

An employee stock ownership plan is either a qualified stock bonus plan, or combination stock bonus and money purchase plan both of which are qualified, that is designed to invest primarily in *qualifying employer securities.* IRC § 4975(e)(7)(A). Additional requirements, prescribed by the Code and by Treasury regulations, are discussed below.

The term, *qualifying employer security*, has a different meaning for the Code's ESOP rules than it does for the Title I prohibited transaction rules. (The special features of ESOPs are governed mainly by the Code.) Here, a qualifying employer security, or employer security (the terms are equivalent under the Code), is common stock issued by the employer, or by a corporation that is a member of the same controlled group, which is readily tradable on an established securities market. IRC § 409(*l*)(1) & 4975(e)(8). Where there is no such readily tradable common stock, employer securities are shares of common stock having voting power and dividend rights, each respectively equal to or greater than the voting power and dividend rights of any other class of stock. IRC § 409(*l*)(2). Noncallable preferred stock that is convertible at any time, at a reasonable conversion price, into common stock that is an employer security, is also an employer security. IRC § 409(*l*)(3).

ESOPs can be valuable tools for corporate finance and corporate planning. An ESOP, for example, can provide equity capital by purchasing newly issued shares, or serve as an inside purchaser of the interest of a shareholder withdrawing from a close corporation. An ESOP can be used, alone or with other investors, to take a company private through a leveraged buyout. An ESOP can improve corporate cash flow, by permitting contributions toward retirement benefits to be made in stock rather than cash. Of course, there are disadvantages. One is that the issuance of new shares to an ESOP dilutes existing shareholder rights. Another is that use of an ESOP in financing still requires compliance with ERISA's fiduciary and other rules.

2. LEVERAGED ESOPS

In an ordinary ESOP, the employer either contributes stock, or contributes money that the ESOP uses to buy stock, on a yearly basis in amounts needed to satisfy current contribution requirements. By contrast, a leveraged ESOP borrows the funds to pay for the acquisition of a large block of

employer securities. The shares are then allocated
to participant accounts as the loan is repaid. The
loan is either obtained from the employer or obtained from another lender and guaranteed by the
employer. The shares may be purchased either
from the employer or on the open market.

There are significant tax advantages for the parties to the loan. To appreciate the most important
one, observe that, if the plan purchases the securities from the employer with a loan from a bank, the
employer gets the loan proceeds from the plan and
the net economic effect of the transaction is that of
a loan to the employer. However, the employer's
annual contributions to the plan for repayment of
principal and interest are deductible in an amount
up to 25% of the annual compensation of the participants (with provisions for carryover of the excess
to subsequent years). IRC § 404(a)(9). By contrast, only interest payments would be deductible
on an ordinary loan to the employer.

The favorable tax treatment of loans for stock
acquisition by ESOPs constitutes a large tax expenditure. It is also controversial. The purpose of the
favorable tax treatment is to encourage ESOPs.
The treatment is justifiable, provided that ESOPs
benefit participants in ways that ordinary plans do
not and significantly contribute to society and the
economy. Assertions that ESOPs provide those
benefits to a sufficiently great extent are subject to
conflicting evidence. Some argue that ESOPs are
harmful to the economy overall, *inter alia* in that

they help subsidize inefficient or dying businesses. Some also argue that, if ESOPs were truly beneficial to employers, they would flourish even without tax incentives.

3. ESOP LOANS

Employer loans to plans and guarantees of loans to plans are prohibited transactions. ERISA § 406(a)(1)(B). Hence, an exemption is needed if leveraged ESOPs are to be possible. Section 4975(d)(3) of the Code (or ERISA § 408(b)(3)) provides it. A loan to an ESOP by a party in interest, or guaranteed by a party in interest, is permitted so long as it is an *exempt loan*, i.e., is primarily for the benefit of the participants and beneficiaries, bears a reasonable rate of interest, and is secured, if at all, only by qualifying employer securities. Regulations clarify these standards.

a. Primary Benefit

To satisfy the requirement that a loan be primarily for the benefit of participants and beneficiaries, its proceeds must be used within a reasonable time, and only to purchase qualifying employer securities or to repay the loan or a prior exempt loan. The effect of the loan may not be to "drain[ ] off" plan assets. Its terms must be at least as favorable as terms of a comparable loan resulting from arm's-length negotiation. Treas. Reg. § 54.4975–7(b)(3) & (4).

The loan must be for a specific term. Treas. Reg. § 54.4975–7(b)(13). It must be without recourse against the ESOP; its only collateral may be qualifying employer securities that either were purchased with the loan or were collateral for a prior exempt loan that was repaid with proceeds of the new loan. The loan may be repaid only with collateral, contributions (other than employer securities) made to meet the loan obligations, and earnings attributable to collateral and investment of contributions. The value of plan assets transferred to the creditor in case of default may not exceed the amount of default. If the lender is a party in interest, the amount transferred may be only what is necessary to meet the repayment schedule. Treas. Reg. § 54.4975–7(b)(5) & (6).

b. Release of Collateral

If the securities purchased with the loan are used as collateral, the loan must provide for the annual release from encumbrance of a number of securities proportional to the amount of the loan repaid in the year. Regulations specify formulas that may be used to determine the number of shares released. Treas. Reg. § 54.4975–7(b)(8).

4. FURTHER ESOP REQUIREMENTS

There are many requirements with which ESOPs must comply. Some of the most important are as follows.

a. Designation

The plan document must specifically designate the plan as an ESOP. Treas. Reg. § 54.4975–11(a)(2).

b. Integration

An ESOP may not be integrated with social security. Treas. Reg. § 54.4975–11(a)(7)(ii).

c. Allocation to Accounts

All assets acquired with proceeds of an exempt loan must initially be placed in a suspense account and then withdrawn as the lender's security interest is released. The assets in the suspense account are assets of the plan. Treas. Reg. § 54.4975–11(c). At the end of each year, the ESOP must consistently allocate to participants' accounts units representing interests in assets withdrawn from the suspense account. Treas. Reg. § 54.4975–11(d)(2). There are limitations on allocations where the employer is an S corporation. IRC § 409(p).

d. Voting Rights

An ESOP must satisfy conditions on the voting of employer stock. IRC § 4975(e)(7). Where the employer has a *registration-type class of securities*, each ESOP participant or beneficiary must be entitled to direct the plan as to the voting of shares allocated to her account. IRC § 409(e)(2). This is

called *pass-through voting*. A registration-type
class of securities is a class of securities required to
be registered under section 12 of the Securities
Exchange Act, or which would be required to be
registered but for an exemption relating to interests
in collective funds issued in connection with qualified plans. IRC § 409(e)(4). (Registration-type securities are essentially publicly traded securities.)
The registration-type securities need not be the
ones held by the ESOP.

If the employer does not have a registration-type
class of securities, participants and beneficiaries
may still be entitled to direct the voting of shares
allocated to their account with respect to mergers,
dissolutions, recapitalizations, and sales of substantially all assets of a business. IRC § 409(e)(3).
This voting requirement is a qualification condition
for defined contribution plans (other than profit-
sharing plans) of employers whose stock is not
readily tradable on an established market, which
have more than 10% of their assets invested in
employer securities. IRC § 401(a)(22). The requirement may be satisfied by allowing each participant one vote and providing that the trustee should
vote the unallocated shares in proportion to the
votes of the participants. IRC § 409(e)(5).

e. Distribution Options

A participant entitled to a distribution from an
ESOP must be able to demand it in the form of
employer securities. IRC § 4975(e)(7) & 409(h)(1).

This prevents ESOPs from being used to keep employer stock in limited hands. The right does not apply to the part of the participant's account that she has diversified. (See below.) If the employer's charter or bylaws restrict ownership of substantially all outstanding employer securities to employees or to a plan, or if the employer is an S corporation, the ESOP may provide for distribution only in cash. IRC § 409(h)(2).

If the securities are not readily tradable, the distributee must have a put option—a right to demand that the employer repurchase the shares under a fair valuation formula. IRC § 409(h)(1)(B) & (4). This rule ensures that the securities will have value to the distributee. The put option cannot bind the plan, but the plan may assume the employer's obligation if it would be prudent for it to do so.

f. Timing of Distributions

If the participant (and spouse, if appropriate) elect, a distribution of her account balance will commence no later than one year after the close of the plan year in which she separates from service because of retirement, disability or death; or which is the fifth year after the plan year in which she otherwise separates from service (and is not reemployed before distribution would be required to begin). IRC § 4975(e)(7) & 409(*o*)(1)(A). Unless the participant elects otherwise, the distribution must be in substantially equal periodic payments, annual or more frequent, over a period not longer than five years (except in cases of very large account balances). IRC § 409(*o*)(1)(C). The account balance of a participant does not include securities acquired with an exempt loan until the close of the plan year in which the loan is repaid. IRC § 409(*o*)(1)(B).

g. Diversification

An ESOP must offer a special investment option to each *qualified participant*—a participant who is at least 55 and has completed at least 10 years of participation—in each of the first six plan years in which she is a qualified participant. Such participant must be able to direct the plan (within 90 days after the close of each plan year) as to the investment of at least 25% of her account in the first five years and 50% in the sixth. The plan must either provide three or more investment options, or distribute the portion of the account subject to the election. IRC § 401(a)(28)(B).

h. Appraisal

All valuations of employer securities that are not readily tradable on an established market must be performed by an independent appraiser. IRC § 401(a)(28)(C).

5. ADDITIONAL TAX ADVANTAGES

We have already discussed the tax advantages pertaining to ESOP loans. Two other important tax-related benefits for ESOPs are discussed here.

a. Dividend Deduction

Dividends normally are not deductible by the issuing corporation. However, in the case of a C corporation, if the dividends are paid on shares of employer stock held by an ESOP, the employer may deduct the amount of any such dividends that are: paid in cash directly to participants and beneficiaries; paid to the plan and then distributed in cash to participants and beneficiaries within 90 days of the close of the plan year; or used to repay the loan by which the securities were acquired. IRC § 404(k). Dividends are also deductible when the participants and beneficiaries are allowed to elect either payment in cash (either directly or through the plan) or reinvestment in additional employer stock held by the plan. IRC § 404(k)(2)(A)(ii); IRS Notice 2002–2.

b. Deferral of Capital Gains

To encourage the sale of all or a substantial portion of the shares of closely held small businesses to ESOPs, IRC § 1042 provides that the sale of stock in a domestic C corporation to an ESOP is eligible for deferral of capital gains tax on the sale proceeds if several requirements are met. First, the corporation must have no stock outstanding that is readily tradable on an established securities market, and the stock in question must not have been received in a distribution from the plan (or through certain other means). IRC § 1042(c)(1).

Second, after the sale, the plan must hold at least 30% of either each class of outstanding stock of the corporation or of the total value of all outstanding stock. IRC § 1042(b)(2). Third, the shareholder must elect deferral. IRC § 1042(a)(1). Fourth, the employer must consent in writing to the application of IRC § 4978, which imposes a tax on it if the ESOP disposes of a certain portion of the shares within three years; and IRC § 4979A, which imposes a tax on certain prohibited allocations of the stock. IRC § 1042(b)(3). Fifth, the shareholder must have held the stock for three years as of the date of sale. IRC § 1042(b)(4). Sixth, within the period beginning three months before the sale and ending 12 months after it, the shareholder must purchase *qualified replacement property*. IRC § 1042(a)(2) & (c)(3). Qualified replacement property is a security of any domestic operating corporation, except the employer or a member of its controlled group, or certain other corporations. IRC § 1042(c)(4). Seventh, no part of the assets acquired by the ESOP may accrue to the benefit of the selling shareholder or members of her family for a period of at least 10 years, or to the benefit of a 25% shareholder at any time. IRC § 409(n). Eighth, the shareholder cannot itself be a C corporation. IRC § 1042(c)(7).

If the criteria for deferral are satisfied, the shareholder recognizes long-term capital gain on the sale only to the extent that the amount realized exceeds the cost of the qualified replacement property. IRC § 1042(a). There are rules providing for the adjustment of the basis of the qualified replacement property by the gain not recognized, and for recapture of gain upon disposition of that property. IRC § 1042(d) & (e).

C. ESOPS AND CORPORATE CONTROL CONTESTS

Many ESOPs are established to defend against tender offers or proxy fights. The defensive value of an ESOP is that it puts a large block of shares in presumably friendly hands. This use has become sufficiently common that the SEC treats certain ESOPs as anti-takeover measures and requires disclosure of information about their defensive character in proxy statements. *SEC v. Evans* (SEC 1989); Securities Exchange Act Release No. 15230.

The defensive use of ESOPs generates troublesome questions about the duties of persons responsible for the ESOP—officers and directors, and plan fiduciaries—to persons who have interests in it— the corporation, shareholders, employees, participants and beneficiaries. We have already examined one such problem: the demands of the duty of loyalty when employer-fiduciaries make critical decisions in corporate control contests (see Chapter 12). In this section we survey others.

1. FIDUCIARY CONSIDERATIONS IN VOTING AND TENDERING

Many ESOPs provide for *mirrored pass-through voting*, an arrangement where participants vote shares allocated to their accounts and the trustee votes unallocated shares in proportion to the participants' votes. There may be analogous provisions for tendering shares. In highly leveraged ESOPs, this can give a participant control of hundreds of unallocated shares for every one allocated to her account. Since employees are likely to support management in takeover and proxy contests, this makes the ESOP a powerful defensive tool. The Department of Labor has taken the position that pass-through voting and tendering are not always appropriate, and that mirrored pass-through voting and tendering may be inconsistent with ERISA's fiduciary rules.

The foundation of the DOL position is that voting and tendering securities held by a plan are fiduciary acts, part of plan asset management. 29 C.F.R. § 2509.94–2. The fiduciary rules demand that voting and tendering decisions be made independently by the fiduciary to whom the relevant authority has been assigned. This responsibility cannot be avoided. *DOL Letter re: Avon Products, Inc. Employees' Retirement Plan* (1988). Any decision on how to vote or tender must be made prudently, and solely in the interests of the participants and beneficiaries and for the exclusive purpose of providing benefits. It is not permissible to take into account other interests, such as ones relating to the participants' employment. *See* Gen. Couns. Mem. 39870 (1992).

The application of these principles to ESOPs (and other plans) with pass-through voting has been controversial. The DOL accepts that participants may direct votes and tenders of allocated shares, but only on the theory that the participant is a limited named fiduciary with respect to such directions. *DOL Letter re: Profit–Sharing Retirement Income Plan for the Employees of Carter Hawley Hale Stores, Inc.* (1984); *DOL Letter re: Polaroid Corp. Stock Equity Plan* (1989). A consequence of the theory is that the plan trustee is a directed trustee and that participant directions must be proper. ERISA § 403(a)(1). Accordingly, while a plan trustee may generally follow participant directions, it must ignore them where participants have been subjected to undue pressure or where following the directions would result in a violation of ERISA. At least one court has agreed, holding that a trustee acted properly when, after a prudent investigation, it chose to tender all allocated shares at an exceptionally favorable price, without consulting the participants. *Central Trust Co. v. American Avents Corp.* (S.D.Ohio 1989). A consequence of the DOL's position is that Title I fiduciary standards can trump the pass-through requirement of IRC § 409(e).

Two arguments can be advanced to justify fiduciary override of participant directions. First, since participants may be subject to direct or indirect employer pressure, override is needed as another means to protect benefit interests. Second, a participant, like an employer-fiduciary, is an interested party. She may decide how to vote or whether to tender on the basis of job concerns, rather than on the basis of providing retirement benefits to herself and others. *See Danaher Corp. v. Chicago Pneumatic Tool Co.* (II) (S.D.N.Y.1986). Because tax subsidies and legal protections are given in order to ensure retirement support, fiduciary override may be proper to ensure that the subsidies and other advantages are not misused.

As to participant failure to exercise the power to vote or tender, the DOL position is that the trustee has full fiduciary responsibility. In particular, it may not blindly proceed in a manner specified in the plan, such as to vote in favor of management or in proportion to the other participants' votes. (A trustee's voting allocated shares for which no directions are received does not violate the pass-through voting requirements of IRC § 409(e). Rev. Rul. 95–57). The DOL takes the same position regarding unallocated shares. The reason is that ERISA § 404(a)(1)(D) requires that plan provisions be followed only to the extent they are consistent with ERISA; in particular, with the duties of prudence and loyalty. *DOL Letter re: Polaroid Corp. Stock Equity Plan* (1989).

One court has substantially agreed with the DOL and held that the trustee had to exercise independent judgment regarding the tendering of unallocated shares, at least where participants did not receive notice that they had responsibility regarding those unallocated shares (because without such notice the participants could not be fiduciaries with respect to those shares). *Herman v. NationsBank*

Trust Co. (Georgia), N.A. (11th Cir.1997). The court, however, disagreed with the DOL's position on undirected allocated shares, holding that participants were named fiduciaries where they had been given proper instructions as to how a failure to direct the shares would be treated.

The DOL has itself confused this area of law by issuing a letter stating that the trustee of a collectively bargained plan must follow plan provisions that require unallocated and non-directed allocated shares to be voted in accordance with participant instructions unless the trustee can advance "well founded reasons" why doing so would violate ERISA. *DOL Letter re: Pass–Through Voting Provisions in Collectively Bargained Employee Stock Ownership Plans* (1995).

Some have argued that the standards urged by the DOL would make little difference. Requiring an independent fiduciary to have responsibility for voting or tendering will not necessarily ensure proper decisionmaking where the fiduciary—usually a bank or investment advisor or manager—is dependent on the employer for retention. Thus, the argument proceeds, such fiduciary may have little incentive to vote against management in a proxy contest or tender shares against management's wishes. Yet while the argument has force, it is important not to overstate it. Although fiduciaries retained by the employer do tend to favor management in proxy contests and tender offers, it is a tendency, not an inevitability. There is still protection to be gained through having decisions made by an independent fiduciary, even one hired by corporate management.

2. STATE CORPORATION LAW

a. The Business Judgment Rule

Some defensive ESOPs have been challenged under state corporation law. The basis for challenge is that the ESOP was established to entrench management, rather than benefit the company, in violation of the directors' corporate fiduciary duty.

Unlike the duty of ERISA fiduciaries to a plan, the fiduciary duty of directors to a corporation is not always a stringent one. Courts generally evaluate director conduct under the business judgment rule: a strong presumption that disinterested directors have acted in good faith, in the best interests of the company, and after reasonable inquiry. When the rule is invoked, a board's decision will be upheld absent abuse of discretion. The establishment of an ESOP before a takeover or other threat emerges is an action that has potential to benefit the company, e.g. through increased productivity. In such cases the business judgment rule is usually invoked and the ESOP upheld. *See Danaher Corp. v. Chicago Pneumatic Tool Co.* (I) (S.D.N.Y.1986). *But see RCM Securities Fund, Inc. v. Stanton* (2d Cir.1991).

However, if a takeover threat has emerged, the establishment of the ESOP is more likely to have been motivated by self interest. The directors' decisionmaking is also more likely to have been rushed. It is not entirely settled how courts should evaluate the ESOP, but many plans established after the emergence of a takeover threat have been held invalid. Generally, the protection of the business judgment rule has been held lost and the ESOP found to have been established primarily (even if not exclusively) to entrench management. *See, e.g., NCR Corp. v. American Telephone & Telegraph Co.* (S.D.Ohio 1991); *Norlin Corp. v. Rooney, Pace Inc.* (2d Cir.1984).

Delaware courts have developed an approach to assessing takeover defenses. They have held that, for the business judgment rule to apply to defenses established after a threat materializes, the directors must establish reasonable grounds for believing that a danger to corporate policy and effectiveness exists. This requires that they act in good faith only after a reasonable investigation. Furthermore, the measures taken must be reasonable in relation to the threat posed. *Unocal Corp. v. Mesa Petroleum Co.* (Del.Super.1985). If the business judgment rule is found inapplicable, the measure will be judged for its "entire fairness" to the corporation.

The meaning of this standard is uncertain. Two non-Delaware decisions applying Delaware law have invalidated defensive ESOPs under it. *NCR Corp. v. American Telephone & Telegraph Co.* (S.D.Ohio 1991); *Buckhorn, Inc. v. Ropak Corp.* (S.D.Ohio 1987). In *Shamrock Holdings, Inc. v. Polaroid*

Corp. (Del.Ch.1989), however, a Delaware court applied the test to uphold a defensive ESOP. There, a corporation, expecting an immediate, unwanted tender offer, established a leveraged ESOP with enough newly issued shares effectively to prevent the offeror from acquiring the 85% of outstanding shares needed under Delaware law (see below) to be able to merge the offeror and target. The company had previously approved a small ESOP as an incentive to employees, but had not implemented it. The court found that the directors had failed to establish reasonable grounds for believing that a danger existed, but upheld the ESOP nonetheless under the entire fairness test. It found that the ESOP would not have an adverse impact on business operations and productivity, that it would not be an ironclad takeover defense, and that it would not have a substantial dilutive effect on existing shareholders. In a subsequent case, the Delaware Supreme Court explained the *Polaroid* decision as based on the ESOP's having been established before the takeover bid. *Paramount Communications, Inc. v. Time Inc.* (Del.Super.1989).

b. Preemption Issues

An unaddressed issue in the state law cases is whether state law should even apply. ERISA preempts any state law to the extent it "relate[s] to" a covered plan. (See Chapter 15.) The state laws in question relate to ERISA plans and so arguably should have been held preempted. If so, the validity of the ESOPs would have to be determined under ERISA (which does not impose fiduciary constraints, since the matter is one of plan establishment; see chapter 12) or else under federal common law.

Another state corporation law that applies to ESOPs, and that may be preempted, is the Delaware statute involved in *Shamrock*. 8 Del. Code § 203 provides that a person who acquires 15% of the shares of a corporation cannot engage in a merger or similar transaction with the corporation for three years unless it obtains 85% of the shares in the transaction by which it obtained 15%. The statute specifies that, for purposes of counting outstanding shares, stock held by ESOPs will not be considered if participants do not have the right confidentially to determine whether shares held by the plan should be tendered. The case for preemption here is strengthened by the fact that, as the DOL urges, ERISA's fiduciary provisions may prohibit participants from determining whether unallocated shares should be tendered.

CHAPTER 15

PREEMPTION

Unlike most statutes, ERISA describes the extent of its preemption of state law. ERISA § 514(a) announces that, with certain exceptions, "the provisions of [title I] and title IV shall supersede any and all State laws insofar as they may now or hereafter relate to any employee benefit plan" covered under ERISA § 4. "State law" includes "all laws, decisions, rules, regulations, or other State action having the effect of law"; "State" includes political subdivisions and "any agency or instrumentality [of a state or subdivision] which purports to regulate, directly or indirectly, the terms and conditions of employee benefit plans covered by [title I]." ERISA § 514(c). Section 514 is the most expansive preemption provision contained in federal law.

It has few exceptions. The major one is subsection (b)(2)(A), which states that, "[e]xcept as provided in subparagraph (B), nothing in this title shall be construed to exempt or relieve any person from any law of any State which regulates insurance." (There is a similar exemption for state banking and securities laws.) State insurance laws are thereby saved from preemption, a result consistent with the policy stated in section 1 of the McCarran–Ferguson Act, that "the continued regulation . . . by the several States of the business of insurance is in the public interest." 15 U.S.C. § 1011. Yet the exception poses a danger: it might be construed to permit state regulation of plans on the theory that plans are insurers. To prevent this, subsection (b)(2)(B) mandates that neither a plan nor its trust "shall be deemed to be an insurance company or other insurer ... or to be engaged in the business of insurance ... for purposes of any law of any State purporting to regulate insurance companies [or] insurance contracts." (There is a similar mandate for banks, trust companies, and investment companies.)

ERISA preemption is one of the most heavily litigated topics in the law of plans. Yet despite its bulk, the law remains unsettled and confused. This chapter surveys the main preemption themes and describes the problems to which ERISA preemption gives rise.

A. "RELATE TO"

1. THE INTERPRETIVE PROBLEMS

514(a) is unusual in that it preempts state laws whether or not they have anything to do with matters governed by ERISA. The test for preemption is whether the state law relates to a *plan*. For several reasons, this yields disturbing consequences. First, the statute itself puts no limits on what "relate[s] to" a plan. Thus, there is no obvious way to set bounds to preemption. Second, ERISA does not contain rules to govern all activity involving a plan. Some state laws are preempted without ERISA supplying new ones in their place. This leaves regulatory gaps.

It is very clear that Congress included a preemption clause to ensure that there would be a domain of exclusive federal regulation, safe from state interference and free from conflicting standards. But it is not entirely clear why Congress chose the present language. All the predecessor bills contained narrower language, for example preempting state laws only "insofar as they may now or hereafter relate to the fiduciary, reporting, and disclosure responsibilities of persons acting on behalf of employee benefit plans." The Conference Committee substituted the present language at the last minute and without much explanation. One reason for the change was concern over disciplinary rules promulgated by state bar associations that would impede the development of prepaid legal plans. (The same concern prompted a broad definition of "State.") Another reason was the desire to prevent states from taxing and licensing health plans, or mandating benefits. Yet those concerns could have been handled through less sweeping language.

Significantly, Congress was aware that the broadened provision might have unexpected consequences. It foresaw a need to adjust the scope of preemption through future legislation. For example, it established a Joint Pension Task Force to study, among other things, preemption policy and

any need for further legislation. ERISA § 3022.
However, the Task Force generated no proposals.
And contrary to what may have been the original
expectation, Congress has modified section 514 very
little since 1974.

2. LIMITS TO PREEMPTION

Some preemption cases are easy. ERISA obviously preempts state laws inconsistent with its provisions. *Alessi v. Raybestos-Manhattan, Inc.* (S.Ct.
1981). More generally, ERISA preempts state laws
that deal, consistently or not, with matters it regulates. For example, in *Local Union 598, Plumbers
& Pipefitters Industry Journeymen & Apprentices
Training Fund v. J.A. Jones Construction Co.* (9th
Cir.1988), a court of appeals held preempted a state
statute requiring minimum levels of contributions
to certain welfare plans. But there are also many
harder cases. The hardest involve state laws that
do not deal with the subjects of ERISA but still
affect or involve plans.

a. "Relate to": The Broad Reading

A line of Supreme Court cases has emphasized
the expansiveness of section 514(a). The crucial
phrase, "relate to," is given its "broad sense" of
having "a connection with or reference to" a plan.
Shaw v. Delta Air Lines, Inc. (S.Ct.1983). Thus,
the Court has held preempted state laws of general
application, such as contract and tort law, to the

extent they affect claims processing or other internal affairs of a plan. *Pilot Life Insurance Co. v. Dedeaux* (S.Ct.1987). Under this line of cases, the Supreme Court has held preempted laws in traditional areas of state regulation, such as family law and community property law, where the laws affected core areas of ERISA such as benefit payment and benefit rights. *Egelhoff v. Egelhoff* (S.Ct.2001); *Boggs v. Boggs* (S.Ct.1997).

The Court has made clear through these cases that preemption is not limited to state laws that affect plans. For example, it is enough that the law presupposes a plan. Thus, in *Ingersoll–Rand Co. v. McClendon* (S.Ct.1990), the Supreme Court held a state wrongful discharge law preempted to the extent it would allow recovery by the employee against the employer for a discharge motivated by the desire to avoid contributions to a pension plan. As the Court explained, "there simply is *no* cause of action if there is no plan." The Court has even held preempted a law that merely refers to plans. In *Mackey v. Lanier Collection Agency & Service, Inc.* (S.Ct.1988), the Court held preempted a section of a state garnishment law that expressly exempted benefit plans from garnishment orders. It was irrelevant that the sole purpose was to make the rest of the law *not* relate to plans. The clause on its face referred to plans covered by ERISA, and that was enough.

One important rule is that a state law claim is preempted if, ignoring the merits, it could be brought under the jurisdictional provisions of ERISA § 502(a). *Pilot Life Insurance Co. v. Dedeaux* (S.Ct.1987). Thus a state law claim for an alleged wrong that would constitute a breach of ERISA or of a plan document is preempted. As the Court explained in *Pilot Life*, "[t]he policy choices reflected in the inclusion of certain remedies and the exclusion of others under the federal scheme would be completely undermined if ERISA-plan participants and beneficiaries were free to obtain remedies under state law that Congress rejected in ERISA." To take a common example, state law tort or contract claims that have the effect of suits for benefits are preempted. *Lister v. Stark* (7th Cir.1989).

b. "Relate to": The Narrower Reading

The tendency of the opinions described above has been to remove limits to preemption. Yet there is a second line of cases in which the Court has sought to give meaning to the common sense idea that some state laws "may affect employee benefit plans in too tenuous, remote, or peripheral a manner to warrant a finding that the law 'relates to' the plan." *Shaw v. Delta Air Lines, Inc.* (S.Ct.1983).

One such limitation to the reach of "relate to" has been implied from ERISA § 502(d). That section allows a plan to sue or be sued as an entity, and it presupposes that judgments against plans can be enforced. In *Mackey v. Lanier Collection Agency & Service, Inc.* (S.Ct.1988), the Court read the section as permitting suits against plans on "run-of-the-mill state-law claims" such as breach of commercial contract, and as permitting state law proceedings to enforce judgments against plans. From this it further concluded (by a 5–4 margin) that section 502(d) must be construed to allow state-law garnishment proceedings against welfare plans to enforce judgments against participants.

A more substantial limitation on ERISA preemption was announced in *New York State Conference of Blue Cross & Blue Shield Plans v. Travelers Insurance Co.* (S.Ct.1995). There, the Court held applicable to ERISA the presumption, operative in implied preemption cases, that "Congress does not intend to supplant state law." The Court further held applicable the principle that state law in areas of traditional state regulation should not be held superseded unless there is clear evidence of Congressional intent to bring about that result. Applying these principles, the Court held not preempted a state law imposing a surcharge on hospital rates for a class of patients who were predominantly covered by ERISA plans. The fact that the law imposing the surcharge had the effect of increasing plan costs was not enough to support a conclusion that it related to plans.

Subsequent to *Travelers*, the Supreme Court held two other state regulatory regimes not preempted, using the same type of analysis. In *California Division of Labor Standards Enforcement v. Dillingham Construction, N.A., Inc.* (S.Ct.1997), the Court held

that a state's prevailing wage law, which permitted
employers to pay lower than prevailing wages to
employees participating in state-approved apprenticeship programs (including programs subject to
ERISA) was not preempted. The Court observed
that the subject matter had traditionally been regulated by states and applied a presumption against
preemption. It held that the impact of the state law
on plans was too tenuous to justify preemption. On
similar grounds, the Court in *De Buono v. NYSA–
ILA Medical & Clinical Services Fund* (S.Ct.1997),
held not preempted a gross receipts tax on hospitals
and health care facilities, to the extent it applied to
a health care facility operated by a plan.

B. A PLAN

Preemption extends only to laws that relate to
plans (subject to title I). It is not enough that the
law relates to benefits if the benefits do not come
from a plan. *Fort Halifax Packing Co. v. Coyne*
(S.Ct.1987). Thus it is important to know what an
ERISA-covered plan is. Caselaw discloses several
very different approaches to answering this question.

1. THE DILLINGHAM TEST

In *Donovan v. Dillingham* (11th Cir.1982), a
court of appeals announced a test for determining
whether an ERISA-covered plan has been established. The test, designed to deal with informal or

largely unwritten benefit arrangements, holds that a plan exists if, from the surrounding circumstances, a reasonable person can ascertain intended benefits, a class of beneficiaries, the source of financing, and the procedures for receiving benefits. The focus is on the definiteness of the arrangement.

The *Dillingham* test appears to rely on a principle of contract law: that contracts, to exist, must have reasonably definite terms. Arguably, that principle accords with ERISA's strong emphasis on certainty in plan terms. The terms required to be determinable are central features of any plan and, by requiring them to be definite, the test helps ensure that a plan can be enforced.

Yet the test has some questionable features. To begin, just as a plan may exist without being written—as a plan in violation of ERISA—a plan arguably may exist without, say, a definite source of financing. It, too, would be plan in violation of ERISA. The *Dillingham* test rejects this characterization in favor of a conclusion that no plan exists, but it is not clear why. The result of the choice is to exclude from ERISA's coverage arrangements in which employees are induced by vague promises of a pension to work for an employer long-term. *See Harris v. Arkansas Book Co.* (8th Cir.1986). Yet these arrangements arguably are among the ones most in need of the protection of ERISA's minimum standards and fiduciary rules.

2.   THE FUNCTIONAL TEST

An alternative approach has been suggested, though not expressly formulated, by the Supreme Court. Observing that the question, What is a plan? is tantamount to the question, What does ERISA regulate? the Court suggested that whether an arrangement is a plan should depend on whether it is something Congress intended to be governed by ERISA. Thus, in *Massachusetts v. Morash* (S.Ct. 1989), the Court held an employer's policy of paying discharged employees for their unused vacation time from general company assets not to constitute a plan. It explained that "ordinary vacation payments ... present none of the risks that ERISA is intended to address. If there is a danger of defeated expectations, it is no different from the danger of defeated expectations of wages for services performed—a danger Congress chose not to regulate in ERISA." As a result, a state law which required payment to discharged employees for their unused vacation time was held not preempted. By contrast, the Court noted, if the benefits had been paid from a separate fund, the arrangement might well be a plan—for ERISA is intended to protect the integrity of such funds.

A similar approach was taken in *Fort Halifax Packing Co. v. Coyne* (S.Ct.1987). There, the Court held a statute requiring a one-time severance payment in the event of a plant closing not preempted because it did not mandate the establishment of a plan. No plan was involved, the Court concluded, because the arrangement for paying the benefit did not "implicate the regulatory concerns of ERISA." The statute mandated only a benefit, not an ongoing arrangement needing administration.

3. GROUP INSURANCE

A benefit commonly provided to employees is coverage under a group health insurance policy. DOL regulations specify that a group insurance arrangement is not a plan where: the employer makes no contributions; employee participation is voluntary; the employer does not endorse the plan; the employer does no more than allow the insurer to publicize the program, and collects and remits premiums; and the employer receives no consideration save reasonable compensation for administrative expenses in collecting and remitting premiums. 29 C.F.R. § 2510.3–1(j). The question then arises: What further employer involvement will give rise to a plan?

The employer's payment of premiums is evidence of a plan, but it is probably insufficient without more. *Kidder v. H & B Marine, Inc.* (5th Cir.1991). There must be further involvement, such as establishing eligibility requirements. *Brundage–Peterson v. Compcare Health Services Insurance Corp.* (7th Cir.1989). On the other hand, employer payment of premiums is not essential. The requisite employer involvement may lie instead, for example, in endorsing the program and providing someone to collect and submit claims forms. *Hansen v. Conti-*

nental Insurance Co. (5th Cir.1991). Some courts treat the dispositive question to be whether the employer's conduct demonstrates an intention to provide benefits on a regular and long term basis. *E.g., Wickman v. Northwestern National Insurance Co.* (1st Cir.1990).

In many cases, the employer purchases the insurance from a multiple employer trust ("MET"). A MET is a commercial enterprise that purchases group insurance policies and sells participation interests to employers that are too small to qualify for group insurance rates. (A MET might instead be self-funded.) The MET is not itself a plan, since it is not established or maintained by an employer for its employees. However, subscribing employers may have established a plan whose benefits are provided through the MET. *Donovan v. Dillingham* (11th Cir.1982).

C. STATE INSURANCE REGULATION

1. "REGULATES INSURANCE"

Even if a state law relates to a plan, it may be saved from preemption if it "regulates insurance". ERISA § 514(b)(2)(A). But what does this mean? Just as with the jurisprudence of the "relates to" language, one can find in the Supreme Court's case law both a broad and a narrower reading of this term. However, the broader reading has clearly come to be dominant.

Initially, the Court drew upon the McCarran–Ferguson Act, 15 U.S.C § 1012, which leaves regu-

lation of the "business of insurance" to states, as
an expression of policy and interpretive guide. Cases
under that act have used three criteria for determining whether a practice constitutes the business
of insurance, to be left to state regulation: whether
the practice has the effect of transferring or spreading policyholder risk; whether the practice is an
integral part of the policy relation between the
insurer and insured; and whether the practice is
limited to entities within the insurance industry.
Union Labor Life Insurance Co. v. Pireno (S.Ct.
1982). In *Metropolitan Life Insurance Co. v. Massachusetts* (S.Ct.1985), the Supreme Court used this
test to clarify the scope of the insurance exception
to ERISA's preemption clause.

In *Metropolitan Life*, the Court held that a state
law requiring insurers to include specific benefits
(for example, minimum mental-health coverage) in
policies sold within the state falls within the insurance exception. Rejecting the argument that mandated benefit laws are health laws, rather than
insurance laws, it concluded that such laws regulate
insurance, as a matter of common sense, and meet
the McCarran–Ferguson criteria for laws regulating
the business of insurance.

The immediate result of the holding is to permit
states indirectly to regulate the benefits offered by
insured medical benefit plans. It thereby legiti-
mizes both interstate and intrastate nonuniformi-
ties in health plan regulation. Interstate nonuniformity results from varying state choices as to

required benefits. Intrastate nonuniformity results from the inability of states to prescribe the benefits of plans not funded through insurance—the "deemer" clause, ERISA § 514(b)(2)(B), ensures that a mandated benefit law will not apply. The Court attributed this heterogeneity to Congressional choice.

In *Pilot Life Insurance Co. v. Dedeaux* (S.Ct. 1987), the Court somewhat narrowed the insurance savings clause, concluding that a law, to be saved from preemption, must be specifically directed toward insurance: impact alone is not enough. This result followed from both a commonsense interpretation of "regulate" and the McCarran–Ferguson factors. On this basis the Court found preempted a state law suit for bad faith in processing disability benefit claims against an insurer from whom a plan purchased a policy. The Court emphasized that it was not enough for the law of bad faith to be associated with the insurance industry. It must regulate it. The Court's finding of preemption was also guided by its conclusion that ERISA's civil enforcement provisions were intended as the exclusive means for enforcing benefit claims, and that allowing state law remedies would interfere with the statutory scheme. On this basis, lower courts have held similar claims against insurers preempted even where they are contained in a state's insurance code. *E.g., Hansen v. Continental Insurance Co.* (5th Cir.1991).

Following *Metropolitan Life* and *Pilot Life*, the Supreme Court developed the law under the insurance savings clause in two ways. First, consistent with both *Metropolitan Life* and the broader reading of the basic preemption provision, the Court has upheld various forms of state regulation of health care, in particular state HMO laws. In *Rush Prudential HMO, Inc. v. Moran* (S.Ct.2002), the Court upheld a state law requiring HMOs to provide independent review of certain benefit denials and to cover services deemed medically necessary by an independent reviewer. The Court rejected the contention that the procedure for independent review conflicted with ERISA's remedial scheme. In *Kentucky Association of Health Plans, Inc. v. Miller* (S.Ct.2003), the Court upheld state laws that prohibit insurers (including HMOs) from excluding from the service network a provider who is willing to meet the insurer's terms for participation. And *Pegram v. Herdrich* (S.Ct.2000), though not a preemption case, based its refusal to hold an HMO's mixed eligibility and treatment decisions to be a fiduciary function in part on a belief that to do so would require the preemption of state malpractice law (see Chapter 12).

The second development has been to simplify the *Metropolitan Life–Pilot Life* test. Those decisions appeared to generate a two part test: a common-sense test, requiring in part that the law be specifically directed at the insurance industry, and a three-part McCarran–Ferguson test. This standard raised perplexities: What is the relationship between the two parts? Must a state law satisfy all three components of the McCarran-Ferguson test?

Just what aspect of the insurance industry must the law be directed toward? In *Kentucky Association of Health Plans, Inc. v. Miller* (S.Ct.2003), the Court rejected uncritical reliance on the McCarran–Ferguson criteria and announced a new standard: a law regulates insurance if it is specifically directed toward entities engaged in insurance, and substantially affects the risk pooling arrangement between insurer and insured.

2.   THE DEEMER CLAUSE

In *FMC Corp. v. Holliday* (S.Ct.1990), the Supreme Court held that the deemer clause, ERISA § 514(b)(2)(B), is as broad as the insurance exception in the sense that a state law initially saved by the insurance exception is ultimately preempted to the extent it relates to plans not funded through insurance. In the Court's view, this results from a straightforward interpretation of the clause. The Court rejected alternative readings that would limit the deemer clause to state laws that are pretexts for regulating plans or to state laws that regulate the insurance business. The effect of the holding is to solidify the difference between the regulatory regimes for insurance plans and for non-insurance plans.

Many self-funded plans purchase stop-loss coverage, under which an insurer issues a policy that covers only claims or an aggregate of claims greater than a certain amount. Courts have generally held that the purchase of a stop-loss policy does not take the self-funded plan out of the scope of the deemer clause. *E.g., Lincoln Mutual Casualty Co. v. Lectron Products, Inc., Employee Health Benefit Plan* (6th Cir.1992); *United Food & Commercial Workers & Employers Arizona Health & Welfare Trust v. Pacyga* (9th Cir.1986). The justifications for the holding vary, but principally focus on the fact that a stop-loss policy does not pay benefits to participants, but instead insures the plan itself against large losses. The plan remains directly responsible for paying claims from its own funds. *Bill Gray Enterprises, Inc. Employee Health and Welfare Plan v. Gourley* (3d Cir.2001).

D. PREEMPTION AND REMEDIES

If section 514(a) appears to preempt a state claim, but ERISA provides no substitute, a court has three options. It can hold the state law not preempted. It can hold the state law preempted and stop there. Or it can hold the state law preempted and fashion a federal common law remedy in its place. There is little general guidance as to what a court should do.

The Sixth Circuit Court of Appeals formerly took the position that state law claims should not be preempted unless ERISA provides a remedy for the wrong. *Perry v. P * I * E Nationwide, Inc.* (6th Cir.1989). This view seems inconsistent with the Supreme Court's expansive approach to preemption and most other federal courts have rejected it. Even the Sixth Circuit has retreated from this position. *Tolton v. American Biodyne, Inc.* (6th Cir.1995).

If a state law claim is preempted, but there is no substitute available under ERISA, the question can always be asked whether courts should supply a federal common law remedy. One extreme position is that courts never should do so. The position is based on statements by the Supreme Court in *Massachusetts Mutual Life Insurance Co. v. Russell* (S.Ct.1985). There, in rejecting an implied right of action under ERISA, the Court characterized ERISA as " 'comprehensive' " and section 502(a) as "carefully integrated," and concluded that one should not "tamper with an enforcement scheme crafted with such evident care as the one in ERISA." In a later case, however, the Court upheld the propriety of courts' developing a federal common law for plans. *Firestone Tire & Rubber Co. v. Bruch* (S.Ct.1989). Despite this language, some lower courts have seized on the pronouncement in *Russell* as a basis for rejecting federal common law remedies. *E.g., Sanson v. General Motors Corp.* (11th Cir.1992).

There are several problems with this reasoning. First, different standards of legitimacy govern federal common law claims and implied rights of action. Whether a right of action should be implied from a statute (the issue in *Russell*) is a question of congressional intent; whether a federal common law remedy should be fashioned is a question of federal court power and the propriety of its exercise.

See Texas Industries, Inc. v. Radcliff Materials, Inc.
(S.Ct.1981). A central function of federal common
lawmaking is to fill gaps in statutory schemes. *See,
e.g., Boyle v. United Technologies Corp.* (S.Ct.1988).
As courts have noted, such gap-filling with respect
to plans is not only essential in light of ERISA's
sweeping preemption provision; it appears to have
been contemplated by Congress. *Kwatcher v. Massachusetts Service Employees Pension Fund* (1st Cir.
1989).

Second, the premise of the argument is flawed
because section 502(a) is anything but carefully and
systematically written. It is a hodgepodge of standing provisions, descriptions of relief, and descriptions of claims, which contains obvious duplication
(such as between sections 502(a)(2) and (a)(3)) and
arguable gaps (such as its failure to specify what
plans, which can sue and be sued, can sue about).
That it is detailed, in some sense, is not a telling
argument against its supplementation. As Judge
Posner observed:

Detailed statutes such as ERISA ... bristle with
interpretive conundra. A statute may be detailed
not because the draftsmen quixotically undertook
to resolve all possible interpretive questions before they arose but because a number of specific
problems were brought to their attention and
they tried to solve them. There may have been
an equal number of problems that were not raised
and therefore—because Congress is too busy to
resolve problems that are entirely hypothetical—

not provided for. It is perverse on the one hand
to penalize draftsmen for having made detailed
provision for the problems that were brought to
their attention by denying them a helping judicial
hand in the problem areas they did not foresee,
and on the other hand to treat a lazily drafted
statute, worded in generalities, as a broad delegation to the judiciary to create a sensible code of
governance.

* * *

It is apparent that Congress, while it gave
careful consideration to a vast number of issues
that might arise in the administration of the new
federal pension law, overlooked a vast number of
other issues . . .

Winstead v. J.C. Penney Co. (7th Cir.1991).

In fact, most courts now agree that it is sometimes proper to recognize federal common law
claims.

On some issues there is fairly wide agreement. An
example is the law of estoppel, discussed in Chapter
11. And some claims that might otherwise be
brought under a federal common law theory (for
example, restitution, *see Provident Life & Accident
Insurance Co. v. Waller* (4th Cir.1990)) may be
brought as equitable claims under ERISA
§ 502(a)(3), still relying on federal common law for
the development of substantive standards. *See Harris Trust and Savings Bank v. Salomon Smith*

Barney, Inc. (S.Ct.2000); *Great-West Life & Annuity Co. v. Knudson* (S.Ct.2002).

Other issues, though, are controversial. For example, courts differ about the propriety of claims for indemnity and contribution among breaching fiduciaries. The split is well illustrated by the majority and dissenting opinions in *Chemung Canal Trust Co. v. Sovran Bank/Maryland* (2d Cir.1991). There the court of appeals distinguished *Russell* as addressing implied rights of action, which it agreed could not serve as a basis for third-party claims. The court then observed that "federal courts have been authorized to develop a federal common law under ERISA, and in doing so, are to be guided by the principles of traditional trust law." It then determined that trust law does permit indemnity and contribution. Finally, it concluded that there was no good reason not to allow indemnity and contribution in connection with fiduciary breaches. In a subsequent case, the court went further, concluding that indemnity and contribution in fact promoted the purposes of ERISA. As it explained, "*Chemung* reflects our belief that ERISA's purpose of deterring pension plan abuse is frustrated when solvent breaching fiduciaries are allowed to escape the consequences of their actions." *Cullen v. Riley (In re Masters Mates & Pilots Pension Plan & IRAP Litigation)* (2d Cir.1992).

The dissent, by contrast, argued that the rationale of *Russell* bars courts from adding remedies to those included in the statute. In its view, the

omission of any provision for indemnity and contribution evidences Congress' positive intent to exclude them.   Other courts that have rejected indemnity and contribution have relied on substantially
the same reasoning.   *See, e.g., Roberts v. Taussig*
(N.D.Ohio 1999).

CHAPTER 16

PROCEDURE

We have already discussed remedies and various aspects of the civil enforcement provisions, ERISA § 502(a), in the course of examining the underlying rights enforced. In this chapter we examine other, more procedural, aspects of plan-related litigation.

A. JURISDICTION, PROCESS AND VENUE

1. SUBJECT MATTER JURISDICTION

ERISA § 502(e)(1) confers on federal district courts subject matter jurisdiction of all suits brought under Title I. The jurisdiction is exclusive of the state courts except for claims under section 502(a)(1)(B) and claims to enforce compliance with qualified medical child support orders. For those claims, jurisdiction is concurrent.

Some claims apparently brought under state law are, in fact, claims under ERISA. Where a putative state-law claim is preempted because it falls within the scope of section 502(a), there is *total preemption* and the claim is "really" federal. What this means in practice is that the well-pleaded complaint rule is no bar to removal. *Metropolitan Life Insurance Co. v. Taylor* (S.Ct.1987).

As one court explained, "[t]he use of the term 'complete preemption' is unfortunate, since the complete preemption doctrine is not a preemption doctrine but rather a federal jurisdiction doctrine." *Lister v. Stark* (7th Cir.1989). Thus, in determining whether there is complete preemption, come courts consider only whether the claim falls within the scope of ERISA § 502(a), leaving the issue of "ordinary" preemption to state courts upon remand. *E.g., Warner v. Ford Motor Co.* (6th Cir.1995). Other courts consider both issues in their analysis of complete preemption. *E.g., Plumbing Industry Board, Plumbing Local Union No. 1 v. Howell Co.* (2d Cir.1997).

Federal common law claims involving plans that do not fall within section 502(a) are not claims under ERISA. Thus, they cannot be brought in federal court under section 502(e)(1). Instead, they must be brought under the general federal question jurisdiction statute, 28 U.S.C. § 1331. Although it is settled that section 1331 permits jurisdiction of at least some federal common law claims, it is not settled which plan common law claims fall within its scope.

One view is that section 1331 allows jurisdiction only over plan common law claims involving matters of "central concern" to ERISA. *Provident Life & Accident Insurance Co. v. Waller* (4th Cir.1990). A broader view is that jurisdiction exists over any claim in which federal common law supplies the rule of decision. *See Northeast Department ILGWU*

Health & Welfare Fund v. Teamsters Local Union No. 229 Welfare Fund (3d Cir.1985). If the narrower view is accepted, the scope of plan-related common law remedies will accordingly be limited to matters of "central concern."

2. PROCESS AND VENUE

One procedural advantage of subject matter jurisdiction under ERISA is that there is nationwide service of process. ERISA § 502(e)(2). By contrast, there is no nationwide service of process for state court actions under section 502(a)(1)(B). Another advantage is broad choice of venue. A suit under ERISA in federal district court may be brought in any district where the plan is administered, where the breach took place, or where a defendant resides or may be found. ERISA § 502(e)(2). These venue provisions are in addition to the general federal question venue provisions of 28 U.S.C. § 1391(b).

When an employee benefit plan is the defendant, it may be served through process on a trustee or administrator in his or her official capacity. In addition, where the SPD has not designated an individual as agent for service of process, the Secretary of Labor may be served, and the Secretary must then notify the administrator or a trustee within 15 days. ERISA § 502(d)(1).

In any suit under ERISA except one brought solely to recover benefits, a copy of the complaint must be served on the Secretaries of Labor and the

Treasury. Either Secretary has the right to intervene, except that the Secretary of the Treasury may
not intervene in fiduciary litigation. ERISA
§ 502(h).

B. LIMITATIONS PERIODS

ERISA § 413 supplies a limitations period for
suits involving violations of part 4 (relating to fiduciary matters). Such a suit must be brought within
the earlier of: (a) six years of the date of the last
action constituting a part of the breach or violation
(or, in the case of an omission, the last date on
which the fiduciary could have cured the breach or
violation); or (b) three years after the earliest date
on which the plaintiff had actual knowledge of the
breach or violation (constructive knowledge is insufficient). Because the fiduciary provisions of ERISA
may be breached without there being any loss, the
date of the wrongful conduct constitutes the date of
the breach or violation. *Ziegler v. Connecticut General Life Insurance Co.* (9th Cir.1990). In the case
of fraud or concealment, the action must be brought
within six years of the date of discovery of the
violation.

ERISA contains no limitations periods for other
actions under Title I, such as benefit claims or suits
under section 510. For these actions, courts select
the most analogous limitations period found in the
state law that would be applicable under choice of
law principles. *Held v. Manufacturers Hanover
Leasing Corp.* (10th Cir.1990). This approach re-

flects a method long used by federal courts where Congress has failed to specify a period of limitations for a statutory claim. However, in recent cases involving statutes other than ERISA, the Supreme Court has held that it may be appropriate to select an analogous limitations period from elsewhere in the statute or from an analogous federal one. *See Agency Holding Corp. v. Malley–Duff & Associates, Inc.* (S.Ct.1987). Courts have not yet considered whether this approach would better serve the purposes of ERISA, in particular that of achieving uniformity in the law.

A plan document might specify a limitations period different from the one that would be borrowed from state law. Courts will generally apply a reasonable limitations period specified in the plan. *E.g., Doe v. Blue Cross & Blue Shield United of Wisconsin* (7th Cir.1997). One decision has held otherwise, though, at least where the provision would be unenforceable under state law. *See Wineinger v. United Healthcare Insurance Co.* (D.Neb.2001).

C.　ATTORNEY'S FEES

ERISA § 502(g)(1) provides that in any suit by a participant, beneficiary or fiduciary under title I, "the court in its discretion may allow a reasonable attorney's fee and costs of the action to either party." Fees may be awarded in connection with both trial court proceedings and appeals. *Sokol v. Bernstein* (9th Cir.1987). Courts generally deny fees for services performed in pursuing the pre-filing plan claims process, but may award fees for services incurred in any remand to a plan. *Peterson v. Continental Casualty Co.* (2d Cir.2002).

Under the prevailing judicial elaboration, a court must consider the following five factors in deciding whether to award fees: the degree of the other party's culpability or bad faith; the other party's ability to satisfy an award; the deterrent effect on other persons in similar circumstances; whether the person requesting fees sought to confer a common benefit on all plan participants and beneficiaries or resolve a significant legal question concerning ERISA; and the relative merits of the parties' positions. *E.g., Armistead v. Vernitron Corp.* (6th Cir.1991). A district court's weighing of the factors is discretionary and will be reviewed only under an abuse of discretion standard. *Jacobs v. Pickands Mather & Co.* (8th Cir.1991). Most courts have rejected any presumption in favor of awarding fees to a prevailing plaintiff. *See Martin v. Arkansas Blue Cross and Blue Shield* (8th Cir.2002) (en banc).

The Seventh Circuit has adopted an approach to section 502(g)(1) slightly different from the five-factor test. Noting that that test is oriented toward prevailing plaintiffs, the court sought a more neutral standard. Borrowing from the Equal Access to Justice Act, 28 U.S.C. § 2412(d)(1)(A), it created a "modest presumption," specifying that fees should be awarded to the prevailing party unless the position of the other party was substantially justified (i.e. unless it had a "solid basis") or special circumstances would make an award unjust. *Bittner v. Sadoff & Rudoy Industries* (7th Cir.1984). Special circumstances may include the five factors. In practice, however, the differences between the approaches may be small. As the Seventh Circuit itself later explained, "[w]hichever approach is used, the bottom-line question is essentially the same: was the losing party's position substantially justified and taken in good faith, or was that party simply out to harass its opponent?" *Meredith v. Navistar International Transportation Corp.* (7th Cir.1991). The court also emphasized that, under the Seventh Circuit standard, one must still take into account ERISA's remedial purpose, which counsels against penalizing participants and beneficiaries for seeking to enforce rights. *Id.*

D. PRIVILEGE

An attorney for a plan or for a plan fiduciary would appear to owe his client the usual duties owed by attorneys to clients, such as loyalty and confidentiality. It would also appear that communications between such an attorney and his client should be privileged. However, because the fiduciaries must act solely in the interest of participants and beneficiaries, it is arguable that the attorney's obligation ultimately runs to them and that there should be no privilege enforceable by the plan or a fiduciary against participants and beneficiaries. Courts have drawn this conclusion.

The first case to consider the issue of attorney-client privilege in the plan context relied on the law of privilege in shareholder derivative suits. It held that the privilege is not available to plans or fiduciaries, at least in fiduciary litigation, where the plaintiff shows good cause why the privilege should not be invoked. The court believed the rule to be premised on trust law principles that were fully applicable to plans, and that the rule appropriately balanced the legitimate need for confidentiality with the legitimate need of participants and beneficiaries to know. *Donovan v. Fitzsimmons* (N.D.Ill.1981).

Subsequent cases have gone further, rejecting the "good cause" requirement and holding that there is no privilege at all in such circumstances: "When an attorney advises a fiduciary about a matter dealing with the administration of an employees' benefit plan, the attorney's client is not the fiduciary personally but, rather, the trust's beneficiaries." *Washington–Baltimore Newspaper Guild v. Washington Star Co.* (D.D.C.1982). The rule denying privilege has even been extended to non-fiduciary litigation, *see Helt v. Metropolitan District Commission* (D.Conn.1986), including criminal prosecutions, *United States v. Evans* (9th Cir.1986).

Since an employer may serve as a fiduciary, the issue arises as to when the employer's plan-related communications with an attorney are protected by privilege. Where the employer is consulting an attorney in its capacity as fiduciary, on matters of plan administration or management, there is no privilege *vis-à-vis* participants and beneficiaries. *Everett v. USAir Group, Inc.* (D.D.C.1985). On the other hand, when the employer consults an attorney in its capacity as sponsor on matters, for example, of plan amendment, there is an enforceable privilege. *Id.* The fact that the employer uses the same lawyer in both capacities does not undermine either rule. *In re Long Island Lighting Co.* (2d Cir.1997).

Courts have held that a fiduciary can invoke the privilege for communications with an attorney hired to represent it in litigation with participants, beneficiaries, or the Secretary, or in other circumstances where its interests and those of the participants and beneficiaries have become adverse. *Martin v. Valley National Bank of Arizona* (S.D.N.Y.1991). One recent case has held that, at least in these circumstances, the fiduciary exception to the attorney-client privilege should be construed narrowly and that "hard cases" should be construed in favor of privilege. *United States v. Mett* (9th Cir.1999).

These privilege rules have been held to apply in ERISA suits brought by the Secretary of Labor. *Donovan v. Fitzsimmons* (N.D.Ill.1981). Presumably the same would be true for suits brought by fiduciaries to protect the interests of participants and beneficiaries.

CHAPTER 17

NONDISCRIMINATION: COVERAGE

An employer might wish to provide a retirement plan for only some employees or, perhaps, cover different groups of employees through different plans. Differential coverage, even if grounded in reasonable business considerations, creates a risk of discrimination against lower paid employees—something federal law has long sought to prevent.

To an extent, preferential coverage of the more highly paid employees is inevitable. Relative to lower paid employees, higher paid ones have more money to save and benefit more from the favored tax treatment of qualified plans. Hence they are more willing to substitute deferred, plan-based benefits for current income. This preference helps drive the formation of plans for those employees. The nondiscrimination rules take advantage of this state of affairs by requiring an employer who establishes a plan covering the more highly paid employees to include some of the lower paid ones, too. In this way, the tax subsidy that primarily benefits more highly paid employees is made to benefit lower paid employees as well.

In this chapter we deal with rules concerning discrimination in plan coverage. The basic rule—a condition of qualification—is that a plan must satisfy at least one of two minimum standards, each of which seeks to ensure that *highly compensated employees* are not covered disproportionately. IRC § 410(b)(1). In the next chapter we examine allied rules concerning discrimination in contributions and benefits.

A. HIGHLY COMPENSATED EMPLOYEES

The minimum coverage standards limit discrimination in favor of highly compensated employees ("HCEs") or, correlatively, against nonhighly compensated employees ("NCEs"). The concept of HCE is a fundamental one for the nondiscrimination rules. In general, an employee is highly compensated for a given year (*the determination year*) if he: (A) was a *5–percent owner* in that year or the preceding one; or (B) in the preceding year received *compensation* from the employer in excess of a sum indexed for inflation ($90,000 in 2003) and, if the employer elects, was in the *top-paid group* of employees for that year. IRC § 414(q)(1). This definition needs extensive elaboration.

1. 5–PERCENT OWNERS

A 5–percent owner of a corporation in a given year is a person who at any time in the year owns more than 5% of the outstanding stock or stock possessing more than 5% of the combined voting power. A 5–percent owner of a non-corporate employer in a given year is a person who at any time in the year owns more than 5% of the capital or profit interest. Ownership includes constructive ownership. IRC §§ 414(q)(2) & 416(i)(1)(B).

2. COMPENSATION

Compensation includes not only wages, salary, commissions and other items includible in gross income, but also elective deferrals under IRC § 402(g)(3) and elective contributions to cafeteria plans and certain other plans. IRC §§ 414(q)(4) & 415(c)(3).

3. TOP–PAID GROUP

A top-paid employee for a year is an employee in the top 20% for that year, ranked by compensation. IRC § 414(q)(3). In determining the number of employees equal to 20%, the following employees are not counted: those who have not completed 6 months of service; those who normally work less than 17 1/2 hours per week; those who normally work no more than 6 months during any year; those younger than 21; certain employees covered by a collective bargaining agreement; and certain nonresident aliens. IRC §§ 414(q)(5) & (8). (An employer may elect less stringent exclusions, or none at all. Temp. Treas. Reg. § 1.414(q)–1, at A–9(b)(2).) Thus, the so-called "top 20%" may consist of fewer than 20% of all employees. The exclusions just described are only for purposes of determining the size of the top 20%, not its membership. A top-paid employee may, for example, have completed only 3 months of service.

4.   FORMER EMPLOYEES

An employee is a *highly compensated former employee* ("HCFE") if he separated from service before the determination year and was an HCE either for the year of separation or any year after he reached age 55. IRC § 414(q)(6).

B. PLANS TESTED FOR NONDISCRIMINATION

A second fundamental concept for the nondiscrimination rules is that of the plan or plan unit tested for compliance. The process of identifying this unit is governed by a complex of rules. The basic ones are described here; others are explained below.

1.   SINGLE PLANS

The basic unit that must satisfy the minimum coverage standard is the *single*, or *separate, plan*. A plan is a single plan if and only if, on an ongoing basis, all of its assets are available to pay benefits to covered employees and their beneficiaries. A single plan may have several benefit structures, several plan documents, several contributing employers, or several trusts or annuity contracts. On the other hand, there exist multiple plans, even under a single document, if a portion of the assets are are not available to pay some of the benefits. Treas. Reg. §§ 1.410(b)–7(a) & 1.414(*l*)–1(b)(1). In the language of the regulations, "[s]eparate asset pools are separate plans." Treas. Reg. § 1.410(b)–7(b).

2. DISAGGREGATION

In identifying the plan units to be tested, certain mandatory disaggregation rules must be applied. A portion of a plan that is a 401(k) plan must be treated as a separate plan from the remainder; a portion of a plan that is an ESOP must be treated as a separate plan from the remainder; a plan that benefits collectively bargained employees must be treated as a separate plan from the remainder, and a portion that benefits employees covered under one collective bargaining agreement is a separate plan from portions that benefit employees covered under other collective bargaining agreements. A plan that benefits employees of more than one employer must be disaggregated into separate plans for each employer. Treas. Reg. § 1.410(b)–7(c). The required disaggregation is only conceptual; plans do not actually have to be restructured.

3. AGGREGATION

An employer may elect to aggregate separate plans (again, only conceptually) for purposes of applying the ratio percentage test and the nondiscriminatory classification test (described below), except where the plans are subject to the mandatory disaggregation rules. Treas. Reg. § 1.410(b)–7(d). This option permits an employer to establish, for example, different plans for salaried employees and hourly employees, without automatically running afoul of the coverage rules. However, if an employer chooses to aggregate plans for the coverage rules, it must also aggregate them for purposes of the nondiscrimination rules of section 401(a)(4) (discussed in chapter 18). IRC § 410(b)(6)(B).

C. THE COVERAGE TESTS

The coverage tests make use of the notions of HCE and plan subject to testing. The basic tests are reasonably straightforward. Their complexities arise mainly from the rules identifying special groups of employees who may or must be counted or ignored.

To meet the coverage standard, a plan must satisfy either (a) the *ratio percentage test*, or (b) both the *nondiscriminatory classification test* and *average benefit percentage test*. IRC § 410(b). Unless the employer elects to designate separate lines of business (see below), testing is by reference to the workforce as a whole.

Both tests are concerned with employees who *benefit* under a plan. In general, an employee benefits under a plan in a given year if he receives an allocation to his account (for defined contribution plans) or an increase in accrued benefits (for defined benefit plans). Treas. Reg. § 1.410(b)–3(a)(1). Former employees may satisfy this definition. For example, a defined benefit plan amendment providing an ad hoc cost of living adjustment benefits former employees. Treas. Reg. § 1.410(b)–3(b)(1).

1.   RATIO PERCENTAGE TEST

The ratio percentage test requires the *ratio percentage* of the plan—the proportion of NCEs who benefit under the plan divided by the proportion of HCEs who benefit under the plan, Treas. Reg. § 1.410(b)–9—to be at least 70%. IRC § 410(b)(1)(B). If, for example, a plan benefits 50% of the HCEs, it must also benefit at least 35% of the NCEs to satisfy the test. A plan automatically satisfies the test if it benefits at least 70% of the NCEs. IRC § 410(b)(1)(A).

2.   NONDISCRIMINATORY CLASSIFI-CATION AND AVERAGE BENE-FIT PERCENTAGE TESTS

The alternative test contains two subtests. One, the nondiscriminatory classification test, requires that the classification used by the plan as a basis for including and excluding employees be both *reasonable* and *nondiscriminatory*. The other subtest, the average benefit percentage test, requires that the *average benefit percentage* of the plan be at least 70%. IRC § 410(b)(2). These tests require substantial unpacking.

a. Nondiscriminatory Classification Test

For purposes of the nondiscriminatory classification test, a classification is reasonable if it is established under objective business criteria. An enumeration of covered employees by name is not a reasonable classification. Treas. Reg. § 1.410(b)–4(b).

There are two ways for a classification to meet the additional requirement that it be nondiscriminatory. One is for the ratio percentage of the plan (which is presumably less than 70%—otherwise the ratio percentage test would be satisfied) to exceed the *safe harbor percentage*. Treas. Reg. § 1.410(b)–4(c)(2). The safe harbor percentage is equal to 50 percent, less 0.75% for each percentage point by which the *nonhighly compensated employee concentration percentage* exceeds 60%. Treas. Reg. § 1.410(b)–4(c)(4)(i). The latter percentage is the percentage of all employees who are NCEs. Treas. Reg. § 1.410(b)–4(c)(4)(iii). A table at Treas. Reg. § 1.410(b)–4(c)(4)(iv) correlates nonhighly compensated employee concentration percentages with safe harbor percentages.

An example shows the operation of this test. Suppose that an employer has ten employees. A plan covers two out of the three HCEs and three out of the seven NCEs. The nonhighly compensated employee concentration percentage is 70%. The table in the regulations shows the corresponding safe harbor percentage to be 42.5%. The plan's ratio percentage is $(3/7) \div (2/3) = 64.3\%$. Since the ratio percentage exceeds the safe harbor percentage, the plan's classification is nondiscriminatory.

The second way that a plan can satisfy the non-discriminatory classification test is by meeting two conditions. First, the plan's ratio percentage must be greater than or equal to the *unsafe harbor percentage*. (If it is less, the classification is automatically discriminatory.) Second, the classification must not be discriminatory in light of the relevant facts and circumstances. Treas. Reg. § 1.410(b)–4(c)(3). The unsafe harbor percentage is 40 percent, reduced by 0.75% for each percentage point by which the nonhighly compensated employee concentration percentage exceeds 60%, but in no case to less than 20%. Treas. Reg. § 1.410(b)–4(c)(4)(ii). The table referred to above also correlates nonhighly compensated employee concentration percentages with unsafe harbor percentages. The regulations identify facts and circumstances of especial relevance to the determination of nondiscriminatory classification. Treas. Reg. § 1.410(b)–4(c)(3)(ii).

b. Average Benefit Percentage Test

The average benefit percentage reflects the benefit structure of the workforce relative to a plan. It is defined as the *actual benefit percentage* of the NCEs divided by the actual benefit percentage of the HCEs. The actual benefit percentage of a group of employees is the unweighted average of the *benefit percentages* of each employee in the group, whether or not a participant in any plan. IRC

§ 410(b)(2)(B); Treas. Reg. § 1.410(b)–5. The benefit percentage for an employee is the employer-provided contribution or benefit under all qualified plans in the *testing group* (i.e. the plan and those that could be permissively aggregated with it under liberalized aggregation rules, *see* Treas. Reg. § 1.410(b)–7(e)), expressed as a percentage of compensation. IRC § 410(b)(2)(C).

To take a simple example, assume that an employer maintains a single defined contribution plan for two highly compensated employees, A and B, and two nonhighly compensated employees, C and D. A earned $100,000 for the year and received a contribution to the plan of $10,000; B earned $80,000 and received a contribution of $16,000; C earned $25,000 and received a contribution of $5,000; and D earned $15,000 and a received a contribution of $2,500. There is only one other employee, E, a nonhighly compensated employee who is not covered by the plan and who earned $20,000. The benefit percentages of the employees are as follows: 10% for A; 20% for B; 20% for C; 16.7% for D; and 0% for E. The actual benefit percentage of the HCEs is $1/2(10\% + 20\%) = 15\%$. The actual benefit percentage of the NCEs is $1/3(20\% + 16.7\% + 0\%) = 12.2\%$. The average benefit percentage is $12.2\%/15\% = 81.3\%$, which is greater than 70%. The average benefit percentage test is satisfied. In practice, the required calculations may be very complicated, both because of the number of employees and the complexity of calculating employee benefit percentages.

If a plan prescribes minimum age and service requirements for participation and excludes from participation all employees not meeting those requirements, the calculation of the average benefit percentage is modified. Either all of those excluded employees must be considered employees for purposes of the calculation (thereby modifying a general exclusion discussed below), or else all employees may be disregarded who would be excluded under the lowest age requirement and lowest service requirement (separately determined) for any of the plans in the testing group. IRC § 410(b)(2)(D) & (4)(A).

There is an additional special rule. A plan (determined without regard to the mandatory disaggregation rule of Treas. Reg. § 1.410(b)–7(c)(5)) that benefits both collectively bargained and noncollectively bargained employees is deemed to satisfy the average benefit percentage test if two conditions hold. First, the of the plan provisions are the same for all participants. Second, the plan would satisfy the ratio percentage test if the rules concerning excludable employees and mandatory disaggregation with respect to plans benefiting collectively bargained employees did not apply. Treas. Reg. § 1.410(b)–5(f).

c. Compensation

For purposes of the average benefit percentage test, as well as other nondiscrimination standards, compensation is defined under IRC § 415(c)(3). *See*

IRC §§ 410(b)(2)(C)(i) & 414(s). Under section 415(c)(3), compensation includes elective deferrals under IRC § 402(g)(3) and amounts contributed or deferred by the employer at the election of the employee, and otherwise not includible in gross income by virtue of IRC §§ 125, 132(f)(4), or 457. However, under section 414(s)(2), the employer may elect to exclude certain of these contributions for purposes of nondiscrimination testing. Alternative definitions of compensation are available under regulations. Treas. Reg. § 1.414(s)–1(c).

Under IRC § 401(a)(17), it is a condition of qualification that a plan not take into account annual compensation in excess of an inflation-adjusted amount ($200,000 in 2003). Thus, an employee's compensation in excess of the statutory maximum is treated as if it were compensation at the maximum amount.

d. Special Rules

A plan maintained by an employer who has no NCEs automatically satisfies the coverage standards, as does a plan that benefits no HCEs. Treas. Reg. § 1.410(b)–2(b)(5) & (6). A plan that benefits only employees covered by a collective bargaining agreement also automatically satisfies the coverage standards. Treas. Reg. § 1.410(b)–2(b)(7).

e. Former Employees

If a plan benefits former employees in a year, the plan is tested separately with respect to present and former employees. In applying the coverage tests to present employees, former employees are disregarded, and vice versa. A plan satisfies section 410(b) with respect to former employees if and only if, under all relevant facts and circumstances, the group of former employees benefiting under the plan does not discriminate significantly in favor of HCFEs. Treas. Reg. § 1.410(b)–2(c).

D. EMPLOYEE INCLUSION RULES

Section 410(b) is concerned with discrimination among employees. Special rules prevent evasion of the standard through manipulation of the category of employee.

1. BUSINESS AGGREGATION RULES

IRC § 414(b) provides that, for purposes of section 410(b) (and other provisions), all employees of all corporations that are members of a *controlled group* of corporations shall be treated as employed by a single employer. The definition of "controlled group" is complex. *See* IRC § 1563. Similarly, section 414(c) provides that employees of trades or businesses, whether or not incorporated, that are under *common control*, shall be treated as employed by a single employer. Again, the definition of "common control" is complex. Treas. Reg. §§ 1.414(c)–1 to 1.414(c)–5. Finally, IRC § 414(m) provides that all employees of members of an *affiliated service group* shall be treated as employed by a single employer. An affiliated service group consists of a service organization and certain other closely related organizations. IRC § 414(m)(2) & (5).

2. LEASED EMPLOYEES

For purposes of section 410(b) (and other provisions), a *leased employee* is treated as an employee of the person for whom his services are provided, and benefits or contributions provided by the leasing organization are attributed to the person for whom the services are performed. IRC § 414(n)(1). A leased employee is a person (other than a common law employee) who provides services to a recipient, where: the services are provided pursuant to an agreement between the recipient and a leasing organization; the person has provided the services on a substantially full-time basis for at least a year; and the services are performed under the primary direction or control of the recipient. IRC § 414(n)(2). There is an exception to this attribution rule for certain cases in which the leasing organization provides a generous, broad-based money purchase plan with immediate participation and full and immediate vesting. IRC § 414(n)(5).

E. EXCLUDABLE EMPLOYEES

To accommodate various special concerns, some employees (*excludable employees*) may be disregarded when applying the coverage tests. Different groups are excluded for different reasons. The most important exclusions are discussed below.

1. COLLECTIVE BARGAINING UNITS

If a plan covers only non-union employees, members of a unit of employees covered by a collective bargaining agreement may be ignored when applying the coverage tests if there is evidence that retirement benefits for them were the subject of good faith bargaining. IRC § 410(b)(3)(A); Treas. Reg. § 1.410(b)–6(d)(1). (There are related exclusion rules for plans that cover both union and non-union employees. *Id.*) The union employees will be disregarded even if no plan was established for them. The rationale for this exclusion is that it permits unions to opt for higher compensation or welfare benefits for its members, in lieu of retirement benefits, without jeopardizing the ability of the employer to establish plans for other employees. This exclusion is not available for bargaining units in which more than 2% of the employees are professionals. Treas. Reg. § 1.410(b)–6(d)(2)(iii)(B).

2. MINIMUM AGE AND SERVICE REQUIREMENTS

If a plan prescribes minimum age and service requirements, and excludes from participation all employees not meeting them, then the plan may disregard those employees for purposes of the minimum coverage tests (except possibly the average benefit percentage calculation—see above). IRC § 410(b)(4)(A). The significance of this rule is that it permits qualified plans to exclude part-time employees.

If some or all employees not meeting ERISA's minimum age and service standards ("otherwise excludable employees") are covered under a plan, the employer may disaggregate the plan into one for the otherwise excludable employees and one for all other employees, and test each separately. In testing each plan under the coverage standards, employees covered by the other may be disregarded. IRC § 410(b)(4)(B); Treas. Reg. § 1.410(b)–6(b)(3).

3.   FORMER EMPLOYEES

In testing coverage of former employees, the employer may exclude those who terminated employment before a certain date and those who were or would have been excludable employees during the plan year in which they became former employees. Treas. Reg. § 1.410(b)–6(h).

F.   SEPARATE LINE OF BUSINESS RULES

The minimum coverage tests are normally applied to the entire workforce. However, an employer may have a diversified business and wish to offer plans to different parts of its enterprise. Thus, under the Code, an employer operating *qualified separate lines of business* ("QSLOBs") may elect to

have the coverage tests applied to employees of each
QSLOB individually. IRC § 410(b)(5). Under this
approach, employees of other QSLOBs are treated
as excludable employees. Treas. Reg. § 1.414(r)–
8(b)(3).

For the approach to be available, all the employer's property and services provided to customers
must be provided through *separate lines of business*
("SLOBs") and every employee must be treated as
an employee of exactly one such line of business.
Treas. Reg. § 1.414(r)–1(b)(1). Moreover, if an employer elects to test one of its plans under the
QSLOB approach, it must so test them all (except
for plans that satisfy the percentage test of IRC
§ 410(b)(1)(A), which may be tested on an employ-
er-wide basis). Treas. Reg. § 1.414(r)–1(c)(2). If
an employer elects to comply with section 410(b) on
a QSLOB basis, it must also comply with section
401(a)(4) on a QSLOB basis, and vice versa. Treas.
Reg. §§ 1.414(r)–1(c)(2)(i) & 1.414(r)–8(c)(1). However, use of the QSLOB method for compliance with
sections 410(b) and 401(a)(4) does not require its
use for compliance with section 401(a)(26), and vice
versa. Treas. Reg. § 1.414(r)–1(c)(2)(i) & (3)(i).

Although each QSLOB is tested separately, the
plan as a whole must still benefit employees on the
basis of a nondiscriminatory classification. IRC
§ 410(b)(5)(B). A plan meets this requirement if it
satisfies either a liberalized version of the nondiscriminatory classification test or the ratio percentage test. Treas. Reg. § 1.414(r)–8(b)(2). The regula-

tions state that, where a classification falls between the safe and unsafe harbors of Treas. Reg. § 1.410(b)–4(c), the fact that the QSLOB requirements, discussed below, are satisfied, will be taken into account as showing nondiscrimination and usually will be dispositive. Treas. Reg. § 1.414(r)–8(b)(2)(ii).

The criteria for a QSLOB are enormously complex. They are described in the form of a three-step procedure that employers must follow. Only the basic requirements can be described here.

1.   LOBS

To begin, an employer identifies its *lines of business* ("LOBs") by designating, for each LOB, the property or services that it provides to customers. An employer's LOBs need not be the same from year to year and a LOB may involve unrelated property and services. Nor is there a requirement that different LOBs provide different property or services; for example, different LOBs may provide the same good in geographically distinct areas or to different classes of customers. The only constraint is that the designation as different of LOBs providing the same or similar property or services must be reasonable. Treas. Reg. § 1.414(r)–2.

2.   SLOBS

Once an employer has identified its lines of business, it must then show that they are organized and

operated separately from each other. A line of
business constitutes a SLOB if it is a separate
organizational unit (e.g., corporation or division) or
group of such; is a separate profit center (or group
of such) with separate books and records; has a
separate employee workforce; and has *separate management*. Treas. Reg. § 1.414(r)–3(b). The separate employee workforce criterion is met only if at
least 90% of the employees who provide services to
the LOB, and who are not substantial-service employees with respect to any other LOB, are *substantial-service employees* with respect to the LOB. (A
substantial-service employee with respect to a LOB
is an employee who provides at least 75% of his
services to it. However, an employer may under
some circumstances treat an employee who provides
at least 50% but less than 75% of his services to a
LOB as a substantial-service employee with respect
to it. Treas. Reg. § 1.414(r)–11(b)(2).) The separate management criterion is met only if at least
80% of the *top-paid employees* with respect to a
LOB are substantial-service employees. (In general, a top-paid employee with respect to a LOB is one
who is within the top 10% by compensation of those
who provide services to that line and who are not
substantial-service employees with respect to any
other LOB. In making the determination of the
group of top-paid employees, the employer may
disregard those employees who provide less than
25% of their services to the LOB. Treas. Reg.
§ 1.414(r)–11(b)(3).)

3. QSLOBS

In order for a SLOB to constitute a QSLOB, it must have at least 50 employees (disregarding those excludable under IRC § 414(q)(5)) on each day of the testing year; the employer must notify the Secretary of the Treasury that it is electing QSLOB treatment; and the SLOB must satisfy at least one safe harbor condition. IRC § 414(r)(2).

The first such condition, prescribed by statute, is that the *highly compensated employee percentage ratio* of the SLOB (i.e. percentage of SLOB employees who are highly compensated divided by percentage of all employees who are highly compensated) is at least 50% but no more than 200%. The 50% prong of this test is deemed met if at least 10% of all HCEs of the employer perform services solely for the SLOB. IRC § 414(r)(3).

There are five other safe harbors established by regulation. One is that the SLOB be in an industry different from every other SLOB of the employer. Treas. Reg. § 1.414(r)–5(c). The IRS has established industry categories for this test, based on Standard Industrial Classification codes. Rev. Proc. 91–64. A second safe harbor is for SLOBs acquired through certain mergers or acquisitions; it may be available for up to four years after the transaction. Treas. Reg.§ 1.414(r)–5(d). A third is for SLOBs that are reported as industry segments on the annual report filed with the SEC, consistently with Financial Accounting Standard 14. Treas. Reg. § 1.414(r)–5(e).

A fourth safe harbor is based on examination of benefit percentages. If the highly compensated employee percentage ratio is less than 50%, the safe harbor is available if the actual benefit percentage of the group of NCEs of the SLOB is at least as great as the actual benefit percentage of the group of all other NCEs of the employer. If the HCE percentage ratio is greater than 200%, the safe harbor is available if the actual benefit percentage of the group of HCEs of the SLOB is no greater than the actual benefit percentage of the group of all other HCEs of the employer. Treas. Reg. § 1.414(r)–5(f).

The final safe harbor, like the prior one, is based on examination of benefits in cases where the highly compensated employee percentage ratio is less than 50% or greater than 200%. In the former case, a specified proportion of the NCEs of the SLOB must accrue a specified minimum benefit or receive a minimum allocation; in the latter case, no HCE of the SLOB may accrue a benefit or receive an allocation in excess of specified limits. Treas. Reg. § 1.414(r)–5(g).

If a SLOB fails to meet any of the foregoing safe harbors, it still may qualify as a QSLOB if the employer requests and receives an individual determination from the IRS. Treas. Reg. § 1.414(r)–6.

G. MINIMUM PARTICIPATION TEST

For defined benefit plans, use of plan aggregation to satisfy the minimum coverage tests is limited by

IRC § 401(a)(26), which requires each qualified defined benefit plan to benefit, on each day of the year, at least the lesser of: (a) 50 employees or (b) the greater of 40% of the workforce or two employees (or, if there is only one employee, that employee). (The requirement is sometimes called the *50–40 rule*.) The purpose of the rule is to prevent discrimination through fragmentation of the workforce into small plans and to simplify the IRS' task of monitoring compliance with discrimination rules. However, it applies even to employers with only a single plan.

1. PLANS TESTED

For purposes of this rule, "plan" means separate plan, as defined above, subject to special disaggregation rules. Treas. Reg. § 1.401(a)(26)–2(c). Among the mandatory disaggregation rules are the following: the portion of a plan that is an ESOP must be treated as a separate plan from the portion that is not an ESOP; the portion of a multiemployer plan that benefits employees covered by collective bargaining agreements must be treated as a separate plan from the portion that benefits employees not covered by any collective bargaining agreement; and a multiple employer plan not covering union employees must be treated as separate plans with respect to each employer. Treas. Reg. § 1.401(a)(26)–2(d)(1). A permissive disaggregation rule is that an employer may elect to treat each portion of a multiemployer plan that benefits employees covered by a given collective bargaining agreement as a separate plan. Treas. Reg. § 1.401(a)(26)–2(d)(2). Unlike as with the coverage standard, aggregation is not permitted.

2. EMPLOYEES CONSIDERED

Not all employees need be taken into account for purposes of the minimum participation test. The section 410(b) rules for excluding employees covered by collective bargaining agreements and employees who have not met minimum age and service requirements generally apply. IRC § 401(a)(26)(B)(i). However, if employees who could be excluded under ERISA's minimum age and service standards are covered under a plan that meets the minimum participation requirements separately with respect to those employees, then those employees may be excluded in determining whether any plan as a whole meets those requirements if: the benefits for such employees are provided under the same plan as the benefits for other employees; the benefits to them are not greater than comparable benefits to other employees under the plan; and no highly compensated employee is included in the group of such employees for more than one year. IRC § 410(a)(26)(B)(ii). If an employer elects to treat its business as divided into QSLOBs, it tests plans separately with respect to employees of each QSLOB, excluding employees of the others. Treas. Reg. § 1.401(a)(26)–6(b)(8). For purposes of this testing, however, the requirement that the QSLOB have at least 50 employees does not apply. IRC § 401(a)(26)(G).

3. OTHER RULES

A defined benefit plan that does not qualify for one of the exemptions discussed below must satisfy one of the following conditions: it provides meaningful benefit accruals to the lesser of 50 employees or 40% of the workforce; or if a comparable number of employees and former employees have meaningful accrued benefits under the plan. Treas. Reg. § 1.401(a)(26)–3.

If a defined benefit plan benefits former employees in a year, it must satisfy either the 50–40 rule with respect to the former employees or else a special test. A plan satisfies the special test if it benefits at least five former employees and either: more than 95% of all former employees with vested benefits benefit under the plan for the year; or at least 60% of the former employees who benefit under the plan for the year are nonhighly compensated former employees. Treas. Reg. § 1.401(a)(26)–4. Former employees may be excluded if they terminated employment before a certain date; were or would have been excludable employees in the year of termination; or have a vested benefit whose present value does not exceed $5,000. Treas. Reg. § 1.410(a)(26)–6(c). The latter exclusion is not available if the special test is used. Treas. Reg. § 1.401(a)(26)–4(d)(2).

4. EXEMPTIONS

A plan (other than a top-heavy plan or a frozen defined benefit plan) that does not benefit any highly compensated employees automatically satisfies section 401(a)(26) if it is not aggregated with other plans to satisfy section 401(a)(4) or 410(b). Treas. Reg. § 1.401(a)(26)–1(b)(1). The portion of a multiemployer plan that benefits only employees in a unit covered by a collective bargaining agreement may be treated as a separate plan satisfying the standard. Treas. Reg. § 1.401(a)(26)–1(b)(2). Other exemptions are contained in the regulations.

CHAPTER 18

NONDISCRIMINATION: CONTRIBUTIONS OR BENEFITS

Even if a plan satisfies the minimum coverage tests, it still might discriminate in favor of HCEs, for example by providing them with relatively greater benefits. IRC § 401(a)(4) prohibits this, requiring as a condition of qualification that a plan not discriminate in contributions or benefits.

The meaning of the requirement is not self-evident and the statute itself provides little guidance. IRC § 401(a)(5)(B) states that contributions or benefits may bear a uniform relation to compensation; e.g., the employer may contribute 2% of annual compensation to each employee's account. And IRC § 401(a)(5)(C) & (D) provide that certain plans which integrate benefits or contributions with Social Security do not for that reason violate the antidiscrimination requirement. But these clarifications themselves require clarification. The IRS has assumed primary responsibility for supplying workable standards.

A. THE BASIC STANDARD

Treas. Reg. §§ 1.401(a)(4)–1 to 1.401(a)(4)–13 contains the "exclusive rules for determining whether a plan satisfies section 401(a)(4)." The regulation is long and complex. Nonetheless, its main features are reasonably straightforward.

Under the regulation, every qualified plan must satisfy three conditions: (1) contributions or benefits must not be discriminatory in amount; (2) benefits, rights, and features under the plan must be made available in a nondiscriminatory manner; and (3) the effect of plan amendments and plan termination must not be discriminatory. Treas. Reg. § 1.401(a)(4)–1(b). A special rule is that a plan benefiting only collectively bargained employees automatically satisfies these conditions. Treas. Reg. § 1.401(a)(4)–1(c)(5).

Qualified plans are also required not to discriminate with respect to the manner in which employees vest in their accrued benefits or the manner in which service is credited. Treas. Reg. § 1.401(a)(4)–11(c) & (d). However, these are treated as parts of the requirement that contributions or benefits not be discriminatory in amount.

The plan subject to testing under section 401(a)(4) is the same as the plan subject to testing under section 410(b)—i.e., the plan as determined after application of mandatory disaggregation, permissive aggregation, and QSLOB rules. Treas. Reg. § 1.401(a)(4)–1(c)(4). Similarly, the leased employee and employee inclusion rules used for the coverage tests are used for the section 401(a)(4) tests as well. Treas. Reg. § 1.401(a)(4)–12. However, unlike as under the coverage tests, only employees who benefit under the plan for the year are considered. *Id.* As with the coverage tests, employees covered by a collective bargaining agreement are excluded from consideration under section 401(a)(4) if retirement benefits for them were the subject of good faith bargaining. IRC § 401(a)(4).

B. NONDISCRIMINATION IN AMOUNT OF CONTRIBUTIONS OR BENEFITS

The most complex of the three basic requirements is that a plan not discriminate in the amount of contributions or benefits. There are a variety of tests for compliance; each test, though, is of one of three formal types. One type is the safe harbor test based on plan design. Once a plan's contribution or benefit structure has been found to comply with such a test, the plan need not be tested again until it has been amended or the law has been changed. A second type is the general test, which requires elaborate calculations each year. Finally, there is an intermediate type, the safe harbor involving limited annual testing of average contribution or accrual rates. Each species of test has advantages and disadvantages, mainly with respect to cost, flexibility in plan design and administration, ease of amendment, and ease of cure in case of noncompliance.

1. DEFINED CONTRIBUTION PLANS

For defined contribution plans there are three basic tests: two safe harbors and a general test. The tests described here are for single, unintegrated plans. The impact of additional factors is discussed later.

a. Safe Harbors

The first safe harbor is based on plan design. A plan does not discriminate in amount of contributions if it allocates contributions and forfeitures based on the same percentage of compensation, the same dollar amount, or the same dollar amount per uniform unit of service. Treas. Reg. § 1.401(a)(4)–2(b)(2). This safe harbor is also available for plans that deviate from strict uniformity in allocation, so long as the deviation complies the requirements of IRC § 401(*l*) (discussed below). Treas. Reg. § 1.401(a)(4)–2(b)(2)(ii).

The second safe harbor, which is partially calculation-based, is for certain *uniform points plans*. A uniform points plan is a defined contribution plan (other than an ESOP) in which an employee receives points based on units of annual compensation, and age or service (or both). Each employee's allocation is equal to the total dollar allocation for all employees multiplied by a fraction equal to his points divided by the total points for all employees. (There are constraints on the method of assigning points.) The safe harbor is available if the average of the *allocation rates* for the HCEs does not exceed the average of the allocation rates for the NCEs. The allocation rate for an employee is the sum of allocations to his account for the year, expressed as either a percentage of compensation or a dollar amount. Treas. Reg. §§ 1.401(a)(4)–2(b)(3) & 1.401(a)(4)–2(c)(2).

As an example, suppose that a uniform points plan grants 10 points for each year of service and 1 point for each $100 of compensation. There are two highly compensated employees. H1 has 25 years of service and earns $100,000; H2 has 10 years of service and earns $150,000. There are three nonhighly compensated employees. N1 has 30 years of service and earns $40,000; N2 has 10 years of service and earns $25,000; and N3 has 3 years of service and earns $20,000. H1 has 1,250 points (250 for service and 1,000 for compensation); H2 has 1,600; N1 has 700; N2 has 350; and N3 has 230. There are a total of 4,130 points. If the total allocation for the year is $41,300, the allocation rates are: H1, 12.5% ($12,500 allocation/$100,000 compensation); H2, 10.7%; N1, 17.5%; N2, 14%; and N3, 11.5%. The average allocation rate of the HCEs is 11.6%. The average allocation rate of the NCEs is 14.3%. The plan satisfies the second safe harbor test.

These safe harbors remain available even in some cases where the plan imposes limits on allocations, uses multiple allocation formulas, or contains other specified provisions. Treas. Reg. § 1.401(a)(4)–2(b)(4).

There are other, more limited, safe harbors. An important one is that an otherwise qualified 401(k) plan is deemed to satisfy the requirement of nondiscrimination in amount of contributions. Treas. Reg. § 1.401(a)(4)–1(b)(2)(ii)(B). Nondiscrimination rules for 401(k) plans are discussed further in Chapter 20.

b. General Test

A defined contribution plan that cannot satisfy one of the safe harbor tests must satisfy the general test, which requires each *rate group* under the plan to satisfy the minimum coverage requirements of section 410(b). A rate group consists of an HCE and all other employees in the plan who have an allocation rate greater than or equal to that of the HCE. Treas. Reg. § 1.401(a)(4)–2(c)(1). For example, in the plan described above, the rate group for H1 consists of H1, N1 and N2; the rate group for H2 consists of the entire workforce.

In applying the section 410(b) tests, each rate group is treated as if it were a separate plan benefiting only the included employees. A rate group may not be aggregated with other rate groups or plans. In applying the nondiscriminatory classification test, the reasonable classification test is deemed met; the facts and circumstances test is deemed met if and only if the ratio percentage of the rate group is greater than or equal to the lesser of the ratio percentage of the plan or the average of the safe and unsafe harbor percentages for the plan. A rate group satisfies the average benefit percentage test if the plan of which it is a part does so (subject to special rules for collectively bargained plans). Treas. Reg. § 1.401(a)(4)–2(c)(3).

2. DEFINED BENEFIT PLANS

For defined benefit plans, there are five safe harbors (four of which are design-based) and two general tests. Again, the tests described immediately below are the basic ones. Complicating factors are discussed later.

a. Safe Harbors

To be able to rely on a safe harbor, a defined benefit plan must satisfy a few preliminary requirements. It must use the same benefit formula and normal retirement age for all employees; provide a normal retirement benefit that is the same form for all employees and the same percentage of average annual compensation or same dollar amount for all employees with the same number of years of service; provide benefits commencing after normal retirement age that are the same percentage of average annual compensation or same dollar amount as would be payable at normal retirement age for the same number of years of service; provide each subsidized optional form of benefit to substantially all employees in the plan; not accept employee contributions; and provide that each employee's benefit must be accrued over the same years of service that are taken into account in applying the plan's benefit formula. Treas. Reg. § 1.401(a)(4)–3(b)(2).

The first safe harbor is for unit credit plans (i.e., those in which participants accrue a unit of retirement benefit for each year of service) that satisfy the 133–1/3 percent accrual rule and in which the benefit formula is solely a function of years of service and, perhaps, average annual compensation. Treas. Reg. § 1.401(a)(4)–3(b)(3). For example, a plan that provides for an accrued benefit of 1.5% of average compensation for the first 10 years of service and 1.75% for years thereafter satisfies the test. Average annual compensation is the employee's highest average of annual compensation over a period of three or more consecutive years (or the full period of service, if shorter) in his compensation history. Treas. Reg. § 1.401(a)(4)–3(e)(2).

A second safe harbor is for unit credit plans using the fractional accrual rule. Such plans must satisfy two additional conditions. First, the accrued benefit before normal retirement age must be equal to the fractional rule benefit (see Chapter 8) times the following fraction: years of service/projected years of service as of normal retirement age. Second, the accrual rate for any participant (except those projected to have more than 33 years of service at normal retirement age) cannot exceed 133–1/3% of the accrual rate for any other participant in the same or any other year. Treas. Reg. §§ 1.401(a)(4)–3(b)(4)(i)(A), (B) & (C)(1). For example, a plan that provides for a normal retirement benefit of 2% of average annual compensation, up to 30 years, with the accrued benefit equal to the fractional rule benefit times years of service/projected years of service, satisfies the test. The highest accrual rate (for those with 30 years of service or less) is 2% of average compensation. The lowest accrual rate considered is the rate for those with 33 years of service. It is equal to the normal retirement benefit divided by 33 years, which is equal to (2% x 30 years x average compensation/33 years), or 2% x (30/33) of average annual compensation (i.e., 1.8%). Thus, the ratio of highest accrual rate to lowest accrual rate is 33/30. In other words, the highest rate is only 110% of lowest rate, and the test is satisfied.

The next two safe harbors are for flat benefit plans using the fractional accrual rule. One requirement is that the accrued benefit before normal retirement age be equal to the fractional rule benefit times the following fraction: years of service/projected years of service as of normal retirement age. A second requirement is that the plan provide a retirement benefit which is a flat benefit; i.e., either the same percentage of average compensation or the same dollar amount for all employees with a minimum number of years of service at normal retirement age, with a pro rata reduction for employees with fewer years of service at normal retirement age. Third, under one safe harbor, a plan must require a minimum of 25 years of service at normal retirement age for an unreduced flat benefit. Treas. Reg. §§ 1.401(a)(4)–3(b)(4)(i)(A), (B) & (C)(2). Under the alternative—a calculation-based safe harbor—the average of *normal accrual rates* for all nonhighly compensated nonexcludable employees must be at least 70% of the average of the normal accrual rates for all highly compensated nonexcludable employees. Treas. Reg. § 1.401(a)(4)–3(b)(4)(i)(C)(3). Normal accrual rate is a complicated concept; in general, it is the annual rate at which the normal retirement benefit accrues. Treas. Reg. § 1.401(a)(4)–3(d)(1)(i).

The final safe harbor is for insurance contract plans that satisfy a special accrual standard and certain other requirements relating to benefit formulas and premiums. Treas. Reg. § 1.401(a)(4)–3(b)(5).

These safe harbors are also available for plans whose benefit formula is not strictly uniform, so long as the deviation from uniformity complies with the requirements of IRC § 401(*l*). Treas. Reg. § 1.401(a)(4)–3(b)(6)(ii). The regulations specify other plan provisions that will not affect satisfaction of a safe-harbor test. Treas. Reg. § 1.401(a)(4)–3(b)(6).

b. General Tests

As with defined contribution plans, a defined benefit plan satisfies a general test for nondiscrimination if each *rate group* under the plan satisfies section 410(b) (modified as in the general test for defined contribution plans). Rate group, however, is defined differently: as the HCE and all other employees who have both a normal accrual rate greater than or equal to that of the HCE and a *most valuable accrual rate* greater than or equal to that of the HCE. Treas. Reg. § 1.401(a)(4)–3(c)(1). Most valuable accrual rate is a complex concept; in general, it is the annual rate at which the most valuable optional form of benefit accrues. Treas. Reg. § 1.401(a)(4)–3(d)(1)(ii).

A plan that does not satisfy the general test may be deemed to do so if: (a) the plan would satisfy the general test by disregarding no more than 5% of the HCEs and (b) the Commissioner determines that, on the basis of all relevant facts and circumstances, the plan does not discriminate with respect to the amount of benefits. Regulations describe factors that may be taken into account in making the latter determination. Treas. Reg. § 1.401(a)(4)–3(c)(3).

3.   CROSS–TESTING

For a plan to be qualified, either contributions or benefits must be nondiscriminatory but not necessarily both. Although it is usual to test a defined contribution plan by reference to contributions and a defined benefit plan by reference to benefits, this need not be the case. A defined benefit plan may be tested by reference to contributions or a defined contribution plan by reference to benefits. Sometimes, there is no choice.

Cross-testing, as this method is called, normally must use one of the general tests. Treas. Reg. § 1.401(a)(4)–8(a). However, safe harbors are available for certain target benefit plans and for defined benefit plans in which benefits are offset by the account balance in a defined contribution plan. Treas. Reg. § 1.401(a)(4)–8(b)(3) & (d).

A defined contribution plan (except for an ESOP) satisfies the general test for nondiscrimination in amount of benefits if each rate group, defined in terms of *equivalent accrual rates*, satisfies section 410(b) (modified as in the general tests described above). An equivalent accrual rate is a translation of an allocation rate into an accrual rate, using one of two methods permitted by the rules. Treas. Reg. § 1.401(a)(4)–8(b)(1)(i)(A) & (2). In addition, the plan must satisfy one of the following three conditions: the plan has *broadly available allocation rates,* i.e., each allocation rate is currently available to a group of employees that satisfies IRC § 410(b) (without regard to the average benefit test); the plan has an age-based allocation rate of a type permitted under the regulations; or else the plan satisfies the *minimum allocation gateway*, i.e., each NCHE has an allocation rate equal to at least 1/3 of the highest NCE allocation rate or equal to at least 5% of her compensation. Treas. Reg. § 1.401(a)(4)–8(b)(1)(i)(B).

A defined benefit plan satisfies the general test for nondiscrimination in amount of contributions if each rate group satisfies section 410(b), where rate groups are defined in terms of *equivalent normal allocation rates* and *equivalent most valuable allocation rates*. Detailed methods are given in the regulations for converting accrual rates into equivalent normal allocation rates and equivalent most valuable allocation rates. Treas. Reg. § 1.401(a)(4)–8(c).

4. COMPLICATING FACTORS

Under some circumstances, special rules apply to the testing of a plan under section 401(a)(4). One important set of rules, those concerning integration and disparities, are discussed in the next section. Others are sketched below.

a. Former Employees

Employees and former employees must be tested separately under the standards described above. Treas. Reg. § 1.401(a)(4)–1(c)(6). Special rules for applying the standards to former employees are set out in the regulations. Treas. Reg. § 1.401(a)(4)–10.

b. Employee Contributions

In general, employee-provided contributions and benefits are tested separately from employer-provided contributions and benefits. Treas. Reg. § 1.401(a)(4)–1(c)(7). Defined benefit plans that include employee contributions not allocated to separate accounts are tested under special rules, both with respect to benefits derived from employer contributions and benefits derived from employee contributions. Treas. Reg. § 1.401(a)(4)–6.

c. Combined Plan

When defined benefit and defined contribution plans are aggregated for testing purposes, special rules are necessary. Safe harbors are unavailable, and cross-testing is required. Treas. Reg. § 1.401(a)(4)–9(b) provides rules for testing such plans.

Unless the combined plan is primarily defined benefit in character (within the meaning of Treas. Reg. § 1.401(a)(4)–9(b)(2)(v)(B)) or consists of broadly available separate plans (within the meaning of Treas. Reg. § 1.401(a)(4)–9(b)(2)(v)(C)), it must satisfy the *minimum aggregative allocation gateway* in order to be eligible for testing on the basis of benefits. Treas. Reg. § 1.401(a)(4)–9(b)(2)(v)(A). The minimum aggregative allocation gateway is satisfied if either the aggregate normal allocation rate for each NCHE is at least 7.5% of her compensation or else a more complicated condition on NCHE allocation rate is satisfied. Treas. Reg. § 1.401(a)(4)–9(b)(2)(v)(D).

d. Plan Restructuring

A plan may be treated as consisting of two or more *component plans* for a year, each of which may be tested as if it were a separate plan. Under this

method, if each component plan satisfies sections
401(a)(4) and 410(b), then the plan as a whole
satisfies section 401(a)(4). It is important to note
that the component plans' compliance with section
410(b) is relevant only to the whole plan's compliance with section 401(a)(4). Even if all the component plans satisfy section 410(b), the plan must still
satisfy section 410(b) as a whole to be qualified.
Treas. Reg. § 1.401(a)(4)–9(c)(1).

A component plan consists of all the allocations,
accruals, and other benefits, rights and features for
a designated group of employees. Any classification
may be used, so long as each employee is included
in exactly one component plan for the year. Treas.
Reg. § 1.401(a)(4)–9(c)(2). In general, the rules applicable to determining whether a plan satisfies
section 401(a)(4) apply to component plans (except
the safe harbor rule for plans with uniform points
allocation formulas, and certain rules for 401(k) and
401(m) plans). Treas. Reg. § 1.401(a)(4)–9(c)(3).
The rules of 410(b) also generally apply, except that
there is no permissive aggregation and the average
benefit percentage test is generally applied to the
whole plan, rather than the component plan, and
without regard for the special rules for collectively
bargained plans. Treas. Reg. § 1.401(a)(4)–9(c)(4).

C. INTEGRATION AND DISPARITIES

The Social Security benefit structure favors lower
paid employees. An employer thus might wish to
skew benefits or contributions under a plan in favor

of HCEs so as to achieve a more uniform relationship between compensation and the total of plan and Social Security benefits (or else the total of plan and FICA contributions). A plan so structured may still comply with section 401(a)(4) through any one of three possible means. It may satisfy the permitted disparity standards of section 401(*l*); it may satisfy one of the general tests, with accruals or contributions adjusted for the permitted disparity; or satisfy the offset formula of section 401(a)(5)(D).

1.   SECTION 401(*l*) PERMITTED DISPARITY

A plan's *disparity* is the amount by which its contribution or benefit formula deviates from a uniform rate so as to favor HCEs. IRC § 401(*l*) permits certain plans with disparities of a prescribed form and within prescribed limits to comply with the section 401(a)(4) requirements concerning amounts of benefits or contributions.

Compliance with section 401(*l*) is intimately connected with plan design. Only plans with specified formal features can satisfy section 401(*l*), and only plans with disparities that satisfy section 401(*l*) can rely on a design-based safe harbor to comply with section 401(a)(4) (in which case the disparities are simply ignored). Treas. Reg. §§ 1.401(a)(4)–2(b)(2)(ii) & 1.401(a)(4)–3(b)(6)(ii). There are different section 401(*l*) standards for different kinds of plans.

a. Defined Contribution Excess Plans

A *defined contribution excess plan* is a defined contribution plan that specifies an *integration level*—which may not be greater than the Social Security taxable wage base, IRC § 401(*l*)(5)(A)(ii)—and sets the employer contribution rate to be higher for portions of employee compensation above that level. Treas. Reg. § 1.401(*l*)–1(c)(16)(ii). The employer contribution rate for amounts up to and including the integration level is called the *base contribution percentage*. Treas. Reg. § 1.401(*l*)–1(c)(4). The rate for amounts above the integration level is called the *excess contribution percentage*. Treas. Reg. § 1.401(*l*)–1(c)(15). Their difference is the disparity. Treas. Reg. § 1.401(*l*)–1(c)(10)(i). For example, a defined contribution plan may specify a contribution rate of 1% of annual compensation up to and including the taxable wage base and 2% for amounts above that level. For this plan, the integration level is the taxable wage base and the disparity is 1%.

A defined contribution excess plan meets the standards of section 401(*l*) if the integration level, base contribution percentage and excess contribution percentage are respectively the same for all employees in the plan (with minor exceptions), and the disparity is no more than the *maximum excess allowance*. The integration level may be either: (i) the taxable wage base; (ii) a dollar amount that does not exceed the greater of $10,000 or 20% of the taxable wage base; or (iii) a figure in between. For integration levels equal to the taxable wage base, or else not greater than the option (ii) limit, the maximum excess allowance is the lesser of the base contribution percentage, or 5.7% (or, if it ever becomes greater, the employer portion of the FICA tax attributable to old-age insurance). For integration levels between 80% and 100% of the taxable wage base, the 5.7% figure is replaced with 5.4%. For integration levels greater than the option (ii) limit, but less than or equal to 80% of the taxable wage base, the 5.7% figure is replaced with 4.3%. IRC § 401(l)(2) & (5)(A); Treas. Reg. § 1.401(l)–2(b) to (d).

b. Defined Benefit Excess Plans

In a *defined benefit excess plan*, an integration level is specified (at or below the taxable wage base) and employer-based accrual rates are greater with respect to average annual compensation above the integration level than below or equal to it. Treas. Reg. § 1.401(l)–1(c)(16)(i). For such a plan to satisfy section 401(l), the disparity—here, the *excess benefit percentage* less the *base benefit percentage*, Treas. Reg. § 1.401(l)–1(c)(10)(ii)—may not exceed the *maximum excess allowance*. IRC § 401(l)(3)(A)(i).

Base and excess benefit percentages are defined analogously to excess and base contribution percentages. Treas. Reg. § 1.401(l)–1(c)(3) & (14). The maximum excess allowance is the lesser of 0.75% or the base benefit percentage. Treas. Reg.

§ 1.401(*l*)–3(b)(2). Thus, for example, if the normal retirement benefit of an employee, whose Social Security retirement age is 65, is 1.25% of average annual compensation up to covered compensation, plus 2% for compensation in excess of covered compensation, then section 401(*l*) is satisfied. The 0.75% figure may be adjusted if the integration level is chosen to be other than an employee's *covered compensation* or if benefits commence other than at the Social Security retirement age (as defined by section 415(b)(8)). Treas. Reg. §§ 1.401(*l*)–3(d)(9) & 1.401(*l*)–3(e)(2). For example, if the plan just described also provides for the payment of 80% of the normal retirement benefit at age 62, then the excess benefit percentage in such case is 1.6% (i.e., 80% of 2%), the base benefit percentage is 1%, and the disparity is 0.6%. For such an early distribution, regulations reduce the maximum excess allowance to 0.6%, and section 401(*l*) remains satisfied.

Covered compensation is the average of the taxable wage bases for the 35 year period ending with the year in which the employee attains or will attain Social Security retirement age. The taxable wage base for any future year is assumed to be the same as that for the present year. Treas. Reg. § 1.401(*l*)–1(c)(7).

c. Defined Benefit Offset Plans

In a *defined benefit offset plan*, the employer-provided benefit is initially determined by the *gross accrual rate* times average annual compensation, but is then reduced by a specified percentage (the disparity, or *offset percentage*) of *final average compensation* up to the *offset level* of the plan. Treas. Reg. § 1.401(*l*)–1(c)(25). For example, an offset plan might provide that the normal retirement benefit is 2% of average annual compensation, less 0.5% of final average compensation up to the employee's covered compensation. Final average compensation is the average annual compensation (up to the taxable wage base) for the 3–consecutive year period ending with the current year or, if shorter, the participant's full period of service. Treas. Reg. § 1.401(*l*)–1(c)(17).

To satisfy section 401(*l*), the disparity may not exceed the *maximum offset allowance*. IRC § 401(*l*)(3)(B). That allowance is generally equal to the lesser of (a) 0.75%; or (b) 50% of *gross benefit percentage* times a fraction (not to exceed 1) equal to average annual compensation divided by final average compensation up to the offset level. Treas. Reg. § 1.401(*l*)–3(b)(3). The gross benefit percentage is the rate at which employer-provided benefits are determined (before application of an offset), as a percentage of average annual compensation. Treas. Reg. § 1.401(*l*)–1(c)(18). The 0.75% figure must be adjusted if the offset level is other than covered compensation or if benefits commence other than at the Social Security retirement age. Treas. Reg. §§ 1.401(*l*)–3(d)(9) & 1.401(*l*)–3(e)(2).

d. Additional Requirements for Defined Benefit Plans

In a defined benefit excess plan, the base and excess benefit percentages must be the same for all employees with the same number of years of service, and in an offset plan, the same gross benefit percentage and same offset percentage must be used for all employees with the same number of years of service. Treas. Reg. § 1.401(*l*)–3(c)(1). The integration or offset level must be determined the same way for each employee (although it need not be the same absolute number). Treas. Reg. § 1.401(*l*)–3(d).

e. Overall Permitted Disparity

The rules above apply in unmodified form only where an employee is covered by one plan, and they apply to only one year. There are additional, aggregate limits on the permitted disparity.

One limit is that, for a given plan year, an employee's *total annual disparity fraction* cannot exceed 1. Treas. Reg. § 1.401(*l*)–5(b)(1). The total annual disparity fraction is the sum of five types of components, one for each plan covering the employee. The first type of component, the *annual defined contribution plan disparity fraction*, is computed for each defined contribution excess plan satisfying section 401(*l*). It is equal to the disparity divided by the maximum excess allowance. Second, the *annual defined benefit excess plan disparity fraction*, computed for each defined benefit excess plan satisfying section 401(l), is equal to the disparity divided by the maximum excess allowance. Third, the *annual offset plan disparity fraction*, computed for each offset plan satisfying section 401(l), is equal to the disparity divided by the maximum offset allowance. Fourth, the *annual imputed disparity fraction*, for plans that rely on an imputed disparity, is equal to one. (Thus, such a plan cannot be combined with any plan that satisfies section 401(l).) Fifth, the *annual nondisparate fraction* is zero for plans that are do not rely on section 401(l) or an imputed disparity to comply with section 401(a)(4). The fractions are calculated after any aggregation of plans for purposes of section 401(a)(4). Treas. Reg. § 1.401(l)–5(b)(2) to (8).

A second limitation is on an employee's cumulative disparity (whether under one or more plans) over his total years of service. This limitation applies only with respect to employees who benefited under a defined benefit plan that either satisfied section 401(l) or that imputed disparities (see below) for plan years beginning after December 31, 1993. For such employees, the *cumulative permitted disparity fraction*—the sum of total annual disparity fractions for all years of service—may not exceed 35. For purposes of this rule, total annual disparity fraction for any plan years before 1989 is 1, and, for simplicity, the employer may presume the fraction in any other year to be 1. Treas. Reg. § 1.401(l)–5(c).

2. IMPUTED DISPARITY

If a plan is integrated, but does not satisfy section 401(l), it may still satisfy section 401(a)(4). However, it must be tested for compliance under one of the general tests. To do this, one uses not the plan's actual allocation or accrual rates but adjusted allocation or accrual rates that take into account the disparities permitted under 401(l). Use of this *imputed disparity* is optional; a plan that does not need it does not have to use it.

a. Adjusted Allocation Rate

The purpose of the adjustment to allocation rates is to develop a hypothetical contribution formula that uses the taxable wage base as integration level and incorporates the maximum permitted disparity. The method is as follows. If an employee's compensation for the year does not exceed the taxable wage base, the *adjusted allocation rate* is equal to the lesser of: twice the unadjusted allocation rate, or the unadjusted allocation rate plus the permitted disparity rate. For employees whose compensation is higher, the adjusted allocation rate is equal to the lesser of: allocations/(compensation for the year— 1/2 taxable wage base); or (allocations + (permitted disparity rate × taxable wage base))/yearly compensation. Treas. Reg. § 1.401(a)(4)–7(b). One then uses these rates in the general test.

An example may help clarify this approach. Assume that A and B are participants in a plan, and that the taxable wage base is $55,500. A's compensation is $25,000 and his allocation is $2,750, or 5%. B's compensation is $100,000 and his allocation is $7,500, or 7.5%. A's adjusted allocation rate is 10%—i.e. the excess contribution percentage the plan could use with a base percentage of 5%. B's adjusted allocation rate is 10.38%, which is the lesser of: (a) $7,500/(100,000 - 1/2(55,500)) = 10.38\%$; and (b) $[7,500 + (5.7\% \times 55,500)]/100,000 = 10.66\%$. (Note that an excess contribution percentage of 10.38% and a base percentage of 5.19%, applied to compensation of $100,000 yields $7,500, the actual contribution for B.) Using the adjusted allocation rates for A, B, and all other participants, one determines rate groups and tests them under the modified 410(b) standard.

b. Adjusted Accrual Rate

A similar method is used to adjust accrual rates. One develops a hypothetical formula and excess benefit percentage, assuming the plan took into account the full permitted disparity in each of the first 35 years of testing and used the employee's covered compensation as the integration level. The method is as follows. For employees whose *average annual compensation* does not exceed covered compensation, the *adjusted accrual rate* is the lesser of: twice the unadjusted accrual rate, or the unadjusted accrual rate + permitted disparity factor. For other employees, the adjusted accrual rate is the lesser of: employer provided accrual/(average annual compensation – 1/2 covered compensation); or (employer provided accrual + (permitted disparity factor × covered compensation))/average annual compensation. Treas. Reg. § 1.401(a)(4)–7(c).

3. SOCIAL SECURITY OFFSET PLANS

IRC § 401(a)(5)(D) provides that a defined benefit plan will not violate section 401(a)(4) merely because the employer-provided accrued benefit is limited to the excess, if any, of the employee's final pay over the employer-derived portion of the Social Security primary retirement benefit attributable to service with the employer. Final pay is highest annual compensation in the final five year period. The portion of the Social Security benefit attributable to service with the employer is equal to years of service with the employer (up to 35) divided by 35. *See* Treas. Reg. § 1.401(a)(5)–1(e)(3)(ii).

D. NONDISCRIMINATION IN BENEFITS, RIGHTS AND FEATURES

The second prong of the section 401(a)(4) standard is that benefits, rights, and features under the plan must be available in a nondiscriminatory manner. This requirement involves two subtests that each benefit, right or feature must separately meet. Treas. Reg. § 1.401(a)(4)–4(a)(1).

First, the group of employees to whom a benefit, right or feature is *currently available* in a plan year must satisfy either the ratio percentage test or the nondiscriminatory classification test. Whether a benefit, right or feature is currently available depends on current facts and circumstances. In determining whether an optional form of benefit or Social Security supplement is currently available, age or service conditions are disregarded (unless, in some cases, the condition must be satisfied within a limited time). Certain other contingencies, such as death, termination of employment, disability and hardship are also disregarded. Treas. Reg. § 1.401(a)(4)–4(b).

Second, the group of employees to whom the benefit, right or feature is *effectively available* must not substantially favor HCEs. Effective availability is determined in light of all the facts and circumstances. Treas. Reg. § 1.401(a)(4)–4(c).

In general, each benefit, right or feature must be tested separately. However, aggregation of any two optional forms of benefit, ancillary benefits, and other rights and features is permissible if two conditions are met. First, one of the two is in all cases inherently of equal or greater value than the other. Second, the one of inherently equal or greater value separately satisfies the requirement of nondiscriminatory availability. Once two optional forms of benefits, ancillary benefits, rights or features have been aggregated to meet the tests, they may be treated as one such benefit, right or feature, and aggregated with yet others for purposes of further testing. Treas. Reg. § 1.401(a)(4)–4(d)(4). The

regulations describe the kinds of benefits, rights
and features for which aggregation is permissible.

E. NONDISCRIMINATION
IN AMENDMENTS

A plan violates section 401(a)(4) if an amendment
or series of amendments discriminates significantly
in favor of HCEs. (Here, amendment includes establishment or termination of a plan.) Whether an
amendment or series of amendments discriminates
is determined in light of all relevant facts and
circumstances. Some factors are listed in the regulations. The test for discrimination is generally
determined as of the time the amendment becomes
effective. Treas. Reg. § 1.401(a)(4)–5(a).

There is a safe harbor for grants of past service
credits. An amendment to such effect is not discriminatory if the period for which the credit is
granted does not exceed the five years immediately
preceding the year in which the amendment becomes effective; the past service credit is granted
on a reasonably uniform basis; the amount of the
credit is determined by applying the current plan
formula to the number of years credited; and the
period of credit represents actual service (or, in
some cases, service imputed for periods of absence).
However, the safe harbor is not available for such
an amendment if it is part of a pattern of amendments that significantly discriminates in favor of
HCEs. Treas. Reg. § 1.401(a)(4)–5(a)(3).

A defined benefit plan must incorporate provisions restricting benefits and distributions. It must provide that, in the event of plan termination, the benefit of any HCE or HCFE is limited to a benefit that is nondiscriminatory under section 401(a)(4). It must also provide that the annual payments to HCEs and HCFEs (optionally limited to the 25 or more most highly compensated for the year) are restricted to an annual amount equal to the payments that would be made on behalf of the employee under a straight life annuity actuarially equivalent to the accrued benefit and other benefits to which the employee is entitled (plus any Social Security supplement). A distribution need not be limited for an employee, however, if: after payment of all benefits to him, the value of plan assets is at least equal to 110% of plan liabilities; the value of benefits payable to him is less than 1% of plan liabilities before distribution; or the value of benefits payable to him does not exceed $5,000. Treas. Reg. § 1.401(a)(4)–5(b).

F. RETROACTIVE CORRECTIONS

Because a plan's compliance or noncompliance with some of the nondiscrimination tests (especially the general tests for nondiscrimination in amount) may not be determinable until after the close of the plan year, the regulations permit amendments that retroactively bring a plan into compliance with sections 401(a)(4) and certain other provisions. Certain corrective amendments are allowed for purposes of bringing the plan into compliance with the minimum coverage requirements; the nondiscriminatory amount requirement; nondiscriminatory plan amendment; and the nondiscriminatory current availability requirement. It is not permitted in order to correct for failure to incorporate the special termination restrictions of defined benefit plans. Treas. Reg. § 1.401(a)(4)–11(g)(2).

There are four conditions on any such retroactive amendment. It may not reduce benefits. It must be effective as of the first day of the plan year. It must be adopted and implemented before the 15th day of the 10th month after the close of the plan year. Finally, the additional allocations or accruals must separately comply with section 401(a)(4) and must benefit a group of employees that separately satisfies section 410(b), unless the amendment is for purposes of conforming the plan to a section 401(a)(4) safe harbor. There are also special conditions for amendments to satisfy the nondiscriminatory availability requirement, and for 401(k) and 401(m) plans. Treas. Reg. § 1.401(a)(4)–11(g)(2).

CHAPTER 19

ADDITIONAL LIMITATIONS ON CONTRIBUTIONS AND BENEFITS

The nondiscrimination rules are not the only ones designed to prevent plan-related advantages from flowing disproportionately to managerial and more highly paid employees. In this chapter we examine yet another: the section 415 limits on amounts of contributions and benefits.

While the nondiscrimination rules limit the *relative* extent to which a plan can favor highly compensated employees, IRC § 415 limits the *absolute* amount that a plan may benefit any employee. IRC § 401(a)(16) makes compliance with the section 415 limits a condition of qualification. A qualified plan, by its terms, must preclude the possibility that those limits will be exceeded. Treas. Reg. § 1.415–1(d).

Section 415 contains limits for both annual contributions to defined contribution plans and annual benefits payable from defined benefit plans. For purposes of section 415, all defined contribution plans of an employer are treated as a single defined contribution plan and all defined benefit plans of an employer are treated as a single defined benefit plan. IRC § 415(f)(1). "Plan," here, includes trusteed plans, annuity plans, annuity contracts and simplified employee pensions. IRC § 415(k)(1). The aggregation rules of section 414 are applied, with modifications that broaden their reach, for purposes of identifying all the plans of the employer. IRC § 415(g) & (h).

A. DEFINED CONTRIBUTION PLANS

The basic limit for defined contribution plans is that the *annual addition*—in general, the employer and employee contributions, plus forfeitures, in the *limitation year*—that increase a participant's account cannot exceed the lesser of $40,000 (subject to future adjustments for inflation), or 100% of the participant's compensation. IRC § 415(c)(1). The amount of the annual addition does not include rollovers or asset transfers from other plans, or repayments by the participant. Treas. Reg. § 1.415–6(b)(3). The meaning of compensation has been discussed above (Chapter 17). Compensation includes elective deferrals. IRC § 415(c)(3)(D). The limitation year is the calendar year, unless the employer elects otherwise. Treas. Reg. § 1.415–2(b).

It follows from the rule that contributions and forfeitures with respect to former employees (who have zero compensation) are not allowed. There is an exception, however, for participants who are permanently and totally disabled. For any such participant who is a NCFE, the employer may elect to treat as her compensation the compensation she would receive if she were paid at the rate she had been paid immediately before becoming permanently and totally disabled, so long as contributions made with respect to such compensation are nonforfeitable when made. Moreover, if the plan provides for continued contributions on behalf of *all* permanently and totally disabled participants for a fixed or determinable period, this exception is not limited to NCFEs and does not require the employer's election. IRC § 415(c)(3)(C).

B. DEFINED BENEFIT PLANS

The basic limit for defined benefit plans is that benefits payable to a participant, expressed as an *annual benefit*, cannot exceed the lesser of an indexed amount ($160,000 in 2003) or 100% of the participant's average compensation for her highest consecutive three years. IRC § 415(b)(1). The limitation does not apply, however, to individuals whose retirement benefits do not exceed $10,000 and who never participated in a defined contribution plan of the employer. IRC § 415(b)(4). In addition, the average compensation limit does not apply to certain participants in non-multiemployer collectively bargained plans that have at least 100 participants and that satisfy various conditions regarding participation, vesting and accrual. IRC § 415(b)(7).

Annual benefit means a benefit payable in the form of a straight life annuity, without ancillary benefits, under a plan in which employees do not contribute and no rollover contributions are allowed. IRC § 415(b)(2)(A). The regulations provide for actuarially adjusting benefits that are payable in other annuity forms and benefits from plans that provide for employee contributions or rollovers. QJSAs, however, are not are not actuarially adjusted, nor are benefits not directly related to retirement benefits (e.g., preretirement disability and death benefits). Treas. Reg. § 1.415–3(b) & (c). The indexed dollar limit is actuarially adjusted for benefits commencing before or after the participant's Social Security retirement age. IRC § 415(b)(2)(C) & (D).

For employees who have fewer than 10 years of participation in a plan, the limits are modified. The indexed dollar limit is reduced by multiplying it by the number of years of participation divided by 10 (but to no less than 10% of the original limitation). IRC § 415(b)(5)(A) & (C). In addition, the limits determined by (a) the average compensation factor used in determining the basic defined benefit limit and (b) the $10,000 figure for those who never participated in a defined contribution plan, are multiplied by a fraction equal to years of service (not participation) divided by 10 (but to no less than 10% of the original). IRC § 415(b)(5)(B) & (C).

C. AGGREGATE LIMITATIONS

The limitations above are limitations for defined contribution and defined benefit plans taken sepa-

rately.   There are different limitations for employees who participate in both defined contribution
and defined benefit plans of an employer.   IRC
§ 415(e).   However, the combined limitations standard has been eliminated for plan years after 1999.
Transition rules are provided in IRS Notice 99–44.

CHAPTER 20

CASH OR DEFERRED ARRANGEMENTS

Cash or deferred arrangements, or CODAs (also known as 401(k) plans), have become increasingly popular as retirement arrangements, whether alone or as supplement to another plan. The distinguishing characteristic of a CODA is that the employee can elect to receive payment from the employer either as cash (usually as current compensation) or as a pre-tax (IRC § 402(e)(3)) contribution to a defined contribution plan. For the employer, an advantage is relative ease of administration. For employees, an advantage is flexibility in allocating income between current compensation and retirement saving.

CODAs can present significant discrimination issues, because highly compensated employees are more likely than non-highly compensated employees to elect to receive a plan contribution instead of current income. Thus, IRC § 401(k), the principal Code section governing CODAs, is mainly concerned with preventing discrimination. This chapter provides an overview of the rules relating to CODAs, with special emphasis on the nondiscrimination standards for these plans.

A. QUALIFIED CASH OR DEFERRED ARRANGEMENTS

1. BASIC QUALIFICATION REQUIREMENTS

A profit-sharing or stock-bonus plan (or pre-ERISA money purchase plan) may include a cash or deferred arrangement. A CODA is an arrangement in which an eligible employee may elect to have the employer make payments either as contributions to the plan (*elective contributions*) or in cash to the employee. If the plan is qualified, the CODA will not cause it to be disqualified, so long as the CODA is a *qualified cash or deferred arrangement*. IRC § 401(k)(1).

A qualified CODA must satisfy three main requirements. First, the CODA may not permit distribution of amounts attributable to elective contributions earlier than age 59½ except in the case of severance from employment, death or disability, certain plan terminations or, in very limited cases, hardship on the employee. IRC § 401(k)(2)(B)(i). The CODA may not distribute amounts attributable to elective contributions merely by reason of the completion of a stated period of participation or the lapse of time. IRC § 401(k)(2)(B)(ii). Second, the employee's interest in amounts attributable to elective contributions must vest immediately. IRC § 401(k)(2)(C). Third, the plan may require no more than one year of service as a condition of participation. IRC § 401(k)(2)(D).

2. CONTRIBUTIONS TO CODAs

Every CODA must provide for elective contributions. For example, a plan may permit eligible employees to defer up to 5% of salary or wages per year. The payment from the employer that is subject to the employee's election ordinarily is his compensation, but it may be a bonus. Treas. Reg. § 1.401(k)–1(a)(3)(vi). Qualification standards limit the amount of an employee's aggregate elective deferrals to a specified maximum dollar amount ($12,000 in 2003.) IRC §§ 401(a)(30) & 402(g)(1). This amount is lower than the total limit on contributions to defined contribution plans (see Chapter 19).

A CODA may also provide for employer and employee contributions of other types as well. A plan may provide for employee after-tax contributions. IRC § 401(m). It may also provide for an employer to make *matching (or partially matching) contributions*. A matching contribution is an employer contribution made on account of an employee's elective deferral (or on account of an employee's contribution to a defined contribution plan). IRC § 401(m)(4)(A). For example, a plan may provide for elective deferrals of up to 10% of compensation and employer contributions that match, dollar-for-dollar, the first 3% of such deferrals. *Qualified matching contributions* are matching contributions that satisfy the vesting and distribution requirements applicable to elective contributions for qualified CODAs. Treas. Reg. § 1.401(k)–1(g)(13)(i).

A CODA may also provide for *nonelective contribution*. These are employer contributions for which there is no employee option to have the contribution instead paid to him in cash. *Qualified nonelective contributions* are nonelective employer contributions (other than matching contributions) that satisfy the vesting and distribution requirements applicable to elective contributions for qualified CODAs. IRC § 401(m)(4)(C); Treas. Reg. § 1.401(k)–1(g)(13)(ii).

3.   OTHER BENEFITS

A CODA may provide for benefits to participants other than those attributable to elective or nonelective contributions. But a qualified CODA may not directly or indirectly condition any benefit, other than matching contributions, on the employee's electing to have the employer make or not make contributions in lieu of his receiving cash. IRC § 401(k)(4)(A). The other benefits in question may include benefits under a defined benefit plan, nonelective contributions under a defined contribution plan, life insurance, plan loans and subsidized retirement benefits. Treas. Reg. § 1.401(k)–1(e)(6).

B.   NONDISCRIMINATION STANDARDS

1.   COVERAGE

For a CODA to be qualified, the employees eligible to benefit under the arrangement (*eligible em-*

ployees) must satisfy the coverage standards of IRC § 401(b)(1). IRC § 410(k)(3)(A)(i). An eligible employee is one who is directly or indirectly eligible to make an election for all or part of the plan year. For example, if an employee need do nothing more than sign an appropriate form to be able to make an election for the year, he is an eligible employee for the year. On the other hand, an employee who must perform additional service to be eligible to make the election is not an eligible employee unless the service is actually performed. Treas. Reg. § 1.401(k)–1(g)(4).

2. CONTRIBUTIONS

a. The Actual Deferral Percentage Test

For a CODA to be qualified, the *actual deferral percentage* ("ADP") for eligible HCEs for the plan year must satisfy one or the other of two tests. It must be the case that: (a) the ADP for eligible HCEs does not exceed 125% of the ADP of all other eligible employees; or (b) the ADP for eligible HCEs does not exceed twice the ADP of all other eligible employees, and the former percentage does not exceed the latter by more than two percentage points. IRC § 401(k)(3)(A)(ii). In applying the test, the ADP for the NCEs is calculated using figures from the prior plan year, unless the employer elects to use the current plan year figures. IRC § 401(k)(3)(A). (For the first plan year, the plan may take as the ADP for the NCEs either 3% or the actual ADP for the current year. IRC § 401(k)(3)(E).) A CODA that satisfies either of the ADP tests satisfies the nondiscrimination standard of IRC § 401(a)(4) with respect to contributions. IRC § 401(k)(3)(C). (However, it must still satisfy the other requirements of IRC § 401(a)(4). Treas. Reg. § 1.401(k)–1(a)(4)(iv).)

A simple example may clarify the tests. If the ADP for eligible HCEs is 12% and the ADP for all other eligible employees is 9%, the plan fails both tests. It fails the first test because 12 is more than 125% of 9 (it is 133%). It fails the second test because, although 12 is less than twice 9, the difference between the figures is more than two percentage points. The plan can comply with the first test by, for example, increasing the ADP of the other employees to 10%. It can comply with the second test by, for example, decreasing the ADP of the HCEs to 11%.

b. Calculating the ADP

To determine the ADP of a group of employees, one first calculates, for each employee, the ratio of: (a) the amount of employer contributions paid to the plan for the year to (b) the employee's compensation for the year. The ADP for the group is the (unweighted) average of these ratios for each member of the group. IRC § 401(k)(3)(B). Thus, for example, if a group consists of two employees, for one of whom the deferral ratio is 10% and for the other 8%, the ADP of the group is 9%.

In determining the individual ratios for purposes of calculating ADP, the salary limitation of IRC § 401(a)(17) applies. Treas. Reg. § 1.401(a)(17)–1(c)(1). For 2003, the limitation is $200,000. Thus, an employee who defers $25,000 of a $250,000 salary has a deferral ratio of 12.5%, not 10%.

In calculating the ADP for a CODA, the employer contributions taken into account always include elective deferrals. IRC § 401(k)(3)(D)(i). The plan, at its option, may also treat as employer contributions all or part of any qualified matching contributions or qualified nonelective contributions. IRC § 401(k)(3)(D)(ii). This option provides flexibility to help the plan to meet the nondiscrimination requirements for a year, by allowing the employer to make and count matching and nonelective contributions. But there are limits to this flexibility. Matching contributions must satisfy a counterpart to the ADP test called the *average contribution percentage test* ("ACP test"). IRC § 401(m)(1) & (2). However, matching contributions used to meet the ADP test cannot be taken into account for purposes of the ACP test. IRC § 401(m)(3). In addition, both of the following must satisfy IRC § 401(a)(4): (a) the total amount of nonelective contributions, including those qualified nonelective contributions treated as elective contributions for purposes of the ADP test; and (b) the amount of nonelective contributions excluding those qualified nonelective contributions treated as elective contributions for purposes of the ADP test or the ACP test. Treas. Reg. § 1.401(k)–

1(b)(5). Other restrictions are contained in the regulations. *Id*.

Some special rules are important. In general, all CODAs included in a plan are treated as a single CODA for purposes of the ADP test. Treas. Reg. § 1.401(k)–1(b)(3)(i). If two or more plans which include CODAs are considered one plan for purposes of IRC § 401(a)(4) or § 410(b), the CODAs included in them are treated as one plan for purposes of the ADP test. IRC § 401(k)(3)(A). Restructuring under Treas. Reg. § 1.401(a)(4)–9(c) is not permitted. Treas. Reg. § 1.401(k)–1(b)(3)(ii). If an HCE is a participant under two or more CODAs of the employer, in determining the deferral ratio of the employee, all such CODAs are treated as one CODA. IRC § 401(k)(3)(A).

c. Safe Harbor

The Code provides a safe harbor for plans that prefer not to use ADP testing. Under the safe harbor, a CODA is treated as satisfying IRC § 401(k)(3)(A)(ii) if it meets two conditions. First, eligible employees must be given written notice of their rights and obligations under the arrangement. IRC § 401(k)(12)(D). Second, the employer must make matching contributions on behalf of each NCE in an amount equal to: (a) 100% of the elective contributions of the employee, up to 3% of compensation; plus (b) 50% of the elective contributions of the employee to the extent that those elective contributions exceed 3% of compensation but do not exceed 5% of compensation; provided that the matching contribution rate for HCEs does not exceed the rate for NCEs. IRC § 401(k)(12)(B)(i) & (ii).

There are two alternative ways for a CODA to meet the second safe harbor requirement. Under one alternative, the rate of matching contributions does not increase as the rate of an employee's elective contributions increases, and the aggregate amount of matching contributions at a given rate of elective contributions is at least equal to the aggregate amount that would be made under the safe harbor formula above. IRC § 401(k)(12)(B)(iii). For example, a match of 100%, up to 4% of compensation, would satisfy this alternative. Under the second alternative, the CODA provides that employer must make nonelective contributions for each eligible NCE in an amount equal to at least 3% of compensation (whether or not the employee actually elects to defer or to make his own contribution). IRC § 401(k)(12)(C).

3. EXCESS CONTRIBUTIONS

Whether a CODA meets the ADP test for a year is partly outside the employer's control, because it depends on the employees' decisions regarding how much income to defer. The option to count qualified matching and qualified nonelective contributions as elective contributions provides a way for the employer to compensate for a disproportionate level of deferral by HCEs. However, use of this option imposes a cost on the employer. An alternative way for the employer to bring a plan into compliance with the ADP test for a year is to return some or all of the amounts contributed to the plan to the employees.

IRC § 401(k)(8)(A) provides that a CODA may meet the ADP test for a plan year if, by the close of the following plan year, the *excess contributions* (and income allocable thereto) are either distributed to employees or treated as after-tax contributions. (There is a 10% excise tax imposed if the plan does not correct the excess contributions within 2½ months after the close of the plan year. Treas. Reg. § 1.401(k)–1(f)(6)(i). If it is not corrected within 12 months, the plan will be disqualified. Treas. Reg. § 1.401(k)–1(f)(6)(ii).) Excess contributions are the excess of the aggregate amount of employer contributions to the plan on behalf of HCEs over the maximum amount permitted under the ADP test. IRC § 401(k)(8)(B). The method of distributing excess contributions is described in the regulations. Treas. Reg. § 1.401(k)–1(f); Notice 97–2. There is no tax under section 72(t) on the distribution of excess contributions. IRC § 401(k)(8)(D).

Similar rules apply if there are *excess aggregate contributions*—aggregate matching and employee contributions that exceed the amounts permissible under the ACP test. IRC § 401(m)(6).

4. CATCH–UP CONTRIBUTIONS

A CODA (and certain other plans that provide for elective deferrals) may permit participants who attain an age of 50 or greater in the taxable year to make *catch-up contributions*. A catch-up contribution is an additional elective deferral in an amount no greater than a statutorily specified amount ($2000 in 2003); the amount of this additional deferral, however, may not exceed the excess of participant compensation over other elective deferrals. IRC § 414(v)(1) & (2)(A). The eligible participant must also have made all other elective deferrals available to him. IRC § 414(v)(5)(B). Plan aggregation rules apply. IRC § 414(v)(2)(D).

Catch-up contributions are not subject to ADP testing and are not subject to the IRC § 401(a)(4) standards for nondiscrimination in amount of contributions, so long as the election is available to all participants who attain age 50 in the taxable year. IRC § 414(v)(3)(B). Nor are they subject to other contribution limits for CODAs (or other plans). IRC § 414(v)(3)(A). It appears that matching contributions may be made on catch-up contributions, but remain subject to ACP testing.

C. SIMPLE 401(k) PLANS

Yet another way for a CODA to meet the requirements of IRC § 401(k)(3)(A)(ii) is for it to be established as a SIMPLE 401(k) plan.

1. ELIGIBLE EMPLOYERS

A SIMPLE 401(k) plan may be established by an employer that, in the plan year, has no more than 100 employees who received compensation of $5,000 or more in the preceding year. IRC § 408(p)(2)(C)(i).

2. SIMPLE PLAN REQUIREMENTS

A SIMPLE 401(k) plan must meet three statutory requirements.

The first set of requirements concerns contributions. Under the plan, an employee may elect to defer a percentage of compensation up to a statutory amount adjusted for inflation ($8,000 in 2003), the employer must match these contributions up to 3% of salary, and there may not be any other contributions. IRC §§ 401(k)(11)(B)(i) & 408(p)(2)(E)(i). As an alternative to the 3% match, the employer may make a nonelective contribution of 2% of compensation for each eligible employee who earns at least $5,000. IRC § 401(k)(11)(B)(ii).

The second requirement is that the SIMPLE 401(k) plan be the exclusive one for eligible employees—that there not be any benefit accruals or contributions under any other qualified plan of the employer for the year. IRC § 401(k)(11)(C). The third requirement is that contributions to the plan vest immediately. IRC §§ 401(k)(11)(A)(iii) & 408(p)(3).

A SIMPLE 401(k) plan is not subject to the top-heavy rules for the year. IRC § 401(k)(11)(D)(ii). Catch-up contributions are permitted, but in amounts less than for regular CODAs or other plans. IRC § 414(v)(2)(B)(ii).

CHAPTER 21

FUNDING AND CONTRIBUTIONS

Concern over the underfunding of pension plans was one of the motivations for the enactment of ERISA. Employers had often failed to set aside reserves adequate to pay promised benefits; the consequences for employees were often sad when the underfunded plans were terminated. Congress saw the misery caused by the spectacularly underfunded Studebaker plan (see Chapter 5) as a lesson in the need for adequate funding. Accordingly, ERISA sets minimum funding standards for defined benefit plans.

Yet underfunding is the not the only funding-related source of concern with plans: overfunding, too, can be problematic, albeit for different reasons. Because employers may deduct contributions in the year they are made, excessive contributions will generate excessive employer tax benefits. Thus, there are rules limiting the annual deduction for contributions to plans. ERISA's funding rules strike a balance between requiring funding in order to protect employees and restricting funding in order to protect the public fisc.

A. BASIC ACTUARIAL PRINCIPLES

In most defined benefit plans, benefit obligations continually accrue. Sufficient funds must be allocated to meet those obligations. To do this systematically is a complex task requiring the services of an actuary.

The annual amount that must be contributed will depend, in large part, on the present value of expected future benefit payments. Calculating the present value of those payments requires assumptions about many factors: the probabilities of current participants surviving until retirement age and their continuing to accrue benefits until that time; the probabilities of new participants becoming covered by the plan; the projected earnings of participants; future inflation rates and interest rates; and future plan expenses. In this section we examine basic principles of actuarial calculation.

1. ACTUARIAL PRESENT VALUE

The concept of present value examined in Chapter 2 is a very simple one, and it is useful only when payment is certain and parameters such as interest rate known. More commonly, there is some uncertainty as to whether payment will take place, and there is a range of values that economic and financial parameters might assume. This is the case for future pensions benefits. Hence, in valuing them for purposes of determining a plan's benefit liabilities, one must determine *actuarial present value*, which takes uncertainty into account.

A simple example can make the concept clear. Suppose that a plan offers an early retirement subsidy of $10,000 to participants who retire at age 55 (but at no other age) with 10 or more years of service. X is a participant, age 50, with 5 years of service. To compute the actuarial present value of the subsidy to X, one must first discount the $10,000 to present value in the usual way. If interest rates are assumed to be 6%, the discount factor is .75. Yet the result—$7500—would be the true present value of the subsidy only if it were certain that X will survive in current employment until age 55. Obviously it is not certain. X might die, become disabled, or leave employment for other reasons before age 55. If the probability of her surviving in employment until age 55 is .80 (an arbitrarily chosen value), the $7500 must be multiplied by .80, to yield the more accurate actuarial present value of $6000.

2. THE CALCULATION OF BENEFIT COSTS

To determine funding levels, one must calculate actuarial present values for certain benefit-related quantities, and systematically allocate those amounts over the chosen funding period.

There are two main kinds of benefit-related costs that must be funded each year. *Normal cost* is the annual cost of benefits and administrative expenses arising from the ongoing accrual of benefits and operation of the plan. ERISA § 3(28). *Past service cost*, by contrast, is the annual cost of amortizing benefit liabilities for past service credits that have arisen through either adoption or amendment of the plan. Both types of cost are calculated according to an *actuarial cost method*, or *funding method*.

A funding method is a recognized actuarial technique for establishing the total annual actuarial cost of plan benefits and expenses. ERISA specifically identifies six acceptable funding methods and two unacceptable ones. ERISA § 3(31). The two unacceptable methods are *terminal funding*, where the whole actuarial value of a participant's total benefit is set aside at the time the participant reaches retirement; and *current disbursement* (or *pay-as-you go*), where no reserves are established and benefits are simply paid out of the employer's current assets. The two most common of the approved funding methods are the *unit credit method* (or *accrued benefit cost method*) and the *entry age normal method*.

a. Unit Credit Method

The unit credit method is quite straightforward. The normal cost for a participant in a given year is the actuarial present value of the portion of her retirement benefit that accrues in the year. Suppose, for example, that a plan provides for an annual accrual of 1% of current compensation. Normal retirement age is 65. In year Y, participant P, age 40, has current compensation of $50,000. P accrues $500 of her total benefit that year. To calculate normal cost, one determines the present value of a $500 single life annuity for P, commencing at age 65, under appropriate interest rate assumptions and estimates of probability of her surviving in service until age 65. (Note that this calculation of normal cost is for participants who work until retirement; that is why survival in service until 65, rather than survival until 65, is the relevant factor. Normal cost for those who terminate employment or become disabled before retirement is usually calculated separately.)

The calculation proceeds as follows. Assume that that present value of the annuity as of age 65, under appropriate assumptions, is $5000. One calculates the actuarial present value of that future $5000 in year Y—the year it accrues. If the interest rate is is assumed to be 8%, and thus the discount rate approximately .15, and the probability of surviving in service to age 65 is .20, the normal cost of the benefit accrued by P in year Y is $5000 × .15 × .20 = $150. The normal cost for the plan in year Y is the sum of the normal costs for all participants.

Past service cost is computed analogously. Assume that, when the plan was adopted, P was credited with 10 years of service, in each of which she earned $30,000. P then has $3,000 in benefits attributable to her past service. Assume that the present value at age 65 of a $3,000 life annuity for P is $30,000. The actuarial present value of this amount as of the plan commencement date (which is not necessarily year Y) is computed using appropriate interest rate and survival assumptions; assume it is $360. This amount must be amortized, normally over 30 years. IRC § 412(b)(2)(B)(ii). Thus, one calculates the annual payments needed to amortize a $360 debt over 30 years, with interest charged on the unpaid portion of the principal. The method is the same as for computing periodic payments on a 30–year mortgage.

b. Entry Age Normal Method

The entry age normal method is probably the most commonly used funding method. It is said to be cost-based, rather than benefit-based, inasmuch it treats the actuarial present value of a participant's total benefit as a cost to be allocated to the various years of service. To compute normal cost under this method, one first calculates a participant's expected total retirement benefit, using tables that project future salary levels, if necessary. Then one determines the *present value of the future benefit* ("PVFB")—the actuarial present value of the expected total benefit. One makes this calculation as of the participant's *entry age* (the year service began to be credited, whether or not the plan had commenced), using appropriate interest rate assumptions and estimates of probability of survival in service until retirement. Next, one amortizes the PVFB over the period of projected credited service. To do this, one divides the PVFB by the value of a *temporary employment-based life annuity* beginning at entry age. This is a single-life annuity continuing until the earlier of death or normal retirement age, in the amount of $1. The quotient is the normal cost: a level annual amount.

With a slight modification, one can use this method to generate a normal cost that is a level annual percentage of compensation. To do so, one computes the PVFB as before, but divides it instead by the value of a different temporary employment-based life annuity—one in which the annuity amount increases from year to year according to the salary scale used in computing the PVFB. The quotient is the *normal cost at entry age*. This figure, divided by the entry age salary, yields the *normal cost percentage*. For each year, the normal cost for a participant is her compensation multiplied by the normal cost percentage.

Past service cost may also be calculated: it is the difference at the time of actual commencement of participation between the present value (as of that time) of the expected total benefit and the present value (as of that time) of all future normal cost accruals. To calculate this difference where normal cost is determined as a level annual percentage of compensation, one proceeds as follows. First, one determines the PVFB as of the date participation begins (not as of entry age). Next, one determines the present value of future normal costs accruals by multiplying the normal cost for the year by the value of a temporary employment-based life annuity in which the periodic amount increases from $1

according to the salary scale. The difference between the amounts is the past service cost for the
participant. It is amortized over 30 years. A similar method is used if normal cost is determined as a
level amount.

An example shows how the entry age normal
method works for normal cost as a level annual
amount. (The numbers are not necessarily realis-
tic.) Suppose that a participant, P, commenced
employment with an employer at age 30. At age
40, the employer instituted a defined benefit plan in
which normal retirement age is 65. P was given
five years of past service credits. Thus, her entry
age is 35. Assume that P's projected benefit at age
65 is $100,000 per year and that the present value
of that annuity for her life, as of age 65, is
$1,000,000. Assume further that, under appropri-
ate interest rate and survival assumptions, the
PVFB at entry age is $50,000. If the value of a
temporary life annuity commencing at entry age is
$25, then the normal cost is $2,000.

To calculate past service cost, assume that the
PVFB as of the date of plan commencement (age
40) is $80,000. The present value of all future
normal cost accruals as of that date is simply $2,000
(the normal cost) times the value of a temporary life
annuity commencing at age 40; assume the annuity
value is $23. Thus, the present value of all future
normal cost accruals is $46,000. The difference
between it and the PVFB as of the same date—

$34,000—is the past service cost. It is amortized just as under the unit credit method.

B. FUNDING STANDARDS

The Title I and Code provisions of ERISA prescribe identical funding standards. The Code standards (which are not qualification conditions) govern all qualified plans except profit-sharing plans, stock bonus plans, *insurance contract plans*, and a few others. IRC § 412(a) & (h). The Title I funding standards apply to all pension plans except defined contribution plans (but not excepting money purchase plans), insurance contract plans, top-hat plans, excess benefit plans, and a few other specialized plans. ERISA § 301(a). An insurance contract plan is a plan funded exclusively by the purchase of insurance contracts, that calls for level premiums with respect to each participant and meets other conditions on premiums and benefits. IRC § 412(i). Because the Treasury Department has the responsibility for implementing and enforcing the funding standards, we shall refer primarily to Code provisions here.

1. THE BASIC FUNDING RULES

a. Required Contribution

The basic funding rule is that, at the end of each plan year, a plan may not have any *accumulated funding deficiency*. The amount of accumulated funding deficiency is the excess (if any) of total *charges* to the *funding standard account* for all plan years to date, over the total *credits* to that account for the same period. IRC § 412(a). An employer who violates the rule is subject to tax. IRC § 4971(a).

b. Funding Standard Account

The funding standard account is a required book-keeping device that is used to keep track of funding charges and credits. IRC § 412(b)(1).

Charges to the account are amounts needed to satisfy benefit and other obligations. There are three main classes of charges. First, there is the normal cost for the plan year. Second, there are the amounts necessary to amortize the following: the unfunded past service liability, over 30 years (40 for plans in existence on January 1, 1974); the net increase in unfunded past service liability resulting from plan amendments adopted in the year, over 30 years; and the *net experience loss* (i.e., the projected economic experience less actual economic experience under the plan) for the year, over 5 years (15 for multiemployer plans); and the net loss resulting from changes in actuarial assumptions, over 10 years (30 for multiemployer plans). Third, there is the amount necessary to amortize each *waived funding deficiency* (see below) for each prior plan year, over 5 years (15 for multiemployer plans). IRC § 412(b)(2).

There are corresponding classes of credits. First, there is the amount considered to be contributed by the employer for the year. Second, there are amounts necessary to amortize the following: the net decrease in unfunded past service liability resulting from amendments adopted in the year, over 30 years; the net experience gain for the year, over 5 years (15 for multiemployer plans); and the net gain resulting from changes in actuarial assumptions, over 10 years (30 for multiemployer plans). Third, there is the amount of the waived funding deficiency for the year. IRC § 412(b)(3).

c. Alternative Minimum Funding Standard

If a plan uses a funding method under which annual contributions are never less than what would be required under the entry age normal method, the plan can maintain an *alternative minimum funding standard account* (along with the regular funding standard account), and will satisfy the minimum funding standard if there is no accumulated funding deficiency with respect to that account. IRC § 412(a) & (g)(1). The charges to the alternative account are: the lesser of normal cost under the plan's funding method and normal cost under the unit credit method; the excess of present value of accrued benefits over fair market value of plan assets; and the excess of credits to the alternative account over charges for all prior years. The account is credited with amounts considered contributed for the year. IRC § 412(g)(2).

If a plan changes from the alternative to the regular funding standard account, then in the first year of the change the regular funding standard account must be credited with the excess of any debit balance in it over any debit balance in the alternative account.   IRC § 412(b)(3)(D).   Then, the credit must be amortized over 5 years through level annual charges to the account.   IRC § 412(b)(2)(D).   The reason for this rule is that contribution levels determined with the alternative funding standard account are generally lower than they would be if determined with the regular account.   Thus, upon return to the regular account there could be a large deficiency.   The rule allows the plan 5 years to eliminate it.

d. Actuarial Cost Methods

In calculating charges and credits, a plan must use one of the statutorily permitted actuarial cost methods.   (However, a collectively bargained plan requiring contributions based on units of service or production may use the *shortfall method*, described in the regulations.   Treas. Reg. § 1.412(c)(1)–2.) In addition, the actuarial assumptions must be reasonable.   Actuarial assumptions and methods must either be reasonable individually, or else result in a total contribution equivalent to that which would result if each assumption and method were individually reasonable.   (For multiemployer plans, the assumptions and methods need only be reasonable in the aggregate.)   Moreover, the assumptions and methods must, in combination, offer the actuary's best estimate of anticipated experience under the plan. IRC § 412(c)(1) & (3). The IRS has challenged what it considers to be unreasonable assumptions and has prevailed in some cases. *See Jerome Mirza & Associates, Ltd. v. United States* (7th Cir.1989). However, courts have generally accepted the view that the "best estimate" standard is procedural only and that actuarial assumptions may properly err on the side of conservatism and overfunding. *See Citrus Valley Estates, Inc. v. Commissioner* (9th Cir.1995); *Rhoads, McKee & Boer v. United States* (6th Cir.1995).

e. Timing

A determination of experience gains and losses, and a valuation of plan assets, must be made at least once a year. IRC § 412(c)(9). For a defined benefit plan other than a multiemployer plan, contributions must be made quarterly and interest is charged on late installments. IRC § 412(m). However, any contributions to such plan made within 8–1/2 months of the close of the plan year are deemed made as of the last day of that year. IRC § 412(c)(10)(A). For multiemployer plans, contributions, to be credited for the plan year, must be made within 2–1/2 months of its close. IRC § 412(c)(10)(B).

2. MODIFICATIONS OF
THE BASIC RULES

a. Additional Funding Requirements

For defined benefit plans (other than multiemployer plans) having more than 100 participants,
the required annual contribution is increased if, for
that year, the *funded current liability percentage* is
less than 90 percent (or, in some cases less than 80
percent). IRC § 412(l)(1) & (9). The funded current liability percentage is the ratio of the value of
plan assets as determined under section 412(c)(2)
(which generally requires reasonable valuation
methods), to current liability (as defined by section
412(l)(7)). IRC §§ 412(l)(8)(A) & (B), 412(l)(9)(C).
Current liability measures the hypothetical liability
of the plan were it to be terminated immediately.
See IRC § 412(l)(7). Future accruals and contingencies are disregarded.

The required increase in contributions is the sum
of the following: (a) the excess (if any) of the *deficit
reduction contribution* over the difference between:
charges to the funding account; and amortization
credits for net increase in unfunded past service
liabilities, net experience gains, and net gains from
changes in actuarial assumptions; plus (b) the *unpredictable contingent event amount*. There is a cap
to the required increase, measured by the funded
current liability percentage. IRC § 412(l)(1). The
deficit reduction contribution is an adjustment that
accelerates the amortization rate for past service

and other liabilities. IRC § 412(*l*)(2)–(4). The unpredictable contingent event amount is an amount needed to amortize *unpredictable contingent event benefits*—benefits not contingent on age, service, compensation, death, disability, or an event that is reasonably and reliably predictable. IRC § 412(*l*)(5)(A) & (7)(B).

b. Full Funding Limitation

The *accrued liability* (or *actuarial liability*) of a plan is the excess of the present value of projected future benefit costs (and administrative expenses) over the present value of future normal cost contributions. ERISA § 3(29). A plan may be said to be fully funded at a time if the accrued liability at that time is equal to the value of plan assets at that time, since present assets plus future normal cost contributions satisfy all benefit obligations. In general, ERISA does not require plans to be more than fully funded.

An additional funding rule implements this principle. If, at the close of a plan year, the accumulated funding deficiency exceeds the *full funding limitation*, the funding standard account is credited with the amount of the excess. IRC § 412(c)(6). This is an obscure way of stating that an employer is not obligated to contribute more than the full funding limitation in an year. The rule operates so that, if a contribution in the amount of the full funding limitation leaves an accumulated funding deficiency, the deficiency is formally eliminated through an ad hoc credit that reduces it to zero.

The full funding limitation is defined as the excess, if any, of the accrued liability over the lesser of the fair market value of plan assets or their value based on a method prescribed by statute. IRC § 412(c)(7). An example shows how the full funding limitation works. Assume that a plan has accrued liability for year Y of $1,000,000, and plan assets of $940,000. The full funding limitation is $60,000. If the funding standard account has a $100,000 deficit, only $60,000 would have to be contributed. The $40,000 difference would be credited to the account so as to bring the balance to zero.

There is one more aspect of the rule. If the accumulated funding deficiency exceeds the full funding limitation, all amounts to be amortized through charges or credits to the funding standard account are deemed fully amortized. In short, all funding-related balances are reset to zero. IRC § 412(c)(6)(B) & (7)(C).

c. Money Purchase Plans

A money purchase plan must maintain a funding standard account, but the only charges and credits to it normally are those for required contributions and actual contributions. Unless there have been past service credits or a funding waiver, there is nothing to amortize. Prop. Treas. Reg. § 1.412(b)–1(a).

3. EMPLOYER INABILITY TO MEET FUNDING STANDARD

An employer who is unable to meet the funding standard for a year has several ways to avoid tax liability.

a. Variances

If the employer (or 10% of the employers contributing to a multiemployer plan) is unable to satisfy the minimum funding standard for a plan year without temporary substantial business hardship (substantial business hardship in the case of a multiemployer plan), and if application of the funding standard would be adverse to the interests of participants, the Secretary of Treasury may waive the funding requirements in whole or in part, except for the portion attributable to a past waiver. Factors that may be taken into account in determining the existence of business hardship include the employer's operating at an economic loss, substantial unemployment or underemployment in the business and industry concerned, depressed or declining sales and profits in the industry, and the likelihood that the plan will be discontinued if the waiver is not granted. No more than 3 waivers (5 for multiemployer plans) are allowed in any 15 consecutive year period. IRC § 412(d). The Secretary of Treasury may also grant, under analogous standards, an extension of the amortization period of up to ten years for an unfunded liability. IRC § 412(e).

Benefits, accruals and vesting rates may not be increased if a funding waiver or extension of an amortization period is in effect. IRC § 412(f)(1).

b. Change in Funding Method

A change in funding method can lower the annual funding cost. If an employer wishes to make such a change, it must obtain approval from the Secretary of Treasury. In certain cases, a defined benefit plan must obtain the approval of the Secretary to change actuarial assumptions used in determining current liability. IRC § 412(c)(5). The Secretary has given general approval to the adoption of certain common funding methods. Rev. Proc. 2000–40, Rev. Proc. 99–45, Rev. Proc. 98–10, Rev. Proc. 95–51.

c. Retroactive Amendments

Notwithstanding the prohibition of amendments that reduce accrued benefits (Chapter 7), an amendment adopted within 2–1/2 months (2 years for multiemployer plans) of the close of the plan year may retroactively reduce accrued benefits for that plan year (but not for prior ones) "to the extent required by the circumstances." No such amendment is effective until the Secretary of Treasury has been notified in writing and has either approved it or failed to disapprove it within 90 days. Approval requires a determination that the amendment is necessary because of a substantial business hardship and that a waiver is either unavailable or inadequate. IRC § 412(c)(8). In general, benefits, accruals, and vesting rates may not be increased within 12 months (24 in the case of multiemployer plans) after the date of such an amendment. IRC § 412(f)(1).

4. NOTICES

ERISA § 101(d) requires any employer maintaining a plan other than a multiemployer plan, who fails to make a required contribution within 60 days of its due date, to notify each participant and beneficiary. No notice is required if there is pending a request for a funding waiver. However, notice is required within 60 days after a denial of such a waiver.

Where an employer requests a waiver, it must notify each affected employee organization, participant, beneficiary and alternate payee. IRC § 412(f)(4). In cases of requests for sufficiently large waivers or extensions with respect to single-employer plans, the Secretary of Treasury must notify the PBGC and give the PBGC and concerned employee organizations the opportunity to submit comments. IRC § 412(f)(3)(B).

5. PENALTIES

If a plan has an accumulated funding deficiency for a plan year, a tax of 10% of the amount of the deficiency (5% for multiemployer plans) is imposed on the employer (or employers). IRC § 4971(a). If the accumulated funding deficiency is not corrected within the *taxable period*, a additional tax of 100% of the deficiency may be imposed. IRC § 4971(b). The taxable period is the period beginning with the end of the plan year in which there is an accumulated funding deficiency and ending on the earlier of the date of the mailing of a notice of deficiency with respect to the 10% tax or the date on which the 10% tax is assessed. IRC § 4971(c)(3). For multiemployer plans, the tax is apportioned according to IRC § 413(b)(6).

Before issuing a notice of deficiency, the Secretary of Treasury must notify the Secretary of Labor, and give the latter a reasonable opportunity to require the employer to eliminate the deficiency or to comment on the imposition of the tax. IRC § 4971(d). The Secretary of Labor or the PBGC may request the Secretary of Treasury to undertake an investigation to determine whether the tax should be imposed. ERISA § 3002(b). The Secretary of Treasury may waive the 100% tax "in appropriate cases." *Id.*; Rev. Proc. 81–44.

Where the aggregate balance of unpaid contributions to a single-employer plan exceeds $1,000,000, a lien in favor of the plan arises on all property of the person or persons who are delinquent in making the contributions. Any such delinquent person must notify the PBGC within 10 days of the due date of the required contribution that triggers the lien. The lien may be perfected and enforced only by the PBGC or its designee. IRC § 412(n).

C. DEDUCTIONS FOR CONTRIBUTIONS

Employer contributions to a plan are deductible if they are ordinary, necessary and reasonable business expenses. IRC § 404(a). *See* IRC §§ 162 & 212. However, there are limits to the amount of deduction allowed.

1. STOCK BONUS AND PROFIT SHARING PLANS

Employer contributions to stock bonus or profit sharing plans are deductible in the year in which paid (not accrued), up to 25% of the total compensation paid or accrued to participants in the plans for the year. IRC § 404(a)(3)(A)(i)(I). (All stock bonus and profit sharing plans of the employer are treated as one. IRC § 404(a)(3)(A)(iv).) There is a separate limit for SIMPLE 401(k) plans. IRC § 404(a)(3)(A)(i)(II). Any excess amounts may be deducted in future years, so long as the total amount deducted in any one year for contributions, past and present, to the plans, does not exceed the 25% (or other statutory) limitation. IRC § 404(a)(3)(A)(ii). Contributions are not deductible to the extent annual additions for the year exceed the section 415 limitation for the year. IRC § 404(j)(1)(B).

Compensation for these purposes consists of "all of the compensation paid or accrued except that for which a deduction is allowable" under a qualified plan.   Treas. Reg. § 1.404(a)–9(b). However, compensation includes elective deferrals under IRC § 402(g)(3). Moreover, such elective deferrals are not subject to the IRC § 404(a)(3) limitation on deductions. IRC § 404(n). There is an indexed upper limit ($200,000 in 2003) to the amount of a participant's compensation that may be taken into account for purposes of computing contribution limits.   IRC § 404(l).

2.   DEFINED BENEFIT AND MONEY PURCHASE PLANS

In general, the deduction for contributions to a defined benefit plan (including an annuity plan, IRC § 404(a)(2)) is equal to the amount necessary to satisfy the minimum funding standard or, if greater, either of two alternative amounts.   One alternative is the amount needed to amortize the remaining unfunded cost of all past and current service credits for all participants, as a level amount or level percentage of compensation, over the remaining future service of each participant.   (However, an adjustment is required if the remaining unfunded cost for any three individuals is more than 50% of the total.)   The other alternative is the amount of normal cost plus the amount necessary to amortize unfunded past service and other supplementary credits in equal annual payments over 10 years.   IRC § 404(a)(1)(A).

There are important qualifications to this basic rule. First, the maximum allowable deduction is the full funding limitation, IRC § 404(a)(1)(A), except that defined benefit plans may deduct at least an amount equal to the unfunded current liability for the year, IRC § 404(a)(1)(D)(i). There are special rules for plans with 100 or fewer participants. IRC § 404(a)(1)(D)(ii). Second, in calculating limits, benefits in excess of the limits imposed under section 415 are not taken into account. IRC § 404(j)(1)(A).

As in the case of profit sharing and stock bonus plans, the nondeductible portion of any contribution may be carried forward to future years. IRC § 404(a)(1)(E).

Money purchase plans, since pension plans, are subject to IRC § 412(a)(1)(A). However, effective in 2002, money purchase plans are subject to the same limitations as stock bonus and profit sharing plans. IRC § 404(a)(3)(A)(v).

3. COMBINATIONS OF PLANS

Where an employer maintains both defined contribution and defined benefit plans, and some employees participate in more than one plan, additional limits apply. In such cases, the maximum total deductible amount is the greater of 25% of the compensation paid or accrued to the participants in the plans, or the amount of contributions to the defined benefit plans up to the amount needed to satisfy the minimum funding standard for each. IRC § 404(a)(7)(A). Again, there is provision for carryover of nondeductible excess contributions. IRC § 404(a)(7)(B).

4. PENALTIES

IRC § 4972(a) imposes a 10% tax on the amount of nondeductible contributions for a year. The tax will continue to be imposed each year to the extent a contribution has not yet been deducted under a carryover provision. IRC § 4972(c). If the contribution was made under a mistake of fact, or conditioned on the plan's initial qualification, or on the contribution's deductibility, the tax can be avoided by return of the excess contribution within one year, so long as ERISA § 403(c)(2) and the plan document permit its return in such cases. Rev. Rul. 91–4.

CHAPTER 22

PLAN TERMINATION

A plan is a form of organized activity; at some point it may come to an end. Yet the central concerns of ERISA remain live even when a plan is terminated. For example, employee expectations might be frustrated at termination because the plan lacks sufficient assets to pay all promised benefits. Or, to take another example, employee expectations might be defeated subsequent to termination because of imprudence in selecting an annuity provider.

ERISA deals with many, but not all, of the problems attendant upon plan termination. In this chapter we examine the problems that Congress and regulators have deemed central and the approaches that have been taken in resolving them.

A. OVERVIEW OF REGULATION

1. INTERNAL REVENUE CODE

Several Code provisions deal with the impact of termination on plan qualification. As we have seen (Chapter 7), the Code requires accrued benefits to vest upon termination or partial termination. This requirement implements the nondiscrimination principle. The Code also requires (as part of the section 401(a) exclusive benefit rule) that a plan be a permanent, rather than temporary arrangement. Hence "the abandonment of the plan for any reason other than business necessity within a few years after it has taken effect will be evidence that the plan from its inception was not a bona fide program for the exclusive benefit of employees in general," Treas. Reg. § 1.401–1(b)(2), and the plan may be retroactively disqualified, Rev. Rul. 69–25. Upon termination of a qualified plan, an employer or administrator will usually seek a determination letter from the IRS confirming that termination has not affected qualified status.

2.   TITLE I

Title I deals very little with plan termination, mainly because termination is not conduct subject to the fiduciary rules (see Chapter 12). However, some conduct incidental to termination is governed by fiduciary standards. For example, the statute expressly provides that fiduciary standards govern the transfer of assets from a terminated plan to a replacement plan, ERISA § 404(d)(1), and cases have made clear that misrepresentations concerning termination may constitute a breach of fiduciary duty (see Chapter 12).

3.   TITLE IV

Plan termination is governed mainly by Title IV. That title, however, deals almost exclusively with problems relating to the termination of underfunded defined benefit plans. To deal with those problems, Title IV establishes a program to guarantee benefits due from such plans; prescribes the conditions under which such plans can be terminated; provides for involuntary termination in cases of severe financial adversity; regulates employer withdrawals from multiemployer plans; and establishes the Pension Benefit Guaranty Corporation ("PBGC") as the regulatory authority. The Title IV regulatory scheme is the focus of the remainder of this chapter.

B.   THE PBGC AND THE BENEFIT GUARANTY PROGRAM

1.   THE PBGC

The PBGC is a governmental corporation established by ERISA. Its role is to carry out the stated purposes of Title IV. Those purposes are: encouraging the continuation and maintenance of pension plans, providing for the uninterrupted payment of benefits to participants and beneficiaries in covered plans, and maintaining premiums at the lowest level consistent with the fulfillment of PBGC obligations. The primary activities of the PBGC are regulating and overseeing the termination of plans covered by Title IV and administering the program of termination insurance. ERISA § 4002.

2. PLANS COVERED

Title IV covers only pension plans and only those that have in fact operated as qualified plans for at least five years or that have received a favorable determination letter from the IRS. ERISA § 4021(a). Even more specifically, it governs only *single employer plans* and *multiemployer plans.* A single-employer plan is a defined benefit plan other than a multiemployer plan: note that this includes non-collectively bargained, multiple employer, defined-benefit plans. ERISA 4001(a)(15). "Defined benefit plan," for purposes of Title IV, is given its broadest interpretation, as any pension benefit plan that is not a defined contribution plan. *In re Defoe Shipbuilding Co.* (6th Cir.1981). A multiemployer plan is a plan maintained pursuant to one or more collective bargaining agreements, to which more than one employer is required to contribute. ERISA § 4001(a)(3). Title IV does not cover, *inter alia*, defined contribution plans, the portion of a defined benefit plan attributable to voluntary employee contributions, top-hat plans, excess benefit plans, and plans of professional service providers that have no more than 25 active participants. ERISA § 4021(b).

3. PLAN TERMINATION INSURANCE

The Title IV benefit guarantee program is called "plan termination insurance." However, it is more a program of social insurance, or transfer payments, than of risk spreading. Under the program, the

PBGC guarantees the payment of nonforfeitable pension benefits in terminated, underfunded single-employer plans, and in insolvent multiemployer plans, up to a prescribed limit. For single-employer plans, the PBGC will actually pay guaranteed benefits; for multiemployer plans, it will loan money to the plan so that the plan can pay them. Funds for the program are derived from a tax on all contributing employers and, if necessary, from loans by the United States government. In addition, the PBGC has a right to reimbursement (described below) when it makes payments under its guarantee.

To implement the program, separate revolving funds for single-employer plans and for multiemployer plans have been established on the books of the United States Treasury. ERISA § 4005(a). Each fund is available to meet benefit guarantees for its associated type of plan. ERISA § 4005(b)(2).

For each single-employer plan, the *contributing sponsor* (i.e., the employer or other person who is or has been responsible for funding the plan, ERISA § 4001(a)(13)) or administrator must pay an annual premium to the PBGC, which is deposited in the single-employer plan fund. Each member of the contributing sponsor's controlled group is jointly and severally liable for the premiums. Similarly, the administrator of each multiemployer plan must pay an annual premium that is deposited in the fund for multiemployer plans. ERISA §§ 4005(b)(1), 4007(a) & (e). The premium rates are specified by Congress on a per participant basis.

Currently, the rate for single-employer plans is $19 per participant, increasing by $9 per $1,000 of unfunded vested benefits. ERISA § 4006(a)(3)(A)(i) & (E). The rate for multiemployer plans is $2.60 per participant. ERISA § 4006(a)(3)(A)(iii).

4. SINGLE-EMPLOYER PLAN BENEFITS GUARANTEED

Not all single-employer benefits are guaranteed by the PBGC. To begin, only *pension benefits* are guaranteed. 29 C.F.R. § 4022.3(b). Pension benefits are benefits payable in annuity form, to a participant (or surviving beneficiary) upon his permanently leaving covered employment, that (alone or with Social Security, Railroad Retirement, or workmen's compensation) provide substantially level income to the recipient. 29 C.F.R. § 4022.2. Moreover, only benefits that are *nonforfeitable* (except those that are nonforfeitable solely on account of termination) are guaranteed. ERISA § 4022(a); 29 C.F.R. § 4022.3(a). A nonforfeitable benefit in this context is one for which all preconditions to entitlement under the plan or ERISA have been fulfilled by the termination date, save possibly the filing of a formal application, retirement, completion of a waiting period, or in some cases death. ERISA § 4001(a)(8); 29 C.F.R. § 4001.2. Finally, the participant or beneficiary must be *entitled* to a benefit for it to be guaranteed. 29 C.F.R. §§ 4022.3(c) & .4. If benefit payment requires consent of the employer, the absence of such consent before termination defeats entitlement. *Hackett v. Pension Benefit Guaranty Corp.* (D.Md.1980).

There are three important qualifications to this guarantee. First, there is an upper limit. The actuarial value of an individual's guaranteed benefits under a plan generally cannot exceed the actuarial value of a single life annuity, commencing at age 65, monthly benefits under which are equal to the lesser of: the average monthly gross income from the employer during the 5 consecutive year period in which gross income was highest; or $750 times a cost-of-living factor. ERISA § 4022(b)(3). For 2003 the maximum guaranteed monthly benefit is $3,664.77. (This amount also serves as a limit on what an individual may receive from the PBGC in guaranteed benefits under all plans. ERISA § 4022B(a).)

Second, the guarantee is effective only for plans that have been in effect at least 60 months at the time of termination, and only for benefit increases resulting from plan amendments made or effective (whichever was later) at least 60 months before the termination. ERISA § 4022(b)(1). However, benefits not meeting these standards are guaranteed to the extent of the number of years (up to 5) the plan or amendment has been in effect multiplied by the greater of 20% of the otherwise fully guaranteed amount or $20 per month. ERISA § 4022(b)(7).

Third, the guarantee is even more limited for *substantial owners*. A substantial owner is the sole proprietor, a 10% partner, or a 10% stockholder.

ERISA § 4022(b)(5)(A). For a substantial owner who is a participant in an unamended plan, the maximum guaranteed benefit is the guaranteed benefit under the foregoing rules (but with no 60-month phase-in, see 29 C.F.R. § 4022.25) multiplied by a fraction (no greater than one) whose numerator is years of active participation and whose denominator is 30. Where the plan has been amended to increase benefits, each benefit increase is treated as if it were provided under a separate plan. ERISA § 4022(b)(5)(B) & (C).

5. MULTIEMPLOYER PLAN BENEFITS GUARANTEED

For multiemployer plans, it is plan insolvency, rather than termination, that triggers the PBGC guarantee. Just as for single-employer plans, it is nonforfeitable pension benefits that are guaranteed. ERISA § 4022A(a).

Again there are important limits on the guarantee. First, only benefits or benefit increases that have been in effect for 60 months are eligible for the guarantee. ERISA § 4022A(b). There is no phase-in rule. Second, the amount of monthly benefit guaranteed is equal to years of credited service times: 100% of the *accrual rate* up to $11, plus 75% of the lesser of $33 or the accrual rate in excess of $11. The accrual rate is essentially the monthly amount of the normal retirement benefit, expressed as a single life annuity, divided by years of credited service. ERISA § 4022A(c).

6.   THE PBGC FINANCIAL POSITION

Until 1996, the PBGC had a deficit in its single-employer fund which, in 1993, reached $2.9 billion. (The multiemployer fund, by contrast, has consistently been in surplus since 1982.) The fund then continued in a surplus position through 2001, attaining an historic peak of $9.7 billion in 2000.

One cause of the elimination of the deficit and the subsequent years of surplus was a set of amendments to ERISA that increased termination insurance premiums and tied their amount in part to the level of plan underfunding. This made plan termination insurance more of a risk-spreading system. Congress also increased the rate at which past-service costs must be amortized (see Chapter 21). Other factors were the decline in the number of terminations, the small number of very large claims, and a period in which the economy was very strong.

Beginning in 2001, the PBGC began to experience significant annual deficits as the economy went into recession and large companies entered bankruptcy. By the end of the 2002 fiscal year, the single-employer fund showed a deficit of $3.6 million; in the early months of fiscal 2003, additional large claims against the single-employer fund deepened the deficit further, and the bankruptcies of large steel companies and airlines threatened to produce additional large claims.

From the inception of the PBGC through the 2002 fiscal year, the corporation experienced $11.0

billion in gross claims; 10 companies accounted for $5.7 billion of this amount. Five of those 10 were steel companies and 3 were airlines. Nearly half of the claims against the single-employer fund since 1975 have been from plans that were less than 50% funded.

C. REPORTING TO THE PBGC

To carry out its responsibilities, the PBGC needs to monitor significant changes in plan financial condition. Thus, events that signal financial troubles must be reported promptly to the PBGC.

There are fifteen categories of such *reportable events* : (1) The issuance of a notice by the Secretary of the Treasury that the plan is no longer qualified, or the determination by the Secretary of Labor that the plan is not in compliance with Title I. (2) The adoption of a plan amendment decreasing some or all benefits. (3) A decrease in the number of active participants by more than 20% in a year, or more than 25% over two years. (4) A determination by the Secretary of the Treasury that there has been a termination or partial termination within the meaning of IRC § 411(d)(3). (5) A failure to meet the minimum funding standard for the year. (6) The inability to pay benefits when due. (7) A distribution of $10,000 or more to a substantial owner, not on account of death, which leaves some nonforfeitable benefits unfunded. (8) A plan merger, consolidation, or transfer of assets, or the prescription by the Secretary of Labor of an alternative method of compliance with the Title I reporting and disclosure rules. (9) A person ceases to be a member of the controlled group. (10) The liquidation or dissolution of a contributing sponsor or a member of its controlled group. (11) The declaration of an extraordinary dividend or the redemption in a 12 month period of 10% or more of the stock, by a contributing sponsor or member of its controlled group. (12) Certain transfers of 3% or more of the benefit liabilities of a plan in a 12 month period. (13) Application made for a minimum funding waiver. (14) Certain loan defaults of $10 million or more by a member of a plan's controlled group. (15) Bankruptcy or insolvency proceedings, or the like, by a member of a plan's controlled group. ERISA § 4043(c); 29 C.F.R. § 4043.20–.35.

In general, the plan administrator or contributing sponsor must notify the PBGC within 30 days after it learns or has reason to know of such an event. ERISA § 4043(a). However, in some cases the contributing sponsor must notify the PBGC within 30 days prior to the event. ERISA § 4043(b); 29 C.F.R. § 4043.61–.68. The PBGC may assess a penalty of up to $1,000 per day for failure to comply with these and other Title IV reporting and notice rules. ERISA § 4071.

In addition to the above requirements, the Secretary of the Treasury must notify the PBGC of an event described under (1), (4) or (5); the Secretary of Labor must notify the PBGC of an event under (1), (5) or (8); and either must notify the PBGC of any event which he believes indicates the plan to be unsound. ERISA § 4043(d) & (e).

D. SINGLE–EMPLOYER PLAN TERMINATIONS

A single-employer plan termination may be either employer-initiated or PBGC-initiated. In the former case, it may be either with or without assets sufficient for the plan to meet all benefit obligations. Different rules govern the three kinds of terminations. The rules for employer-initiated termination must be complied with strictly. Failure to do so invalidates termination and leaves the plan ongoing. *Phillips v. Bebber* (4th Cir.1990); 29 C.F.R. §§ 4041.31 & .41(b).

1. STANDARD TERMINATIONS

A *standard termination* is the method for voluntarily terminating a plan whose assets are sufficient to meet *benefit liabilities*—i.e., the "benefits of employees and their beneficiaries under the plan," ERISA § 4001(a)(16), whether fixed or contingent.

The procedure for standard termination is designed to require as little PBGC involvement as possible. To initiate it, the administrator must give written notice of the intent to terminate to every participant, beneficiary of a deceased participant, alternate payee, and employee organization. ERISA § 4041(a)(2). The notice must be given at least 60, but no more than 90, days before the proposed termination date. 29 C.F.R. § 4041.23(a). Within 180 days after the proposed termination date, the administrator must file with the PBGC a Form 500, Standard Termination Notice. ERISA § 4041(b)(2)(A); 29 C.F.R. § 4041.25. Within the same period, the administrator must send written notice to each participant or beneficiary specifying and explaining the amount of his benefit. ERISA § 4041(b)(2)(B); 29 C.F.R. § 4041.24. During this period, the plan generally continues to operate as normal, subject to restrictions designed to protect the plan's sufficiency for benefit liabilities. 29 C.F.R. § 4041.22.

Within 60 days of the notice to the PBGC (or any longer period agreed to by the PBGC and administrator, or resulting from a suspension of review pending the submission to the PBGC of additional information) the PBGC may issue a notice of non-compliance if it has reason to believe that plan assets will not be sufficient to meet benefit liabilities or if the notification and filing requirements were not met. If such a notice is issued, the termination may not proceed. ERISA § 4041(b)(2)(C); 29 C.F.R. §§ 4041.26 & .31. Absent notice of non-compliance within the prescribed period, the administrator may commence distribution of plan assets so long as they are in fact sufficient for benefit liabilities as of the termination date. ERISA § 4041(b)(2)(D); 29 C.F.R. § 4041.28(c). Distribution must be completed within 180 days after the end of the PBGC review period or, in some cases, within 120 days of the receipt of a favorable deter-

mination letter from the IRS. 29 C.F.R.
§ 4041.28(a). The PBGC must be notified that
distribution has been completed properly and that
all benefit liabilities have been satisfied, within 30
days of completion. ERISA § 4041(b)(3)(B).

2. DISTRIBUTION OF PLAN ASSETS

ERISA § 4044(a) prescribes an order for the distribution of plan assets in single-employer plan terminations. Assets are allocated to *priority categories* in the following order.

First, to the portion of an individual's accrued
benefit derived from his voluntary contributions.
(These highest-priority benefits are not guaranteed
by the PBGC. ERISA § 4021(b)(12).) Second, to
the portion of each individual's accrued benefit derived from his mandatory contributions. (These
benefits may or may not be guaranteed, depending
on whether they meet the criteria for guaranteed
benefits, discussed above). Third, to benefits payable as an annuity, that either were in pay status as
of the beginning of the three year period ending on
the termination date, or would have been in pay
status at that time had the participant retired and
elected to commence payment before the beginning
of that three year period. For such benefits, the
amount allocated is determined on the basis of the
plan provisions (in effect during the five years before termination) under which the benefit would be
the least. (These benefits, too, may or may not be
guaranteed.) Fourth, to other guaranteed benefits

and to benefits that are nonguaranteed because of the substantial owner limitation.

Having satisfied the fourth priority category, the plan will have satisfied all guaranteed benefits. The remaining categories consist of wholly non-guaranteed benefits. The fifth category consists of all other benefits that were nonforfeitable before the date of termination. The sixth consists of all other accrued benefits. This category includes accrued benefits that become nonforfeitable upon termination and benefits payable only upon plan termination.

To distribute plan assets to participants and beneficiaries, the administrator must purchase annuities from an insurer or otherwise follow the terms of the plan and applicable regulations. ERISA § 4041(b)(3)(A); 29 C.F.R. § 4041.28(c) & (d).

The Supreme Court has held that this allocation scheme does not itself create any benefit entitlements. It merely provides for the orderly distribution of benefits, the rights to which are determined under plan provisions or other provisions of Title I or the Code. *Mead Corp. v. Tilley* (S.Ct.1989).

If the plan permits and no law prohibits, any assets remaining after allocation (other than those attributable to employee contributions) may be distributed to the employer. ERISA § 4044(d). If the plan provides for any residual assets to be distributed to participants, the sponsor may purchase a *participating group annuity contract*—a contract that provides annuities for the participants and beneficiaries, and an opportunity for the sponsor to share in favorable investment and actuarial experience under the contract. However, the premium for the participating feature may not be taken into account in determining the amount of residual assets and may not be paid from the residual assets allocable to participants. 29 C.F.R. § 4041.28(c)(4).

3.   DISTRESS TERMINATIONS

A single-employer plan that is not eligible for a standard termination (because of insufficient assets) may terminate under a *distress termination* in statutorily specified circumstances. Both distress termination and standard termination are unavailable when termination would violate the terms of a collective bargaining agreement. ERISA § 4041(a)(3). In such a case, termination must be initiated by the PBGC.

The procedure for distress termination is as follows. First, the administrator must provide a written notice of intent to terminate to all affected parties, including the PBGC, no less than 60 and no more than 90 days before the proposed termination. ERISA § 4041(c)(1); 29 C.F.R. § 4041.41. The PBGC will review the notice and tentatively determine whether it was issued in compliance with the statute and regulation. The PBGC may also request information so that the it can determine whether to commence involuntary termination proceedings. 29 C.F.R. § 4041.44.

Within 120 days after the proposed termination date, the administrator must submit to the PBGC a Form 601, Distress Termination Notice, and Schedule EA–D, Distress Termination Enrolled Actuary Form. These forms provide information that allows the PBGC to determine whether the criteria for a distress termination are met, and information concerning plan assets and liabilities. Where assets have not been certified as sufficient to meet guaranteed benefits or benefit liabilities, additional information must also be provided about participants and benefits. ERISA § 4041(c)(2)(A); 29 C.F.R. § 4041.45.

On the basis of the information submitted, the PBGC determines whether the criteria for a distress termination are satisfied. The criteria are met if each contributing sponsor and member of the sponsor's controlled group (within the meaning of ERISA § 4001(a)(14)) meets any one of the following conditions: liquidation proceedings are pending with respect to such person; reorganization proceedings are pending with respect to such person and the bankruptcy or other court approves the termination after notice to the PBGC; or the person demonstrates to the PBGC that, without a distress termination, it will be unable to continue in business, or that the costs of providing pension coverage have become unreasonably burdensome solely as a result of a decline in the covered workforce. ERISA § 4041(c)(2)(B). The PBGC notifies the administrator of its conclusion. ERISA § 4041(c)(2)(C); 29 C.F.R. § 4041.46.

As soon as practicable after determining that the criteria for a distress termination are met, the PBGC must attempt to determine whether the plan has sufficient assets to (a) pay guaranteed benefits and (b) meet benefit liabilities; and then notify the administrator. ERISA § 4041(c)(3)(A); 29 C.F.R. § 4041.47(a). If the PBGC determines that the plan is sufficient for benefit liabilities, or determines that the plan is sufficient for guaranteed benefits but not for benefit liabilities, the administrator may proceed to issue benefit notices and distribute benefits. 29 C.F.R. § 4041.47(c). Otherwise, the PBGC will commence involuntary termination proceedings. ERISA § 4041(c)(3)(B). If the administrator subsequently finds that the assets of the plan are insufficient to provide for benefits at the level determined by the PBGC, it must notify the PBGC. If the PBGC agrees that assets are insufficient for guaranteed benefits, the termination will proceed as an involuntary termination. ERISA § 4041(c)(3)(C)(ii).

In the period between the administrator's initial notification to the PBGC and the PBGC's determination regarding asset sufficiency, restrictions on plan administration apply. The administrator may not distribute plan assets or otherwise take steps to implement the proposed termination; may pay benefits attributable to employer contributions only in the form of an annuity (except for death benefits); may not purchase irrevocable commitments from an insurer; and, commencing on the proposed termination date, must limit benefits to those guaranteed

by the PBGC or those to which assets are required
to be allocated. The same restrictions apply if the
administrator, in the course of distributing assets,
finds that assets are or will be insufficient to pay
guaranteed benefits. ERISA § 4041(c)(3)(D); 29
C.F.R. § 4041.42.

4. LIABILITY FOR UNDERFUNDING

Even if plan assets are sufficient to pay guaranteed benefits, the contributing sponsor and members of the controlled group remain liable to the
PBGC for the amount of unfunded benefit liabilities
as of the termination date, plus interest. ERISA
§ 4062(b)(1). A person may also be liable if, within
five years before the termination, the person entered into a transaction (e.g., sale of the business
for the employees of which the plan was established), a principal purpose of which was to evade
liability for underfunding. ERISA § 4069(a).

The liability to the PBGC is payable in cash or
securities as of the termination date; however, liability in excess of 30% of the collective net worth of
all persons liable may be paid on commercially
reasonable terms. ERISA § 4062(b)(2). If a person so liable fails to pay the amount due after
demand, a lien for the liability arises in favor of the
PBGC upon all property of the person. The
amount of the lien, however, is limited to 30% of
the collective net worth of all persons liable.
ERISA § 4068(a).

The PBGC may bring a civil action in federal district court to enforce the lien. ERISA § 4068(d)(1). The lien has the same priority as a federal tax lien, and is treated as such in bankruptcy proceedings. ERISA § 4068(c).

The PBGC will pay to participants and beneficiaries in a terminated plan a percentage of the *outstanding amount of benefit liabilities*—the value of plan benefit liabilities as of the termination date, less the value of benefits that are guaranteed or for which plan assets are allocated at termination. ERISA § 4001(a)(19). The percentage the PBGC will pay is the *recovery ratio*. ERISA § 4022(c)(1). This is the average, with respect to prior plan terminations, of the percentage of unfunded benefit liabilities recovered by the PBGC. ERISA § 4022(c)(3).

5.   INVOLUNTARY TERMINATIONS

a.   Triggering Events

Under some circumstances, the PBGC *may* institute proceedings to terminate a plan. It may do so when it determines that: the plan has not met the minimum funding standard (or when it has been notified that the Secretary of Treasury has mailed a notice of deficiency with respect to the initial funding deficiency tax); the plan will be unable to pay benefits when due; a reportable event has occurred; or the possible long-run loss to the PBGC may be expected to increase unreasonably if the plan is not terminated. Where the PBGC determines that the plan does not have assets available to pay benefits currently due, it *must* initiate termination proceedings. ERISA § 4042(a).

Unlike as in voluntary terminations, the PBGC may initiate proceedings irrespective of any provision in a collective bargaining agreement. ERISA § 4041(a)(3).

b. Appointment of Trustee

The PBGC may seek to have a trustee appointed for the terminating plan, before or simultaneous with its petitioning for termination. ERISA § 4042(b)(1). Commonly, the administrator and PBGC agree to such an appointment, and usually the PBGC becomes the trustee. ERISA § 4042(b)(3). Where there is no agreement, the PBGC may petition a federal district court for appointment of a trustee. ERISA § 4042(b)(1). On appointment, the trustee is invested with administrative and asset management responsibility for the plan. ERISA § 4042(d)(1)(A).

c. Termination Proceedings

The PBGC initiates termination proceedings by petitioning a federal district court for a decree that the plan should be terminated "to protect the interests of the participants or to avoid any unreasonable deterioration of the financial condition of the plan or any unreasonable increase in the liability of

the [benefit guaranty] fund." ERISA § 4042(c).
The petition may be filed notwithstanding the pendency of bankruptcy or similar proceedings with
respect to the plan or its property. ERISA
§ 4042(e). As soon as practicable, the trustee must
give notice of the proceedings to interested parties
(including the administrator, participants, employers who may be subject to liability, and employee
organizations). ERISA § 4042(d)(2). However,
neither notice to interested parties nor a hearing is
required if the administrator consents to the termination. *Jones & Laughlin Hourly Pension Plan v.
LTV Corp.* (2d Cir.1987). Once the decree has been
entered, the court assumes exclusive jurisdiction of
the plan and its property and may stay any other
pending proceedings with respect to plan property.
ERISA § 4042(f).

Once the decree has been entered, the trustee
assumes the power to marshal assets and distribute
them to participants. ERISA § 4042(d)(1)(B). In
general, the trustee has the same duties as a bankruptcy trustee under 11 U.S.C. § 704. ERISA
§ 4042(d)(3).

d.   Sponsor Liability

A contributing sponsor and the members of its
controlled group have liabilities to both the trustee
and to the PBGC in cases of involuntary termination. The liabilities to the PBGC for unfunded
benefit liabilities have been discussed above. The
liabilities to the trustee are for the outstanding

balance of the accumulated funding deficiency, the outstanding balance of waived funding deficiencies, and the outstanding balance of decreases in the accumulated funding deficiency that resulted from extensions of amortization periods. This liability is due as of the date of termination, and payable in cash or securities. ERISA § 4062(c).

6. PLAN RESTORATION

The PBGC has extensive authority to restore a plan. Where a plan is being terminated or is about to be terminated, the PBGC, on the basis of circumstances it "determines to be relevant," may halt the termination and take whatever action is necessary and within its power to restore the plan to its prior status. Even where the plan has been terminated, the PBGC make take whatever action is necessary to restore the plan to its prior status, where the PBGC determines that such action is "appropriate and consistent with its duties under [Title IV]." ERISA § 4047.

The PBGC has used (or threatened to use) its restoration power in cases where the sponsor has established (or proposed to establish) a *follow-on plan*. A follow-on plan is a new benefit arrangement that, when combined with the guaranteed benefits under a terminated plan, provides a package of benefits substantially the same as those under the terminated plan. The PBGC takes the position that follow-on plans are abusive, as attempts to use the plan termination insurance program to subsidize an ongoing retirement program. The PBGC's use of its restoration powers for this purpose has been upheld by the Supreme Court. *Pension Benefit Guaranty Corp. v. LTV Corp.* (S.Ct. 1990).

When the PBGC issues a restoration order, it also issues a restoration payment schedule for the plan sponsor. That schedule provides for amortization of relevant charges and credits over a period of no more than 30 years. 29 C.F.R. § 4047.3; Treas. Reg. § 1.412(c)(1)–3. In addition, amounts previously paid by the PBGC for guaranteed benefits and related expenses become a debt of the restored plan, to be repaid according to terms prescribed by the PBGC. 29 C.F.R. § 4047.5.

E. REVERSIONS

A reversion is possible only if funds remain in the plan after payment of all benefit liabilities. One major cause of surplus funds is investment experience or economic factors proving more favorable (at least in the short run) than had been assumed when funding levels were set. Another cause of surplus assets is termination itself: funding levels necessarily were based on the assumption of an ongoing plan and were tied to projected benefits and future salary levels; but benefit liabilities at termination are based on currently accrued benefits and current salary levels. Thus, some or all of the surplus may represent the value of anticipated future accruals. In light of these causes, surplus assets in a sense constitute found money. It is no surprise that employers, employees and the Treasury stake competing claims to them.

The employer position, which is substantially a refrain of the employer-property theory of plans (Chapter 4), is that plan assets constitute employer money used for a dedicated purpose. Once the use ceases, anything that remains should be returned to the rightful owner. A further, policy-based argument for the employer is that the availability of a reversion is an incentive to plan formation. The participant position is also based on familiar themes: that plan funds represent payment for services rendered, and that participants have benefit expectations beyond what is measured by accrued benefits at termination. The Treasury position is that, since plan funds represent the tax-free accumulation of money for which the employer has already obtained a deduction, the tax benefit with respect to any surplus should be restored.

Quite clearly, the resolution of these competing interests is a difficult policy problem, analogous to that of resolving the competing interests in ongoing plans. Regrettably, a systematic method of dealing with residual assets has not yet emerged. The relevant statutes merely pose the fundamental question of who is entitled to excess funds. They permit a distribution to the employer only if "all liabilities of the plan to participants and their beneficiaries have been satisfied," ERISA §§ 403(c) & 4044(d); or only after the "satisfaction of all liabilities with respect to employees and their beneficiaries," IRC § 401(a)(2). But they do not answer the fundamental question, since they do not clearly identify the "all liabilities" which must be satisfied or, correlatively, identify the residual funds available for reversion to the employer.

At first sight, an answer is given by Treas. Reg. § 1.401–2(b)(1), which limits the amount of the reversion to amounts resulting from "erroneous actuarial computations." However, the regulation explains that the amount resulting from erroneous actuarial calculation is just the "surplus arising because actual requirements differ from the expected requirements," and further explains that that surplus is the amount left over after benefit liabilities have been paid. Thus, the limitation is only apparent.

Much of the law developed to date favors the employer interest in surplus assets. In general, the benefit liabilities that must be satisfied prior to reversion have been identified with accrued benefits as of termination. *See, e.g.*, Rev. Rul. 83–52. Arguments that participants have an expectation of the continuation of the plan and of future benefit accruals, which ought to be enforced as a plan liability, have been rejected by courts, *Blessitt v. Retirement Plan For Employees of Dixie Engine Co.* (11th Cir.1988), and the ERISA enforcement agencies, *e.g.*, PBGC Opinion Letter No. 87–11. Nonetheless, there are counter-tendencies that work to the advantage of employees.

First, an exception to the general principle limiting benefit liabilities to accrued benefits is the rule (see Chapter 7) that early retirement subsidies cannot be eliminated by plan amendment or termination for those participants who satisfy the eligibility conditions before or after the amendment or termination. ERISA § 204(g)(2). Before taking a reversion, the employer must either purchase annuities to cover the contingent liability for the subsidy, or amend the plan to provide subsidized benefits without regard to the conditions precedent. Rev. Rul. 85–6.

Second, there are formal limitations on reversions. A plan amendment authorizing a reversion, or increasing its amount, is ineffective until five years after adoption. ERISA § 4044(d)(2). A reversion may be prohibited by a collective bargaining agreement or other document. *Delgrosso v. Spang & Co.* (3d Cir.1985). Courts also may apply a presumption against reversions in construing plan documents. *Rinard v. Eastern Co.* (6th Cir.1992).

Third, there are statutory deterrents. To discourage reversions and to recover tax benefits, a 20% tax is imposed on the amount of any reversion. IRC § 4980(a). The tax increases to 50% if the employer fails to establish a *qualified replacement plan* or else increase benefits to a prescribed degree. IRC § 4980(d)(1). A qualified replacement plan is one that (a) covers at least 95% of those active participants in the terminated plan who remain as employees, (b) receives at least 25% of the amount the employer could have received as a reversion (less the amount of certain benefit increases) directly from the terminated plan, and (c) if a defined contribution plan, satisfies other conditions. IRC § 4980(d)(2). The benefit increases required to avoid the 50% tax are pro rata increases in participant benefits that take effect immediately upon termination. They must have an aggregate present value of at least 20% of the maximum reversion that would be allowed under the plan. IRC § 4980(d)(3).

F. THE PURCHASE OF ANNUITIES

Assets are usually distributed at termination through the purchase of annuities. However, ERISA does not address the problem of an annuity provider—usually an insurance company—becoming unable to meet its commitments. Instead, it substantially leaves the matter to state insurance regulation. The failures of some insurance companies have challenged this approach.

The PBGC's position is that it is not required or even permitted to guarantee annuities issued in connection with a plan termination. In the view of the PBGC, the only insurable event under Title IV is plan termination itself, and the premium structure is based on that presumption. The PBGC has estimated that its potential exposure could be substantial were it to insure against the failure of insurance companies. PBGC Letter on PBGC Liability for Payment of Benefits in Case of Annuity Contract Failure (1991).

In response to problems in the insurance industry, the PBGC has issued regulations that compel administrators of single-employer plans to include, in the notice of an intended standard termination, a statement that the PBGC's guarantee ends upon distribution of plan assets and an identification of the insurer, if any, from whom annuities will be purchased. 29 C.F.R. § 4041.23(b)(5) & (9). In addition, each participant and beneficiary must ultimately receive a copy of the annuity contract or certificate through which benefits will be provided (or equivalent information). 29 C.F.R. § 4041.28(d). There are comparable requirements for distress terminations. The rationale of the disclosure requirements is to provide affected parties with an opportunity to take appropriate preventative or remedial action. The PBGC has also taken the position in regulations that the selection of an annuity provider is governed by the Title I fiduciary standards. 29 C.F.R. § 4041.28(c)(3).

The DOL, too, has long taken the position that the purchase of annuities for a plan is a fiduciary function, since it involves the discretionary exercise of control over plan assets. An especial concern is that an employer-fiduciary might be tempted to purchase inexpensive, but risky annuities, upon termination rather than the safest ones available, so as to maximize the amount of the reversion. In the early 1990s, suits were brought by individuals and the Secretary of Labor, alleging breach of duty through improper annuity purchases. *See, e.g., In re Budd Co. Pension Plan Litigation* (E.D.Pa.1991); *Martin v. Raymark Industries Inc.* (D.Conn.1992). Most of these suits were precipitated by the defaults of Executive Life Insurance Company. In 1994, Congress amended ERISA's enforcement provisions to allow the Secretary of Labor, fiduciaries, and former participants and beneficiaries to bring suit for appropriate relief where the purchase of insurance contracts or annuities in connection with a termination violates fiduciary standards or the terms of the plan. ERISA § 502(a)(9).

G. WITHDRAWAL LIABILITY

With respect to multiemployer plans, Title IV's main concern is employer withdrawal from them. The principal aim of the Title IV multiemployer plan rules is to ensure that, upon withdrawal, an employer contributes its proportionate share of the amount of underfunding. The rules are extraordinarily complex and can only be sketched here.

A participating employer *completely withdraws* from a multiemployer plan when it permanently ceases to have an obligation to contribute (e.g., because the union is decertified) or permanently ceases all covered operations under the plan. ERISA § 4203(a). An employer *partially withdraws* if there is a 70% contribution decline (as defined by statute) or a partial cessation of the contribution obligation (e.g., because it ceases to have an obligation to contribute under some, but not all, collective bargaining agreements). ERISA § 4205(a). Special standards for complete and partial withdrawal govern certain industries. A withdrawal does not occur merely because of a bona fide sale of assets provided that the purchaser has an obligation to continue contributions and certain safeguards are met. ERISA § 4204(a)(1).

If an employer withdraws from a plan, it is liable to the plan for its allocable amount of unfunded vested benefits, subject to various adjustments. ERISA § 4201. There are complex formulae for determining the allocable amount of unfunded vested benefits, ERISA § 4211, and for adjusting it to take into account the extent of withdrawal (if only partial), ERISA § 4206, and other factors. *See* ERISA § 4201(b). The amount of liability is determined by the sponsor, which also sets a schedule for payment. ERISA §§ 4202 & 4219(b)(1). The employer may ask the sponsor to review the determination. ERISA § 4219(b)(2). All disputes must be resolved through arbitration, with a presumption of correctness attaching to the sponsor's determination. ERISA § 4221(a). An action may be brought in federal district court to enforce, modify or vacate any award. ERISA § 4221(b)(2). In the absence of arbitration, the liability an employer may be enforced by an action brought in state of federal court. ERISA § 4221(b)(1).

The PBGC is authorized by statute to establish a fund to reimburse plans for uncollectible withdraw-

al liability payments. ERISA § 4222. However, it
has never exercised this authority.

INDEX

ACCOUNTING
Pension costs, 51–52
Retiree medical benefits, 52

ACCRUAL OF BENEFITS
    See also Benefits; Vesting of Benefits
Accrued benefits,
    Defined benefit plans, 99
    Defined contribution plans, 98
    Early retirement benefits, 108–09
    Early retirement subsidies, 109
    Welfare benefits, 107
Age discrimination rules, 106
Amendments,
    Accrued benefits, 107–08, 446–47
    Future accruals, 110–11
Anti-backloading rules,
      In general, 100
    Fractional rule, 104–05
    Insurance plans, 105
    133–1/3% rule, 102–04
    3 percent rule, 100–02
    Top-heavy plans, 106–07
Anti-cutback rule, 108–10
Backloading, 98, 111–12
Cash balance plans, 111–14
Cash outs, 129–130

485

ACCRUAL OF BENEFITS—Cont'd
Difference between accrual and vesting, 81–83

ACTUARIAL ASSUMPTIONS AND METHODS
See Funding Standards and Methods; Valuation

AGE DISCRIMINATION
Benefit accrual, 106
Eligibility to participate in plan, 97
Retirement age, 37, 80

ALIENATION OF BENEFITS
Anti-alienation rule, 141–42
Bankruptcy, 143–44
Benefits in pay status, 148
Loans to participants, 148
Participant wrongdoing, 148–49
Qualified domestic relations orders,
    Alternate payee, 145
    Rationale, 145
    Requirements, 145–47
    Rollovers, 160–61
Welfare benefits, 142–43

AMENDMENTS
Accrued benefits, 108–11
Fiduciary conduct, 253
Future accruals, 110–11
Nondiscrimination, 408–09
Oral amendments, 95, 217–19
Oral plans, 217
Retroactive, 409–10, 446–47

ANNUITIES
    See also Benefits, Spousal Protection; Valuation
Annuity forms,
        In general, 119–21
    Joint life, 119–20
    Participating group annuity contract, 467–68
    Qualified joint and survivor, 123–24
    Qualified preretirement survivor, 123–24
    Single life, 119
    Straight-life, 120
Annuity starting date, 124–25, 151
Definition, 118
Fiduciary responsibility, 481–82
Normal annuity form, 120

ANNUITIES—Cont'd
Plan termination, 480–82
Present value, 23–25, 119–120
Subsidized annuities, 120–21
Survivor annuities,
    Fully subsidized, 127
    Incidental benefit rule, 136–37
    Qualified joint and survivor annuity, 123–24
    Qualified preretirement survivor annuity, 123–24
    Reasons for requirement, 121–22
    Spouses, 125, 147
    Waiver, 125–27
    Written explanation, 126–27
Taxation,
    Amounts not received as an annuity, 153–54
    Amounts received as an annuity, 151–52
    Basic rule, 151–52
    Separate contracts, 154–55
    Simplified Exclusion Method, 152–53

ASSETS
See Fiduciary Standards; Funding Standards and Methods; Plan
    Assets

BANKRUPTCY
Exclusion of plan interest from estate, 143–44
PBGC lien, 442
Retiree medical benefits, 95

BENEFIT SUITS
See Civil Remedies

BENEFITS
    See also Accrual of Benefits; Annuities; Claims Procedures;
        Distributions, Nondiscrimination in Contributions or
        Benefits; Social Security; Taxation; Valuation; Vesting
        of Benefits
Early retirement benefits, 108–09, 120–21
Employee compensation, 45–48
Formulas,
    Career average, 3
    Final average, 3
Limitations, 411, 413–14
Non-retirement benefits (pension plans),
    Death benefits, 136–38
    Defined benefit and money purchase plans, 135–36

BENEFITS—Cont'd
Non-retirement benefits (pension plans)—Cont'd
   Defined contribution plans, 135
   Incidental benefit rule, 136–38
   Retiree medical benefits, 135–36
   Survivor annuities, 137–38
Normal retirement age, 80
Normal retirement benefit, 80–81, 120
Payroll practices, 47
Protection of benefit rights in workplace,
       In general, 114–17
   Group protection, 116
   Medical and disability plans, 116–17
Retiree medical benefits, 8, 93–95, 135–36
Severance benefits, 92–93
Welfare benefits, 7

CASH OR DEFERRED ARRANGEMENTS
Definition, 6, 417
Qualification rules,
   Basic rules, 417
   Catch-up contributions, 426
   Elective contributions, 418
   Matching contributions, 418
   Nondiscrimination,
      Contributions, 420–24
      Coverage, 419–20
      Excess contributions, 424–26
SIMPLE plans, 426–28

CIVIL REMEDIES
   See also Claims Procedures; Federal Common Law; Penalties
Attorney-client privilege, 354–56
Attorney's fees, 352–54
Benefit suits,
   Exhaustion of claims procedures, 166–69, 177–78
   Federal policy, 178–79
   Jury trial, 189–90
   Labor-law model, 179–80
   Review of claim denial,
      Abuse of discretion review, 181–82, 183–84, 187–88
      Conflict of interest, 186–87
      Contra-proferentum, 184–85
      Fiduciary discretion, 183
      De novo review, 184–85
      Review of facts, 185

CIVIL REMEDIES—Cont'd
Benefit suits—Cont'd
    Trust-law model, 181–82
Breach of fiduciary duty,
    Civil penalties, 279
    Liability of non-fiduciaries, 280–81
    Plan remedies, 251, 275–78
    Standing, 275, 278–79
Claims procedures, 190–93
Damages,
    Awards to participants and beneficiaries, 193, 278
    Awards to plans, 275–78
Equitable relief, 276, 278–79
Federal common law,
    Contribution and indemnity, 346–47
    Estoppel claims, 219–23, 345
    Preemption, 342–45
    Restitution, 345–46
Limitation periods, 351–52
Plan information, 209–11
Plan termination, 471–72, 474–75
Preemption of state law remedies, 329–31, 342–45
Procedural wrongs, 190–93
Process and venue, 350–51
Prohibited transactions, 280–81, 297–98
Subject matter jurisdiction, 348–50
Withdrawal liability, 482–84

CLAIMS PROCEDURES
    See also Benefits; Civil Remedies
Exhaustion, 166–69, 177–78
Minimum standards,
    Standards common to all plans
        Basic standards, 170–71
        Initial determination, 171
        Review of adverse determination, 171–71
    Group health plans
        Initial determination, 173–75
        Post-service claim, 173
        Pre-service claim, 173
        Review of adverse determination, 175–77
        Urgent care claim, 173–74
    State-law procedures, 177–78
Requirement of claims procedure, 165–66

COMPENSATION
    See also Benefits; Contributions; Nondiscrimination in Con-
        tributions or Benefits; Nondiscrimination in Coverage;
        Pre–ERISA Law and Practice; Social Security; Taxa-
        tion
Annual limit, 368
Highly compensated employees, 359
Nondiscrimination standards, 367–68

CONTRIBUTIONS
    See also Funding; Nondiscrimination in Contributions or
        Benefits
Deductibility in general, 449
Limitations on contributions, 411–13
Limitations on deductions,
    Combination of plans, 451–52
    Defined benefit and money purchase plans, 450–51
    Stock bonus and profit sharing plans, 449–50
Penalties for nondeductible contributions, 452
Plan assets, 237–39
Timing, 441
Transfer of property to plan, 285–86

COVERAGE
See ERISA; Nondiscrimination in Coverage; Participation in
    Plan

CRIMINAL SANCTIONS
Appointment of ex-convict to plan position, 247–48
Reporting and disclosure, 209–11

DEATH BENEFITS
See Benefits; Taxation

DEFINED BENEFIT PLANS
See Plans

DEFINED CONTRIBUTION PLANS
See Employee Stock Ownership Plans; Plans

DISCRIMINATION
See Age Discrimination; Nondiscrimination in Contributions or
    Benefits; Nondiscrimination in Coverage

DISTRIBUTIONS
    See also Annuities; Benefits; Loans to Participants; Nondis-
        crimination in Contributions or Benefits; Taxation
Consent, 130, 139

DISTRIBUTIONS—Cont'd
Death distributions, 140–41, 160
Early distributions, 139, 162–64
Employee stock ownership plans, 312–13
Employer securities, 156–57, 312–313
Lump sum distributions,
    Definitions, 155–56
    Employer securities, 156–57
    Five-year averaging, 157
    Ten-year averaging, 157
Non-annuity distributions,
    Cash outs, 129–30
    Lump sum option, 127–28
    Spousal consent, 130
Plan termination, 466–68, 472, 480–82
Rollover distributions,
    In general, 157–58
    Eligible retirement plans, 158
    Eligible rollover distributions, 158
    Surviving spouse, 160–161
    Transfer to a new plan, 159–60
    Trustee-to-trustee transfer (direct transfer of rollover distribution), 162
    Withholding tax, 161
    Written explanation, 161–62
Timing,
    Death distributions, 140–41
    Participant delay, 139–40
    Required beginning, 139
Trustee-to-Trustee transfers (direct transfer of rollover distribution), 162

DIVERSIFICATION
See Employee Stock Ownership Plans; Fiduciary Standards

EARLY RETIREMENT
See Accrual of Benefits; Annuities; Benefits; Distributions

EMPLOYEE STOCK OWNERSHIP PLANS (ESOPs)
Allocation of shares, 311
Corporate control contests, 317–25
Corporate finance, 307
Definition, 306
Distributions, 312–13
Diversification of participant accounts, 314
Exempt loans, 309–10

EMPLOYEE STOCK OWNERSHIP PLANS (ESOPs)—Cont'd
Leveraged ESOPs, 307–09
Minimum participation standard, 378
Nondiscrimination in coverage, 361
Policy, 300–01
Qualifying employer security, 301–02
Requirements, 306–07, 310–14
State law,
    Business judgment rule, 322–24
    Preemption 324–25
Tax advantages, 308–09, 314–17
Voting and tendering of share, 311–12, 317–22

EMPLOYEES
See Highly Compensated Employees; Nondiscrimination in Con-
        tributions or Benefits; Nondiscrimination in Coverage;
        Participants and Beneficiaries; Participation in Plan

EMPLOYER SECURITIES
See Distributions, Employee Stock Ownership Plans; Prohibited
        Transaction Rules, Taxation

EMPLOYERS
See Benefits; Employee Stock Ownership Plans; ERISA; Fiducia-
        ries and Fiduciary Responsibility; Parties in Interest; Plan
        Sponsor; Plans; Pre–ERISA Law and Practice

ENFORCEMENT
See Civil Remedies; Criminal Sanctions; ERISA; Penalties

ERISA
    See also Pre–ERISA Law and Policy
Amendment to statute, 18–19, 76–77, 122, 145, 148–49, 243
Coverage,
        In general, 1–2
    Title I, 9–11
    Title III, 11–12
ERISA Reorganization Plan, 21–22
Incompleteness of statute, 74–76, 344–45
Legislative history,
    Benefit suits, 178–79
    Fiduciary standards, 248–49
    Joint Explanatory Statement, 212
    Meaning of [ ] citations, 74
    Preemption, 328–29
    Reporting and disclosure, 195–96
    Writing requirement, 212–13

ERISA—Cont'd
Policies underlying statute, 72–74
Reasons for enactment, 70–72, 74–75, 429
Regulation by government agencies, 21–22
Title I (in general), 16–19
Title II (in general), 19–20
Title III, 16
Title IV (in general), 20–21

EXCLUSIVE BENEFIT RULE
See Fiduciary Standards; Pre–ERISA Law and Practice; Prohibited Transaction Rules

FEDERAL COMMON LAW
Alienation of benefits, 142
Benefit suits, 179
Preemption, 342–45
Remedies,
    Contribution and indemnity, 346–47
    Estoppel claims, 219–23, 345
    Need for, 342–45
    Restitution, 345–46
    Subject matter jurisdiction, 349–350

FIDUCIARIES AND FIDUCIARY RESPONSIBILITIES
Administrator, 229–230
Allocation and delegation of responsibility, 228–29, 270–71
Attorney-client privilege, 354–56
Attorneys and professionals, 234
Bonding, 245–47
Cofiduciary responsibility, 269–70
Employer, 235–36, 253–55, 257–62
Fiduciaries in general, 224–26
General standard, 14–15, 232–34
Investment advisor, 231
Investment manager, 14, 228, 230–231
Limitations on fiduciary responsibility,
    Allocation and delegation of responsibility, 270–71
    Directed trustees, 272–73
    Exculpatory provisions, 273
    Insurance and indemnification, 273–74
    Participant-directed accounts, 274–75
Named fiduciary, 226–27
Persons convicted of crimes, 247–48
Plan administration, 253–55
Plan establishment or amendment, 253

FIDUCIARIES AND FIDUCIARY RESPONSIBILITIES—Cont'd
Plan termination, 253, 454, 481–82
Relationship with sponsor, 54–55, 321–22
Term of office, 236–37
Trust law, 224–26
Trustees and trustee responsibilities,
     In general, 227
    Directed trustees, 228–29, 272–73
    Non-delegation, 228

FIDUCIARY STANDARDS
    See also Civil Remedies; Plan Assets; Pre–ERISA Law and
        Practice; Prohibited Transaction Rules
Cofiduciary standards, 269–70
Diversification, 265–66, 305–06
Eligible individual account plans, 305–06
Employer securities, 305–06
Fiduciary duty in general, 248–50
Loyalty (exclusive benefit),
     In general, 250–51
    Conduct subject to duty, 253–57
    Conflicts of interest, 257–62
    Employer conduct, 253–55, 257–62
    Impartiality, 252–53
    Owed to plan, 251–52
Non-deviation, 267
Non-inurement, 244–45
Plan administration, 253–55
Plan establishment or amendment, 253
Plan termination, 254, 454, 480–82
Prudence, 263–65
Purchase of annuities, 480–82
Trust requirement, 243–44
Truthfulness and information, 267–69
Voting and tendering of shares, 257–62, 265, 317–22
Writing requirement, 211–12

FORFEITURE
See Accrual of Benefits; Amendments, Vesting of Benefits

FUNDING
    See also Contributions, Funding Standards and Methods;
        Pension Benefit Guaranty Corporation; Termination of
        Plans; Termination of Single–Employer Plans; With-
        drawal Liability

FUNDING—Cont'd
Overfunding,
    In general, 429
Underfunding,
    In general, 71, 429
    Liability to PBCG, 471–72

FUNDING STANDARDS AND METHODS
    See also Contributions; Funding; Valuation
Actuarial cost methods (funding methods),
    Change in methods, 446
    Current disbursement (pay-as-you-go) method, 432
    Definition, 432
    Entry age normal method, 434–37
    Shortfall method, 440
    Terminal funding, 432
    Unit credit method, 432–34
Actuarial principles and concepts,
    Accrued liability (actuarial liability), 443
    Actuarial present value, 430–31
    Funded current liability percentage, 442
    Normal cost, 431–37
    Past service cost, 431–37
Additional funding requirements,
    Deficit reduction contribution, 442–43
    Unpredictable contingent event contribution, 442–43
Full funding limitation, 443–44, 451
Minimum funding standards,
    Accumulated funding deficiency, 437–38
    Actuarial assumptions, 440–41
    Alternative minimum funding standard account, 439–40
    Coverage, 437
    Experience gains and losses, 438–39
    Extension of amortization period, 446
    Funding stand account, 438–39
    Liabilities in involuntary terminations, 474–75
    Penalties for accumulated funding deficiency, 447–49
    Retroactive amendments, 446–47
    Waivers, 438, 445–46
Money purchase plans, 444

HIGHLY COMPENSATED EMPLOYEES
    See also Nondiscrimination in Contributions or Benefits;
        Nondiscrimination in Coverage
Compensation, 359
Definition, 358–60

HIGHLY COMPENSATED EMPLOYEES—Cont'd
Former employees, 360

INCIDENTAL BENEFIT RULE
See Benefits

INDIVIDUAL RETIREMENT ACCOUNTS
See Distributions; Plains

INFORMATION
Conflicts between Plan Document and Summary Plan Description,
    In general, 213–16
  Disclaimers, 215
  Reliance, 215–16
Determination letters, 207–08
Disclosure to participants and beneficiaries,
    In general, 204–07
  Examination of documents, 206
  Exemptions, 207
  Requests by participant or beneficiary, 206–07
  Summary Annual Report, 206, 207
  Summary of Material Modifications and Changes, 205
  Summary Plan Description, 205–06
Insurance information, 201
Notice,
  Denial of claim for benefits, 171–74, 176–77
  Distress termination, 468–69
  Failure to make required contribution, 447
  Request for waiver of funding standard, 447
  Standard termination, 464–65, 481
Oral representations,
    In general, 218
  Actuarial soundness of plans, 220
  Estoppel claims, 219–23
  Retiree medical benefits, 95
Recordkeeping, 208–09
Remedies and sanctions, 209–11
Reporting and disclosure,
    Policy, 194–96
  Relation to fiduciary and enforcement provisions, 195–96
Reporting to government agencies, 203–04
Reporting to PBGC,
  Distress termination, 468–69
  Reportable events, 462–64
  Standard termination, 465–66

INFORMATION—Cont'd
Reports and documents,
    Annual Report, 199–202
    Plan Document, 211–12
    Summary Annual Report, 202–03
    Summary of Material Modifications and Changes, 199
    Summary Plan Description, 197–98
    Terminal Report, 209
Rollover distributions, 161–62
Survivor annuities, 126–27
Trustee-to-trustee transfers, 161–62
Writing requirement,
    Fiduciary standards, 211–12, 267
    Purposes, 211–13

INSURANCE AND INSURERS
See Annuities, Benefits; Fiduciaries and Fiduciary Regulation;
    Fiduciary Standards; Information; Plan Assets; Plan Ter-
    mination Insurance; Plans; Preemption

JOINT AND SURVIVOR ANNUITIES
See Annuities; Spousal Protection

LOANS TO PARTICIPANTS
Alienation of benefits, 148
Prohibited transaction rules, 131–32, 286, 293
Qualification rules, 132–33
Rationale, 130–31
Risks, 130–31
Spousal consent, 134
Taxation, 133–34

LUMP SUM DISTRIBUTIONS
See Distributions; Taxation

MULTIEMPLOYER PLANS
See Plans; Nondiscrimination in Contributions or Benefits; Non-
    discrimination in Coverage; Plan Termination Insurance;
    Plans; Pre–ERISA Law and Practice; Withdrawal Liability

NONDISCRIMINATION IN CONTRIBUTIONS OR BENEFITS
Allocation rates, 386
Basic standard, 382–84
Collective bargaining agreements, 384
Imputed disparity,
    Adjusted accrual rate, 405–06
    Adjusted allocation rate, 404–05

NONDISCRIMINATION IN CONTRIBUTIONS OR BENEFITS
  —Cont'd
Nondiscrimination in amendments, 408–09
Nondiscrimination in amount,
    Cross-testing, 392–94, 395
    Defined benefit plans, 388–92
    Defined contribution plans, 385–88
    Employee contributions, 394–95
    Former employees, 394
    General tests, 384, 387–88, 391–92, 393
    Plan restructuring, 395–96
    Safe harbors, 384, 385–87, 388–91
Nondiscrimination in benefits, rights and features,
    Aggregation, 407–08
    Current availability, 406–07
    Effective availability, 407
Permitted disparity,
      In general, 397
    Cumulative permitted disparity fraction, 403
    Defined benefit excess plan, 399–400
    Defined benefit offset plan, 400–01
    Defined contribution excess plan, 398–99
    Disparity, 397
    Integration level, 398
    Offset level, 401
    Total annual disparity fraction, 402
Plans tested, 383–84
Rate group, 387, 392, 393–94
Retroactive corrections, 409–10
Social security offset plans, 406
Vesting, 383

NONDISCRIMINATION IN COVERAGE
    See also Participation in Plan
Affiliated service group, 369–70
Collective bargaining agreements, 367, 368
Common control, 369
Compensation, 367–68
Controlled group, 369
Coverage tests,
      In general, 362–63
    Actual benefit percentage, 365
    Average benefit percentage test, 362, 363, 365–67
    Benefit percentage, 365–66
    Collective bargaining agreements, 367, 368

NONDISCRIMINATION IN COVERAGE—Cont'd
Coverage tests—Cont'd
    Former employees, 368–69
    Nondiscriminatory classification test, 362, 363–65
    Ratio percentage test, 362, 363
    Safe harbor percentage, 364
    Unsafe harbor percentage, 365
Employees benefiting under a plan, 362–63
Excludable employees,
    Collective bargaining agreements, 371
    Former employees, 372
    Minimum age and service requirements, 367, 371–72
Highly compensated employees, 358–60
Leased employees, 370
Plans tested,
    Aggregation, 361–62
    Cash or deferred arrangements, 361
    Disaggregation, 361
    Employee stock ownership plans, 361
    Single (or separate) plans, 360–61
Reasons for discrimination, 357
Separate line of business rules,
    In general, 372–77
    Qualified separate lines of business, 376–77

NORMAL RETIREMENT AGE
See Accrual of Benefits; Vesting of Benefits

PARTICIPANTS AND BENEFICIARIES
In general, 13

PARTICIPATION IN PLAN
    See also Nondiscrimination in Coverage
Eligibility, 96–97
Minimum participation standard,
    Collective bargaining agreements, 378–79, 381
    Defined benefit plans, 380
    Employee stock ownership plans, 378
    Employees considered, 379–80
    Exemptions, 381
    50–40 rule, 380
    Qualified separate lines of business, 379–80
    Plans tested, 378–79

PARTIES IN INTEREST (DISQUALIFIED PERSONS)
    See also Prohibited Transaction Rules; Penalties

500   *INDEX*
References are to Pages

PARTIES IN INTEREST (DISQUALIFIED PERSONS)—Cont'd
    See also Prohibited Transaction Rules; Penalties—Cont'd
        In general, 15, 282–83
Categories, 282–83

PENALTIES
    See also Civil Remedies; Criminal Sanctions; Taxation
Accumulated funding deficiency, 447–49
Breach of fiduciary duty, 279
Nondeductible employer contributions, 452
Plan information, 209–11
Prohibited transactions, 298–99

PENSION BENEFIT GUARANTY CORPORATION
    See also Plan Termination Insurance; Termination of Plans;
        Termination of Single-Employer Plans; Termination of
        Single—Employer Plans; Withdrawal Liability
Deficit, 461–62
Purposes, 455
Reporting requirements, 462–64
Trustee in involuntary terminations, 473

PENSION PLANS
See Plans

PLAN ASSETS
    See also Fiduciaries and Fiduciary Responsibility; Fiduciary
        Standards; Prohibited Transaction Rules
Bonding, 245–47
Corporate finance, 48–52
Guaranteed benefit policies, 240–43
Identification, 237–38
Impact on economy, 53–55
Investment in other entities, 239–40
Mutual fund shares, 239
Non-inurement, 244–45
Time of acquisition, 238–39
Trust requirement, 243–44

PLAN SPONSOR
    In general, 13
Administrator, 229
Contributing sponsor, 457, 471, 474

PLAN TERMINATION INSURANCE
    See also Pension Benefit Guaranty Corporation; Termination
        of Plans; Termination of Single-Employer Plans

PLAN TERMINATION INSURANCE—Cont'd
Annuities, 480
Benefit guarantees,
    Multiemployer plans, 460
    Single employer plans, 458–59
Characteristics, 456–58
Premiums, 457–58

PLANS
Criteria for existence,
    Dillingham test, 333–34
    Functional test, 335–36
    Group insurance arrangements, 336–37
    Statute, 2
Employer programs, 2, 33–38
Financial intermediaries, 53–55
Independence from employer, 50
Internal Revenue Code terminology, 6–7
Non-qualified plans, 31–32
Oral plans, 217–18
Permanence, 454
Retirement security programs, 38–44
Types of plans,
    Cash balance plans, 6
    Cash or deferred arrangements (401(k) plans), 6, 417
    Church plans, 10
    Defined benefit excess plans, 399–400
    Defined benefit offset plans, 400–01
    Defined benefit plans, 3–4
    Defined contribution excess plans, 398–99
    Defined contribution (individual account) plans, 4–6
    Disability plans, 10
    Eligible individual account plans, 302–03
    Eligible retirement plans, 159
    Employee stock ownership plans, 6, 300–01, 306
    Excess benefit plans, 10–11
    Flat (fixed) benefit plans, 4
    Follow-on plans, 475
    Government plans, 9–10
    Individual retirement accounts and annuities, 11–12
    Insurance contract plans, 437
    Keogh plans, 11
    Leveraged ESOPs, 307–09
    Money purchase plans, 5
    Multiemployer plans, 8–9, 456

PLANS—Cont'd
Types of plans—Cont'd
    Multiple employer plans, 8–9
    Pension plans, 3, 7
    Profit sharing plans, 5
    SIMPLE plans, 12, 427
    Simplified employee pensions, 12
    Single employer plans, 456
    Single (or separate) plans, 360–61
    Social security offset plans, 406
    Stock bonus plans, 5–6
    Taft–Hartley plans, 63
    Target benefit plans, 5
    Top-hat plans, 17
    Top-heavy plans, 90
    Uniform points plans, 385
    Unit benefit plans, 3
    Welfare plans, 7–8
Workforce management, 35–38

PREEMPTION
"Regulates insurance,"
    In general, 337–41
    Deemer clause, 341–42
"Relate to,"
    In general, 327–29
    Legislative History, 328–29
    Limitations to preemption, 329–33
State law remedies, 178–79, 329–31, 342–47
State regulation of ESOPs, 324–25
Total preemption, 348–49

PRE-ERISA LAW AND PRACTICE
    See also ERISA
Benefit suits, 62–64, 178
Common law theories,
Contract law, 59–60
    Deferred compensation, 62
    Employer property, 58–59
    Fairness, 60–61
    Restitution, 62
    Trust law, 62–64
Development of plans, 33–36
Employee expectations, 56–57
Internal Revenue Code, 64–66
Labor Management Relations Act, 61, 63, 66

PRE-ERISA LAW AND PRACTICE—Cont'd
Securities laws, 67–69
Welfare and Pension Plans Disclosure Act, 66–67, 195–96

PROFIT SHARING PLANS
See Employee Stock Ownership Plans; Plans

PROHIBITED TRANSACTION RULES
See also Parties in Interest; Fiduciaries and Fiduciary
Responsibility; Fiduciary Standards
In general, 283–89
Employer real property, 302
Employer securities,
Acquisition, 303–05
Adequate consideration, 304–05
Eligible individual account plans, 302–03
Qualifying employer securities (Title I), 301–02
Qualifying employer securities (IRC), 306–07
Title I definition, 301
Exemptions
Administrative, 295–97
Banks and insurers, 294
Class, 296–97
Contracts for office space and services, 293
Loans to ESOPs, 309–10
Loans to participants, 131–32, 293
Necessity, 292
Qualifying employer securities, 303–05
Kickbacks, 291–92
Party in interest rules,
In general, 284
Contribution of property to plan, 285–86
Employer securities and real property, 287–88, 303–05
Furnishing of goods, services or facilities, 286
Loans, 286
Sale, exchange or lease of property, 285–86
Transfer or use of assets, 287
Purpose, 282
Remedies for violation,
Civil remedies, 297–98
Taxes, 298–99
Self-dealing rules, 288–92
Statutory clarification, 294–95

PROTECTION OF RIGHTS IN WORKPLACE
See Benefits

PRUDENCE
See Fiduciary Standards

QUALIFICATION
See also Contributions; Distributions; Nondiscrimination
in Contributions or Benefits; Nondiscrimination in
Coverage; Pre–ERISA Law and Practice; Taxation
In general, 19
Determination letters, 207–08, 453–54
Loans to participants, 132–33
Non-qualified plans, 31–32
Permanence, 454
Plan termination, 453–54

QUALIFIED DOMESTIC RELATIONS ORDERS
See Alienation of Benefits; Distributions

REPORTING AND DISCLOSURE
See Information

RETIREE MEDICAL BENEFITS
See Accounting; Benefits; ERISA; Vesting of Benefits

RETIREMENT
See Accrual of Benefit; Age Discrimination; Annuities; Benefits;
Distributions; ERISA; Taxation

ROLLOVER DISTRIBUTIONS
See Distributions; Taxation

SEPARATE LINES OF BUSINESS
See Nondiscrimination in Coverage

SEVERANCE BENEFITS
See Benefits

SOCIAL SECURITY
See also Nondiscrimination in Contributions or Benefits
In general, 39–40, 43, 44
Integration,
ESOPs, 311
Imputed disparity, 404–06
Permitted disparity, 397–403
Social security offset plans, 406

SPOUSAL PROTECTION
Loans to participants, 134
Non-annuity distributions, 130

SPOUSAL PROTECTION—Cont'd
Qualified domestic relations orders, 145–49
Rationale, 121–22
Survivor annuities, 123–27

STOCK-BONUS PLANS
See Employee Stock Ownership Plans; Plans

SURVIVOR ANNUITIES
See Annuities; Spousal Protection

TAFT-HARTLEY PLANS
See Plans; Pre–ERISA Law and Practice

TAXATION
See also Benefits; Contributions; Distributions; Penalties
Accumulated funding deficiency, 447–49
Annuities,
Amounts not received as an annuity, 153–54
Amounts received as an annuity, 151–53
Basic rule, 151–52
Exclusion ratio, 151
Expected return, 151
Investment in the contract, 151–52
Separate contracts, 154–55
Simplified exclusion method, 152–53
Early distributions, 162–64
Loans to participants, 133–34
Lump sum distributions,
Employer securities, 156–57
Five-year averaging, 157
Ten-year averaging, 157
Nondeductible employer contributions, 452
Prohibited transactions, 298–99
Retirement policy, 39, 41–43
Rollover distributions,
In general, 157–62
Eligible retirement plans, 158, 159
Eligible rollover distributions, 158–59
Surviving spouse, 160–61
Transfer of property, 160
Withholding tax, 161
Tax advantages,
ESOPs, 308–09, 314–17
Firm, 30–32, 50–52
Individual, 27–30

TAXATION—Cont'd
Trustee-to-trustee transfers, 157–58, 162

TERMINATION OF PLAN
    See also Pension Benefit Guaranty Corporation; Plan Termi-
        nation Insurance; Termination of Single–Employer
        Plans
Fiduciary standards, 253, 454, 481–82
Qualification, 453–54
Title IV coverage, in general, 454–55

TERMINATION OF SINGLE–EMPLOYER PLANS
    See also Pension Benefit Guaranty Corporation; Plan Termi-
        nation Insurance; Termination of Plans
Benefit liabilities, 464
Distress terminations, 468–71
Distribution of assets to participants and beneficiaries,
    Annuities, 480–83
    Outstanding amount of benefit liabilities, 472
    Priority categories, 466–67
Involuntary terminations,
    Initiation by PBGC, 472–73
    Liabilities to trustees, 474–75
    Proceedings, 473–74
    Trustee, 473
Liabilities of sponsor and others, 471–72, 474–75
Restoration of plan, 475–76
Reversions, 467, 476–80
Standard terminations, 464–66
Terminal report, 209

TOP-HEAVY PLANS
See Accrual of Benefits; Contributions; Vesting of Benefits

TRUST AND TRUSTEES
See Fiduciaries and Fiduciary Status; Fiduciary Standards; Plan
    Assets; Plans; Pre–ERISA Law and Practice

UNDERFUNDING
See Funding; Funding Standards and Methods

VALUATION
Actuarial present value, 119, 430–31
Mortality tables, 119–20
Pensions, 25–27
Present value,
    Annuity, 24–27, 119–21

VALUATION—Cont'd
Present value—Cont'd
Future payment, 24–25

VESTING OF BENEFITS
Coverage of vesting rules, 91–92
Nondiscrimination, 383
Forfeiture,
Bad-boy clauses, 87
Death of employee, 86
Normal retirement benefit, 80–81
Policy, 78–79
Plan termination or partial termination, 88–90, 453–54
Relationship to other protections, 78–79, 96
Retiree medical benefits, 93–95
Severance benefits, 92–93
Vesting schedules,
In general, 81–83
Break in service, 85–86
Cliff vesting, 83
Graded vesting, 83
Matching contributions, 83–84
Top-heavy plans, 90–91
Year of service, 84–85

WELFARE AND PENSION PLANS DISCLOSURE ACT
See ERISA; Pre–ERISA Law and Practice

WELFARE BENEFIT PLANS
See Accrual of Benefits; Alienation of Benefits; ERISA; Plans, Vesting of Benefits

WITHDRAWAL LIABILITY
See also Pension Benefit Guaranty Corporation; Plan Termination Insurance; Termination Insurance; Termination of Plans
In general, 482–84

WRITING REQUIREMENT
See Fiduciary Standards; Information

†